Dilemmas and Connections

Dilemmas and Connections

Selected Essays

—

CHARLES TAYLOR

THE BELKNAP PRESS OF HARVARD UNIVERSITY PRESS
Cambridge, Massachusetts, and London, England
2011

Library of Congress Cataloging-in-Publication Data

Taylor, Charles, 1931–
Dilemmas and connections : selected essays / Charles Taylor.
p.   cm.
Includes bibliographical references (p.) and index.
ISBN 978-0-674-05532-2 (alk. paper)
I. Title.
B995.T31   2010
191—dc22   2010020424

To Aube

Contents

Part I

ALLIES AND INTERLOCUTORS

Iris Murdoch and Moral Philosophy

I

I cannot pretend to give an account of Iris Murdoch's contribution to moral philosophy, much less sum it up or give some verdict on it. Her contribution is much too rich, and we are much too close to it. What I want to do, instead, is talk in a more personal vein and say what Dame Iris's work has meant for me. This is inevitably going to be idiosyncratic, and Dame Iris may not recognize herself in my remarks. But I think it does touch on some important issues.

Dame Iris's work had meaning for me partly as someone involved in the world of analytic philosophy. This world has lots of good qualities. But one of its drawbacks is a tendency to narrowness on certain questions. And one of the most marked sites of this narrowness was in moral philosophy. The narrowness concerns more than just the range of doctrines considered, though it also consists in that. But, more fundamentally, it has restricted the range of questions that it seems sensible to ask. In the end it restricted our understanding of what morality is. I have tried to sum this up by saying that Anglo-Saxon moral philosophy has tended to see morality as concerned with questions of what we ought to do and to occlude or exclude questions about what it is good to be or what it is good to love. The focus is on obligatory action, which means that it turns away from issues in which obligation is not really the issue, as well as those where not just actions but ways of life or ways of being are what we have to weigh. Another shorthand way of putting this point is that this philosophy tended to restrict itself to the "right" at the expense of the "good." If issues of the good life were allowed, independent of the issue of what is right, they were seen as a second zone of practical consideration, lacking the urgency and high priority of the moral. (Jürgen Habermas has formulated this priority, which shows that this philosophical temper has gone beyond the Anglo-Saxon world.)

From within this narrow perspective, it could seem that moral philosophy had two main intellectual tasks: (1) to try to work out exactly what the considerations are which tell us which action is right and (2) to try to show that these are the right considerations, against other rival candidates. The first has a place because our sense of what is right starts off fuzzy and powerful, with strong but unclear intuitions; it stands in need of clarification. The second task is the exercise of founding. It is not surprising that within this philosophical climate, the two main contenders were utilitarianism and Kant. For some writers, the main philosophical debate seems to be between these two outlooks. John Rawls, in some sense inspired by Kant, seemed to assume in his original *Theory of Justice* that the rival he had to defeat was utilitarianism. The rest of the philosophical universe was given much shorter shrift. These two schools are popular because they do come up with clear answers to (1) and (2). Moreover, in each case, the answer to the first has the intellectually satisfying property of being a single criterion. Morality can be derived from one source.

Now a countermovement has begun in analytical philosophy in recent years. To some extent, it is the revenge of Nietzsche (Bernard Williams is important here). In another way, it reflects a return of Aristotle. In either case, it wants to restore the wider focus. One way of stating this is to introduce the stipulative distinction, whereby "morality" is used for the narrower domain concerned with obligatory action, and "ethics" for the wider domain, including issues of what is a good or worthwhile life. The influence of Nietzsche is at work here, but using this vocabulary does not mean we have to reject morality; it can be seen as a legitimate part of the larger domain of ethics. What it cannot be anymore for the users of this vocabulary is the whole, or the one ultimately serious domain of the practical, trumping all others.

Iris Murdoch was criticizing the narrowness of moral philosophy well before the present counterwave—and not entirely on the same grounds. Indeed, her reflections would lead us to make a further extension of the ethical, beyond those proposed by neo-Nietzscheans and neo-Aristotelians. Put briefly, while these take us beyond morality to issues about the good life, they stop there. Murdoch seems to me to take this first step, but then goes one further. Beyond obligatory action, she opens up the question of what it is good to be. But she takes this beyond the question of a good and satisfying life to the consideration of a good which would be beyond life, in the sense that its goodness cannot be entirely or exhaustively explained in terms of its contributing to a fuller, better, richer, more satisfying human life. It is a good that we might sometimes more appropriately respond to in suffering and death, rather than in fullness and life—the domain, as usually understood, of religion.

Put another way, in the terms I suggested above, this takes us beyond the question of what we ought to do to that of what it is good to be, and then beyond that again, to what can command our fullest love. (But I'm already sneaking in a Christian rather than a Buddhist discourse here. There is a disagreement between Dame Iris and me about this, which I want to return to later.) I would like to use an image here: We were trapped in the corral of morality. Murdoch led us out not only to the broad fields of ethics but also beyond that again to the almost untracked forests of the unconditional. (The forest is a Buddhist image.) I want to talk about these two stages, more about the first, because I understand it better, but also some about the second, because there lie many important questions which Murdoch has opened up for us.

2

Let me start with the first liberation: from morality to ethics, from the narrow corral to the wider pasture. In order to liberate ourselves fully, we have to understand what was going for the narrow focus on morality. Two important orders of reason converged to encourage the shift: One was moral, one epistemological.

One can still sense the force of the moral reasons in the rhetoric of contemporary philosophers. If one objects to a utilitarian that one might legitimately put, say, one's own integrity before the obligation to do the act which has the highest utility consequences, one invites the retort that one is self-indulgent and not really single-mindedly committed to human happiness, as one ought to be. We can see here in secularized form the traces of the Christian origins of this philosophy. If Aristotelian ethics starts with the question of what constitutes a good and worthwhile life, and then raises the issue of what one owes to others within this frame, it has seemed to a certain Christian temper, present in all ages but particularly strong during the Reformation and early modern period, that the demands of charity are unconditional, that they override fulfillment. Concentrate not on your own condition, but on practical benevolence.

This temper was strengthened by the cultural revolution which I have called the affirmation of ordinary life, which dethroned the supposedly higher activities of contemplation and the civic life and put the center of gravity of goodness in ordinary living, production, and the family. It belongs to this spiritual outlook that our first concern ought to be to increase life, relieve suffering, foster prosperity. Concern above all for the fullness of life smacked of pride, of self-absorption. And beyond that, it was inherently not egalitarian, since the alleged "higher" activities could only be carried out by an elite minority, whereas leading one's ordinary life rightly was open to everyone.

There is a moral temper to which it seems obvious that our major concern must be our dealings with others, in justice and benevolence; and these dealings must be on a level of equality. One can emphasize more justice (Kantians) or benevolence (utilitarians), but there is a shared perspective which is inimical to the ancient primacy of ethics and which draws us powerfully to the corral.

The second motive is epistemological. It concerns the demands of disengaged reason. I mean here self-monitoring reason, reasoning which can turn on its own proceedings and examine them for accuracy and reliability. We can scrutinize these proceedings to any degree of clarity, even up to the undeniably binding. This is the great contribution of Descartes, which he expressed in terms of *les idées claires et distinctes*. Disengaged reason is opposed to uses of reason which try to get a good purchase on some domain analogous to perception, but also to discerning the qualities of a piece of music, being able to tell what people are about, how they stand to the matter and to you, and so on. We do not tend to call these things "reason," but they have analogies to *to logistikon* of Plato. Disengaged reason means that we cease to rely on our engaged sense, our familiarity with some domain, and take a reflexive turn. We put our trust in a method, a procedure of operation. The sense of freedom and power which goes with this is part of the motivation. This move connects with the primacy of instrumental reason.

In this outlook, the prospect of a single criterion is very exciting. At last the fuzzy intuitions of common sense can be reduced to clarity. What is more, all incommensurabilities, and, hence, difficult decisions, can be ironed out. Utilitarianism both satisfies demand for rigor and homogeneity and fits well with the disengaged stance of instrumental reason. Think of the rhetorical self-portrayal of disengaged reason, daring to withdraw from the hold of sacred hierarchies, to stand back from them, and assess them coldly, in the light of how much *good* they do. And this good can be clearly measured. Here clarity, rigor, disengagement, and also philanthropy come together. But Kantianism also gets a charge from being rigorous and homogeneous. Part of the immense success of Rawls's *Theory of Justice* when it was first published came from this sense that after all it showed that rigorous modes of reasoning (e.g., game theory) can be of use in ethics.

So we have the complex standing behind morality: the primacy of justice-benevolence with equality, and also disengaged reason, rigor, clarity. Single-term moralities offer us a homogeneous, calculable domain of moral considerations. This seems right to their protagonists (1) because the exaltation of justice-benevolence over issues of fulfillment and the good life simplifies the domain of the moral and (2) because the calculability fits with the dominant models of disengaged reason. Now there is reason to think that principle (2) is not a cogent *argument* but, rather, a good cultural *explanation* for the popularity of single-term theories. Principle (1) is questionable, but one might find it convincing in some form. Even so, this is not a good ground for holding to single-criterion moralities, because even if you grant (1), you still cannot simply put *all* questions to do with justice-benevolence in a single category, to be decided without reference to any external considerations. You cannot just say, as Kant does with his categorical imperative, that this set of considerations *always* has priority. This would exclude all questions of importance and put the most trivial demands of justice-benevolence over the most weighty of fulfillment.

Principle (1) is *one* sense that can be given to the slogan "The right has priority over the good." And analogies and close relations emerge in political theory. So, for example, we entrench rights and we say: Protecting these takes precedence over all other considerations, for example, of the public good, happiness, and so forth. A project is being pursued in this entrenchment which we would all agree with. That is, with really essential rights, there should not be any derogation for mere advantage: No one should condemn an innocent person, or torture someone, or deprive people of the right to speak their minds just because the gross national product will go up or because most people will have more satisfying lives, or live in greater security. But these provisions have to be applied with a sense of how to distinguish the important from the trivial. One of the cases fought under the Canadian Charter of 1982, which won in first instance, was by a man who objected to the Alberta law requiring the wearing of a seat belt.

There are also other reasons for adopting single-term moralities. These deal with (3) questions of fairness and justice between people. And these seem to many people more clear-cut, more capable of satisfying and unchallengeable solution than issues about fulfillment and the good life. These latter seem to allow an indefinite proliferation of possible solutions, whereas issues of justice seem to allow for clear-cut resolution. Anybody can fantasize about possible fulfillments: I can decide that I ought to spend my life like Simon Stylites atop a pillar. Are you sure you can tell me I am wrong? But I cannot just decide that I need your car, and that makes it all right for me to take it. Whether there is anything at all to this, plainly it is what people think. No one thought Rawls was out of his mind to try to decide between different principles of justice with the aid of rational choice theory. (Correction: Some of us did question this, but we were a distinct minority, as the Rawls boom showed.) But people would have been stunned if he had proposed to settle in this way questions of the good life. Modern Western culture has made issues of epistemology central, and this has generated some skepticism about morality. But the skeptical sense falls unequally on the different kinds of considerations. Questions of the good life are more easily declared insoluble than those of justice.

Another reason for distinguishing justice from the good life concerns (4) our respect for people's freedom, another central good of modern Western culture. Determining what constitutes the good life means being able to tell people that they are mistaken when they propose another model for themselves. This is the reason for part of the suspicion of Aristotle among moderns. He is telling us that a certain way of life is the truly human one. That means that people who live other ways are declared wrong. It is thought that a real respect for their autonomy requires being agnostic on their way of life, allowing them the space to design their own lives without forfeiting the respect and even support of their fellows. But plainly this courtesy cannot be extended to issues of justice, as the point above about my needing your car shows. Moral restrictions intervene where we have to direct the traffic between people seeking to fulfill life plans, and give everybody a chance. However, these restrictions ought not intervene *within* the itinerary of any one agent. So a morality showing respect for freedom (itself an issue of justice) will make a sharp distinction between questions of justice and those of the good life, and will moralize the first and leave the second unregulated. And so we generate the single-term moralities concerned with justice-benevolence. Clearly (4) is in a relation of mutual support with (3).

There is a variant of (4) which returns as a principle of political theory. Someone may deny (3) as a principle of ethics, that is, they can think that there are universal truths about the good life. Some people are wrong, and are living tawdry and contemptible lives, and we are perfectly at liberty to tell them so. Nevertheless, these thinkers hold (5) that political society must give everyone the space to develop on his or her own, and that this society should not espouse one or another view of the good life. R. M. Dworkin holds something like this. This is a political transposition of a single-term morality. It is a basic definition of liberal society for some, but it does not require that these people hold to a single-term morality.

Staying with moral theory—hence leaving aside (5)—it does not seem to me that (3) or (4) do anything to make single-term moralities more plausible. Indeed, (4) may be thought to be incoherent. If there is a real issue of what is the good life for some person X—and why would there be a reason to take seriously his decisions on it if it weren't?—then why can he not be wrong? But these reasons help explain something else about these theories: their thinness. They have a narrow view of what morality is as a dimension of human life.

Let us try to get at this issue by taking up the question, What is involved in being a moral agent? Everyone would probably agree that a moral agent is sensitive to, responding to, certain considerations, the ones we think of as moral;

or, an agent who is capable of responding to these considerations. To speak a dialect of Heideggerese, the agent has moral meanings in his or her world. So what is it to have these meanings? Much contemporary Anglo-Saxon moral philosophy concentrates on the agent's having a sense that she or he ought to do certain things. The focus is on what we are obliged to do. The intellectual interest concentrates on getting clear what the things we are obliged to do have in common. One theory says that they all involve maximizing human happiness; another says that they all involve our not acting on maxims which are not universalizable. Another way of putting this is: Philosophy is seeking here a way of deriving our obligations, seeking a test by which we can see what we are morally obliged to do.

But ethics involves more than what we are obligated to do. It also involves what it is good to be. This is clear when we think of other considerations than those arising from our obligations to others, questions of the good life and human fulfillment. But this other dimension is there even when we are talking about our obligations to others. The sense that such and such is an action we are obliged by justice to perform cannot be separated from a sense that being just is a good way to be. If we had the first without any hint of the second, we would be dealing with a compulsion, like the neurotic necessity to wash one's hands or to remove stones from the road. A moral obligation comes across as moral because it is part of a broader sense which includes the goodness, perhaps the nobility or admirability, of being someone who lives up to it.

The obligation to do and the goodness in being are two facets, as it were, of the same sense. Each totally without the other would be something very different from our moral sense: a mere compulsion, on one hand; a detached sense of the superiority of one way over another, on the other hand, comparable to my aesthetic appreciation of cumulus over nimbus clouds, not making any demands on me as an agent. Contemporary philosophy has explored one facet at length but has said almost nothing about the other. But this too can be articulated; more can be said about the goodness of different ways of being. Traditionally, philosophical theory has explored this in the language of virtue. But even more important for our moral consciousness has been the portrayal of good and bad lives in exemplary figures and stories. Our moral understanding would be crippled if we had to do without such portrayals. Christian moral theology without the Gospel would be an even stranger affair than it is. Nevertheless, this whole domain of the articulation of the good, whether philosophical or narrative, has been relatively neglected in Anglo-Saxon moral philosophy. Why?

One answer could be the hard-headed reason that we do not need to explore this in order to know what to do. Philosophy should help us clarify obligation. So finding out that what really makes an action obligatory is that it furthers the general happiness is really useful stuff. Just being more articulate about the kind of good person you are when you do this adds nothing. It is a form of self-indulgence. But this will not really stand up. We often need to be clearer on the goods involved in order to deliberate well. Take the domain favored by single-term morality itself: justice-benevolence. There is an internal tension that can arise here, between the two terms. The issue can arise: When should we override justice in the name of benevolence? Should we ever override it at all? Traditionally put, this is the issue of justice versus mercy. To answer these questions, we may find ourselves looking at what kind of good it is to be a just person and what it is to be benevolent. We will be thinking of how to place these two virtues in our lives. This is the case, a fortiori, when it is a matter of thinking how to combine justice-benevolence and the virtues of fulfillment or of the good life. The belief that all the moral deliberation we need can be effected with a calculus of obligated action is another illusion of the erroneous single-term moralities, and only makes sense on condition that their homogeneous domain exhausts the moral. Ethical thinking, to use this term for the broader domain, sometimes also requires deliberation about what it is good to be in order to determine what to do in certain circumstances.

An example is inspired by some arguments of Bernard Williams. Let us say that the course of action with the highest utility consequences clashes with that which my integrity would demand. I am minister of forests in the red-green coalition government. I am also head of the Green Party. I am reluctantly persuaded that the least bad course of action really available in the situation is to chainsaw a section of rain forest. But I ask the Prime Minister to relieve me of my portfolio. Let someone else do the deed. Deciding this involves weighing not just actions and their consequences but also qualities of being, that is, assessing the action also by how it fits into a whole life, constituted not only of other actions but also of feelings, commitments, solidarities, and so forth. The same order of considerations is in play if you think that I am just indulging my image here and ought to take responsibility for what has to be done. In either case, I need to get clear on what it is good to be and how important this is relative to the other considerations in play.

Single-term morality perpetrates a drastic foreshortening of our moral world, by concentrating only on what we are obligated to do. But the reduction is even more drastic than I have described hitherto. I spoke of the things it is good to be, of virtues as "life goods" in *Sources of the Self.*[1] I also distinguished there what I called "constitutive goods." By that I mean features of ourselves, or the world, or God, such that their being what they are is essential to the life goods being good. Examples in well-known traditional views are: God having created us and calling us is a constitutive good for Judeo-Christian-Islamic theism; the Idea of the Good is one such for Plato; for Aristotle, our being animals having logos is one. In these well-understood traditional ethics, articulating the life goods quite naturally leads to spelling out the constitutive goods. And, moreover, getting clear on these helps to define more clearly and vividly the life goods. This is obvious in the theistic case, where among the most important life goods are the love and worship of God. But we can also see it in Plato, where a deeper understanding of the life dominated by reason has to pass through attaining a vision of the Idea of the Good. The truly good person is inspired to model himself or herself on the order shaped by the Good. Similarly, for Aristotle we come to see better how to order the goods in our lives when we understand that we are animals possessing logos.

Now it might be thought that constitutive goods figure only in theistic or metaphysical ethics, that they have no place in a modern humanistic outlook. But this would be a mistake. In a modern humanistic ethic, the locus of the constitutive good is displaced onto the human being itself. In Kant, the sense of the dignity of human life, as rational agency soaring above everything else in the universe, is an example of the identification of a constitutive good in a humanist ethic. My claim is that something like this sense of the dignity and value of human life, of the nobility of rational freedom, underpins the ethical consciousness of our contemporaries and plays the two roles we can see it occupying in Kant's philosophy: it defines why the human being commands our respect when she or he is the object of our action; and it sets us an ideal for our own action.

And just as defining the virtues helps us to deliberate, understanding better as we do what it is good to be, so this understanding can be further aided by clarifying the constitutive goods. We help to clarify what it is good to be by getting clearer on just what is noble or admirable about the human potential. Here again, we have two facets of the same exploration. On one, we are defining the virtues, the qualities of life we want to have; on the other, we are looking at what is, the human being endowed with its potential in its world, and taking inspiration from what we find worthy in this. There is, indeed, an important difference from the earlier theological or metaphysical ethics, insofar as on this second facet these incorporated elements which go beyond human potential, for example, God or the Good. But there is also a substantial overlap, and thinking on these two facets remains part of our moral understanding. We are in some way *moved* by human powers; this forms part of the moral meanings in our world, along with our sense of what it is good to be, and what we ought to do—just as the theist is moved by the love of God.

The foreshortened single-term morality misses not only life goods but constitutive goods. It neglects not just the unarticulated know-how but misses a lot of what we need to articulate in order to know what to do. But there is an even more serious omission. I have been talking mainly as though the point of articulation were to help one see what to do. But some of our articulations not only help us to define better what we want to be and do, they also move us, as I have just indicated. Articulating a constitutive good not only helps us fine-tune what we want to be and do, it also inspires and moves us to want to be and do it. And articulating the virtues can have a similar effect. This is nowhere more evident than in the recounting of the models and paradigms, exemplary people and actions, in real life or story, which both inspire and guide us. Both functions frequently come together in these narrations, which also involve articulating goods of both kinds. Exemplary figures body forth life goods, but in some cases—the Gospels, the life of the Buddha—part of what is being conveyed is a constitutive good.

Moreover, these two functions are in part interdependent. Seeing better what a certain good involves can change your stance toward it—in either direction, of course. It may increase or decrease your attachment to it. Even more important, appreciating what is good about a good can be an essential condition of making finer discriminations about what it means to realize it. This is the point made by Aristotle when he holds that the *phronimos* has to have the right dispositions in order to discern the good. Bad moral dispositions do not destroy our understanding of mathematics, he says, but they do weaken our grasp of the *arche* or starting points of moral deliberation.[2] To put it in more Platonic language, in many situations really to know what to do you have to love the good, and there is thus something self-defeating in confining ethics to the issue of what to do.

If we give the full range of ethical meanings their due, we can see that the fullness of ethical life involves not just doing, but also being; and not just these two but also loving (which is shorthand here for being moved by, being inspired by) what is constitutively good. It is a drastic reduction to think that we can capture the moral by focusing only on obligated action, as though it were of no ethical moment what you are and what you love. These are the essence of ethical life.

One of the reasons for shying away from all this, besides the many enumerated above, is the confused inarticulacy of modern naturalism. This comes from a deep reticence in talking about foundations and an inability to determine how to talk about them (which obviously strengthens the reticence). After clarifying what we ought to do, utilitarians and contemporary neo-Kantians are left uncertain how to talk about the basis for accepting the whole range of obligations. Sometimes they just shift into another register, like John Mackie,[3] and give a sociobiological account of how it is understandable that we have the norms we do. But that is not articulating the good, because it in no way makes clearer what is good or admirable about what we seek; it just tries to explain in a quasi-scientific way why we seek it. (Although sometimes it is confusedly taken in the latter manner, and then becomes part of the support for a reductive instrumentalist ethic.) Some writers just terminate with the brute fact that our intuitions are what they are.

This is partly because of a confusion about what arguing "foundations" could be. This word is bad, because it implies something to the philosophical ear which is impossible. It implies that you could argue someone who shared absolutely no moral sense at all into morality. "Foundations" means you would have to take him from point zero of moral commitment to the full sweep of obligations you generate by your calculus. This cannot be done, but there is no reason to think that it ought to be, that something terrible is missing because it cannot be.[4] The point of articulating our moral sense cannot be to provide foundations in this sense, though it can be a very powerful tool in real moral argument. The famous line from Dostoyevsky, "If God does not exist, then everything is permitted," is often taken as an assertion that foundations have to be given. If I think God does not exist, I feel I can do anything; then you convince me he does, and I suddenly see that there are moral limits. But I think the sentence can be taken as a statement of the constitutive good that someone (Dostoyevsky?) recognizes, without supporting a foundationalist view. What is the difference?

Articulating the good is in a way providing reasons, but not in either of the senses which are generally recognized by much contemporary moral philosophy. Let me outline the two senses. The first is giving a basic reason. I want to speak of a basic reason where we argue for doing A on the grounds that it amounts to doing B, and where this justification is asymmetrical. Basic reasons parallel the structure of purposive action. I am phoning George. You ask why? Because he is going to give me a job. Why do I want a job? Because I need the income to live. The action has several descriptions: (1) phoning George, (2) getting a job, (3) finding the means to live. But these are not on the same footing. The description (3) is basic; I only go for (2) because it amounts in this situation to (3), and similarly with (1). If I could live on the dole or find a job some other way, I would not be phoning. It is one of the self-given tasks of much modern moral theory to identify a basic reason in this sense. Pursuing the greatest happiness of the greatest number is one such. The minister of finance is (1) balancing the budget. She is (quite properly in this context) operating under utilitarian principles, so she is doing it (2) in order to reduce inflation, because (3) she believes that reduced inflation will increase economic well-being. Reason (3) is the basic reason. If you convince her that the conjuncture requires a return to Keynesian policies, she will run a deficit.

So one way of arguing for something is giving a basic reason. But when you have identified the basic reason, and your interlocutor is not moved by it, where do you go from there? It seems you have to set yourself another task: giving him that basic reason, that is, bringing it about that he takes on that basic reason as his own. Now you need to give reasons of the foundationalist sort. But the articulation of life and constitutive goods is reason-giving in neither of the above senses. It does not give a basic reason for a policy described in less-than-basic terms, as increasing economic welfare does for balancing the budget. The two descriptions, pre- and post-articulation, of some life or constitutive good are not related in this way. One gives a fuller, more vivid, or clearer, better defined understanding of what the good is.

On a theistic view, God's will does not stand to loving my neighbor as (3) does to (2) and (1) in the examples above. Or, rather, it does so only in the rather warped Occamite theologies which caused such havoc in early modern thought. In this view, the various actions open to us do not have moral value in themselves, but this is only imparted to them by the command of God. On a less strained and alien view (for instance, Thomist, but not only Thomist), invoking God's will is further expanding what is good about this, which I initially grasp as good by natural reason. So you do not articulate a basic reason here. Nor can you cause another person to acquire a basic reason from a standing start. You have to draw on the interlocutor's moral understanding. How you can nevertheless carry out an argument which can bring the interlocutor over to you, I tried to outline in "Explanation and Practical Reason." The distorted understanding of practical reason is one of the grounds which have moved moral philosophy of a naturalist temper to make both kinds of goods an intellectual no-go area. But there also are confusions about what is entailed in the "anti-metaphysical" stance of naturalism itself.

Drawing this together, we can see a link between two main lines of criticism offered here of single-term moralities: (1) their attempt to develop high-definition decision procedures, denying the need for phronêsis, and (2) their foreshortening of the moral domain. We see what is wrong with the first when we note that our judgments of what to do take place in the context of a grasp of the good which is largely unarticulated. It consists largely of background understanding. Or else it is presented to us in paradigm persons or actions or in internalized habitus. It can be articulated to some degree in descriptions of the good, and this can be very important, both for our knowing what to do or be and because it can move us to do or be it. But these descriptions are only understood in the context of background understanding, acquired habits and paradigms, which can never be transcended or escaped. When we see what the domain is which permits this articulation, we are induced to burst the boundaries of the foreshortened moral world and recognize the relevance for this world of what we are and love, as well as what we do. We thus conceive the place of articulacy in ethical life very differently. We not only see (1) its restricted scope; but also (2) its plurality of function—not only helping us know what to do but also know what we want to be, and even more crucially makes us love the good; and we similarly see (3) that the forms of articulacy are more widely varied, that philosophical definition is one mode, but that our understanding (including philosophical understanding) would be badly impoverished without moral narrative and admiring attention to exemplars.

3

Now I want to talk, all too briefly, about the second move, from field to forest. It is hard to talk about this, and it is, above all, hard to talk about it clearly and in a recognized common language. The forest is virtually untracked. Or, rather, there are old tracks; they appear on maps which have been handed down to us. But when you get in there, it is very hard to find them. So we need people to make new trails. That is, in effect, what Iris Murdoch has done.

We need, partly, new trails because we have changed. We have grown into a different civilization from our medieval and even early modern forebears. We moderns may differ among ourselves as to what has happened in this phenomenon we call "modernity," but it seems agreed by all that something important has changed. It is as though an earthquake has shifted the fields, and we can no longer enter the forest in the same way. Something like this seems to be Murdoch's assumption in *Metaphysics as a Guide to Morals,* because she frequently refers to what we can no longer believe, what is a thing of the past. She writes, for example, "Our general awareness of good, or goodness, is with us unreflectively all the time, as a sense of God's presence, or at least existence, *used to be* to all sorts of believers" (p. 509, emphasis added).

Now I disagree with Murdoch in her actual conclusions here, particularly her ontological proof of the nonexistence of God. ("Any existing God would be less than God. An existent God would be an idol or a demon"; p. 508.) But the general idea that today we have to start from somewhere other than where our ancestors did seems to me very right. Just what the difference is, we will disagree on, and this is partly because of our different readings of the change we gesture at with the term "modernity."

But that is not the whole story. We also need new tracks because human beings are different. People are constantly blazing new trails, even in so-called ages of faith. We have to accept as an *ultimate surd* that people find very different ways to God, or the Good, or Nirvana, ways that seem to involve incompatible assumptions (hence the need for some disjunctive expression like the ones I have just used to designate the destination), and yet that these are not simply different destinations, like being clever and being rich, but different attempts to articulate the same call. It is obvious that people of great spiritual depth and dedication and, beyond this, people of holy lives, are drawn to very different paths. Someone who wanted to follow all the people they admire today might be tempted to try to take them all. But this is impossible, in that a fuller spiritual life involves engaging on a path, and they are sufficiently different that one cannot be on more than one. This is not to say that there cannot be selective borrowings, as some Christians have learned from Buddhist meditation techniques. It is just that there remain unbridgeable differences, such as whether your focus is God or the Good.

My contention is that this kind of difference cannot be understood simply as one of premodern versus modern but is another manifestation of that puzzling multiplicity of paths which seems to be a perennial feature of the human condition. Many faiths, not least the one I share in, have spent centuries trying to deny this multiplicity. It is now time to discover, in humility and puzzlement, how we on different paths are also fellow travelers. It is in that spirit that I have found Iris Murdoch's work tremendously helpful and illuminating, as much because of as in spite of our differences. And it is in this spirit that I want to try to bring out part of the difference between us, by giving my own account of Western modernity in its relation to what one might call faith, or in any case what the image of the forest is meant to convey. I am going to try the impossible and say what this image only gestures at. I can think of three ways, and I am going to start with the one which most runs against the civilization of Western modernity.

Entering the forest is acknowledging that life is not the whole story. There is one way to take this expression, which is as meaning something like: Life goes on after death, there is a continuation, our life does not totally end in our deaths. I do not mean to deny what is affirmed on this reading, but I want to take the expression here in a somewhat different (though perhaps related?) sense. What I mean is something more like: The point of things is not exhausted by life, the fullness of life, even the goodness of life. This is not meant to be just a repudiation of egoism, the idea that the fullness of my life (and perhaps those of people I love) should be my concern. Let us agree with John Stuart Mill that a full life must involve striving for the benefit of humankind. Entering the forest is seeing a point beyond that.

One form of this is the insight that there can be in suffering and death not merely negation, the undoing of fullness and life, but also the affirmation of something which matters beyond life, on which life itself originally draws. The last clause seems to bring us back into the focus on life. It may be readily understandable without leaving the fields how one could accept suffering and death in order to give life to others. In a certain view, that too has been part of the fullness of life. But entering the forest involves something more. What matters beyond life does not matter just because it sustains life; otherwise it wouldn't be "beyond life" in the meaning of the act. (For Christians, God wills human flourishing, but "thy will be done" does not reduce to "let human beings flourish.")

This is the way of putting it which goes most against the grain of contemporary Western civilization. There are other ways of framing it. One which goes back to the very beginning of Christianity is a redefinition of the term life to incorporate what I'm calling beyond life, for example, the New Testament evocations of eternal life, and John 10:10. Or, we could put it in a third way: entering the forest means being called to a change of identity. Buddhism gives us an obvious reason to talk this way. The change here is quite radical, from self to "no-self" *(anatta)*. But Christian faith can be seen in the same terms: as calling for a radical decentering of the self in relation with God. ("Thy will be done.") This way of putting it brings out a similar point to my first way, since most conceptions of a flourishing life assume a stable identity, the self for whom flourishing can be defined.

So entering the forest means aiming beyond life or opening yourself to a change in identity. But if you do this, where do you stand in relation to the fields? There is much division, confusion, and uncertainty about this. Historic religions have in fact combined concern for field and forest in their normal practice. It has even been the rule that the supreme achievements of those who went beyond life have served to nourish the fullness of life of those who remain on this side of the barrier. Thus, prayers at the tombs of martyrs brought long life, health, and a whole host of good things for the Christian faithful. Something of the same is true for the tombs of certain saints in Muslim lands, while in Theravada Buddhism, for example, the dedication of monks is turned, through blessings, amulets, and so forth, to all the ordinary purposes of flourishing among the laity.

Against this, there have recurrently been "reformers" in all religions who have considered this symbiotic, complementary relation between renunciation and flourishing to be a travesty. They insist on returning religion to its "purity," and posit for everyone the goals of renunciation from the pursuit of flourishing. Some are even moved to denigrate the latter pursuit altogether, to declare it unimportant or an obstacle to sanctity. But this extreme stance runs athwart a very central thrust in some religions. Christianity and Buddhism will be my examples here. Renouncing, aiming beyond life, not only takes you away but also brings you back to flourishing. In Christian terms, if renunciation decenters you in relation with God, God's will is that humans flourish, and so you are taken back to an affirmation of this flourishing, which is biblically called *agape*. In Buddhist terms, Enlightenment does not just turn you from the world; it also opens the floodgates of *metta* (loving kindness) and *karuna* (compassion). There is the Theravada concept of the *Paccekabuddha,* concerned only for his own salvation, but he is ranked below the highest Buddha, who acts for the liberation of all beings. Thus, outside of the stance which accepts the complementary symbiosis of renunciation and flourishings, and beyond the stance of purity, there is a third one, which I could call the stance of *agape/karuna.*

I have gone into this to set the stage for my account of the conflict between modern culture and forest-dwelling. There is going to be some corner-cutting and oversimplification, but I believe that a powerful constitutive strand of modern Western spirituality is involved in an affirmation of life. It is perhaps evident in the contemporary concern to preserve life, to bring prosperity, to reduce suffering worldwide, which is I believe without precedent in history. This arises historically out of the affirmation of ordinary life which I referred to above as a consequence related to, but distinct from, the focus on morality. This affirmation originally was a Christian-inspired move. It exalted practical agape and was polemically directed against the pride, elitism one might say, and self-absorption of those who believed in higher activities or spiritualities. Consider the Reformers' attack on the supposedly "higher" vocations of the monastic life. These were meant to mark out elite paths of superior dedication, but were in fact deviations into pride and self-delusion. The really holy life for the Christian was within ordinary life itself, living in work and the household in a Christian and worshipful manner.

There was an earthly, one might say earthy, critique of the allegedly "higher" here which was then transposed and used as a secular critique of Christianity and, indeed, religion in general. Something of the same rhetorical stance adopted by Reformers against monks and nuns is taken up by secularists and unbelievers against Christian faith itself. This allegedly scorns the real, sensual, earthly human good for some purely imaginary higher end, the pursuit of which can only lead to the frustration of the real, earthly good, to suffering, mortification, repression, and so forth. The motivations of those who espouse this "higher" path are thus, indeed, suspect. Pride, elitism, and the desire to dominate play a part in this story, too, along with fear and timidity (also present in the earlier Reformers' story, but less prominently). In this critique, of course, religion is identified with the second, purist stance above, or else with a combination of this and the first "symbiotic" (usually labeled "superstitious") stance. The third, the stance of *agape/karuna,* becomes invisible. That is because a transformed variant of it has in fact been assumed by the secularist critic.

Now one must not exaggerate. This outlook on religion is far from being universal in our society. One might think that this is particularly true in the United States with its high rates of religious belief and practice. And, yet, I want to claim that this whole way of understanding things has penetrated far deeper and wider than simply to card-carrying, village-atheist-style secularists, that it also shapes the outlook of many people who see themselves as believers. What do I mean by this way of understanding? Well, it is a climate of thought, a horizon of assumptions, more than a doctrine. That means that there will be some distortion in the attempt to lay it out in a set of propositions. But I am going to do that anyway, because there is no other way of characterizing it that I know. If it were spelled out in propositions, it would read something like this: (1) that for us life, flourishing, driving back the frontiers of death and suffering are of supreme value; (2) that this was not always so; it was not so for our ancestors and for people in other earlier civilizations; (3) that one of the things which stopped it being so in the past was precisely a sense, inculcated by religion, that there were "higher" goals; and (4) that we have arrived at (1) by a critique and overcoming of (this kind of) religion.

We live in something analogous to a postrevolutionary climate. Revolutions generate the sense that they have won a great victory and identify the adversary in the previous regime. A postrevolutionary climate is one which is extremely sensitive to anything which smacks of the ancient regime and sees backsliding even in relatively innocent concessions to generalized human preferences. This can be seen, for example, in the Puritans who saw the return of Popery in any ritual, or Bolsheviks who compulsively addressed people as "comrade," proscribing the ordinary appellation "mister." I would argue that a milder, but very pervasive, version of this kind of climate is widespread in our culture. To speak of aiming beyond life is to appear to undermine the supreme concern with life of our humanitarian, "civilized" world. It is to try to reverse the revolution and bring back the bad old order of priorities, in which life and happiness could be sacrificed on the altars of renunciation. Hence, even believers are often induced to redefine their faith in such a way as not to challenge the primacy of life.

My claim is that this climate, often unaccompanied by any formulated awareness of the underlying reasons, pervades our culture. It emerges, for instance, in the widespread inability to give any human meaning to suffering and death, other than as dangers and enemies to be avoided or combated. This inability is not just the failing of certain individuals; it is entrenched in many of our institutions and practices, for instance the practice of medicine, which has great trouble understanding its own limits or conceiving some natural term to human life.

What gets lost, as always, in this postrevolutionary climate is the crucial nuance. Challenging the primacy of life can mean two things. It can mean trying to displace the saving of life and the avoidance of suffering from their rank as central concerns of policy. Or, it can also mean making the claim, or at least opening the way for the insight, that more than life matters. These two are obviously not the same. It is not even true, as people might plausibly believe, that they are causally linked, in the sense that making the second challenge "softens us up," and makes the first challenge easier. Indeed, I want to claim (and did in the concluding chapter of *Sources of the Self*) that the reverse is the case: that clinging to the primacy of life in the second (let us call this the "metaphysical") sense is making it harder for us to affirm it wholeheartedly in the first (or practical) sense.

But I do not want to pursue this claim here. The thesis I am presenting is that it is in virtue of its postrevolutionary climate that Western modernity is very inhospitable to forest-dwelling. This, of course, runs contrary to the mainline Enlightenment story, according to which religion has become less credible thanks to the advancement of science. There is, of course, something in this, but it is not in my view the main story. Moreover, to the extent that it is true, that is, that people interpret science and religion as at loggerheads, it is often because of an already felt incompatibility at the moral level. It is this deeper level that I have been trying to explore here. In other words, to oversimplify again, the obstacles to belief in Western modernity are primarily moral and spiritual, rather than epistemic. I am talking about the driving force here, rather than what is said in arguments in justification of unbelief. That is why I feel I want to demur when Murdoch invokes in *Metaphysics* things in which we allegedly can no longer believe. In one sense, I don't think there are such things. Even the grossest superstitions survive in advanced societies, and these were on the other hand always condemned by minorities. On another level, if we want to talk about things it is *hard* to believe, things that go against the grain, then I think this is true today of forest-dwelling in general, whether one is on their path or mine. Talking about what cannot be believed seems to accept that the revolution is epistemically driven, whereas I think that the motor of change is elsewhere.

I want to extend a little farther what is involved in this "take" on our age. For those who reject the metaphysical primacy of life, this outlook can itself seem imprisoning. The field is turned into another corral. From my perspective, human beings have an ineradicable bent to respond to something beyond life; denying this stifles. This perspective is, of course, radically at odds with that of secular humanism. But there is a feature of modern culture which fits my perspective. This is the revolt from within unbelief, as it were, against the primacy of life. It is not now in the name of something beyond, but really more just from a sense of being confined, diminished by the acknowledgment of this primacy. This has been an important stream in our culture, something woven into the inspiration of poets and writers, for example, Baudelaire (but was he entirely an unbeliever?) and Mallarmé. But the most influential proponent of this kind of view is undoubtedly Nietzsche. And it is significant that the most important anti-humanist thinkers of our time, for example, Foucault, Derrida, Bataille, all draw heavily on Nietzsche.

Nietzsche, of course, rebelled against the idea that our highest goal is to preserve and increase life, to prevent suffering. He rejects this both metaphysically and practically. He rejects the egalitarianism underlying this whole affirmation of ordinary life. But his rebellion is in a sense also internal. Life itself can push to cruelty, to domination, to exclusion, and indeed does so in its moments of most exuberant affirmation.

So this move remains within the modern affirmation of life in a sense. There is nothing higher than the movement of life itself (the *Will to Power*). But it chafes at the benevolence, the universalism, the harmony, the order. It wants to rehabilitate destruction and chaos, the infliction of suffering and exploitation, as part of the life to be affirmed. Life properly understood also affirms death and destruction. To pretend otherwise is to try to restrict it, tame it, hem it in, deprive it of its highest manifestations, what makes it something you can say "yes" to. A religion of life which proscribes death-dealing, the infliction of suffering, is confining and demeaning. Nietzsche thinks of himself as having taken up some of the legacy of pre-Platonic and pre-Christian warrior ethics, their exaltation of courage, greatness, elite excellence. Modern life-affirming humanism breeds pusillanimity. This accusation frequently recurs in the culture of counter-Enlightenment.

Of course, one of the fruits of this counterculture was Fascism, to which Nietzsche's influence was not entirely foreign, however true and valid Walter Kaufman's refutation of the simple myth of Nietzsche as a proto-Nazi. But in spite of this, the fascination with death and violence recurs, for example, in the interest in Bataille, shared by Derrida and Foucault. (Bataille was also a prewar fascist sympathizer.) Jim Miller's book on Foucault shows the depths of this rebellion against "humanism," as a stifling, confining space one has to break out of.[5] My point here is not to score off neo-Nietzscheanism, as some kind of antechamber for Fascism. A secular humanist might want to do this. But my perspective is rather different. I see these connections as another manifestation of our (human) inability to be content simply with an affirmation of life. The Nietzschean understanding of enhanced life, which can fully affirm itself, also in a sense takes us beyond life; and in this it is analogous with other, religious notions of enhanced life (like the New Testament's eternal life). But it takes us beyond by incorporating a fascination with the negation of life, with death and suffering. It does not acknowledge some supreme good beyond life and in that sense sees itself rightly as utterly antithetical to religion.

I am tempted to speculate further and to suggest that the perennial human susceptibility to be fascinated by death and violence is at base a manifestation of our nature as *homo religiosus.* From the point of view of the forest-dweller, it is one of the places this aspiration for the beyond most easily goes when it fails to take us to the forest. This does not mean that religion and violence are alternatives. On the contrary, it means that most historical religions have been deeply intricated with violence, from human sacrifice down to intercommunal massacres, because most historical religion remains only very imperfectly oriented to the forest. The religious affinities of the cult of violence in its different forms are indeed palpable. What it might mean, however, is that the only way fully to escape the draw toward violence is to enter the forest, that is, through the full-hearted love of some good beyond life. A thesis of this kind has been put forward by René Girard, for whose work I have a great deal of sympathy, although I do not agree on the centrality he gives to the scapegoat phenomenon.[6]

On the perspective I am developing here, no position can be set aside as simply devoid of insight. We could think of modern culture as the scene of a three-cornered—perhaps ultimately a four-cornered—battle. There are secular humanists, there are neo-Nietzscheans, and there are those who acknowledge some good beyond life. Any pair can gang up against the third on some important issue. Neo-Nietzscheans and secular humanists together condemn religion and reject any good beyond life. But neo-Nietzscheans and forest-dwellers are together in their absence of surprise at the continued disappointments of secular humanism, together also in the sense that its vision of life lacks a dimension. In a third lineup, secular humanists and believers come together in defending an idea of the human good, against the anti-humanism of Nietzsche's heirs.

A fourth party can be introduced to this field if we take account of the fact that the forest-dwellers are divided. Some think that the whole move to secular humanism was just a mistake, which needs to be undone. We need to return to an earlier view of things. Others, among whom I place myself, think that the practical primacy of life has been a great gain for humankind, and that there is some truth in the revolutionary story; this gain was in fact unlikely to come about without some breach with established religion. (We might even be tempted to say that modern unbelief is providential, but that might be too provocative a way of putting it.) But we nevertheless think that the metaphysical primacy of life is wrong, and stifling, and that its continued dominance puts in danger the practical primacy.

I have rather complicated the scene in the last paragraphs. Nevertheless, the simple lines sketched earlier still stand out. Both secular humanists and anti-humanists concur in the revolutionary story, that is, they see us as having been liberated from the illusion of a good beyond life and thus enabled to affirm ourselves. This may take the form of an Enlightenment endorsement of benevolence and justice; or it may be the charter for the full affirmation of the will to power, or "the free play of the signifier," or the aesthetics of the self, or whatever the current version is. But it remains within the same postrevolution-ary climate. For those fully within the climate, the forest becomes all but invis-ible. I have been exploring in my own way the terrain that I believe Iris Mur-doch has opened up for us. My map is not the same as hers. But then what two maps of largely untracked wilderness can ever be identical? I would like this exploration to be a tribute to the courage and insight of one who was origi-nally, and has remained, one of my teachers.

CHAPTER TWO

Understanding the Other: A Gadamerian View on Conceptual Schemes

The great challenge of this century, both for politics and for social science, is that of understanding the other. The days are long gone when Europeans and other Westerners could consider their experience and culture as the norm toward which the whole of humanity was headed, so that the other could be understood as an earlier stage on the same road that they had trodden. Now we sense the full presumption involved in the idea that we already possess the key to understanding other cultures and times.

But the recovery of the necessary modesty here seems always to threaten to veer into relativism, or a questioning of the very ideal of truth in human affairs. The very ideas of objectivity that underpinned Western social science seemed hard to combine with that of fundamental conceptual differences between cultures; so that real cultural openness appeared to threaten the very norms of validity on which social science rested.

What does not often occur to those working in these fields is the thought that their whole model of science is wrong and inappropriate. Here Gadamer has made a tremendous contribution to twentieth-century thought. He has in fact proposed a new and different model, which is much more fruitful, and shows promise of carrying us beyond the dilemma of ethnocentrism and relativism.

In *Wahrheit und Methode,* Gadamer shows how understanding a text or event that comes from our history has to be construed not on the model of the "scientific" grasp of an object but rather on that of speech partners who come to an understanding *(Verständigung)*. Following Gadamer's argument here, we come to see that this is probably true of human science as such. It is not simply knowledge of our own past that needs to be understood on the "conversation" model, but knowledge of the other as such, including disciplines like anthropology, where student and studied often belong to quite different civilizations.

This view has come to be widely accepted today, and it is one of the great contributions that Gadamer has made to the philosophy of this and succeeding centuries. I would like to lay out here why this is so.

First, I want to contrast the two kinds of operation: knowing an object and coming to an understanding with an interlocutor. Some differences are obvious. The first is unilateral, the second bilateral. I know the rock, the solar system; I don't have to deal with its view of me or of my knowing activity. But beyond this, the goal is different. I conceive the goal of knowledge as attaining some finally adequate explanatory language, which can make sense of the object and will exclude all future surprises. However much this may elude us in practice, it is what we often seek in science: we look for the ultimate theory in microphysics, where we will finally have charted all the particles and forces, and we do not have to face future revisions.

Second, coming to an understanding can never have this finality. For one thing, we come to understandings with certain definite interlocutors. These will not necessarily serve when we come to deal with others. Understandings are party-dependent. And then, frequently more worrying, even our present partners may not remain the same. Their life situation or goals may change and the understanding may be put in question. True, we try to control for this by binding agreements and contracts, but this is precisely because we see that what constitutes perfect and unconstrained mutual understanding at one time may no longer hold good later.

Third, the unilateral nature of knowing emerges in the fact that my goal is to attain a full intellectual control over the object, such that it can no longer "talk back" and surprise me. Now this may require that I make some quite considerable changes in my outlook. My whole conceptual scheme may be inadequate when I begin my inquiry. I may have to undergo the destruction and remaking of my framework of understanding to attain the knowledge that I seek. But all this serves the aim of full intellectual control. What does not alter in this process is my goal. I define my aims throughout in the same way.

By contrast, coming to an understanding may require that I give some ground in my objectives. The end of the operation is not control, or else I am engaging in a sham designed to manipulate my partner while pretending to negotiate. The end is being able in some way to function together with the partner, and this means listening as well as talking, and hence may require that I redefine what I am aiming at.

So there are three features of understandings—they are bilateral, they are party-dependent, they involve revising goals—that do not fit our classical model of knowing an object. To which our "normal" philosophical reaction is: quite so. These are features unsuited to knowledge, to real "science." The content of knowledge should not vary with the person who is seeking it; it can't be party-dependent. And the true seeker after knowledge never varies in her goal; there is no question of compromise here. Party-dependence and altered goals are appropriate to understandings precisely because they represent something quite different from knowledge; deal cutting and learning the truth are quite distinct enterprises, and one should never mix the two on pain of degrading the scientific enterprise.

How does Gadamer answer these "obvious" objections? His answer contains many rich and complex strands. I want to mention two here, leaving aside others that are equally, perhaps even more, important (such as the whole issue of "linguisticality," which is another of Gadamer's crucial contributions to the thought of our time).

The first is a negative point. Gadamer does not believe that the kind of knowledge that yields complete intellectual control over the object is attainable, even in principle, in human affairs. It may make sense to dream of this in particle physics, even to set this as one's goal, but not when it comes to understanding human beings.

Gadamer expresses this, for instance, in his discussion of experience. Following Hegel, he sees experience, in the full sense of the term, as "Erfahrung der Nichtigkeit" (Experience of Negation).[1] Experience is that wherein our previous sense of reality is undone, refuted, and shows itself as needing to be reconstituted. It occurs precisely in those moments where the object "talks back." The aim of science, following the model above, is thus to take us beyond experience. This latter is merely the path to science, whose successful completion would take it beyond this vulnerability to further such refutation. "Denn Erfahrung selber kann nie Wissenschaft sein. Sie steht in einem unaufhebbaren Gegensatz zum Wissen und zu derjenigen Belehrung, die aus theoretischem oder technischem Allgemeinwissen fliesst" ("for experience itself can never be science. Experience stands in an ineluctable opposition to knowledge and to the kind of instruction that follows from general theoretical or technical knowledge").[2] Now Gadamer sees it as part of the finitude of the human condition that this kind of transcending of experience is in principle impossible in human affairs. To explain fully why would involve talking a great deal about linguisticality, which I have no space for here. But perhaps the main point can be made tersely in terms of the place of culture in human life. Whatever we might identify as a fundamental common human nature, the possible object of an ultimate experience-transcending science is always and everywhere mediated in human life through culture, self-understanding, and language. These not only show an extraordinary variety in human history, but they are clearly fields of potentially endless innovation.

Here we see a big watershed in our intellectual world. There are those who hope to anchor an account of human nature below the level of culture, so that cultural variation, where it is not trivial and negligible, can be explained from this more basic account. Various modes of sociobiology and accounts of human motivation based on the (conjectured) conditions in which human beings evolved share this ambition. They have the necessary consequence that most cultural variation is placed in the first category and seen as merely epiphenomenal, a surface play of appearances. And then there are those who find this account of human life unconvincing, who see it as an evasion of the most important *explananda* in human life, which are to be found at this level of cultural difference.

Gadamer is one of the major theorists in the second camp, and hence he sees the model of science that I opposed above to understanding as inapplicable to human affairs.

This may help explain why he refuses this model, but not the adoption of his alternative based on interpersonal understanding. How does he justify party-dependence, and what analogue can he find to revising goals?

The first can be explained partly from the fact of irreducible cultural variation. From this, we can see how the language we might devise to understand the people of one society and time would fail to carry over to another. Human science could never consist exclusively of species-wide laws. In that sense, it would always be at least in part "idiographic" as against "nomothetic." But for Gadamer party-dependence is more radical than that. The terms of our best account will vary not only with the people studied but also with the students. Our account of the decline of the Roman Empire will not and cannot be the same as that put forward in eighteenth-century England, or those that will be offered in twenty-fifth-century China, or twenty-second-century Brazil.

It is this bit of Gadamer's argument that often strikes philosophers and social scientists as scandalous and "relativist," abandoning all allegiance to truth. This interpretation is then supported by those among Gadamer's defenders who are in a "postmodern" frame of mind.

But this grievously misunderstands the argument. Gadamer is anything but a "relativist" in the usual sense of today's polemics. To see this, we have to bring out another way in which Gadamer breaks with the ordinary understanding of "science."

As we often have been led to understand it in the past, scientific explanation deploys a language that is entirely clear and explicit. It is grounded in no unthought-out presuppositions, which may make those who speak it incapable of framing certain questions and entertaining certain possibilities. This false view has been largely dispelled in our time by the work of such thinkers as Kühn and Bachelard. We now understand that the practices of natural science have become universal in our world as the result of certain languages, with their associated practices and norms, having spread and been adopted by all societies in our time.

But what has been less remarked upon is that these languages became thus universally diffusible precisely because they were insulated from the languages of human understanding. The great achievement of the seventeenth-century scientific revolution was to develop a language for nature that was purged of human meanings. This was a revolution because the earlier scientific languages, largely influenced by Plato and Aristotle, were saturated with purpose and value terms. These could only have traveled along with a good part of the way of life of the civilizations that nourished them. But the new austere languages could be adopted elsewhere more easily.

We can see how different the situation is with the languages of "social science." These too have traveled, but very much as a result of the cultural influence and cultural alignment of the "West." Moreover, the languages of social science seem incapable of achieving the kind of universality we find with natural sciences. The study of human beings remains in a preparadigmatic condition, where a host of theories and approaches continue to compete, and there is no generally recognized "normal" science.

This difference in the fate of the two kinds of "science" is connected to the fact that the languages of human science always draw for their intelligibility on our ordinary understanding of what it is to be a human agent, live in society, have moral convictions, aspire to happiness, and so forth. No matter how much our ordinary everyday views on these issues may be questioned by a theory, we cannot but draw on certain basic features of our understanding of human life, those that seem so obvious and fundamental as not to need formulation. But it is precisely these that may make it difficult to understand people of another time or place.

Thus we can innocently speak of people in other ages holding opinions or subscribing to values without noticing that in our society there is a generalized understanding that everyone has, or ought to have, a personal opinion on certain subjects—say, politics or religion; or without being aware of how much the term "value" carries with it the sense of something chosen. But these background understandings may be completely absent in other societies. We stumble into ethnocentrism, not in virtue so much of the theses that we formulate, but of the whole context of understanding that we unwittingly carry over unchallenged.

Now this is not a danger that we can conjure once and for all by adopting a certain attitude. That is because the context that will give its sense to any theoretical account of human life we are entertaining will be the whole, tacit, background understanding of what it is to be a human being. But this is so wide and deep that there can be no question of simply suspending it and operating outside of it. To suspend it altogether would be to understand nothing about human beings at all. Here is where the striking contrast with the languages of natural science emerges. There it was possible to develop languages for the objects of science that bracketed out human meanings and still think effectively, indeed, more effectively, about the target domain. But bracketing out human meanings from human science means understanding nothing at all; it would mean betting on a science that bypassed understanding altogether and tried to grasp its domain in neutral terms, in the language of neurophysiology, for instance.

If our own tacit sense of the human condition can block our understanding of others, and yet we cannot neutralize it at the outset, then how can we come to know others? Are we utterly imprisoned in our own unreflecting outlook? Gadamer thinks not. The road to understanding others passes through the patient identification and undoing of those facets of our implicit understanding that distort the reality of the other.

At a certain point, we may come to see that "opinions" have a different place in our life-form than in those of others, and we will then be able to grasp the place of beliefs in their life; we will be ready to allow this to be in its difference, undistorted by the assimilation to "opinions."

This will happen when we allow ourselves to be challenged, interpellated by what is different in their lives, and this challenge will bring about two connected changes: we will see our peculiarity for the first time, as a formulated fact about us and not simply a taken-for-granted feature of the human condition as such; and at the same time, we will perceive the corresponding feature of their life-form undistorted. These two changes are indissolubly linked; you cannot have one without the other.

Our understanding of others will now be improved through this correction of a previous distortion, but it is unlikely to be perfect. The possible ways in which our background could enframe them distortively cannot be enumerated. We may still have a long way to go, but we will have made a step toward a true understanding; and further progress along this road will consist of such painfully achieved, particular steps. There is no leap to a disengaged standpoint which can spare us this long march.

Wird ein Vorurteil fraglich . . . so heisst dies mithin nicht, dass es einfach beiseite gesetzt wird und der andere oder das Andere sich an seiner Stelle unmittelbar zur Geltung bringt. Das ist vielmehr die Naïvität des historischen Objektivismus, ein solches Absehen von sich selbst anzunehmen. In Wahrheit wird das eigene Vorurteil dadurch recht eigentlich ins Speil gebracht, dass es selber auf dem Spiele steht. Nur indem es sich ausspielt, vermag es den Wahrheitsanspruch des anderen überhaupt zu erfahren und ermöglicht ihm, das er sich auch ausspielen kann.

(If a prejudice becomes questionable . . . this does not mean that it is simply set aside and the text or other person accepted as valid in its place. Rather historical objectivism shows its naivete in accepting this disregarding of ourselves as what actually happens. In fact our own prejudice is properly brought into play by being put at risk. Only by being given full play is it able to experience the other's claim to truth and make it possible for him to have full play himself.)[3]

We can now see how our grasp of the other, construed on the model of coming to an understanding, is doubly party-dependent, varying not only with the object studied but also with the student: with the object studied, because our grasp will have to be true to them in their particular culture, language, way of being. But it will also vary with the student, because the particular language we hammer out in order to achieve our understanding of them will reflect our own march toward this goal; it will reflect the various distortions that we have had to climb out of, the kinds of questions and challenges that they in their difference pose to us. It will not be the same language in which members of that culture understand themselves; it will also be different from the way members of a distinct third culture will understand them, coming as they will to this goal through a quite different route, through the identification and overcoming of a rather different background understanding.

That is why the historiography of the Roman Empire, carried out in twenty-fifth-century China or twenty-second-century Brazil, is bound to be different from ours. They will have to overcome different blocks to understanding; they will find the people of that time puzzling in ways which we do not; they will need to make them comprehensible through a different set of terms.

The coming-to-an-understanding model fits here, with its corollary of party dependence, because the language of an adequate science of the Ys for the Xs reflects both Xs and Ys. It is not, as with the knowledge-of-object model, a simple function of the object, the scientific theory that is perfectly adequate to this reality. It is a language that bridges those of both knower and known. That is why Gadamer speaks of it as a "fusion of horizons." The "horizons" here are at first distinct, they are the way that each has of understanding the human condition in their nonidentity. The "fusion" comes about when one (or both) undergo a shift; the horizon is extended so as to make room for the object that before did not fit within it.

For instance, we become aware that there are different ways of believing things, one of which is holding them as a "personal opinion." This was all that we allowed for before, but now we have space for other ways and can therefore accommodate the beliefs of a quite different culture. Our horizon is extended to take in this possibility, which was beyond its limit before.

But this is better seen as a fusion rather than just as an extension of horizons, because at the same time we are introducing a language to talk about their beliefs that represents an extension in relation to their language. Presumably, they had no idea of what we speak when we use the phrase "personal opinions," at least in such areas as religion, for instance. They would have had to see these as rejection, rebellion, and heresy. So the new language used here, which places "opinions" alongside other modes of believing as possible alternative ways of holding things true, opens a broader horizon, extending beyond both the original ones and in a sense combining them.

Here we see the full force of the Gadamerian image of the "conversation." The kind of operation described here can be carried out unilaterally and must be when one is trying to write the history of the Roman Empire, for instance. But it borrows its force from comparison with another predicament, in which live interlocutors strive to come to an understanding, to overcome the obstacles to mutual comprehension, to find a language in which both can agree to talk undistortively of each. The hermeneutical understanding of tradition limps after this paradigm operation; we have to maintain a kind of openness to the text, allow ourselves to be interpellated by it, take seriously the way its formulations differ from ours; all things which a live interlocutor in a situation of equal power would force us to do.

Horizons are thus often initially distinct. They divide us, but they are not unmovable; they can be changed, extended. I want to discuss this notion of horizon next, but first I must say a word about why this picture of a language for science that varies with both knower and known is quite different from the common idea of "relativism" and has a clear place for the concepts of correctness and truth.

Relativism is usually the notion that affirmations can be judged valid not unconditionally but only from different points of view or perspectives. Proposition p could be true from perspective A, false from perspective B, indeterminate from C, and so forth; but there would be no such thing as its being true or false unconditionally.

It does not seem to me that Gadamer is into this position at all. If the historiography of the Roman Empire in twenty-fifth-century China is different from our own, this will not be because what we can identify as the same propositions will have different truth values. The difference will be rather that different questions will be asked, different issues raised, different features will stand out as remarkable, and so forth.

Moreover, within each of these enterprises of studying Rome from these different vantage points, there will be such a thing as better or worse historiography.

Some accounts will be more ethnocentric and distortive than others, still others will be more superficial. Accounts can be ranked for accuracy, comprehensiveness, nondistortion, and so forth. Some will be more right than others, will approach closer to the truth.

But beyond this, we can also see a possible ranking between accounts from different starting points. Let us say that twenty-fifth-century Chinese historians take account of the work of Gibbon, Symes, Jones, Peter Brown, and so forth. They will be trying not just to fuse horizons with the Romans but also with us as we try to do the same thing. The fusion will not only be bipolar but triangular, or if we see Gibbon as a distinct standpoint, quadrangular.

We can see now that there is another virtue here of accounts. They can be more or less comprehensive in a new sense; not depending on how much detail and coverage they offer of the object studied, but rather on their taking in and making mutually comprehensible a wider band of perspectives. The more comprehensive account in this sense fuses more horizons.

The ideal of the most comprehensive account possible ought in a sense to take the place of the old goal of a point-of-view-less nomothetical science that grasps all humanity under one set of explanatory laws. Instead we substitute the ideal of languages that allow for the maximum mutual comprehension between different languages and cultures across history. Of course, this is a goal that can in the nature of things never be integrally realized. Even if, *per impossibile,* we might have achieved an understanding to which all cultures to date might sign on, this could not possibly preempt future cultural change, which would require the process of fusion to start over again.

But it is nevertheless an important ideal both epistemically and humanly: epistemically, because the more comprehensive account would tell more about human beings and their possibilities; humanly, because the language would allow more human beings to understand each other and to come to undistorted understandings.

For human affairs, the model of scientific theory that is adequate to an object is replaced by that of understanding, seen as a fusion of horizons. "Verstehen *ist* immer der Vorgang der Verschmelzung . . . vermeintlich für sich seiender Horizonte" ("understanding is always the fusion of these horizons supposedly existing by themselves").[4]

Gadamer's concept of "horizon" has an inner complexity that is essential to it. On one hand, horizons can be identified and distinguished; it is through such distinctions that we can come to grasp what is distorting understanding and impeding communication. But on the other hand, horizons evolve, change. There is no such thing as a fixed horizon. "Der Horizont ist vielmehr etwas, in das wir hineinwandern und das mit uns mitwandert. Dem Beweglichen verschieben sich die Horizonte" ("The horizon is, rather, something into which we move and that moves with us. Horizons change for a person who is moving").[5] A horizon with unchanging contours is an abstraction. Horizons identified by the agents whose worlds they circumscribe are always in movement. The horizons of A and B may thus be distinct at time *t* and their mutual understanding imperfect. But A and B by living together may come to have a single common horizon at $t+n$.

In this way "horizon" functions somewhat like "language." One can talk about the "language of modern liberalism," or the "language of nationalism," and point out the things they cannot comprehend. But these are abstractions, freeze frames of a continuing film. If we talk about the language of Americans or Frenchmen, we can no longer draw their limits a priori; for the language is identified by the agents who can evolve.

This way of understanding difference and its overcoming through the complex concept of a horizon is to be contrasted with two others. On one hand, we have the classic model that comes from the epistemological tradition, whereby our grasp of the world is mediated by the inner representations we make of it, or the conceptual grid through which we take it in. This way of construing knowledge easily generates the conjecture that there may be unbridgeable differences. What if our inner representations diverge, even as we stand before the same external objects? What if our conceptual grids are differently constructed, through which all the information we receive is filtered? How will we ever be able to convince each other, even understand each other? Any consideration that one may adduce in argument will already be represented or enframed by the other in a systematically different way. All reasoning stops at the borders of conceptual schemes, which pose insurmountable limits to our understanding.

In reaction to this, there is the attempt to establish the possibility of universal communication through an outright rejection of the idea of a conceptual scheme, as famously proposed by Donald Davidson.[6] Davidson means his argument to be taken as a repudiation of the whole representational epistemology. "In giving up the dualism of scheme and world, we do not give up the world, but re-establish unmediated touch with the familiar objects whose antics make our sentences and opinions true and false."[7]

As a rejection of the old epistemology (or at least attempted rejection; I am not sure that Davidson shakes off the shackles of the representational view), this is welcome. And Davidson's argument against the idea that we could be imprisoned in utterly incongruent schemes, invoking the "principle of charity," is obviously a powerful one. Davidson's principle of charity requires that I, the observer/theorist, must make sense of him, the subject studied, in the sense of finding most of what he does, thinks, and says intelligible; else I cannot be treating him as a rational agent and there is nothing to understand, in the relevant sense, at all.

What this argument shows is that total unintelligibility of another culture is not an option. To experience another group as unintelligible over some range of their practices, we have to find them quite understandable over other (very substantial) ranges. We have to be able to understand them as framing intentions; carrying out actions; trying to communicate orders, truths, and so forth. If we imagine even this away, then we no longer have the basis that allows us to recognize them as agents. But then there's nothing left to be puzzled about. Concerning nonagents, there is no question about what they are up to and hence no possibility of being baffled on this score.

The problem with this argument is that it is in a sense too powerful. It slays the terrifying mythical beast of total and irremediable incomprehensibility. But what we suffer from in our encounters between peoples are the jackals and vultures of partial and (we hope) surmountable noncommunication.

In this real-life situation, Davidson's theory is less useful, mainly because it seems to discredit the idea of "conceptual schemes" altogether—this in spite of the fact that the argument only rules out our meeting a totally unintelligible one. But in dealing with the real, partial barriers to understanding, we need to be able to identify what is blocking us. And for this we need some way of picking out the systematic differences in construal between two different cultures, without either reifying them or branding them as ineradicable. This is what Gadamer does with his image of the horizon. Horizons can be different, but at the same time they can travel, change, extend—as you climb a mountain, for instance. It is what Davidson's position as yet lacks.

Without this, Davidson's principle of charity is vulnerable to being abused to ethnocentric ends. The principle tells me to make the best sense of the other's words and deeds as I can. In translating his words into my language, I should render him so that as much as possible he speaks the truth, makes valid inferences, and so forth. But the issue is to know what counts as "my language" here. It can mean the language I speak at the moment of encounter, or it can mean the extended language, the one that emerges from my attempts to understand him, to fuse horizons with him. If we take it in the first way, it is almost certain that I will ethnocentrically distort him.

The problem is that the standing ethnocentric temptation is to make too quick sense of the stranger, that is, sense in one's own terms. The lesser breeds are without the law because they have nothing we recognize as law. The step to branding them as lawless and outlaw is as easy as it is invalid and fateful. So the conquistadores had an easy way of understanding the strange and disturbing practices of the Aztecs, including human sacrifice. While we worship God, these people worship the devil.

Of course, this totally violates Davidson's intent. But the problem is that we need to understand how we move from our language at the time of encounter, which can only distort those we encounter, to a richer language that has place for them, from making the "best sense" in our initial terms, which will usually be an alien imposition, to making the best sense within a fused horizon. I cannot see how we can conceive of or carry out this process without allowing into our ontology something like alternative horizons or conceptual schemes. This I think marks the superiority of Gadamer's view over Davidson's.

Davidson's argument is nonetheless very valuable in pointing out the dangers, even the paradoxes, involved in using any such terms. We can see this when we ask the question, what does the concept "scheme" contrast with? The term "content" is certainly bad, as though there were stuff already lying there, to be framed in different schemes. There is certainly a deep problem here.

It belongs to the very idea of a scheme, in the sense one is tempted to use it in intercultural studies, that it indicates some systematic way in which people are interpreting or understanding their world. Different schemes are incombinable such ways of understanding the same things.

But what things? How can you point to the things in question? If you use the language of the target society to get at them, then all distinction between scheme and content disappears. But what else can you use? Well, let us say our language, that of the observer/scientists, about this target area. But then we still will not have got at the "content" we share in common, which would have to be somehow identifiable independently of both schemes.

The point is well taken and needs to be kept in mind in order to avoid certain easy pitfalls, such as thinking that one has a neutral, universal categorization of the structures or functions of all societies, for example, "political system," "family," "religion," and so forth, which provide the ultimately correct description for what all the different fumbling cultural languages are aiming at, the noumena to their phenomenal tongues. But the notion of two schemes, one target area, remains valid and indeed indispensable.

Let's go back to the case of the conquistadores and the Aztecs. We might say that one thing the conquistadores had right was that they recognized that ripping out of hearts in some way corresponded in Spanish society to the Catholic Church and the Mass, and that sort of thing. That is, the right insight, yielding a good starting point for an eventual fusion of horizons, involves identifying what something in the puzzling life of an alien people can usefully be contrasted with in ours. In Gadamerian terms, what we are doing is identifying that facet of our lives which their strange customs interpellate, challenge, offer a notional alternative to.

An example will show what is at stake here. A few years ago a wildly reductivistic American social scientist produced a theory of Aztec sacrifice in which it was explained "materialistically" in terms of their need for protein. On this view the right point of comparison in Spanish society would be their slaughterhouses rather than their churches. Needless to say, from such a starting point, one gets nowhere.

The fruitful supposition is that what went on atop those pyramids reflected a very different construal of an X, which overlaps with what Christian faith and practice is a construal of in Spain. This is where thinking and inquiry can usefully start. It has one powerful—and in principle challengeable—presupposition: that we share the same humanness and that therefore we can ultimately find our feet in Aztec sacrifice, because it's a way of dealing with a human condition we share. Once this is accepted, then the notion of two schemes, same X, becomes inescapable. Only we have to be careful what we put in the place of the "X."

In a general proposition, we might say that what we put in place of the X is dimension, or aspect of the human condition. In the particular case, it is much more dangerous to specify. "Religion" would be an obvious candidate word. But the danger is precisely that we happily take on board everything this word means in our world and slide back toward the ethnocentric reading of the conquistadores. So we perhaps retreat to something vaguer, like "numinous," but even this carries its dangers.

The point is to beware of labels here. This is the lesson to be learned from attacks on the scheme-content distinction. But that the Mass and Aztec sacrifice belong to rival construals of a dimension of the human condition for which we have no stable, culture-transcendent name is a thought we cannot let go of, unless we want to relegate these people to the kind of unintelligibility that members of a different species would have for us. If rejecting the distinction means letting this go, it is hardly an innocent step.

The conception of horizons and their fusion shows how the "science" we have of other times and people is, like the understandings we come to, party-dependent. It will differ both with the object and the subject of knowledge.

But how about the analogue to the other property of understandings I mentioned above, that they may involve changing our goals? The analogous point here is that in coming to see the other correctly, we inescapably alter our understanding of ourselves. Taking in the other will involve an identity shift in us. That is why it is so often resisted and rejected. We have a deep identity investment in the distorted images we cherish of others.

That this change must occur falls out from the account of the fusion of horizons. To recur to our example: we come to see that attributing "opinions" to them is distortive. But we only ever did so originally, because it seemed to go without saying that this is what it meant to have beliefs in certain areas. To get over the distortion, we had to see that there were other possibilities, that our way of being isn't the only or "natural" one, but that it represents one among other possible forms. We can no longer relate to our way of doing or construing things "naively," as just too obvious to mention.

If understanding the other is to be construed as fusion of horizons and not as possessing a science of the object, then the slogan might be: no understanding the other without a changed understanding of self.

The kind of understanding that ruling groups have of the ruled, that conquerors have of the conquered—most notably in recent centuries in the far-flung European empires—has usually been based on a quiet confidence that the terms they need are already in their vocabulary. Much of the "social science" of the last century is in this sense just another avatar of an ancient human failing. And indeed, the satisfactions of ruling, beyond the booty, the unequal exchange, the exploitation of labor, very much includes the reaffirmation of one's identity that comes from being able to live this fiction without meeting brutal refutation. Real understanding always has an identity cost—something the ruled have often painfully experienced. It is a feature of tomorrow's world that this cost will now be less unequally distributed.

The cost appears as such from the standpoint of the antecedent identity, of course. It may be judged a gain once one has gone through the change. We are also enriched by knowing what other human possibilities there are in our world. It cannot be denied, however, that the path to acknowledging this is frequently painful.

The crucial moment is the one where we allow ourselves to be interpellated by the other; where the difference escapes from its categorization as an error, a fault, or a lesser, undeveloped version of what we are, and challenges us to see it as a viable human alternative. This unavoidably calls our own self-understanding into question. This is the stance Gadamer calls "openness." As against the way I stand to what I see as an object of science, where I try "sich selber aus der Beziehung zum anderen herauszureflektieren und dadurch von ihm unerreichbar zu werden" ("reflecting [myself] out of [my] relation to the other and so becoming unreachable by him"),[8] "Offenheit für den anderen schliesst . . . die Anerkennung ein, dass ich in mir etwas gegen mich gelten lassen muss, auch wenn es keinen anderen gäbe, der es gegen mich geltend machte" ("Openness to the other . . . involves recognizing that I myself must accept some things that are against me, even though no one else forces me to do so").[9]

Gadamer's argument in *Wahrheit und Methode* deals with our understanding of our own tradition, the history of our civilization, and the texts and works which belong to this. This means that what we study will be in one way or another internal to our identity. Even where we define ourselves against certain features of the past, as the modern Enlightenment does against the "Middle Ages," this remains within our identity as the negative pole, that which we have overcome or escaped. We are part of the *Wirkungsgeschichte* of this past, and as such it has a claim on us.

My point in this essay has been that Gadamer's account of the challenge of the other and the fusion of horizons applies also to our attempts to understand quite alien societies and epochs. The claim here comes not from their place within our identity, but precisely from their challenge to it. They present us different and often disconcerting ways of being human. The challenge is to be able to acknowledge the humanity of their way, while still being able to live ours. That this may be difficult to achieve, that it will almost certainly involve a change in our self-understanding and hence in our way, has emerged from the above discussion.

Meeting this challenge is becoming ever more urgent in our intensely intercommunicating world. At the turn of the millennium, it is a pleasure to salute Hans-Georg Gadamer, who has helped us so immensely to conceive this challenge clearly and steadily.

CHAPTER THREE

Language Not Mysterious?

I AGREE profoundly with the Wittgensteinian thrust of Robert Brandom's exciting work. We can see this as a multidimensional holism. Like Wittgenstein, and others who ultimately relate back to Kant, such as Hegel, Heidegger, and Merleau-Ponty, Brandom offers a devastating critique of the atomism which is implicit in the mainstream post-Cartesian epistemology.

This, as I have argued elsewhere, can be seen as a (partly justified) method which has been illegitimately projected onto ontology. The method is one which is meant to check and verify our too hastily drawn conclusions, and consists in breaking the problematic area down into its smallest parts, and checking each of these and their connections. The illegitimate ontological projection issues in the idea that this is how we in fact think, deep down.

So we accredit the idea (1) that one could first take in one piece of information, then another; then link them, and see the correlation; and hence make inferences. Then (2) one could pass to another plane, and start communicating these "ideas"; to which end one would "invent" language. This too proceeds atomistically: first one word is invented, then another, then another. See Condillac's famous treatise.[1]

Process (1) doesn't make sense for Brandom. How could we take in an isolated piece of information? What sense could we make of such an isolated bit of information? Well what sense *do* we make of it? Elder says: "go, Scout, and see if there are any tiger tracks." Scout comes back: "Elder, I saw a paw track in the sand!" That's a particulate bit, but it makes sense here within our whole general grasp of our situation, which includes forest, tigers, the consequent danger of being eaten, our collaborative efforts to avoid this and other dangers, and so on.

This bit is relevant because it will license multiple inferences, practical and factual. Included among the former would be here: "Let's not go there now." So Brandom's opening move in *Making It Explicit* is absolutely crucial. He dethrones representation as the primary building-block of thought and language. What is crucial is inferences.

Here he joins up with the holism of Heidegger and Merleau-Ponty, who insist on a primacy of our whole grasp of things; in Kant-speak: the transcendental unity of apperception over the elementary bits.

Process (2) likewise doesn't make sense. Again, what could we do with, what sense could we make of, a single word? Here both Brandom and Wittgenstein connect back to Herder in his famous critique of Condillac. The French thinker tried to explain the origin of language through his famous fable of two children in the wilderness. It was part of their natural endowment that they tended to cry out when frightened. The cry was in a sense a natural sign of danger. The children come in time to use this as a word for danger; they treat this as an "instituted" sign in Condillac's terms.

Herder protests that the really difficult issue has been covered up. How do they become capable of understanding what a "word," an "instituted" sign, is, what it involves? Building on both Kant and Frege, Wittgenstein unpacks something of what is involved, that is, the background of practices and activities and the understanding they suppose, which make possible, by making sense of, our uses of language. Meaningful language requires a context of action.

Canonically, we can see this consciousness developing in our philosophical tradition over the last two centuries or so, gradually undoing the tunnel vision abstractions of the main line of modern epistemology (Descartes, Hobbes, Locke, Hume, Condillac). Brandom's *Tales of the Mighty Dead* sets out one interesting version of this canon.[2] I offer a simplified version here. Kant introduced the primacy of the judgment, that is, you can't understand what it is to master a word, or concept, without mastering the feat of making judgments. Frege develops this point further with his enunciation of the primacy of the sentence: "Nur im Zusammenhang des Satzes hat ein Wort Bedeutung."

But Wittgenstein takes us well beyond this, because he sees that making judgments, cast in the form of sentences, is only one among many language games. More accurately, there is a family of such games, which have in common that they put in play "prepositional contents," combinations of reference and predication, which can be used to make empirical claims ("Sam smokes"), to ask questions about how things are ("does Sam smoke?"), and to give commands ("Sam, smoke!").[3] But lots of other things are going on in language. We also establish intimacy or distance; open contact and close it off; cry for, and give or withhold sympathy; disclose the beauty of the world, or the depths of our feelings, or the virtues of the good life, or the nature and demands of God or the gods, and so on.

Some of these other activities are going on in and through the enunciation of sentences, and the making of judgments: "Die Welt ist tief" (Nietzsche);[4] "God is Great!" But a lot else is going on which we won't get if we just focus on the judgments qua judgments. A great deal is carried in the rhetorical stance, tone of voice, body language, choice of words with a given resonance: these are clearly determinative of intimacy or distance, giving or withholding sympathy, and much else besides. Moreover, the disclosive power of our words in poetry is plainly something we often can't bring to light just by fixing clearly the reference and predication of the judgments we can identify (sometimes, indeed, the force depends on the very uncertainty attending these).

All these points suggest that the boundaries of language as we ordinarily take it, that is, speech in words, are perhaps too restrictive. Some of the disclosive work of poetry, rhetorical exhortation, the projection of ideals, the revelation of beauty, and so on, has close analogies to what goes on in painting, in music, in dance, in gesture. Perhaps to get clear on the whole phenomenon of human language, we need to see how the narrower phenomenon (speech in words) relates to the broader field of the whole range of "symbolic forms," in Cassirer's terms.

Wittgenstein takes the context-building of Kant and Frege (judgment or sentence as the context for word-meaning), and in turn embeds this in a wider frame: as one set of language games among others; and he sets the language games in the all-encompassing frame of a form of life.

There is another dimension of Wittgenstein's contextualization, which goes beyond Frege and Kant (though not Hegel, to take an important figure from Brandom's *Tales of the Mighty Dead*). Language games are social; they are developed and played out in exchange. If a word can't have meaning outside of the capacity of making judgments, this capacity itself can only arise within games of exchange, what Brandom calls games of "giving and asking for reasons." The primacy of sentence over word turns out to mean also the primacy of the dialogical over the monological.

Much of the above, in particular this latter point, is brilliantly developed in Brandom's work. We are all very much in his debt, so that it is almost churlish to enter caveats and cavils here. But philosophy is in a sense a perpetual disturbance of the peace, and so I plunge on.

I have set the stage in the above which should allow me to identify the area in which (I think) our disagreement lies. The stage is set by the story I have been telling, which seems close to Brandom's story, of our slow and difficult emergence from the hole that modern epistemology and the primacy of monological representation dug for us. The climbing gear, the pick and pitons, which have enabled this are the identifications of essential contexts. The isolated bit of information cannot be outside of the framework of judgments, which means also a framework of exchange, a particular language game, eventually a way of life.

The question that needs to be asked here is, how far must this embedding in necessary contexts go? There is a set of language games, whose goal is to make, exchange, and check claims about the factual state of things, and draw inferences about other states, or practically about what to do. Plainly this is a package deal. One can't imagine a language capacity which would consist of deploying just isolated moves in this set of games—say, a single person having a single bit of information, then finding a word for it, then communicating it to another; or people just having representations, then making inferences.

But is this package—let's call it the "everyday fact-establishing and practical" package—itself self-sufficient? Or can we only make sense of our having this set of capacities if we set them in the context of our ability to operate through the whole range of symbolic forms which I gestured at above?

Right away this question might appear ill-formed, until we are able to define the boundaries of "fact-establishing." Does it include establishing "facts" about the beauty of things, the depth of feelings, the virtues of the good life, the existence and will of gods? After all, about these matters we may also give and ask for reasons. But to take the term in this broad sense would in effect foreclose the question I'm trying to pose. The answer would have to be negative.

Let me set out my reasons for this last claim, because they are crucial to my argument here. A serious attempt in prose to set out true judgments about the beauty of things (aesthetics), the virtues of life (ethics), or the nature of God (theology) has to draw on uses of language, in Cassirer's broad sense, which are disclosive. I mean the uses which either without asserting at all, or going beyond their assertive force, make something manifest through articulating it.

Let me say something about this distinction assertoric/disclosive that I have been invoking here. This is meant to mark a contrast. A pure case of the disclosive would be where we use language, or some symbolic form to articulate and thus make accessible to us something—a feeling, a way of being, a possible meaning of things—without making any assertion at all. For me, Chopin's Fantaisie-Impromptu in C Sharp Minor articulates a certain as yet indefinable longing; it draws me into it, and makes it part of my world. I daresay I am not alone in seeing this in the music, and that this was not foreign to the inspiration Chopin had in composing it. A human possibility is articulated and disclosed here, but nothing at all is asserted.

At the other end, when the cook shouts out of the kitchen to the men in the yard, "Soup's on!," something is asserted, but nothing is disclosed. But the contrast does not simply hold between "pure" uses of language or symbols. For an immense range of human speech and symbol, there is both assertion and disclosure. Very obviously, this is the case in poetry and novels, but it is clearly present also in works of philosophy, as soon as one is attentive to their rhetorical dimension, and the range of literary reference they draw on. In these cases, we can speak of the disclosive dimension of a work, for instance, the stance to the world that an author is articulating for us, that he may even be drawing us into, convincing us to adopt, so powerful is his portrayal, the stance which I as a reader critic might capture in my own assertoric prose, defining it by describing its essential features, but which is not so described in the novel. Tolstoy offers a useful example, because he could not resist being his own critic, and offering long moralistic descriptions in *War and Peace,* driving home is assertoric form what was meant to be disclosed in the narrative.

Now my claim here is that there are certain matters which can't be properly explored without recourse to the disclosive dimension. That is, there couldn't be an intelligent discussion of the beauty of landscape which didn't either deploy, or draw on, our familiarity with, say, certain paintings, or certain powerfully evocative descriptions. There couldn't be a discussion of Christian piety which didn't draw on, say, the music of Bach, or certain hymns, or Chartres Cathedral, or an evocative life of Saint Francis, or the *Divine Comedy,* or . . . the list could be extended almost indefinitely. Treatises on ethics either draw on disclosive works, or move at some or other point into an evocative-disclosive key ("the starry skies above and the moral law within"; or the contrast between the social virtues and the "monkish" virtues). The notion of a totally rhetoric-free work on ethics is close to absurdity. Few books are more unintentionally comic than the moral treatises of fiercely (on epistemic grounds) anti-rhetorical, metaphor-mistrusting philosophers, like Hobbes or Bentham. The reader is offered a feast of powerful images—Leviathan, lives which are "nasty, brutish and short," "two sovereign masters, pain and pleasure"—all in the name of sober, purified reason.

So there is no point even asking the question, whether the fact-establishing and practical family of games could exist on its own, unless we draw the boundaries pretty narrowly. One way of drawing them would be to fence in the zone in terms of the everyday practical issues dealt with. In this zone, we establish the state of things and make inferences of an everyday practical kind. The practical inferences draw on norms that are treated as unproblematic, and remain unproblematized, or else on the uncontroversial behavioral meanings of things.

Examples of the first might be: "I'm invited to dine with the Governor-General, so I'd better fetch my tux from the cleaners"; of the second: "there's a tiger loose in the woods, so don't go there," or "it's going to rain, so take an umbrella." This class might also include: "Patricia says the paintings are beautiful, so we'll go to the Exhibition." Brandom's examples are mainly drawn from this everyday domain.

Beyond this, there are more specialized domains, where the things taken for granted in the everyday domain might be challenged. For instance, we might question, and hence transform, our practices of fact-finding (science, among other things, does this). Or we might question our norms—maybe I should follow the example of Evo Morales, and wear a sweater to dinner with the Governor-General, to make a political point? And are we sure that Patricia knows beautiful painting when she sees it? Of course, the boundaries are fluid here, but some rough distinctions of level can be made, defining the everyday as the domain of the unproblematized.

Now we might hope to treat the everyday package so defined as self-sufficient, as not dependent on the disclosive dimension of language, and thus on the wider range of symbolic forms. We might then make another move: extend the boundary to allow in the specialized domains of (natural?) science, because these by their very nature operate on a set of exclusions which demand that we sideline the disclosive, that is they function without drawing on metaphysical, theological, aesthetic considerations, or on moral values, and without being swayed in one's reasonings by the rhetorical force of the expressions used.

We would then arrive at a familiar grouping, the language games of science and everyday life, which the Vienna positivists already identified as their zone of unproblematic meaningfulness, over against "metaphysics," "poetry," religion, and the like.

But within this general zoning proposal, there are harder and softer versions. There are hard-line materialists, for instance, who frown on sciences of the human which aren't taken from the beginning as reducible to some level of natural science (minds to be explained by the functioning of brains, emotions by endocrinology). And there are more permissive versions which leave these questions open. One very severe version, which wants to admit only natural science–style causation into its ontology, and which appeals to what Quine called "a taste for desert landscapes," is denounced by Brandom under the name "naturalism." He insists, against them, that we have to introduce norms into our account of language. Naturalism consists in the attempt to "bake a normative cake with non-normative ingredients," and is bound to fail.[5] Here Brandom stands in a very important modern tradition, with Russell, Husserl, and others in their denunciation of "psychologism," and their recognition that this type of reduction makes nonsense of logic.

Moving farther in an inclusive direction, some philosophers want to fence in certain reasonings about ethics, in fact what is usually called "morals"—

that is, norms which regulate our actions toward each other. This inclusion can be justified by the claim that we can define a morals on the basis of "reason alone," independent of metaphysics, theology, or people's conceptions of the good life. Such attempts in our day usually draw either on Benthamite or Kantian traditions, and they include some of the most influential of today's moral philosophers: for example, Rawls (in one of his stages), Habermas, Scanlon. I, alas, haven't read all of Brandom's work, but I suspect that he has some sympathy for a position of this range.

But even a broad-gauge ontology, which would allow norms, and even moral norms, into the bounded area, would still possibly be able to leave the disclosive uses of language outside, and hence could lay claim to a positive answer to my above question, whether the fact-establishing practical family can be seen as at least potentially self-sufficient.

Before I come to grips with Brandom's work, I'd like to explore a bit further the reasons for defining such a bounded frame for fact-establishing discourse. Of course, part of it may be the familiar "secularist" outlook that wishes to separate itself from the religious and metaphysical beliefs which have dominated the human past. But the crucial idea involved here is a concept of "reason alone" ("die blosse Vernunft," in Kant's famous formulation).[6] By this I mean a notion of human reason, which can suffice to tackle the whole range of inescapable human problems, but which can do so without relying on the deliverances of religion or metaphysics. This is not synonymous with, but can easily evolve into, a notion of reason that doesn't have to have recourse to the disclosive-articulative dimension of human language in the broad sense.

The bridges between these two formulations are, first, that religious claims, and often also metaphysical ones, rely heavily on alleged truths derived from this dimension. But second, there is the fact that the canons of argument can be made much more rigorous and conclusive, if one leaves the disclosive aside. We can more easily agree on the conclusions of natural science, and certain facts about human desires and aspirations, as well as the rules of logic, while differences on the nature of beauty, on the highest virtues, on the existence of God, and the like, seem quite intractable. By stripping down its range of operation, reason can become more effective in reaching common conclusions.

Behind this mode of thinking stands obviously the spectacular success of natural science since Galileo, which has been won precisely by factoring out the whole culturally varied domain of the human meanings of things, and frames the phenomena to be studied in neutral terms in a stance of disengagement. This has obviously been the model inspiring the aspiration to a more restricted, and for this reason more effective reason, although only the most radical, materialist versions would make natural science the royal road to all valid truth.

So we can see that here are powerful motivations to believe in a family of fact-establishing practical language games, whose scope is drawn narrowly enough to exclude the disclosive. Now the hope here is that this narrowed realm of reason can suffice to decide all the inescapable issues of human life. It follows that what the disclosive dimension yields is not essential for these issues. This can be assured, on one hand, by declaring certain deliverances of the disclosive dimension as without any real object (religion, metaphysics), and by declaring others as expressive of legitimate differences of taste and temperament (ethics, i.e., modes of the good life, as against moral rules; and aesthetics, the beautiful, what moves us in art and nature). We will differ on these latter questions, but there is no common object to agree about; what moves us reflects our own variable natures, not some common independent reality.

So one of the strongest strands of the motivation to this narrowed reason is epistemological, that certain questions would be easier to resolve if the really divisive issues could be legitimately left aside. In this, there is an echo of the original epistemological tradition, whose errors can also be seen as epistemologically driven. I argued above that we can see the original positing of particulate bits of information as a kind of reflection of what was seen as a good method. This is the one which Descartes sets out in the *Rules for the Direction of the Mind,* and involves our breaking any issue down into its smallest elements, and then building up to the global solution by careful steps.[7] The error was to project this resolutive-compositive method onto the mind, not just as a good way of proceeding in certain questions, which it undoubtedly is, but as how the mind really works. We ontologized the method.

The question arises, whether something similar isn't happening here, in this narrowing of reason. It would be handy epistemically, if a restricted definition of reason alone really panned out, that is, really could solve all the inescapable questions; so we jump too quickly to the belief that this is how things are.

The original mistake had two sides: first, ontologizing the method; but then, as a result, applying it universally, even where it didn't work at all. So atomism was applied everywhere, to thoughts in our minds, to "impressions" of the world (Hume), to words invented one by one to form language (Condillac), and to societies as broken down into individuals (Hobbes). Some of these applications turned out to be crippling, and we are only slowly climbing out of them. (We still hear of "methodological individualism" in politics and sociology.)

In the case we're looking at here, our understanding of human language, it might also be true that the mistake has two sides: first, ontologizing the method, that is believing that this narrower reason really can resolve all inescapable problems; and then, because of this, applying it to areas where it is disastrously mal-adapted (like the study of societies with quite different cultures, or of ethical ways of life, or of religions, etc.).

But is it a mistake? We mustn't draw the parallels too close. Of course, if we look at the actual phylogenesis of human language-users, and the ontogenesis of human agents, it is clear that this stripped-down reason has not been operating from the start. A plausible account of phylogenesis, like that of Merlin Donald, for instance, would see our hominid ancestors developing a culture of linguistic communication through stages; involving, first, mimesis, ritual, and dance; and then perhaps later, myth and narrative; finally developing what we think of now as speech, with the capacity to operate on the meta-level, making second-order judgments about the validity of first-order ones.[8] The very possibility of conceiving stripped-down reason only appears at the third level, and is realized over centuries of development.

Something parallel is obviously true for ontogenesis, where the mimetic and the narrative have a big role early on, before the child grows beyond what Piaget calls "egocentrism."

Now such phylo- and ontogenetic considerations immediately invalidate the epistemological-atomist claim, because that tried to tell us how the mind always works. But "reason alone" isn't vulnerable to this. It can allow for a genesis in which it emerges out of more primitive modes of thought. We slough off these earlier forms, and the assumptions about the cosmos and God on which they depend, and we become adult and independent reasoners. We have grown beyond our "self-inflicted nonage" ("selbstbeschuldigte Unmündigkeit," as Kant called it),[9] and can reason in this way.

The issue of false ontologization here is quite independent of our genetic story; it amounts to this: can we conceive of a viable way of human life in which the fruits of the articulative-disclosive dimension are clearly segregated from public reason and relegated to the zone of differential personal experience? (which of course wouldn't prevent us from mutual communication and exchange about them). The second question, that about the scope of this "reason alone," takes up the same issue from another direction. Does this stripped down reason constitute a good method for deciding only a certain restricted range of questions, for instance, those of natural science, where no one would contest its appropriateness? Or is it also omnicompetent, that is, sufficient for all inescapable questions to be resolved by reason? These questions are closely related, but, as we shall see below, slightly different.

Oĸ, why am i going on at length about this, when I should be talking about Robert Brandom? I crave the reader's indulgence, the more so in that I want to go a little bit longer talking at this level. The issue I'm addressing is this: after all the discoveries we have made (and Brandom helped make) about the necessary contexts of our ordinary uses of language, is there one more contextualization we have to make? Are our everyday fact-establishing practical games of giving and asking for reasons, which we have shown to be the essential context for all the micro-moves within them, themselves only possible in a broader context, that of the range of symbolic forms which run the full range from pure assertoric to pure disclosive?

And a good reason for asking this question is that there has been a strong temptation to answer it in the negative, to assert the self-sufficiency of the factual-practical. We saw one range of motives for this, following the reasoning of the Vienna Circle, and another (overlapping) range, which springs from a deep investment in the idea of a post-metaphysical way of life grounded on "reason alone."

But there is also another very influential view, which draws its motivation from a certain biologism. Human beings should be explicable, like other animals, in terms of their biology. The exigencies of human survival and the hazards of evolution have wired into our natures a certain number of goals. These can be established, as for any other species, by observing us.

If we think of humans as another animal species, seeking survival, then the development of language can appear as a great advantage. Imagine that a group of hominids regularly hunts mammoths. They surround the great beast and attack from several sides; or try to scare it into a trap. What an inestimable boon it would be to develop a mode of communication permitting something like our factual-practical family of language games. You could shout out: "Watch out! He's turning left!" This is the context in which some theorists seem to think of the evolution of language. For instance, Steve Pinker in *The Language Instinct*.[10]

And Bernard Williams in *Truth and Truthfulness* argues plausibly that these two goals, establishing reliable truth, and communicating it reliably to one's fellows, would be highly prized in early human societies.

So from the evolutionary biological standpoint, there is already a positive reason to see the factual-practical family as the crucial gain over their hominid ancestors that language offered homo sapiens.

And negatively, there is a reason to look askance at the disclosive. We saw above that this cannot be avoided if we want to make a serious attempt to establish what is really beautiful, or really good, or really Godly. But the aim of the sociobiological approach is to bracket these questions. True, people seek what they call truth, beauty, goodness, and often think of these in relation to God. But the "scientific" approach disregards the language, and looks at the actual patterns of behavior. In this way, following Hume, we can establish the patterns of reaction called "morality": actuated by sympathy, they feel or react positively to actions which enhance the general utility. We can also quite well understand how this kind of pattern would have been selected for in evolution: bad team players must have been given a hard time, and had a short life.

Similarly, rather than focusing on the issue of what true love is, and the fidelity it requires, we note that pair-bonding as a behavior pattern has been selected for. An obvious "just-so" story suggests itself why the gene for this would become preponderant. And, of course, another "just-so" story can explain why, while upholding the general rule, so many men want to "cheat." Having multiple partners spreads one's genes wider.

Obviously, to practice this kind of sociobiological explanation, the disclosive offers no help. It can only distract from the main story, which is the selection of certain patterns of external behavior, however rationalized in terms of goodness and beauty. The stripped-down picture of human life now looks like this: through evolution humans have acquired a tendency to desire certain patterns of action: pair-bonding of men with women, some degree of mutual aid, and to react positively to actions which increase the general utility. But these are not sufficient to determine their behavior, because they can and often must reason how to encompass these goals, or manifest these reactions. Moreover, thanks to language they can deliberate together, and also pursue enquiry, so that over time their rational calculations become more effective and far-reaching.

All this points to the thought that what is crucial about human language is just the "Viennese" combination above: the fact-finding pragmatic family of language games, augmented by empirical science.

So we have isolated three motivations to assert the self-sufficiency of the factual-practical family: the "Vienna" one (all other uses are meaningless); the "postmetaphysical" one (we are acceding to a culture based on "reason alone"); and the sociobiological one.

But why talk about all this in an essay on Robert Brandom? Because I suspect that I might have been talking about him after all, that in other words he subscribes to some version of the self-sufficiency of fact-establishing practical language games, or otherwise put, of stripped-down reason.

And the evidence?—Well, remember, I just said "suspect." We aren't at the stage of an indictment here, let alone a conviction.—Yes, but the evidence?

Twofold: first, certain statements which belong very much to the vocabulary of the stripped-down version. Which ones? Well, statements like this, about the norms that we have to suppose at the heart of language games, that "their existence is neither supernatural [n]or mysterious."[11] Or, again about norms, as products of social interaction; as such, they "are not studied by the natural sciences—though they are not for that reason to be treated as spooky or supernatural."[12]

Secondly, in defense of these demurrals, Brandom seems to want to insist on how norms are somehow our creatures. Normative attitudes, he says, "have been appealed to in explaining where discursive norms came from—how sapience could have arisen out of the primordial nondiscursive ooze of mere sentience. For it has been claimed not just that we discursive beings are creatures of norms but also that norms are in some sense creatures of ours . . ."[13] Now in some sense this last sentence must be true; the "creating" goes both ways. But I believe that there is also an asymmetry here, which this phrase doesn't quite capture, and which has very much to do with the issue of stripped-down reason.

All right, maybe I am hypersensitive, pathologically suspicious, jumping to conclusions about Brandom's real meaning. So for the remainder of this discussion, let me switch tack. I want to say what I think is wrong with both of these claims, and leave undecided whether Brandom puts them forward in the sense that I am denying them.

Take the first group: "spooky" is too vague; and "supernatural" is odd, even absurd (what is part of the "natural order" if not fish swimming, birds flying, humans talking?). So let me focus on "mysterious." It seems to me a very apt word to characterize human language, and its emergence in the course of hominid-to-human evolution.

I want to distinguish three facets of the meaning of this widely used word, not all of which are always in play, of course. (1) We use it to designate something which defies understanding, something we can't explain, which even seems impossible given how we (think we) know things work, but nevertheless happens. This is the sense in which a novel is a "murder mystery." (2) It can also mean something which is (1), but also given a great importance, because the puzzling matter is something of great depth and moment; what is still barely understood here would reveal something of great moment about us, the cosmos, God, or whatever. (3) If we draw on the etymology, which relates the word to what is hidden, and then also to the process of initiation, in which secrets are revealed, then another facet comes to the fore: here we are dealing with the way that we could come to know more about the matter in question. Something is a "mystery" in this sense, when we can't come to understand it by taking a disengaged stance to it, applying already articulated concepts, but when we have to open ourselves to our experience of it, explore it by immersing ourselves in it. For example, the behavior of people of another culture can be mysterious, but we can learn to understand it by immersing ourselves in it, interacting with the people, remaining open to their values, norms, ways of talking. If we remain fixed within our initial judgments about them: strange, coarse, barbaric, etc., we will impede the learning, and never grasp what they're about. Or the appeal of a work of art can be baffling, until we allow ourselves to be led by the articulations of a helpful friend and give our full attention to it.

Now it is clear that some things can be (1) without being (2) or (3) (murder mysteries). Some things are both (1) and (3), without being (2) (a work of art which is itself not terribly profound). But some things are at once (1) and (2) and (3). Leaving aside the mysteries of religion, I would nominate human language and its genesis as the prime example of such a three-faceted mystery. It seems to me (1) that we haven't got a clue how these capacities of mimesis, narrative, and then descriptive speech emerged out of earlier life-forms and only a very incomplete grasp of how they relate to each other. Then (2) that there are few matters which touch more profoundly on what it is to be a human being. We are in sum the "zôon echon logon" of which Aristotle speaks, but giving "logos" its fuller sense englobing both speech and reason. And then, to the extent that articulating to disclose is crucial to language, it is the very realm where (3) holds, where we have to engage with things (works of art, modes of human life, our relation to God) in a stance of openness and potential neologism, in order to articulate what they're about.

So that saying that language and/or its genesis isn't mysterious is like saying that Atlas isn't strong, or Aphrodite isn't beautiful. It sounds weird.

Yes, but if we could sidestep the articulative-disclosive, then (3) would not hold; and also (1) would be less true, because one of the more unfathomable aspects of language would be sidelined. That's what makes me attribute the narrower view to people who say this kind of thing. I know that we could look at it all on a rhetorical level. That the repudiation of mystery and the supernatural is there to balance the (to materialists shocking) idea that norms can't be reduced to causal processes like those in inanimate nature. It's meant to express some kind of agreement in spite of the difference. But around what? I will return to this in a minute.

But first, I admit that my reaction to the denial of mystery as just weird depends on my substantive view on the main issue. I want to answer this question with a resounding negative: the factual-practical can't be self-sufficient. Our ability to operate with this family of language games depends on our operating in the whole range of symbolic forms. The articulative/disclosive is the essential background to our most immediately "practical" discourse.

In other words, I remain convinced that the articulative cannot be peeled off from the public giving of and asking for reasons, and hence that (3) applies. Why not? Because even in those narrow areas where a stripped-down reason appropriately applies, as in natural science, or logic and mathematics, there is a continuing and I believe irremovable presence of the articulative-disclosive.

There's a big case to argue here, and not very much space to lay it out, so let me just mention some subclaims which are meant to back up the bigger claim. Here are a few, which tackle one form of the question:

a. Even in the exchanges about natural science, rhetoric is being deployed. It doesn't seem possible to argue, to try to convince each other, without framing the debate rhetorically, with such phrases as "everyone agrees that"; "surely, the crucial issue is"; and the like.

b. The practice of this austere type of enquiry is sustained and guided by an ethic, a certain notion of human excellence, of dedication to the truth, of unflinching facing of unwelcome findings, of full communication. Indeed, this connects back to (a), in that rhetorical stances in these exchanges often try to position the speaker as a paragon practitioner of this ethic (and/or the opponent as grievously failing in this department).

c. Becoming the kind of person who can operate under this ethic is inseparable from a development of self-consciousness and self-examination. It's not by accident that this science develops first in a culture which is simultaneously developing radical self-scrutiny, and a sense of my own responsibility.

What is emerging here is the way in which very stripped-down fact-establishing language games still need a Sitz im Leben, in a life in which the kind of self-understandings which can only develop through articulation and disclosure play an ineliminable role. The claim is not that considerations about these disclosures, say, about the ethic that science demands, play a direct role as premises in the arguments deployed—except negatively, that your words are disqualified if you're violating these precepts. It is rather that the fact-establishing game can't be carried on except within a richer form of life that includes considerations which it can't deploy itself in the giving and asking for (its kinds of) reasons. Science with agents who couldn't understand and respond to this ethic is a human impossibility, though it might be imagined in a strange faraway galaxy in a science fiction story.

The argument for this contextualization is not the same directly evident one which we saw in the deconstruction of atomistic epistemology, viz., that something like a particulate representation, prior to inference, doesn't make any sense. You could write a science fiction story about scientists who were ethical zombies, as I said above; this proves that in some sense it is imaginable. But it is humanly impossible.

So much for the argument against ontologization of this stripped-down reason. But we can also argue against the other side of the stripped-down claim, which holds that this reduced reason can handle all inescapable issues. Here my considerations will already be familiar. (i) It seems to me wildly implausible that we can ever come to understand human society in history, especially cultures very different from ours, without heavy reliance on the articulative-disclosive dimension of language. (ii) It also seems implausible that we can develop a morality based on "reason alone" without a consideration of the features which make life a good one, and these, I would argue, can't be adequately considered without articulation. (iii) I can't accept a theory of art which voids all objective value and understands value purely in terms of our responses. (iv) And, of course, I don't start from atheist premises in considering religion. I realize that all these reasons will not be equally cogent for readers, but just one suffices to upset the belief in an omnicompetent stripped-down "reason alone."

These are my reasons for seeing language as a paradigm case of mystery in the richest, three-faceted sense above. Let me now turn to the other claim that Brandom makes: we create norms as much as they create us.

Now there are different cases here. Sometimes, we really create norms out of whole cloth. We invent a new game, or transform an old one; say, we follow the legendary account of how rugby arose out of a "foul" in a game of soccer. Someone picked up the ball and ran, and then people got the idea of making this the central activity in a new game. (It's supposed to have happened at Rugby School; the rest is history.)

But how about the fact-establishing games of giving and asking for reasons? Well, in a sense, we don't just establish the rules of this game, because it has already a telos. In fact, we repeatedly redesign the rules of enquiry and exchange throughout human history, in order to be truer to what comes to seem to us to be the telos. Hence the revolutions in paradigms, and even in the description of the enquiry itself, as we saw in the seventeenth century. There is invention here, but it takes the form of better realizing what is seen as a preexisting goal. It is hard to know what to say here, because the goal is defined in quite a new way; but the sense of improving on what others were aiming at before us is crucial here, and differentiates this case from inventing rugby, for instance.

Something similar is true of moral renewals and revolutions. There is a widespread Western narrative of "secularization" which goes something like this: formerly people took their values from the divine or the cosmos; then they awoke, and realized that we are on our own. So they took it into their own hands to establish their values. This makes moral/political change seem like inventing rugby. It pleases us to do things this way. But this seems to me wildly distorted as an account. The thinkers who developed the first contract theories, understanding societies as founded by individuals, and not as preexisting orders, had a strong sense that the foundation must conform to the norms they called "Natural Law," and very often that this law was backed by God. The atheists of the French Revolution appealed to Nature; the Bolsheviks to the historical development of freedom. They recognized demands they had to meet.

There is an asymmetry on these serious issues. Our revolutions, redesignings, always come in response to a demand which is seen as prior; be it that of grasping reality (science), or that of building a properly human way of political life. The demands are prior in two senses. First they are demands made on us as human beings, which are valid, independent of our choices. But second, just because they address human beings as such, we can see earlier understandings of the kind of demand in question (enquiring about the nature of things, building the good society) as faulty versions of what we now identify (more) correctly.

This is even more clearly the case, if we think of the ontogenesis of each one of us. We all enter a world in which certain goals, values, goods, ways of talking, thinking, enquiring are established. We only learn these activities because we take these as given, at first unquestionable. Then we may come to innovate, even in revolutionary fashion. But we are altering what is there in order to bring it more into true with its inherent telos.

But there is one way in which we could have a real sense of creating our norms; suppose we could arrive at a point of perfect transparency; we could understand by reason why our present norms have to be the way they are, given the inescapable telê of human life. What grasping the world means is studying it with the methods of natural science. What the good society means is one organized by norms, which themselves are dictated by "reason alone."

There are two variant bases for this sense of transparency. The first, of Humean origin, is illustrated by the sociobiological approach. We discover the ends of human life when we grasp how humans have evolved, and with what built-in ends. Enquiry then concerns the factual nature of the world, and deliberation deals with the best way of responding to this factual nature given our ends. True, this is not what "science" meant to earlier ages, when it was still deeply involved with metaphysics and theology, but we now see that there is nothing further we need to understand (except in detail) about our predicament and the kind of giving and asking for reasons that it requires. There is no place for a sense of mystery.

The second basis is inspired by Kant. Here the key notion is that our norms can be established by reason alone; or else that reason establishes the form of all moral norms, and we only need to fill in the facts to come to determinate conclusions about what we ought to do. There would be no simple brute acceptance of certain ultimate goods, such as human rights, democracy, equality, where we couldn't see by transparent reason alone why these have to be the criteria of right. Since we are reasoning beings, there is no constraint in our being guided by reason alone.

This is the Kantian dream, and it has seduced many "and the best of them," to quote Pound.[14] It would really establish a symmetry because the norms which create us, as free rational beings, would themselves be dictated by free rationality.

In other words, some variant of the post-metaphysical, or the sociobiological approach, which would establish the self-sufficiency of the factual practical family of language games, might succeed in taking the mystery out of language.

BUT I'M WANDERING too far. I mention these possibilities not because I'm convinced that Brandom adopts either one, but because each in its own way would establish a real symmetry between the way we are made by our culture, our norms, our language, and the way it makes us, a symmetry of the kind that Brandom seems to espouse.

He does reject one kind of "naturalism," one which would claim to give an adequate account of norms in terms of natural science. But there are other forms—sociobiological, for instance—on which I find it hard to interpret him.

What Brandom actually says seems to suggest more something like the rugby analogy. "Discursive deontic statuses are *instituted* by the practices that govern scorekeeping with deontic attitudes."[15] He also says that while normative statuses are instituted by practical attitudes, their being correct or incorrect doesn't just depend on these attitudes.[16] But something like this distinction holds for games, too. We invent our new game of rugby, we design the rules, but this doesn't determine who wins. The important issue is whether this designing of rules responds to an unrefusable telos which precedes our design.

In fact, the mystery resides in our having certain ends of life, which we endlessly redefine, without their even becoming totally transparent, that is, without our ever fully understanding the reasons for them.[17]

I HAVE TAKEN the reader very far afield, and, I recognize, very far away from Brandom's agenda, rather concentrating on questions that bother me, perhaps an inappropriate response to his impressive body of writing, like Evo Morales wearing his sweater to meet King Juan Carlos. I was induced to do so nonetheless because of the great richness of Robert Brandom's work, both the wealth of detail and the striking general architecture. The latter, which in fact draws us up out of the tunnel vision of the Cartesian tradition, and shows the dimensions of the house of language which we inhabit, is what encouraged me to raise a further question about the shape of this remarkable (and I think mysterious) dwelling.

Celan and the Recovery of Language

I

Celan stands in the stream of modern poetics, in particular the stream which arises in Germany in the 1790s. But in continuing it, he had to alter it; he had at least to try to rescue it, but only by transforming it. This wasn't entirely a free choice on his part; he couldn't take up the heritage in any other way. In fact, he reaches out to connect with this stream in a condition of crisis, which his life made him feel with unparalleled intensity.

This poetics arises out of a sense of the constitutive power of language. It starts in the Hamann-Herder understanding that words don't just acquire meaning through the designation of things we already experience. On the contrary, speech, linguistic expression, makes things exist for us in a new mode, one of awareness or reflection ("Besonnenheit," to use Herder's term).

This idea is then transformed by the writers of the 1790s—for instance, the Schlegel brothers, and Novalis—into a new understanding of poetics. In much ordinary speech, words do indeed seem to function according to the old, designative, view. Forgetting the global relation to the world that language itself constitutes, we can easily believe that words like, for instance, "hand," "stick," "water" just stand for things we already know. But for a range of higher things, the "infinite," the "invisible," our predicament is obviously different.

This emerges perhaps most clearly in their doctrine of the "symbol." The crucial point about the "symbol" was that it was that whereby alone a domain was disclosed; we could say: that whereby alone certain meanings come to exist for us. The highest things, things to do with the infinite, with God, with our deepest feelings, can only be made objects of thought and consideration for us through expression in symbols. How can the infinite be brought to the surface, to Erscheinung? asks A. W. Schlegel. "Nur symbolisch, in Bildern und Zeichen," he answers. Poetry is what achieves this: "Dichten . . . ist nichts anderes als ein ewig Symbolisieren: wir suchen entweder fur etwas Geistiges eine äussere Hülle oder wir beziehen ein Äusseres auf ein unsichtbares Inneres" ("Writing poetry is perpetual symbolizing: either we seek an outer shell for something spiritual or we relate something external to an invisible inner reality").[1]

We can get a better sense of what was meant by these higher, "invisible" things, if we think, as a first approximation, of the things that couldn't figure in our experience at all if we weren't language beings. Take "spirit" (Ruach, Pneuma). Well, wind would be there for us, even if we had remained pre-linguistic animals; we might seek shelter from it. And breathing would be there, as we gasp for breath running.

But spirit? Not that gift, that rushing, that onset of strength to reach for something higher, something fuller. This sense of the force of the incomparably higher only takes shape for us in the name. Spirit enters our world through language; its manifestation depends on speech. The term "spirit" is a symbol in Schlegel's sense. And the uses of language whereby these words are first launched into circulation are called in the above quote "Dichten," the creation of poetry.

On this view, there is something performative about poetry; through creating symbols it establishes new meanings. Poetry is potentially world-making; that is the understanding of poetics which comes down to us from the 1790s, in whose succession Celan stands.

Understanding poetics in this way brings about a shift of register, which opens up a new gamut of possibilities. Think of "spirit" again: it enters our world through the Bible and related texts and sayings; its reality fixed in narrative and doctrine. The new poetics involves a reflexive move, which points to the way the Bible itself is not a simple narration of events which were already there for, for example, the people of Israel, before these events were recorded. It points to the way that these events themselves have been made manifest, and given shape, in language. This reflexive turn, so typical of modernity, brings an awareness of the conditions of awareness, of making the "Invisible" manifest.

A gamut of possibilities opens here. Reflexive awareness can bring about subjectivism, and a collapse of transcendence, but doesn't need to. At one, subjectivist, extreme, the manifestations in language can be seen just as effects of language. The poet's straining to find the right word is not seen as an attempt to be faithful to a reality beyond language. At another point on the spectrum, this language is understood as an attempt to define something which transcends language, but is still quite intraworldly. The poet articulates human nature, or the human condition. Then at the other extreme, the full, original understanding is retained: our language strives to render God, or something which transcends humanity.

All too often, it is just assumed that the reflexive turn of modern poetics entails or inevitably issues in the first, subjectivist, stance. But there is no necessity to this. Traditional theism and modernist poetics can work together, as, for instance, Hopkins and Eliot attest. There is long theological warrant for the fragile, constructed nature of all our names for God. But it is in the very nature of this poetics to allow for an ontological indeterminacy. The language can be taken in more than one sense, ranging from the fullest ontological commitment to the transcendent to the most subjective, human—even language centered. We can see this in the reception of Wordsworth's poetry in the nineteenth century.[2]

I SAY THAT Celan is in the stream of this modern poetics, because he accepts the central goal of "Dichtung," its performative power to manifest hitherto inaccessible reality and possibilities of being. His description of poetry as "actualized language" ("aktualisierte Sprache"), and his claim that "poems are sketches for existence," attest to this.[3] A key word in his famous speech of 1960, on receiving the Büchner Prize, is "setting free" ("freisetzen").[4] "Geh mit der Kunst in deine allereigenste Enge. Und setze dich frei" (20). He glosses the term "actualized language" with the clause "freigesetzt unter dem Zeichen einer zwar radikalen, aber gleichzeitig auch der ihr von der Sprache gezogenen Grenzen, der ihr von der Sprache erschlossenen Möglichkeiten eingedenk bleibenden Individuation" (17) ("actualized language, set free under the sign of a radical individuation, which at the same time stays mindful of the limits drawn by language, the possibilities opened by language"). A few lines later he says what this poetry could be: "Dann ware das Gedicht—deutlicher als noch bisher—gestaltgewordene Sprache eines Einzelnen,—und seinem innersten Wesen nach Gegenwart und Präsenz" (17) ("Then a poem would be—even more clearly than ever before the language-become-form of a single person and, following its inmost nature, presentness and presence").[5]

But poetry as self-definition, self-free-setting, is also a contact with another:

> Das Gedicht ist einsam. Es ist einsam und unterwegs. Wer es schreibt, bleibt ihm mitgegeben. Aber steht das Gedicht nicht gerade dadurch, also schon hier, in der Begegnung—im Geheimnis der Begegnung? Das Gedicht will zu einem Andern, es braucht dieses Andere, es braucht ein Gegenüber. Es sucht es au, es spricht sich ihm zu. (18)

("The Poem is lonely. It is lonely and underway. Whoever writes one stays mated to it. But in just this way doesn't the poem stand, right here, in an encounter—in the mystery of an encounter? The poem wants to reach an Other, it needs this Other, it needs an Over-against. It seeks it out, speaks towards it.")

Earlier, Celan makes the claim that it is a hope of poetry to speak in the cause of another, perhaps even in that of a wholly other (16) ("velleicht in eines ganz Anderen Sache"). And below he speaks of poems as "Wege, auf denen die Sprache stimmhaft wird, es sind Begegnungen, Wege einer Stimme zu einem wahrnehmenden Du, kreatürliche Wege, Daseinsentwürfe vielleicht, ein Sich-vorausschicken zu sich selbst, auf der Suche nach sich selbst . . . Eine Art Heimkehr" (22) ("paths on which language gets a voice, they are encounters, paths of a voice to a perceiving Thou, creaturely paths, sketches of existence perhaps, a sending oneself ahead towards oneself, in search of oneself . . . a kind of homecoming"). Self-freeing, self-discovery, self-definition, real home-coming, are all inseparable from finding the other. "Das Gedicht . . . wird Gespräch" ("conversation"; 18). This is crucial to Celan's poetics, as we shall see further below.

Celan stands within the space of ontological indeterminacy, inseparable from modern poetics. But his stance is not quite neutral; there is a longing, a straining, a yearning (as I read him) toward the fullest ontological commitment, the "wholly other" as God. But there are also tremendous obstacles on the road, both despair and reticence, and much else besides, which make straight affirmation impossible, beyond the range of authentically "free-setting" language. He is compelled to remain ambivalent, giving with one hand what he takes with the other.

2

Before undertaking a discussion of some of Celan's poetry, I should like to make a few more general remarks about the tradition of modern poetics he stood within, especially as it came to be understood in the twentieth century. The reflexive awareness, that we open up contact (Celan says "Begegnung") with something higher or deeper (be it God, or the depths of human nature, desire, the Will to Power, or whatever) through language, shows the fragility of this contact. Poetry as Dichtung can be seen as an event with performative force, words which open up this contact, make something manifest for the first time. But what is this event?

Outside of the most subjectivistic interpretations, it has an objective side: something language-transcendent is manifested, set free. But it also has an inescapably subjective aspect. This reality is made manifest to us, who speak this language, have this sensibility, have been prepared by previous speech or experience. So this new word resonates in/for us; that the word reveals what it does is *also* a fact about us, even though it is more than this. It *could* in principle eventually resonate for everyone, but only because they will have been inducted into the language and the human meanings within which it can resonate. This is the sense of Shelley's phrase "subtler language," in which he describes the medium of modern poetry. Unlike the references of earlier poems, which were guaranteed by established public meanings (the Chain of Being, Divine history, and the like), modern poetry doesn't rely on already recognized structures. It opens new paths, "sets free" new realities, but only for those for whom it resonates.[6]

This is what makes for the fragility of this "poetic" language. What reveals by resonation can cease to. The language may go dead, flat, become routinized, a handy tool of reference, a commonplace, like a dead metaphor, just unthinkingly invoked. We see this, of course, with traditional religious language, as also its opposite. The opposite, the continuing, ever-renewed force of a language, can be sustained in a living religious tradition. "Come Holy Spirit, our hearts inspire," sing generations of worshippers, ever-renewing the fullness of meaning. But these same prayers can become dead, routine; people just go through the motions when saying/singing them; or else they take an aura of comfort, of familiarity of links with family, lineage, and the past, which has little to do with their original revelatory force.

The fruit of the reflexive turn can be that this deadness, routine, which used to be seen as a lack in the worshipper, can now come to be blamed on the language. The very demand for authenticity—quintessentially modern—seems to drive us toward new languages, which can resonate within us.

In relation to the poetic tradition itself, the danger looms that poetic language lose its force, like all those Shakespearean or biblical metaphors buried in ordinary speech, that it become leveled down—in other words, that the difference between ordinary, routine, everyday descriptive and calculating-operative speech, on one hand, and poetic creation, on the other, be lost; the second absorbed into the first. In relation to the literary canon, the idea is that great poetry, in order to resonate again, needs a new context; otherwise put, it needs a range of contemporary voices, which can serve as its interlocutors, with which it can resonate. Otherwise its force is in danger of being lost. (Celan as one of the twentieth century's great translators of poetry illustrates marvelously this co-resonation through difference, which brings the foreign alive.)

This fear of language going dead, of its losing its resonance, is recurrent in modern culture, and not just in relation to literature. We see it in Heidegger, for instance, in his contrast between empty conformist "Gerede" ("idle talk") and authentic speech. It is a quintessentially modern worry, because it depends on the modern sense of the potential of language as Gedicht, and the resulting distinction between creative and ordinary speech. Only in relation to this high vocation of poetic language, can this fear of falling arise. The fear is of a loss of the performative power. It is coeval with modern poetics. It was expressed by the founding thinkers of the 1790s, and has recurred ever since, along with the hope that new poetic creation can reverse the fall. This was the sense of Mallarmé's homage to Edgar Allan Poe for having assumed the vocation of "donner un sens plus pur aux mots de la tribu" ("give a purer meaning to the words of the tribe").[7] And the sense that language is in constant danger of being lowered, besmirched, becoming inauthentic, is constant. We see it in different ways in the early twentieth century with Karl Kraus and George Orwell. In the realm of art, a word has been coined for this collapse into banality and empty sentiment: kitsch.

But there are a couple of features of this fragility of language which have been especially thematized in the twentieth century, and which are central to Celan's work. The original Romantic idea of the poet as creator and seer could suggest a monological view. The resonance which really matters is that in the poet's soul or being. But more and more a dialogical understanding of language (implicit in the founding theories of Hamann, Herder, and Humboldt) makes its way, and it becomes clear that the resonances which matter are those which link speaker and hearer, writer and readers, and eventually (perhaps) whole communities. Poets may fail to be heard, but the end of the writing is to reach others and to effect a coming together in the Being revealed, or set free.[8]

This sense is central to Celan, as we saw above. In so many of his poems, the breaking through to a free-setting word coincides with the moment of address to a "du." Buber's work resonated profoundly with Celan. He underlined some sentences of Buber in a book Celan bought about him. Among them this: "Creatures stand within the secret of Creation, of Speech. . . . We can say thou, because thou is also said to us"; and this: "Spirit is not in the I, but between I and Thou."[9]

Parallel to the isolation of the "I" is the focus on the single poetic Word. Just as there is a partial insight behind monologism (a single poet creates), so there is some truth in this focus on a single word. The breakthrough to renewed performative power can come to fruition in a crucial moment, even a word. This happens frequently in Celan's poetry. It is part of what he means to capture through his term "Atemwende" (breath-turn), which he gave as the title to one of his collections. It is the moment where, in the turn of breathing, as it were, the free-setting word comes.

But the partiality of this view comes clear when we see what Celan never forgets, how this concentrated breakthrough in a word is only made possible through a host of others, references, invocations, questionings, against which background the performative power can act in this word. Just as resonance occurs not in the single poet but between him/her and a Thou, so the power to make us resonate builds through a whole constellation, before erupting (as it may) in a single word or phrase. Just as the poem as a whole can make us resonate, but only thanks to the whole intertextual setting; the kind, indeed, that we constantly try to build anew so that our classics can continue to live for us.

The meaning is in the chain of meanings: there is something much more here than the banal Saussurean observation that the meaning of each term depends on the skein of distinctions in which it is set. "Dans la langue, il n'y a que des différences et pas de termes positifs" ("in language, there are only differences, and not isolated positive terms").[10] "Red" would mean something different were there no notions of "scarlet" or "crimson." Here we're talking about how a word can serve to open a new space, reveal a new reality, make contact with the hidden or lost. And this power only comes against a whole background of complementary meanings, which is itself altered by the introduction of the new word.

THIS FRAGILITY of the word is a crucial part of the background to twentieth-century poetics. How does this affect Celan? One is reminded here of the half-joke that Jews are just like everyone else, only more so. Just like everyone else, Celan faces this fragility. Except that already, the "just like everyone else" sounds inadequate here, because from the beginning, even before the catastrophe, an uncommonly strong poetic vocation was evident in the young Paul Antschel. From early on, he wanted to continue/renew the tradition. He was inspired by Hölderlin and Rilke.

Another old saw comes to mind: what happens when the irresistible force hits the immovable object? The irresistible force here was Celan's poetic vocation. The immovable object(s) were the all-but-insurmountable obstacles in the path of this vocation.

This brings us to the "only more so." What makes it possible to practice such a vocation is being rooted in some literary, spiritual, or community tradition. There were three of these which were relevant for the young Antschel: the community, whether practicing or laicized, of East European Jewry, more specifically in the "borderlands" where Czernowitz was situated; the spiritual tradition of Judaism, which although not central to his family was definitely present; and the German language as a vehicle for great literature, that his mother inducted him into.

Now of these, the first was destroyed and scattered; while the second was deeply problematical for him, for a host of reasons, but at least partly because like many Jews (and some Christians) he found it hard after the Shoah to believe in the god who would save Israel. The third tradition, for its part, was threatened with pollution.

This third threat takes us way beyond the usual danger of the fragility of language. This was and is often conceived as the threat that language succumb to the banal, the routine, the inauthentic, mere posing; that literature slide to kitsch. But for Celan the unfeeling banality of postwar German was just part of the problem. The major stumbling-block was that this language, using the full gamut of references in its literary tradition, had served to articulate, plan, and execute the most execrable crimes, the crimes indeed which in different ways had caused his exile from the first two traditions.

It is not just a matter of banality, but of a language whose resonances had been deeply poisoned by its complicity in evil. We shouldn't be fooled here by Hannah Arendt's celebrated phrase about the "banality of evil." This certainly exists; indeed, it has its place in the cycle of evil, as Dostoyevsky saw. But whoever wants to forget that evil can also be exhilarating should think of Hitler inciting vast audiences with a counter-gospel of scapegoating hatred, and rousing them to dark heights of fantasy-murder, which then became real in the hidden machinery of the Holocaust.

There is a connection here to banality. Because the exhilaration with evil, with the self-affirming power of scapegoating and persecution, unlike the exaltation of the Spirit, leaves one on the morning after, as it were, with a sense of emptiness and futility. In the absence of repentance, this can only be filled by even more extreme exhilaration over evil, like the progress of a drug addiction; which partly accounts for the sliding of the "eliminative" anti-Semitism of the Nazi leadership toward ever more and more horrible forms of evil; or else it can end in suicide, as Dostoyevsky portrays it in the case of Smerdyakov in *The Brothers Karamazov*, who has death embedded in his name. Goebbels and Hitler had no other option come the final defeat in 1945.

Or else one can avoid facing either of these extremes by dumbing oneself down, by a kind of desensitizing routinization, which covers up both horror and excitement. One is, after all, only doing one's job, only following orders.[11]

So the banality of evil is a real phenomenon. But only at one end of the cycle; it is not the whole. The real horror of what Victor Klemperer called the LTI (his code word "Lingua Tertii Imperii"; in German "Sprache des dritten Reiches") lies at the other end of the spectrum. It is where language functions as a performative, revealing, free-setting Word, but in relations to the depths of scapegoating anger and hatred that the human soul can fall prey to. This is the fact that Heidegger utterly failed to see, for all the mutual sympathy with Celan around the goal of renewing the language, for all that Celan had borrowed from the older man's philosophy to articulate this goal for himself, as we see in terms like "freisetzen" and in the relating of Denken and Dichten.

The greatest sin against the language in Heidegger's time was not a banal falling into everyday Gerede, but an incandescent performative Word of evil. This total inability on Heidegger's part even to perceive the elephantine fact which dominated his time estranged him irremediably from Celan, who had waited in vain for "a thinker's/(un-/delayed coming)/word/in the heart" ("einer Hoffnung, heute,/auf eines Denkenden/(un-/gesäumt kommendes)/Wort/im Herzen" ("Todnauberg," in *Lichtzwang*).

And so we have a language in danger of pollution. Not only by its original use for Words of darkness, but also by the way the guardians of a truer tradition, people like Heidegger and Benn, had lived with this while hiding it from view. Not only in its terrible deviancy, but in its blindness to this deviancy, the pollution was contagious, threatening to spread through the whole system.

In fact the original Nazi-speak, or LTI, itself was a mixture of horror and banalization, in that a rhetoric of mobilization to hatred and destruction coexisted with a bland euphemization which was meant to hide its worst consequences—words like "Endlösung" or "Gleichschaltung," for instance. As J. M. Coetzee put it in an article on Celan, the German language was "corrupted to the bone during the Nazi era by euphemism and a kind of leering doublespeak."[12] The postwar cover-ups just continued in paths already laid down by the regime.

So the irresistible force hits the immovable object—only more so. As the ancient Israelites were condemned to make bricks without straw, so this twentieth-century Jew from Eastern Europe, whose mother tongue was German, had to rebuild a tradition, without the most elementary building blocks. He had to recreate the materials as well as construct with them. He had to reconstitute the language in order to recover contact with destroyed or estranged traditions.

I want now to note some of the ways he attempted this.

3

The first I will call itineracy, the kind of movement which Celan captured in the image of the Meridian. As he introduced the image in his Bremen talk, he speaks of himself as seeking the place of his origin, seeking it on a children's map. "Keiner dieser Orte ist zu finden, es gibt sie nicht, aber ich weiss, wo es sie, zumal jetzt, geben müsste, und . . . ich finde etwas!" The passage continues a little later: "Ich finde das Verbindende und wie das Gedicht zur Begegnung Führende. Ich finde etwas—wie die Sprache—Immaterielles, aber Irdisches, Terrestrisches, etwas Kreisförmiges, über die beiden Polen in sich selbst Zurückkehrendes und dabei—heitererweise—sogar die Tropen Durchkreuzendes—: ich finde . . . einen *Meridian*" (23) ("I find something that binds and leads to encounter, like a poem. I find something—like language—immaterial yet earthly, terrestrial, something circular, returning upon itself by way of both poles and thereby—happily—even crossing the tropics (and tropes): I find . . . a *meridian*").[13]

A meridian is not a place. It is a no-place, a u-topia—a word that also occurs in this talk. A meridian is a line drawn on a map, connecting places, not a real line in the world, but one linking representations of places on the map. What is it that this image points to, and what does it set free? What is gone are those places: Czernowitz, the Bukovina, Prague. What can still live is the movement of a life which emerges from those lost places, and continues in the existing loci of Paris, Normandy, Bremen. The places can exist again, linked in the memory-and-anticipation of this life which still runs forward. But not if this movement itself is broken into fragments, the earlier parts inaccessible and without communication with the rest.

A meridian is a moving line which reconnects. It is a running through of the broken place-fragments which reconstitutes a unity across time and restores the integrity or wholeness of a life, either of a person, or of a people. The performative power of the language is its ability to restore the contact across the lines of fracture, and thus reconstitute the underlying integrity. The power of Celan's poetry lies partly in the creation/revelation of a gathered time, bringing together what has been dispersed. Almost magically, the movement connects places/times.

> Die Silbermünze auf deiner Zunge schmilzt,
> Sie schmeckt nach Morgen, nach immer, ein Weg
> Nach Russland stegit dir ins Herz,
> Die karelische Birke
> Hat
> Gewartet,
>
> . . . . .
>
> Wie heisst es, dein Land
> Hinterm Berg, hinterm Jahr?
> Ich weiss, wie es heisst,
>
> . . . . .
>
> Es wandert überall hin, wie die Sprache,
> Wirf sie weg, wirf sie weg,
> Dann hast du sie wieder, wie ihn,
> Den Kieselstein as
> der Mährischen Senke

den dein Gedanke nach Prag trug,
aufs Grab auf die Gräber, ins Leben

längst
ist er fort, wie die Briefe, wie alle
Laternen, wieder
Musst du ihn suchen, da ist er,
Klein ist er, weiss,
Um die Ecke, da liegt er,
Bei Normandie-Njemen—in Böhmen,
Da, da, da,
Hinterm Haus, vor dem Haus,
weiss ist er, weiss, er sagt:
Heute—es gilt.

("ES IST ALLES ANDERS," IN *DIE NIEMANDSROSE*)

(The silver shekel melts on your tongue,
it tastes of Tomorrow, of Always, a path
to Russia rises in your heart,
the Karelian birch
is still
waiting,

.　.　.　.　.

what is it called, your land
back of the mountain, back of the year?
I know what it's called.

.　.　.　.　.

it wanders everywhere, like language,
throw it away, throw it away,
then you'll have it again, like
that pebble from the Moravian Basin
your thought carried to Prague,
on the grave, on the graves, into life.

it's
long gone, like the letters, like all those
lanterns, you must
seek it again, here it is,
it is small, white,
round the corner, it lies here
at Normandy-Niemen—in Bohemia,
here here here
back of the house, front of the house,
white it is white, it says:
Today's the day.)

The place-times come together into the movement, as the dry bones connect in Ezekiel 37. It is perhaps significant that gathered time is the main understanding of eternity that emerges from the Bible, as expressed in an eschatology of resurrection, where all come together, living, for God—something very different from the eternity of Plato, the ever-unchanging.

This meridian connection is similar, but also very different from the juxtaposition of alien fragment images releasing an epiphany, which modernist poetry made familiar in the early twentieth century. We can think of Eliot: "These fragments have I shored against my ruin." When Eliot says:

> Unreal City,
> Under the brown fog of a winter dawn,
> A crowd flowed over London Bridge
> I had not thought death had undone so many.
>
> ("The Waste Land," 60–63)

the line from Dante's *Inferno* sliding into a contemporary scene releases all the desolation, the slide into nothingness, that the bustle conceals. The juxtaposition releases something behind the images, something normally hidden behind each separately.

With Celan, what is set free is not something beyond the place-references; rather it is their unity-in-movement. This is both restored and revealed; this is what "setting free" seems to mean in this context.

But the gathering of times is also the reconnection of persons, the restoration of a lost, or never possessed, mutual presence. This is what the eruption of a "Du" in Celan's poetry often signals. Gathered time restores a kind of simultaneity across epochs, in which we can speak to each other. And that is part of its point, in itself, and for Celan. This poet understood the dialogical nature of language. In its fullness it is conversation (Gespräch), as we saw above. If language in its resonating in us, can release the meanings of things, then the fullest release comes in the completion of language, in dialogue. A meaning shared in friendship or love is a meaning more intensely felt, understood, and lived. All poetry presumes this in its call (implicit or explicit) to an addressee.

That is why the renewed contact with Czernowitz and his origins is often for Celan also a recovery of contact with his mother, sometimes the ability to resume the conversation with her, brutally interrupted by her deportation and murder. Sometimes the gathering movement takes him to the point where he can address her again. "Du" is sometimes said to her.

But there is another burst of joy in shared meaning in Celan's discovery of Mandelshtam, a kindred spirit, Jewish, pan-European, whose world too was devastated before he was killed; but who fought to the end to save/renew the language. The passage quoted above from "ES IST ALLES ANDERS," which runs in part: "ein Weg/nach Russland stegit dir ins Herz,/ die karelische Birke/hat/gewartet," continues: "der Name Osip kommt auf dich zu, du erzählst ihm,/was er schon weiss, er nimmt es, er nimmt es dir ab, mit Händen" ("the name Osip comes toward you, you tell him/what he already knows, he takes it, he takes it off you with hands").[14]

Time gathered to the point of dialogue, gathering in movement "paths (Wege) on which language finds a voice, ... paths of a voice to a perceiving thou" (Büchner Prize talk, p. 22, quoted above in German); these paths are what the meridian image points to; the meridian as a line drawn, hence a movement. That is what I mean by "itineracy."

THE EXAMPLES above have concentrated on the restored unity in Celan's life. But time-gathering goes further. In "DU SEI WIE DU" *(Lichtzwang)*, we contemporaries are connected again with Isaiah, through an intermediate link in Meister Eckhart.

But the linking itineracy occurs in a number of forms in Celan's poetry, not just connecting biographies and generations. The sense of path. Movement, journey, is often there, often moving toward a moment of gathering; sometimes seeming to get there, sometimes falling agonizingly short (and what exactly is the difference? A good question I want to address below). See for instance "HINAUSGEKRÖNT" or "Hüttenfenster" or "IN DER LUFT" (all from *Die Niemandsrose*).

And sometimes the Word itself is on a path, hurtling toward the point where it can set a soul's sense free ("EIN WURFHOLZ," in *Die Niemandsrose*).

4

Sometimes the movement reaches a turning point, an Atemwende, when in a word or phrase the gathering is made; as in "NAH IM AORTENBOGEN" or "WENN ICH NICHT WEISS, NICHT WEISS (both in *Fadensonnen*). As in these two poems, the gathering moments come with key words of the Jewish tradition; we suddenly have the power to say and hear them again. Sometimes there are images hallowed by long tradition, as with the "temples" in "Engführung" *(Sprachgitter):*

Also
stehen noch Tempel. Ein
Stern
Hat wohl noch Licht.

Nichts,
nichts ist verloren.

. . . . .

Ho-
sanna.

(Therefore
temples still stand. A
star may still give light.
Nothing, nothing is lost. Ho-
sanna.)[15]

Sometimes it is less immediately understandable, but one can sense the gathering: "ES WAR ERDE" *(Niemandsrose).*

But often the turning word is "Nothing"; or else a term connected with it, like "Niemandsrose." Here is a place of radical indeterminacy. We can read this (1) against a long apophatic tradition, a negative theology which reminds us of the inadequacy of all our names for God. This apophatic tradition is also linked to a certain understanding of death: the process of dying is that wherein we are forced to relinquish all our cherished illusions, the screens that separate us from God. The moment of death can be the moment of truth.

But this constellation of ideas was transvalued, was given a quite new sense in the modern poetic tradition. The key figure here is (2) Mallarmé. "Le néant" (in his mind borrowed from Hegel) is now a crucial reference point in an atheist universe. What survives the transition is a similar sense of the privileged standpoint of death on life. Already, before he lost his faith, Mallarmé shared what came to be called the symbolist sense that poetry was higher than mere life, that it required turning one's back on life:

> Ainsi, pris du dégoût de l'homme à l'âme dure
> Vautré dans le bonheur, où ses seuls appétits
> Mangent . . .
> Je fuis et je m'accroche à toutes les croisées
> D'où l'on tourne le dos à la vie, et béni,
> Dans leur verre, lavé d'éternelles rosées,
> Que dore la matin chase de l'Infini
>
> Je me mire et me vois ange! et je meurs, et j'aime
> —Que la vitre soit l'art, soit la mysticité—
> A renaître, portant mon rêve en diadème,
> Au ciel antérieur où fleurit la Beauté!

(LES FENÊTRES, 21–32)

(Thus, seized with disgust for the man of hard heart,
Sprawled in the happiness in which only his appetites
Feed, . . .
I flee, clinging to all the window frames
From which one can turn one's back on life;
And blessed in their glass, bathed in eternal dews,
Adorned by the chaste morning of the Infinite.

I gaze at myself and I see an angel! And I die, yearning
—Be the window pane art, be it mysticism—
To be reborn, bearing my dream as a diadem,
Under the former sky where Beauty once flourished.")[16]

In this early poem, you can still see the original religious sources of this dissatisfaction with bare life. The image of the window, invoked repeatedly in different forms, divides the universe into a lower and higher. The lower is likened to a hospital, life is a kind of putrefaction; but above and beyond is the river, the sky, and the images which invoke this are still saturated with the resonances of the religious tradition: *Infini, ange, mysticité.*

But later, after his crisis, Mallarmé emerges with something like a materialist view of the universe. Underneath everything we see is *le Rien, le Néant.* But the poet's vocation is none the less imperious. He will even speak of it in terms which borrow from the Romantic tradition of an original, perfect language. (Poetry is concerned with "l'explication orphique de la Terre.")

In terms of belief, Mallarmé has joined the Enlightenment, and even a rather extreme, materialist version of it. But in terms of the point of human existence, he couldn't be further removed from it. The primacy of life is decisively rejected, treated with revulsion. What emerges is something like a counter-primacy of death.

It is clear that for Mallarmé the realization of the poetic vocation, achieving the purified language, essentially involves something like the death of the poet; certainly the overcoming of all particularity, but this process, it seems, is consummated only in actual death: "Tel qu'en Lui-même enfin l'éternité le change."

"Tout ce que, par contre coup, mon être a souffert, pendant cette longue agonie, est inénarrable, mais heureusement je suis parfaitement mort, et la région la plus impure où mon Esprit puisse s'aventurer est l'éternité, mon esprit, ce Solitaire habituel de sa propre Pureté, que n'obscurcit plus même le reflet du Temps."[17]

("All that my being has suffered as a reaction during that slow death is beyond recounting, but fortunately I am utterly dead, and the most impure region where my spirit can venture is Eternity—my Spirit, that recluse accustomed to dwelling in its own Purity, which is no longer darkened even by the reflection of Time.")[18]

MALLARMÉ becomes the first great modern poet of absence ("aboli bibelot d'inanité sonore"), followed in that by others, including Eliot and Celan himself. The absence, clearly, of the object ("Sur les crédences, au salon vide: nul ptyx"), but this is something which can only be attained via the absence, in a sense the death, of the subject ["(Car le Maître est allé puiser des pleurs au Styx / Avec ce seul objet dont le Néant s'honore)"]. A strange parallel is set up with the earlier religious tradition, but within the framework of denied transcendence.

Death and the moment of death have an ineradicable place in the religious traditions: death as the giving up of everything, of one's very self, in Christianity; the hour of death as a crucial moment, therefore ("pray for us now and at the hour of our death"); a status it has as well in most Buddhist traditions. In Christian terms: the locus of death, as the place where one has given everything, is the place of maximum union with God; and therefore, paradoxically, the source of most abundant life.

In this new post-Mallarmé perspective, the locus of death takes on a new paradigm status. The Christian paradox drops away: death is no longer the source of life. But there is a new paradox: there seems to be a renewed affirmation of transcendence, of a point to life beyond life. But at the same time, this is denied, in the sense that this point has absolutely no anchorage in the nature of reality. To search for this point in reality is to encounter only le Néant.

This paradoxical idea, which we could call immanent transcendence, is one of the principal themes of the immanent counter-Enlightenment. Death offers in some sense the privileged perspective, the paradigm gathering point for life. This idea recurs again and again in our culture—not necessarily derived from Mallarmé. Heidegger's Sein-zum-Tode is a famous example, but the theme is taken up in rather different forms in Sartre, Camus, and Foucault, was echoed in "the death of man" fad, and so on. And in the variant which spoke of "the death of the subject," the paradoxical affinities with certain religious outlooks—perhaps most obviously Buddhism—were patent.

In Mallarmé's version it seems that the true meaning of things, which poetry strives to articulate, comes from the standpoint of death or absence, things as they stand to each other beyond the screen of lived involvement.

There is a purity in the moment of death, of stripping down of lived meanings. Perhaps we find something analogous in Beckett, whom Celan never met, but greatly admired, and felt some kinship with.

Now this atheist view is partly enhanced and partly screened by (3) another modern stance which is much more widespread, an atheism which prides itself on courageously facing the emptiness of the universe, and soldiering on with the human meanings it endorses in the teeth of this cosmic indifference, perhaps transmuting the loss and the sadness into the elegiac beauty of a Housman.

CELAN'S "NOTHING" has to be understood against this whole background. How to hear it?

> Niemand knetet uns wieder aus Erde und Lehm,
> niemand bespricht unsern Staub.
> Niemand.
>
> Gelobt seist du, Niemand.
> Dir zulieb wollen
> wir blühn.
> Dir
> entgegen.
>
> Ein Nichts
> waren wir, sind wir, werden
> wir bleiben, blühend:
> die Nichts-, die
> Niemandsrose

> ("PSALM," IN *DIE NIEMANDSROSE*)

> (No one kneads us again out of earth and clay
> no one incants our dust.
> No one.
>
> Blessed art thou, No One.
> In thy sight would
> we bloom.
> In thy
> Spite.
>
> A Nothing
> we were, are now, and ever
> shall be, blooming:
> the Nothing-, the
> No-One's-Rose.)

In these poems invoking Nothing, there is often protest, moments of dis-abused disillusion.

> Es war Erde in ihnen, und
> sie gruben.

Sie gruben und gruben, so ging
ihr Tag dahin, ihre Nacht. Und sie lobten nicht Gott,
der, so hörten sie, alles dies wollte,
der, so hörten sie, alles dies wusste.

Sie gruben un hörten nichts mehr;
sie wurden nicht weise, erfanden kein Lied,
erdachten sich keinerlei Sprache.
Sie gruben.

(There was earth inside them, and
they dug.

They dug and dug, and so
their day went past, their night. And they did not praise God,
who, so they heard, wanted all this,
who, so they heard, witnessed all this.

They dug and heard nothing more;
they did not grow wise, invented no song,
devised for themselves no sort of language.
They dug.)

The diggers invoke irresistibly the camps, their prisoners, and forced labor. The tone thus far in the poem is one of total abandonment. God's only role here is as the one who allegedly knows and wills all this. Reading these lines, one feels pulled toward (3), the modern atheist stance, moved by despair and disillusion. But how to read the last stanza of this poem?

O einer, o keiner, o niemand, o du:
Wohin gings, da's ging nirgendhin?
O du gräbst und ich grab, und ich grab mich dir zu,
und am Finger erwacht uns der Ring.

("ES WAR ERDE IN IHNEN," in *Die Niemandsrose*)

(O none, o none, o no one, o you:
Where did it go then, making for nowhere?
O you dig and I dig, and I dig through to you,
and the ring on our finger awakens.)[19]

A poem like "Mondorla" (*Die Niemandsrose*) might be pulled in a Mallarméan direction. But in poems like "DAS NICHTS" and "DIE POSAUNENSTELLE" (*Zeitgehöft*), after passing through a landscape of despair, there comes a faint but unmistakable note of affirmation.

In fact, the powerful thrust of so much of Celan's poetry toward gathered time tells rather in the direction of (1), a kind of renewal of the apophatic tradition.

Save that . . . ? It is hard to say exactly. Save that nothing in this poetry guarantees that we have reached the end, the ultimate version of the story, the definitive interpretation of things. Rather there is a gamut of places in which an Atemwende brings us close to a gathering point, and to a Gatherer. Some of these are more joyous and confident, others despairing, almost cynical. What seems undeniable in this poetry is the *direction toward* a gathering. What seems forever unresolved is whether we have in fact found that one exists. The indeterminacy is never eradicated. The poetry remains on its way (unterwegs).

5

I have been talking about one important vector of Celan's poetry, that toward gathering. But there are others. I would like briefly to mention one which is especially prominent in the later cycles. It is as though the attempt to purify the language took the form of an austere paring down, an abandonment of all lush images and of the feelings they invoke, even going so far as to break words down into their component elements, in order to rebuild anew.

Already early on, there is an image which recurs from time to time in Celan's poetry which seems to point to this kind of self-contained purity. It is that of the stone:

> Wohin mir das Wort, das unsterblich war, fiel:
> in die Himmelsschlucht hinter der Stirn,
> dahin geht, geleitet von Speichel und Müll,
> der Siebenstern, der mit mir lebt.
>
> Im Nachthaus die Reime, der Atem in Kot,
> das Auge ein Bilderknecht—
> Und dennoch: ein aufrechtes Schweigen, ein Stein,
> der die Teufelsstiege umgeht.
>
> ("WOHIN MIR," IN *DIE NIEMANDSROSE*)

> (Where the word, that was undying, fell:
> into heaven's ravine behind my brow,
> led by spittle and dreck, there goes
> the sevenbranch starflower that lives with me.
>
> Rhymes in the night house, breath in the muck,
> the eye a thrall to images—
> And yet: an upright silence, a stone
> evading the devil's staircase.)[20]

This drive to austerity arose inevitably out of Celan's situation. Adorno has famously said that it was impossible to write lyric poetry after Auschwitz. One can certainly see the point of this remark, but it amounts to a surrender of humanity before darkness. To renounce lyric poetry is to give up something essential to our existence as human beings. Celan felt this with every fiber of his being. Moreover his lyric had to go to the very places and times which threatened to silence it forever, places returned to in his most famous poems, like "Todesfuge" *(Mohn und Gedächtnis)* and "Engführung" *(Sprachgitter)*.

But the point behind Adorno's "harshest judgement"[21] (which the philosopher eventually withdrew) remained valid, and Celan was acutely aware of it. What Adorno had meant to warn against was a kind of aestheticization of the cruelty and horror, a transfiguration which beautified or hid the ugly face of evil. Some critics attacked "Todesfuge" on these grounds. Celan was extremely sensitive to this criticism; that was because he better than anyone else had measured the dangers here, and striven to avoid them. Indeed, Celan's greatness partly consists in that he could break the silence, and venture into these forbidden areas without trivializing them under an aesthetic gloss. But this venture itself required a certain reserve, a silence, "ein aufrechtes Schweigen," as he puts it here. Over against the idolatrous eye, "a slave to images," this silence takes as its icon the stone, which "avoids the devil's stairway."[22]

Much of Celan's later poetry seems to be heeding this call for sparseness and reserve, sometimes finding its forms and images in the art of etching, which his wife practiced:[23]

> Weggebeizt vom
> Strahlenwind deiner Sprache
> das bunte Gerede des An-
> erlebten—das hundert-
> zungige Mein-
> gedicht, das Genicht.
>
> ("WEGGEBEIZT," in *ATEMWENDE*)

> (Etched away from
> the ray-shot wind of your language
> the garish talk of rubbed-
> off experience—the hundred-
> tongued pseudo-
> poem, the noem.)[24]

Here the etching has eaten away at "the hundred-tongued pseudo-poem, the noem," getting beyond the babble of self-feeling and expression ("das bunte

Gerede" recalls Heidegger). It is as though Celan is striving for a purity which will take him beyond the merely human:

> Fadensonnen
> über der grauschwarzen Ödnis.
> Ein baum-
> hoher Gedanke
> greift sich den Lichton: es sind
> noch Lieder zu singen jenseits
> der Menschen.
>
> ("FADENSONNEN," IN *ATEMWENDE*)

> (Thread suns
> above the grey-black wilderness.
> A tree-
> high thought
> tunes in to light's pitch: there are
> still songs to be sung on the other side
> of mankind.)[25]

In the further verses of "WEGGEBEIZT," whose opening lines were cited above, we are taken through ice and snow to "den gastlichen / Gletscherstuben und -tischen"; in the glacier, there awaits "ein Atemkristall." "KEIN HALB-HOLZ" *(Lichtzwang)* takes us from the wood and thyme of the slopes to the "Grenzschnee" which declares our ordinary limits and signposts dead.

But what is remarkable about this later poetry is that the process we see in the earlier work has been taken a stage further. Celan has always been breaking down received images, and reconstituting new ones through a recombination of the elements. Now he does the same with words: "das hundert- / zungige Mein- / Gedicht, das Genicht." He remakes the poetic language afresh. He is well aware that poetic words with performative force only live in a web of connections; but he takes the risk of breaking many of these established skeins, in order to set up new ones. Erich Kahler, author of the "Disintegration of Form in the Arts," in describing Celan's language, spoke of its reduction to "primary-wordedness . . . bare signs and ciphers, stuntedness."[26] Celan's task as a lyric poet after catastrophe demanded nothing less.

I have evoked here only two of the many vectors of Celan's poetics. What animates them all is a striving for a triple reconnection. The aim on one level was to restore and renew the tradition of modern poetics, in particular its German-language form, within which he stood. But animating this was a striving to recover the lost voices of his East European Jewish inheritance, and beyond this to restore/renew his roots in Judaism itself. It was in one sense a triple mission impossible, or at least not possible without ambivalence, and a recurring sense of failure. But until the final despair, he never gave up; and the attempt has yielded a rich array of signposts, luminous and arresting, which we shall try to follow, limping and uncertain, during the coming century.

Part II

SOCIAL THEORY

CHAPTER FIVE

Nationalism and Modernity

NATIONALISM is much talked about these days. I suppose it's obvious why. The post-Communist massacres in the ex–Soviet Union and ex-Yugoslavia are reason enough. And suddenly this kind of frightening outburst seems in danger of becoming more the rule than the exception. For some people this is all the more shocking in that it seems like a throwback. The Bosnian savagery comes across to these people as an atavistic return, as though primeval identities and ageless mutual hatreds were being resurrected at the end of the twentieth century. But this can't be quite the right take on things, because so much in nationalism is quintessentially modern. The Serb-Croat wars disconcert us because they mix an unquestionably modern discourse—self-determination, rule by the people, et cetera—with other elements that seem to us alien to (what we understand as) modernity.

Can we hope to understand this? Is there even a "this" to understand here? Is there a single phenomenon? Maybe we're making things even harder for ourselves by assuming that there is something called "nationalism" that is the same wherever people make demands in the name of ethnic/cultural self-determination, so that Bosnian Serbs and Québécois are placed in the same category.[1] The differences are explained by the first being more "extreme" than the second, just as neat whiskey knocks you out, but diluted whiskey makes you mellow.

I want to argue that there are big differences here but also some links. Sorting this out will require thinking in more than one register. One-line theories of nationalism are as bad as such theories invariably are in social science. I am going to try to explore the ways in which various nationalisms are linked to modernity, both to central features of its political culture and to the stresses and malaise to which it gives rise.

Some explanations take up this topic from this latter perspective. Nationalism is an outbreak of emotion that is understandable when people are under strain because of, say, a disorienting social and economic transition, especially if this is accompanied by hard times. So we understand why lots of Russians voted for Zhirinovsky in the last election, even though we deplore it, just as we understand why Algerians voted for the Islamic Salvation Front in their last election. Now if things had been going better, if people had felt more secure, or if there hadn't been so much unemployment and hardship, these extreme and dangerous parties wouldn't have made the headway they did.

There is very often a lot of truth in this last counterfactual proposition. But it doesn't tell us what is really interesting to know: why nationalists or Islamic "fundamentalists" are the candidates waiting to take up the angry, disoriented protest vote. And this has a lot to do with the progress of what I am calling "modernity," even, perhaps especially, where it seems to take "antimodern" forms.

So I want first to trace the ways in which nationalism arises out of modern society and the modern state form. Ernest Gellner has an interesting theory of just this kind.[2] His is in a sense a functional account. It concentrates on modern societies as economies, which by their very nature need to be serviced and (to some degree) managed by the state.

A modern economy is by definition one undergoing growth and change. As such it requires a population that is mobile, both occupationally and geographically. People no longer will necessarily stay in the same métier throughout their whole careers, and certainly there cannot be the hereditary handing down of métier from parent to child that characterized many premodern societies. This flexibility can be attained only by a high level of general education, literacy, and numeracy, one unmatched by any previous society in history. The modern division of labor is multiform but shallow. That is, it is taken for granted that people can be retrained or at least that their children can. Vocations are no longer linked with the standing status divisions that marked many earlier societies, of which the extreme case is the traditional Indian caste system.

Moreover, this generalized and high level of culture has to be homogeneous. We need people who can communicate with each other and generally understand each other without having to rely heavily on familiarity with particular contexts of family, clan, locality, provenance, et cetera. To "do business" with each other, operate a system of courts, run a bureaucratic state apparatus, and the like, we need millions who can communicate without difficulty in a context-free fashion. A standard language must replace all the local and class dialects that abounded earlier.

Society needs in a sense a homogeneous culture, one into which people have to be inducted to be able to do business with each other across all the particularities of context and background. But how can they be inducted into this culture? Here is where the modern state takes on an especially important role.

In earlier "agro-literate" societies, the high culture was confined to a class, the literati and perhaps other top strata. The job of handing on this culture could be assumed by families in some cases or by special institutions that might be at some distance from the state (for example, the Church in premodern Europe). But in the modern context, the task of educating everybody up to scratch is too imposing and too vital to be left to the private sector. Both the scale of the educative enterprise and its essential uniformity dictate that it be assumed by the state. Modern societies/economies are all serviced, inescapably, by a state system of education.

A homogeneous language and culture is fostered and diffused and hence also to some degree defined by the state. Modern societies necessarily have official languages, almost official cultures. This is a functional imperative. Gellner takes issue with Elie Kedourie: it is not so much that nationalism as a sentiment, as a political aspiration, has imposed homogeneity. Rather, homogeneity is a requirement of the modern state, and it is this "inescapable imperative [that] eventually appears on the surface as nationalism."[3]

Now up to this last quote, I think Gellner is basically right. There can be differences in the detailed account, but it seems to me an undeniable feature of modern-market, growth-oriented, industrial economies, embedded as they are in bureaucratic polities, that they force a kind of homogeneity of language and culture, both designedly, as through the education system, and by the very way they operate, as through their media. And it seems that this couldn't very well be otherwise. The demands of this kind of society in trained personnel—above all in *retrainable* personnel, capable of taking on ever-new technologies and operating by ever-new methods—and the need for intercommunication across vaster and vaster networks push inevitably to the diffusion of standardized, context-free languages, embedding within themselves a multiplicity of expert "language games." As a consequence of this, earlier "network" identities, linked to family, clan, locality, and provenance, tend to decline, and new "categorical" identities, which link us to a multitude of others nationally or even globally—on the basis of confession, profession, citizenship—take on more and more importance.[4]

Compared with earlier societies, which tended to be divided between a "high" culture, and appanage of a restricted class, and a set of partly overlapping "folk" cultures, this modern form tends to universalize a species of "high" (literate) culture, putting a larger and larger proportion of its population through tertiary education, inculcating into many of them a "canon," as "high" cultures have always tended to do to their initiates. As Gellner puts it, "a high culture pervades the whole of society, defines it, and needs to be sustained by that polity. *That* is the secret of nationalism."[5]

All this seems true, but how does it account for nationalism? This seems evident enough to Gellner. If a modern society has an "official" language, in the fullest sense of the term—that is, a state-sponsored, inculcated, and defined language and culture, in which both economy and state function—then it is obviously an immense advantage to people if this language and culture are theirs. Speakers of other languages are at a distinct disadvantage. They must either go on functioning in what to them is a second language or get on an equal footing with speakers of the official language by assimilating. Or else, faced with this second distasteful prospect, they demand to redraw the boundaries of the state and set up shop in a new polity/economy where their own language will become official. The nationalist imperative is born.

People have raised objections to Gellner's theory on a number of grounds, most notably that it seems to have trouble explaining the rise of nationalism in preindustrial contexts, such as nineteenth-century Eastern Europe and twentieth-century Africa. But I don't want to dwell on these difficulties, for which there are probably answers anyway. What concerns me is the incompleteness of the explanation.

Some people assimilate; they go without much protest into the mix-master of school and army and lose their regional dialects. They enter as peasants and emerge as Frenchmen.[6] Why do some put up a fight and create nationalist movements while others do not? Or again, if there are two languages widely spoken in a given state, why is it so difficult to come to some arrangement around a form of bilingualism? This does happen, of course, but alas, much more rarely than it should, and it is often fraught with strife and difficulty even where it has been adopted. Why should this be so?

Some people might think that the problematicity of bilingualism needs no explanation. It's so much easier to operate in a single language. The subsequent question is, easier than what? If everyone were willing to agree happily to operate in a single language, we'd be crazy to insist on two. But if the alternative is strife, resentment, separatist movements, perhaps even the dissolution of the state, well, bilingualism isn't really that complicated. In my (admittedly jaundiced) experience of living in a bilingual state, pleas about the trouble and expense of bilingualism are generally technological pretexts for a chauvinism that dares not declare itself openly.

But if that is so, then the crucial explanatory bit is missing from Gellner's account. The reason why some minorities assimilate and others fight back has to be referred to the nationalism of the latter. The reason bilingual solutions are hard isn't because they're so complicated and expensive but because they're resisted (for example, under the bad faith pretext that they're complicated and expensive) on fundamentally nationalist grounds. That is, nationalism is still figuring in the account as an explanans, not as a successfully accounted for explanandum.

What Gellner has done, which is very valuable, is define some of the very important stakes of nationalist struggle. Just because the modern state does sustain an official language/culture, it becomes of ultimate significance to those with a strong national identity to get some kind of control of a state. The state focus of so much modern national sentiment and national identity, which Gellner makes a matter of definition, is thereby partly explained, and this is no small matter. But the original energy fueling these struggles remains to be understood. Unless one takes the cynical view (espoused, for instance, by Pierre Trudeau in relation to Quebec independentism) that the whole thing is powered by the ambition of social elites to establish a monopoly of prestigious and remunerative jobs. The refusal of bilingualism is then easily explained: Under this regime, members of our gang get 50 percent of the jobs; under unilingualism, we get 100 percent.

Once again, this certainly explains something but far from everything. It can't explain, for instance, why non-elites are so easily recruited into the nationalist enterprise. Nor does it explain the solidarity of the elites themselves. If you are one of those holding down a top job within the 50 percent allocated to your language group, why should you upset everything so that some as-yet-unfavored compatriots can take over the other 50 percent? Why side with compatriots against fellow top jobholders? Of course, not everybody does, but one of the remarkable things about the moral pressures of nationalism is that many feel they should and lots do. Where does nationalism get its moral thrust? Totally cynical explanations are powerless to illuminate this.

Last, I wonder if we should make the state focus definitional for modern nationalism as Gellner does. Granted, nationalism overwhelmingly takes this form, but not invariably. Thus French-Canadian nationalism, from the nineteenth into the twentieth century, had two forms, of which the dominant one was turned away from the state and promoted nonstate institutions, especially the Church. The more familiar state-centered mode was also there, at least since the rebellion of 1837, but it remained the less powerful strand—that is, until the turnover of 1960, after which it has taken over the whole field, with the resultant rise of independentism and the identity switch from "Canadien-français" to "Québécois." Nevertheless, during those many decades before 1960, there were people whom everybody, including themselves, referred to as "nationalistes" who lacked the state focus. The emotional and moral sources on which they drew were different but not totally distinct from those drawn on by Quebec nationalists today. We gain nothing by excluding this phenomenon from our purview by definitional fiat.

So the ultimate sources of modern nationalism still escape us. (Perhaps they always will.) But at least we understand better some of the things at stake in modern nationalist struggles, and hence their focus, thanks to Gellner's account. Before I try my hand at defining the sources, I would like to supplement Gellner's picture of what is at stake by bringing to the fore other functional requirements of the modern state.

Modern nation-states are "imagined communities," in Benedict Anderson's celebrated phrase.[7] We might say that they have a particular kind of social imaginary—that is, socially shared ways in which social spaces are imagined. There are two important features of the modern imaginary, which I can best bring out by contrasting them in each case with what went before in European history.

First, there is the shift from hierarchical, mediated-access societies to horizontal, direct-access societies. In the earlier form, hierarchy and what I am calling mediacy of access went together. A society of ranks—"society of orders," to use Alexis de Tocqueville's phrase—like seventeenth-century France, for instance, was hierarchical in an obvious sense. But this also meant that one belonged to this society via belonging to some component of it. As a peasant, one was linked to a lord who in turn held power from the king. One was a member of a municipal corporation that had a standing in the kingdom or exercised some function in a parliament with its recognized status, and so on. By contrast, the modern nation of citizenship is direct. In however many ways I am related to the rest of society through intermediary organizations, I think of my citizenship as separate from all these. My fundamental way of belonging to the state is not dependent on or mediated by any of these other belongings. I stand, alongside all my fellow citizens, in direct relationship to the state that is the object of our common allegiance.

Of course, this doesn't necessarily change the way things get done. I know someone whose brother-in-law is a judge or an MP, and so I phone her up when I'm in a jam. We might say that what has changed is the normative picture. But underlying this, without which the new form couldn't exist for us, is a change in the way people imagine belonging. There were certainly people in seventeenth-century France and before for whom the very idea of direct access would have been foreign, impossible to clearly grasp. The educated had the model of the ancient republic. But for many others, the only way they could understand belonging to a larger whole, like a kingdom or a universal church, was through the imbrication of more immediate, understandable units of belonging (parish, lord) into the greater entity. Modernity has involved, among other things, a revolution in our social imaginary, the relegation of these forms of mediacy to the margins, and the diffusions of images of direct access.

This has come about in a number of forms: the rise of a public sphere, in which people conceive of themselves as participating directly in a nationwide (sometimes even international) discussion; the development of market economies, in which all economic agents are seen as entering into contractual relations with others on an equal footing; and, of course, the rise of the modern citizenship state. But we can think of other ways as well in which immediacy of access takes hold of our imaginations. We see ourselves as in spaces of fashion, for instance, taking up and handing on styles. We see ourselves as part of the worldwide audience of media stars. And while these spaces are in their own sense hierarchical—they center on quasi-legendary figures—they offer all participants an access unmediated by any of their other allegiances or belongings. Something of the same kind, along with a more substantial mode of participation, is available in the various movements (social, political, religious) that are a crucial feature of modern life and link people translocally and internationally into a single collective agency.

These modes of imagined direct access are linked to—indeed, are just different facets of—modern equality and individualism. Directness of access abolishes the heterogeneity of hierarchical belonging. It makes us uniform, and that is one way of becoming equal. (Whether it is the only way is the fateful issue at stake in much of today's struggles over multiculturalism.) At the same time, the relegation of various mediations reduces their importance in our lives; the individual stands more and more free of them and hence has a growing self-consciousness as an individual. Modern individualism, as a moral idea, doesn't mean ceasing to belong at all—that's the individualism of anomie and breakdown—but imagining oneself as belonging to ever wider and more impersonal entities: the state, the movement, the community of humankind. This is the same change—seen from another angle—that I described above in terms borrowed from Craig Calhoun: The shift from "network" or "relational" identities to "categorical" ones.

The second important feature of the modern social imagery is that it no longer sees the greater translocal entities as grounded in something other, something higher, than common action in secular time. This was not true of the premodern state. The hierarchical order of the kingdom was seen as based in the Great Chain of Being. The tribal unit was seen as constituted as such by its law, which went back "since time out of mind" or perhaps to some founding moment that had the status of a "time of origins" in Mircea Eliade's sense. The importance in premodern revolutions, up to and including the English civil war, of the backward look, of establishing an original law, comes from this sense that the political entity is in this sense action-transcendent. It cannot simply create itself by its own action. On the contrary, it can act as an entity because it is already constituted as such, and that is why such legitimacy attaches to returning to the original constitution.

Seventeenth-century social contact theory, which sees a people as coming together out of a state of nature, obviously belongs to another order of thought. But it wasn't until the late eighteenth century that this new way of conceiving things entered the social imaginary. The American Revolution is in a sense the watershed. It was undertaken in a backward-looking spirit, in the sense that the colonists were fighting for their established rights as Englishmen. Moreover, they were fighting under their established colonial legislatures, associated in a Congress. But out of the whole process emerged the crucial fiction of "we, the people," into whose mouth the declaration of the new Constitution was placed.

Here the idea is invoked that a people or, as it was also called at the time, a "nation" can exist prior to and independently of its political constitution so that this people can give itself its own constitution by its own free action in secular time. Of course, the epoch-making action rapidly comes to be invested with images drawn from older notions of higher time. The "Nova Ordo seclorum," just like the new French revolutionary calendar, draws heavily on Judeo-Christian apocalyptic beliefs. The Constitution founding comes to be invested with something of the force of a "time of origins," a higher time, filled with agents of a superior kind, which we should ceaselessly try to reapproach. But nevertheless, a new way of conceiving things is abroad. Nations, people, can have a personality, can act together outside of any prior political ordering. One of the key premises of modern nationalism is in place, because without this the demand for self-determination of nations would make no sense. This just is the right for peoples to make their own constitution, unfettered by their historical, political organization.

What is immensely suggestive about Anderson's account is that it links these two features. It shows how the rise of direct-access societies was linked to changing understandings of time and, consequently, of the possible ways of imaging social wholes. Anderson stresses how the new sense of belonging to a nation was prepared by a new way of grasping society under the category of simultaneity:[8] society as the whole consisting of the simultaneous happening of the myriad events that mark the lives of its members at that moment. These events are the fillers of this segment of a kind of homogeneous time. This very clear, unambiguous concept of simultaneity belongs to an understanding of time as exclusively secular. As long as secular time is interwoven with various kinds of higher time, there is no guarantee that all events can be placed in unambiguous relations of simultaneity and succession. The high feast is in one way contemporaneous with my life and that of my fellow pilgrims, but in another way it is close to eternity, the time of origins, or the events it prefigures.

A purely secular time understanding allows us to imagine society "horizontally," unrelated to any "high points," in which the ordinary sequence of events touches higher time, and therefore it does not recognize any privileged persons or agencies—such as kings or priests—who stand and mediate at such alleged points. This radical horizontality is precisely what is implied in the direct-access society, where each member is "immediate to the whole." Anderson is undoubtedly right to argue that this new understanding couldn't have arisen without social developments like that of print capitalism, but he doesn't want to imply by this that the transformations of the social imaginary are sufficiently explained by these developments. Modern society also required transformations in the way we figure ourselves as societies. Crucial among these has been this ability to grasp society from a decentered view that is no one's. That is, the search for a truer and more authoritative perspective than my own doesn't lead me to center society on a king or sacred assembly, or whatever, but allows for this lateral, horizontal view, which an unsituated observer might have—society as it might be laid out in a tableau without privileged nodal points. There is a close inner link between modern direct-access societies, their self-understandings, their refraction in categorical identities, and modern synoptic modes of representation in "the Age of the World Picture": society as simultaneous happenings, social interchange as an impersonal "system," the social terrain as what is mapped, historical culture as what shows up in museums, et cetera.[9]

WHAT LIGHT can these considerations about the social imaginary throw on modern nationalism? They can help illuminate what is at stake in nationalist struggles, just as Gellner's account did, an account that these considerations in a sense complement. Gellner showed the phenomenon of a state-fostered official language as a functional requirement of a modern state and economy. And in an analogous way there are functional requirements that attend the modern social imaginary.

The horizontal, direct-access society, given political form by an act of the people, forms the background to the contemporary source of legitimate government in the will of the people. This principle is getting harder and harder to gainsay in the modern world. It comes close to being the only acceptable basis for any regime that doesn't declare itself as merely temporary or transitional, with the partial exception of so-called Islamic regimes—although this doesn't prevent it from being used to justify the most terrible tyrannies. Communist regimes were also supposedly based on popular sovereignty, and fascism was supposed to emanate from the united will of a conquering people.

Now this has certain functional requirements. Let's first of all take the case where the attempt is made to live out the principle of popular sovereignty through a representative democracy. The nature of this kind of society, as in any other free society, is that it requires a certain degree of commitment on the part of its citizens. Traditional despotisms could ask of people only that they remain passive and obey the laws. A democracy, ancient or modern, has to ask more. It requires that its members be motivated to make the necessary contributions: of treasure (in taxes) and sometimes blood (in war); and it expects always some degree of participation in the process of governance. A free society has to substitute for despotic enforcement with a certain degree of self-enforcement. Where this fails, the system is in danger. For instance, democratic societies where the level of participation falls below a certain threshold cease to be legitimate in the eyes of their members. A government elected in an election with a turnout of 20 percent can't claim to have the mandate of the people. It can only claim to have gotten there by the rules, which is a much weaker defense if ever it faces a crisis.

So democracies require a relatively strong commitment on the part of their citizens. In terms of identity, citizenship has to rate as an important component of who they are. I am speaking in general, of course; in any society, there will be a wide gamut of cases, stretching from the most gung ho and motivated to the most turned-off internal exiles. But the median point of this gamut has to fall closer to the upper than the lower limit. This membership has to be one that matters. In particular, it has to matter more than the things that can divide the citizens.

In other words, the modern democratic state needs a healthy degree of what used to be called "patriotism," a strong sense of identification with the polity, and a willingness to give of oneself for its sake. That is why these states try to inculcate patriotism and to create a strong sense of common identity even where it did not previously exist. And that is why one thrust of modern democracy has been to try to shift the balance within the identity of the modern citizen, so that being a citizen will take precedence over a host of other poles of identity, such as family, class, gender, even (perhaps especially) religion. This may be promoted in a deliberate way, on the basis of an express ideology, as in the case of French Republicanism. Or it may be fostered in more indirect ways, as a consequence of the injunction to render other modes of description—gender, race, religion, et cetera—irrelevant in the operation of public life.[10]

But the effect is the same, and we can see that it complements the factors Gellner highlights. Parallel to the homogeneity of language and culture that the modern state economy can't help fostering is this homogenization of identity and allegiance that it must nourish for its survival. In both cases, the features that divide us, that distinguish us into subgroups and partial publics, fade, either altogether or at least in their importance and relevance.

How does this connect with nationalism? One obvious link is that nationalism can provide the fuel for patriotism. So much so that we can have trouble distinguishing them from each other. But it is important to keep them distinct if we want to understand our history. If we think of patriotism as a strong citizen identification, then nationalism is one basis for patriotism but not the only one. We can speak of nationalism when the ground of the common political allegiance is some ethnic, linguistic, cultural, or religious identity that exists independently of the polity. If I am a nationalist, I owe allegiance to this state because it is the state of the Xs, where X is my national identity, one I would bear whether or not we were lucky enough or strong enough or virtuous enough to have a state. The whole nationalist idea supposes this prepolitical identity, as I said above.

But patriotism can also have the meaning it had for the ancients. I love my fatherland, and what makes it essentially mine is its laws. Outside of these, it is denatured and no longer really mine. There is no reference to a prepolitical identity here; on the contrary, the patria is politically defined. Now this is important, because this was the form that patriotism took initially in the two great inaugural revolutions of the liberal age, the American and the French. Neither was initially nationalist. The nation either was taken as given out of previous history or was constructed, in the American case, out of an alliance based on an obvious commonality of historical predicament, and in both cases the patriot was one who sought the nation's freedom. It was later, when (the elites of) other peoples began to feel that they couldn't attain real freedom by simply revolutionizing the existing (often imperial) political structures or finding their place within a liberal empire (of Napoléon), that nationalism raised its head.

But subsequently, so much did nationalism become the rule, as a basis for patriotism, that the original prenationalist societies themselves began to understand their own patriotism in something like nationalist terms. Instead of seeing liberal institutions as uncomplicatedly universal, nationalism accredited the idea that in each society they must be tailored to the particular genius of the people. But then even in their original countries of origin where they were at first understood universalistically, they now come to be seen as colored by particular circumstances and history.

Be that as it may, nationalism has become the most readily available motor of patriotism, so that when leaders want to unite a country and lift people out of their warring partial allegiances they appeal to a broader national identity, telling a story that makes this central to the history of their society rather than the partial identities they are trying to supersede. Thus Nehru, in his *Discovery of India,* tells a narrative of Indian identity, the basis of a pan-Indian secular nationalism that would take precedence over the potentially warring communal allegiances, Hindu and Muslim.

There is thus a sort of dialectic of state and nation. It is not just that nations strive to become states; it is also that modern states, in order to survive, strive to create national allegiances to their own measure. This is a point parallel to

Gellner's correction of Kedourie above. Nationalism is not only the motor behind the homogenization of modern societies; it can also sometimes be the upshot. In order to see this, we have to keep in mind the functional requirement of patriotism.

But this still doesn't "explain" modern nationalism because lots of nationalisms arise outside of this state-building process,[11] and we still have to explain why some state-sponsored enterprises of patriotism succeed and other founder on unconquerable existent identities. (Is the Nehruvian secular Indian nationalism among the casualties?) The ultimate insight still eludes us.

It does, however, further define the form of the struggles to which nationalism gives rise and clarifies what is at stake in them in a way parallel and complementary to Gellner's account. This showed how the modern economy and bureaucratic state pushed toward a state-fostered common language and culture and thus showed that if a given minority group did not want to assimilate and the majority was unwilling to give them a place through some regime of bilingualism, then the minority faced the unenviable position of being forever disadvantaged. Feeling the assimilative pressure on their members inseparable from this position, they ultimately risked the feared outcome of assimilation. Trouble and strife are built into such a situation.

Analogously here, we see that the modern state must push for a strong common identity. And thus if a group feels that this identity doesn't reflect it and the majority will not accommodate it by modifying the definition of common identity to include this group, then its members feel like second-class citizens and consequently experience an assimilative pressure. Trouble of some sort must follow.

What this doesn't tell us is what makes these "if" clauses true when they are. What it does help us to see is that once they are true, the distressing scenarios of nationalist struggles—separatist movements, assimilation policies, tense compromises, and the like—are not just the result of gratuitous bloody-mindedness, even less the result of some regression to premodern tribal identities, but are very much the product of a situation of rivalry that is quintessentially modern in its structure and stakes.

A further word here might be helpful about how this latter kind of struggle plays itself out, based on further reflections on the functional requirements of democratic rule. The model of democratic legitimacy requires that the laws we live under in some sense result from our collective decisions. "The people" for these purposes is thought to form a collective unit of decision. But we do more than decide on issues that are already clear-cut. If that were the case, the best way to do things would be to put everything to a referendum. We also have to deliberate, clarify things, make up our minds. So "the people" also has to be conceived as a collective unit of deliberation.

Now in the meaning of the act, "the people" is also seen as made up of equal and autonomous members, because to the extent that this is not the case and some are dependent on others the decision would be held to emanate from the influential part and not from the whole people.

If we put these two together, we have the idea of a process of deliberation and decision in which everybody can be heard. Of course, if we were very exigent, this would always turn out to be utopian. In fact, democratic societies are usually satisfied with some approximation of principle to this norm. But if it appears that, in some systematic way, there are obstacles to certain sections of the population being heard, then the legitimacy of democratic rule in that society is under challenge.

Now there are a number of ways a case can be made that a certain segment of the population is being systematically unheard. A case of this kind was made on behalf of the working class in earlier times, could be made today with great plausibility on behalf of the nonworking marginalized poor, and is often vigorously made on behalf of women. What concerns me here is the way that a case of this kind can be made in relation to an ethnic or linguistic group.

A minority group can come to feel that their way of seeing things is different from the majority, that this is generally not understood or recognized by the majority, and, consequently, that the majority is not willing to alter the terms of the debate to accommodate this difference, and therefore the minority is being systematically unheard. Their voice cannot really penetrate the public debate. They are not really part of the deliberative unit.

Understanding of how this feeling could arise must emerge from our ever-deferred search for the sources of nationalism. But we can see from here how destabilizing this type of challenge is in a modern democratic society, because it strikes at the very basis of legitimacy in this kind of society. Part of understanding modern nationalism is seeing how vulnerable our societies are to it.

THAT BEING SAID, can we now come to the sources of nationalism? If I could listen to the voice of prudence, I would now plead lack of space and leave this to some other occasion. But I am going to ignore the trembling of angels and rush in anyway. Nationalism, I have wanted to say, can't be understood as an atavistic reaction. It is a quintessentially modern phenomenon. One might think that the above discussion clears the way for a picture of it as both. What is modern would be the context of nationalistic struggles, the stakes and predispositions to struggle, given national sentiment, as these have been outlined by Gellner, supplemented by my remarks (in turn inspired by Anderson). What is primeval would be the sentiment itself, and so the two can be neatly combined.

But I think that even the sentiment is one that could only arise in modernity, and that is what I now want to explain. Why does nationalism arise? Why couldn't the Germans just be happy to be part of Napoléon's liberalizing empire, as Hegel would have liked? Why didn't the Algerians demand the full French citizenship to which they would have been entitled according to the logic of "l'Algérie, c'est la France" instead of going for independence? And so on, through an immense range of similar questions.

First, it's important to see that in a great many situations the initial refusal is that of certain elites, generally the ones who are most acquainted with the culture of the metropolis they are refusing. Later, in a successful nationalist movement, the mass of the people is somehow induced to come on board. This indicates that an account of the sources of such a movement ought to distinguish between these two stages.

So let me try to tackle the first phase. Why do the elites refuse metropolitan incorporation, even, perhaps especially, when they have accepted many of the values of the metropolis? Here we have to look at another facet of the unfolding process of modernity.

From one point of view, modernity is like a wave, flowing over and engulfing one traditional culture after another. If we understand by modernity, inter alia, the developments discussed above—the emergence of a market-industrial economy, of a bureaucratically organized state, of modes of popular rule—then its progress is, indeed, wavelike. The first two changes, if not the third, are in a sense irresistible. Whoever fails to take them or some good functional equivalent on will fall so far behind in the power stakes as to be taken over and forced to undergo these changes anyway. There are good reasons in the relations of force for the onward march of modernity so defined.

But modernity as lived from the inside, as it were, is something different. The institutional changes just described always shake up and alter traditional culture. They did this in the original development in the West, and they have done this elsewhere. But outside of those cases where the original culture is quite destroyed and the people either die or are forcibly assimilated—and European colonialism has a number of such cases to its discredit—a successful transition involves a people finding resources in their traditional culture to take on the new practices. In this sense, modernity is not a single wave. It would be better to speak of alternative modernities, as the cultures that emerge in the world to carry the institutional changes turn out to differ in important ways from each other. Thus a Japanese modernity, an Indian modernity, and various modulations of Islamic modernity will probably enter alongside the gamut of Western societies, which are also far from being totally uniform.

Looking at modernity from this perspective, we can see that it—the wave of modernity—can be felt as a threat to a traditional culture. It will remain an external threat to those deeply committed against change. But there is another reaction among those who want to take on some version of the institutional changes. Unlike the conservatives, they don't want to refuse the changes. They of course want to avoid the fate of those aboriginal people who have just been engulfed and made over by the changes. What they are looking for is a creative adaptation, drawing on the cultural resources of their tradition that would enable them to take on the new practices successfully. In short, they want to do what has already been done in the West. But they see, or sense, that that cannot consist in just copying the West's adaptations. The creative adaptation using traditional resources by definition has to be different from culture to culture. Just taking over Western modernity couldn't be the answer. Or otherwise put, this answer comes too close to engulfment. They have to invent their own.

There is thus a "call to difference" felt by "modernizing" elites that corresponds to something objective in their situation. This is part of the background to nationalism. But there is more. The call to difference could be felt by anyone concerned for the well-being of the people involved. But the challenge is lived by the elites concerned overwhelmingly in a certain register, that of dignity.

Western modernity has been a conquering culture because the changes described above confer tremendous power on the societies adopting them. In the relation of conquest, there grow presumptions of superiority and inferiority that the conqueror blithely accepts and the conquered resist. This is the challenge to dignity. To the extent that traditional elites can remain insulated from the relationship, they feel the challenge less. But those involved in modernization, whether it be in a colony or a country overshadowed and threatened, have before them constantly what they also see as a state of backwardness that they are concerned to make up for. The issue is whether they can.

Thus the urge on the part of elites to find their own path is more than a matter of concern for their compatriots. It is also a matter of their own dignity. Until they can find their own creative adaptation and take on the institutional changes while remaining themselves, the imputation of inferiority against the culture they identify with remains unrefuted. And, of course, the imputation is liberally made by members of the dominant societies. Their word tends (irrationally but understandably) to have weight just because of their success and power. They become, in a sense, important interlocutors whose recognition would count for a lot if they gave it. In the face of nonrecognition, this importance will frequently be denied, but sometimes with a vehemence that makes the denial suspect.

I am trying to identify the source of the modern nationalist turn, the refusal—at first among elites—of incorporation by the metropolitan culture, as a recognition of the need for difference but felt existentially as a challenge, not just as a matter of valuable common good to be created but also viscerally as a matter of dignity, in which one's self-worth is engaged. This is what gives nationalism its emotive power. This is what places it so frequently in the register of pride and humiliation.

So nationalism can be said to be modern because it's a response to a modern predicament. But the link is also more intimate. I said above that nationalism usually arises among "modernizing" elites. The link can be understood as more than accidental. One facet of nationalism, I have been arguing, is a response to a threat to dignity. But modernity has also transformed the conditions of dignity.

These in effect could not but change in the move from hierarchical, "mediated" societies to "horizontal," direct-access ones. The concept of honor, which was in place in the earlier forms, was intrinsically hierarchical. It supposed "preferences," in Montesquieu's terms. For me to have honor, I had to have a status that not everyone shares, as is still the case with an "honors list" of awards today. Equal direct-access societies have developed the modern notion of "dignity." This is based on the opposite supposition that all humans enjoy this equally. For instance, the term as used by Kant designates what is supposed to be the appanage of all rational agents. Philosophically, we may want to attribute this status to all, but politically, the sense of equal dignity is really shared by people who belong to a functioning direct-access society together.[12] In this typically modern predicament, their dignity passes through their common categorical identity. My sense of my own worth can no longer be based mainly on my lineage, my clan. A goodly part of it will usually be invested in some other categorical identity.

But categorical identities can also be threatened, even humiliated. The more we are inducted into modern society, the more this is the form in which the question of dignity will pose itself for us. Nationalism is modern because it is a typically modern way of responding to the threat represented by the advancing wave of modernization. Elites have always been able to experience a dramatic loss of dignity in the face of conquering power. One way of responding is to fight back or come to terms with the conquerors out of the same traditional identity and sense of honor. Another is to force a new categorical identity to be the bearer of the sought-for dignity. It is (a subspecies of) this second reaction that we call nationalist. But it is essentially modern. The 1857 rebellion in India was in part an attempt to expunge this perennially available loss of dignity in a premodern context. In this sense, it was not a nationalist movement, as the later Congress was.

The modern context of nationalism is also what turns its search for dignity outward. No human identity is purely inwardly formed. The other always plays some role. But it can be just as a foil, a contrast, a way of defining what we're not, for better or for worse. So the aboriginals of the newly "discovered" world figured for post-Columbian Europeans. The "savage," the other of civilization, provided a way for Europeans to define themselves, both favorably (applying "civilized" to themselves in self-congratulation) and sometimes unfavorably (Europeans as corrupted in contrast to the "noble savage"). This kind of other reference requires no interaction. Indeed, the less interaction, the better, or else the stereotype may be resisted.

But the other can also play a role directly, where I need his or her recognition to be confident of my identity. This has been standard for our relation to our intimates, but it wasn't that important in relation to outsiders in the premodern period. Identities were defined by reference to the other but not out of the other's reactions. Where this latter becomes so, of course, the way we interact is crucial. Perhaps we should correct this statement: because of the big part played by illusion, the way the interaction is seen by the parties is crucial. But the key point is that the interaction is understood to be crucial by the identity bearers themselves.

I would like to argue that identities in the modern world are more and more often formed in this direct relation to others, in a space of recognition. I can't argue the general case here,[13] but I hope that this is evident for modern nationalism. Modern nationalist politics is a species of identity politics. Indeed, it is the original species: national struggles are the site from which the model comes to be applied to feminism, to the struggles of cultural minorities, to the gay movement, et cetera. The work of someone like Frantz Fanon,[14] written in the context of the anticolonial struggle but whose themes have been revived in the other contexts, illustrates the connections. Strong national sentiment among elites usually arises in the first phase because an identity is threatened in its worth.

This identity is vulnerable to nonrecognition, at first on the part of the members of the dominant societies, but later there has developed a world public scene, on which peoples see themselves as standing, on which they see themselves as rated, and which rating matters to them. This world scene is dominated by a vocabulary of relative advance, even to the point of having to discover periodic neologisms in order to euphemize the distinctions. Hence what used to be called the "backward" societies began to be called "underdeveloped" after the war, and then even this came to be seen as indelicate, and so we have the present partition: developed/developing. The backdrop of modern nationalism, that there is something to be caught up with, each society in its own way, is inscribed in this common language, which in turn animates the world public sphere.

Modern nationalism thus taps into something perennial. Conquest or the threat of conquest has never been good for one's sense of worth. But the whole context in which this nationalism arises—that of successive waves of (institutional) modernization—and the resultant challenge to difference—that of the growth of categorical identities as well as the creation of the world public sphere as a space of recognition—are quintessentially modern. We are very far from atavistic reactions and primal identities.

HENCE THE FIRST PHASE of modern nationalism, the refusal of incorporation, arises from the felt need for difference in the context of modernization, but lived in the register of dignity, of an identity potentially threatened in its worth, and in a growing space of recognition.

Let's suppose this is all true (a proposition with a very low antecedent probability); it still accounts only for the first phase. How does nationalism become generalized and galvanize whole populations? How does it spread beyond the elites?

The answer to this question will be even more unsatisfactory than the answer to the previous question. There does not seem to be a single mechanism. Sometimes a charismatic leadership with great imaginative power can make nationalism a mass movement by linking the national aspiration to a host of existing complaints. This was true in the case of Gandhi during the Salt March, for instance. Often the movement spreads slowly down from the original elites to those who strive to emulate them, accede to them, and take them as their model. And when we take account of the fact that modernity itself, as we saw above, tends to generalize a transformation of the original high culture, we can understand how more and more strata of the population may come to experience their situation in the terms originally espoused by elites.

These are ways in which the mass of the people can come to share in the original nationalist aspiration and sense of vulnerable identity. But there are other ways in which nationalism can become a mass movement, in which ordinary people are recruited into it without necessarily sharing the original outlook. Sometimes active minorities, themselves actuated by nationalist fears and aspirations, can contrive to sow discord, distrust, and hatred between populations that hitherto had lived in some amity side by side. Terrorist killings can accomplish this, as can atrocities committed by armed gangs, identified as from one group, against the members of the other community. Then uninvolved people can begin to mistrust their neighbors, even though they may be uninvolved as well. Each community draws together among its own members, in fear and for protection. But the result is that they begin to condone or at least not protest the action of their self-appointed "self-defense" squads, as these perhaps begin to clear out the now-untrustworthy neighbors. The scenario is all too depressingly familiar; we have only to think of the breakup of Yugoslavia in the 1990s.

At the end of the day, each community is ranged against the other, perhaps even geographically separated into "ethnically cleansed" pockets, full of a hatred and fear fed on atrocity stories and often feeling betrayed and bewildered. Each community is now in the grip of a powerful nationalism, hell-bent on its own form of ethnically pure "self-determination," but for the masses the motivation may have little to do with a call to difference and a sense of threatened identity. This is a nationalism born of a sense of physical threat, of the fear of displacement, even extermination, by a hostile other. Each community has the sense that the other united first against its unsuspecting members and that its own mobilization is secondary and defensive in nature. The tragedy is that often neither is right; the split was in a sense engineered by determined and violent minorities, playing a game of provocation and counterprovocation, objectively allied in gradually unraveling ties of conviviality, even intermarriage, which may be of centuries' standing.[15]

Many of today's mass nationalisms are of this secondary and defensive variety, a response to the perceived threat of expulsion or genocide. The infernal circles of killings between Armenians and Azeris, Georgians and Abkhazi, and so on, are of this kind. But this is not to say that such nationalisms are of an entirely different kind. Because somewhere in the causal story is usually the action of minority elites, who were actuated by the classic motivation to difference that I described above. What does distinguish them, however, is that the diffusion of the nationalist movement doesn't come through more and more strata coming to share the original aspiration, through a conversion to the nationalist vision, as with Gandhi and the Salt March, but rather through the (often-manipulated) politics of division and mutual threat—not an identity threat in this case but a physical threat of exile or annihilation. I want to call this kind of mass nationalism defensive, but we have to remember that usually at its origin lies a minority nationalism of aspiration. And of course it may also happen that over time, in a third phase, a mass nationalism of defense can be gradually won over to some version of the original aspiration.

The rise of communal "nationalisms" in India illustrates these mechanisms. Before the mass agitations of the twentieth century, Hindus and Muslims often enjoyed a degree of conviviality difficult to imagine today. Both communities participated in a form of syncretism. In certain parts of the subcontinent, Hindus would attend the celebration of Moharram, and Muslims would attend Dussehra feasts. Protests around the turn of the century began to come from elites in both communities, who wanted to create and propagate a purer, more consistent version of their respective religious identities.

The motivations for religious reform and purification are, of course, always plural and complex. But I would maintain that part of the motivation is the one I described above. Hindu reform, for instance, from Rammohan Roy on, was partly stimulated by the fact of domination, by admiration for the powers of discipline and organization of the dominators, and by the desire to find

Hindu sources for an identity that could sustain the same reformed practices. It was an unavoidable by-product of this that popular syncretism, along with many other practices of popular Hinduism, was judged unacceptable. In Arya Samaj terms, it was "idolatry."

A similar approach, couched in the same terms, comes from the side of Muslim reform. These reform movements, which turned to a purer, often more Sharia-oriented Islam and condemned various popular practices, sometimes including various aspects of Sufism, have been a feature of the last century or so. Indeed, they began somewhat earlier if we include the Wahhabi. Again, it would be a wild oversimplification to explain them entirely as the response to a "call to difference." But the need to respond to a conquering West and the wounds to Islam's self-esteem as itself an erstwhile conquering civilization have almost certainly given a stimulus to these movements.

The move to sever syncretic conviviality, then, comes from elites concerned, at least in some important part, with the call to difference and the threat to identity. And indeed, the Arya Samaj did call for Hindus to cease participating in Moharram, and to complete the connection, members of the Arya Samaj formed part of the nucleus out of which emerged the Rashtriya Swayamsevak Sangh and later the Bharatiya Janata Party, standard-bearers of contemporary Hindu communalism.

But between pure-minded calls to renounce syncretism and the present communal violence and mistrust lies the second phase. My argument is that, unlike the pan-Indian nationalism of Gandhi, followed by Nehru, which was popularized by diffusion of the aspiration concerned, communalism made inroads into syncretic conviviality mainly through clashes and conflicts that raised ever-stronger reactions of defense. For Jinnah and those around him, the impulse to form Pakistan had a lot to do with the preservation of a modernized (and, in Jinnah's case, rather secularized) Muslim identity against the danger of being overwhelmed in a Hindu state. Their own "call to difference" risked being drowned out, they feared, by India's answer to its own call. But when the Muslim League swept the Muslim areas of India in the elections of 1941, the popular slogan was "Islam in danger!" What was being conjured up here was a threat of a more direct and aggressive kind. The ideology of Pakistan propagated itself as a defensive nationalism.

Of course, since then, in a third phase, the original positive aspiration may have propagated itself downward in Pakistani society. It is not easy to judge the extent to which this is so because defensiveness and threat still seem important mainstays of Pakistani unity.

I HAVE BEEN trying to plug the explanatory hole that I saw in Gellner's account and my Anderson-inspired complement to it. These told us something about the context of modern nationalist struggles, even about what can make them virtually inevitable. But the sources of nationalist aspirations escaped us. They offered us Hamlet without the prince. I have tried to explain the missing bit by invoking the context of expanding modernity and the call to difference it raises among peoples in the path of that expansion. This call, lived by elites in the register of dignity, can become the basis of a mass movement in a number of ways, including some rather sinister and destructive ones that have little to do with the call itself.

What does this tell us about the kinds of nationalism? Can we think of it as something homogeneous? Here there are lots of difficulties, and I can see my theory already in danger of unraveling because it places phenomena like the various modes of Islamic "fundamentalism" in the Third World (Iran, Algeria) in the same category as nationalism. Indeed, insofar as I am trying to account for nationalism as a call to difference in face of the wave of "modernization," lived in the register of threatened dignity, and constructing a new, categorical identity as the bearer of that dignity, I could also be talking of the rise of Marxist parties in certain Third World contexts.

This doesn't by itself worry me. As Liah Greenfeld argues (and I feel my account has a lot in common with hers),[16] this may even be a point in favor of my argument. We shouldn't make a fetish of our preliminary vocabulary of distinctions. So what if the categories that emerge from the explanation include more than what we antecedently called "nationalism"? If some common element is really illuminated, then we have gained.

Now with the very important reservation that I don't want to reduce Islamic integrism to a single mode of explanation, as we are dealing with a complex, many-sided, overdetermined reality, I nevertheless would like to argue that its various manifestations have some features of the profile I have just outlined. The sense of operating on a world scene in the register of threatened dignity is very much present, as are the overvehement rejection of the West (or its quintessence, America, the "great Satan") and the tremendous sensitivity to criticism from this quarter, for all the protestations of hostility and indifference. Islamic societies are perhaps, if anything, more vulnerable to a threat to their self-esteem from the impact of superior power in that Islam's self-image, as indicated above, was of the definitive revelation, destined to spread outward without check. The Islamic sense of Providence, if I may use this Christian expression, can cope with the status of conquerors but tends to be bewildered by the experience of powerlessness and conquest.

Again, for all the protestations of faithfulness to the origins, this integrism is in some respects very modern. It mobilizes people in a modern fashion in horizontal, direct-access movements; it thus has no problem using the "modern" institutional apparatuses of elected legislatures, bureaucratic states, and armies. While it would reject the doctrine of popular sovereignty in favor of a species of theocracy, it has also delegitimated all the traditional ruling strata. The Iranian revolution was carried out against the Shah. Those enjoying special authority are exclusively those who "rationally" merit this, granted the nature and goals of the state—namely, the experts in God's law (not to speak of Ayatollah Khomeini's media-oriented abuse of the Islamic judicial forms in issuing his fatwa against Salman Rushdie).

Indeed, it seems true of all fundamentalisms that they paradoxically are most modern when they think they are most faithful to tradition, starting with the original home of the term, in the Protestant sectarian doctrines of biblical inerrancy. This is, in fact, a doctrine defended only in recent centuries. But more important, one can doubt that the issue would even have been clearly understood by Christians in earlier centuries. It supposes a modern conception of the literal truth in secular time that owes something to our social imaginary and our science. Christians of earlier centuries lived in a world in which secular time was interwoven with various orders of higher time, various dimensions of eternity. From within this time sense, it may be hard to explain just what is at stake in the question whether "day" in Genesis means "literally" the twenty-four hours between sunset and sunset, let alone convince someone that he or she should be concerned about it.

Moreover, seeing nationalism, proletarian internationalism, and religious fundamentalisms in the same register may help us to understand their interaction, that they are so often, in fact, fighting for the same space. Arab nationalism gives way to Islamic integrism,[17] just as the demise of Soviet Marxism opens the way for virulent nationalisms. The search for a categorical identity, to answer the call to difference and be the bearer of the sought-for dignity, can take many forms. It is understandable that the discrediting of some strengthens the appeal of others.

Moreover, this kind of diversity and rivalry shades into that between different definitions of nationalism. In many countries, fewer and more inclusive national identities have vied for people's allegiance: Québécois and Canadian, Slovak and Czecho-Slovak, Scots and British. Indeed, one could class the struggle between Nehruvian and "Hindutva" nationalism in India as another such rivalry rather than as a struggle between a national and a religious identity. In all the struggles invoked in this and the preceding paragraph, it is as though there were a space waiting to be filled. It is this that I am trying to cast light on.

So I'm not unduly worried that my account may lead us to bring together things that we now class under different headings. Understanding nationalism in terms of a "call to difference" allows for a great variety of different responses. The aspiration to take on certain forms of modernity on the basis of one's own cultural resources can obviously be played out in many different ways, depending on what you want to take over and what cultural resources you hope to sustain it with. The considerations Gellner adduces, as well as others, certainly explain why one thing people generally want to take over is state power; hence the near-universal validity of his definition of nationalism. But we can also see why in special circumstances a phenomenon like pre-1960 Quebec "nationalism" can arise.

But one difference is worth noting here: that between liberal nationalism—for example, contemporary Quebec independentism—and what we saw in Bosnia. There are some common roots, as captured in my scheme, but there are also clear qualitative differences. The idea that these are both manifestations of the same force but differing in virulence is a serious mistake. It is not just that the second phase in Bosnia was a purely "defensive" one, in my sense. More fundamentally, nationalisms differ, as I have just said, in regard to what they want to take over.

Now in some nationalisms part of what is defined as the desirable modernity is the liberal regime of rights and equal citizenship, attributed to all members of the political unit, regardless of differences, even of ethnicity. These nationalisms have taken over—one might better say, have never lost—the aspirations to patriotism of the founding revolutions anterior to nationalism. The original "nations" these revolutions sought to liberate were held to consist of all free men living in the historically defined societies. The fact that "free men" excluded women in one way and Afro-American slaves in another, more grievous way didn't totally blunt the force of this principle. On the contrary, this force was part of the complex of factors that eventually led to the lifting of these exclusions.

The first wave of nationalisms in Europe that grew up in opposition to the Holy Alliance were of this liberal sort. They retained the original *Verfassungspatriotismus* of the revolutions; their sense of nation incorporated the constitutional principles of liberalism. Contemporary Quebec nationalism is of this kind.

Of course, liberal nationalism suffers strains. All are citizens without distinction, and yet the state has its raison d'être in a cultural nation to which not all citizens belong. There are tensions here to be managed. But there is no question of sacrificing universality on the altar of the nation, for this would be a betrayal of identity.

Quite different are the modes of nationalism where what is to be taken over does not include this liberal patriotism, even in some cases, as in proto-Nazi German movements, where this patriotism is rejected as an alien element, a bit of "Zivilisation" that is contrary to the "Kultur" of the nation, or where liberal politics has never had a toehold, as in the Balkans. There one can have forms where the aspiration includes state power, economic development, even something like an abolition of traditional hierarchies in the name of popular sovereignty. But nothing stands in the way of defining the nation purely ethnically, even racially. Where this is so, the elements of modern politics taken up are no help. Rather, they aggravate things. At least traditional societies recognized some moral limits, however frequently transgressed, in the treatment of outsiders. But in the face of the sovereign national will, source of all right, nothing else can stand.

Premodern societies often incorporated different groups in a sort of hierarchy of complementarity, where each one had its niche—as Greeks, for instance, were frequently merchants in the Ottoman Empire. This was a far cry from equal rights, but it did confer a semisecure status. But the outsider has no place in a regime of popular sovereignty, where the people are ethnically defined. Moreover, under the rules of self-determination, outsiders in sufficiently large numbers can contest one's right to the territory. Add to this the sense of threat in defensive nationalism and the scene is set for ethnic cleansing.

It is clear that this type of nationalism, while having partly similar roots to the liberal one and growing and operating within the context of modernity, is nevertheless a wholly different animal, obeying a different dynamic. The account I'm offering should not only lead us to see other phenomena (for example, some "fundamentalisms") as very similar to nationalism but also help us to distinguish rather different modes within the category.

I have not addressed all sorts of other objections. But enough is enough. I have tried to present an account of nationalism on two levels, as it were: on one level, I have attempted to describe the social and state context in which national struggles are played out and by which the stakes of these struggles are defined; and on a second level, which it was more foolhardy to venture onto, I have tried to say what gives rise to nationalist aspirations and national movements. Whatever the inaccuracy of my remarks on this second level (or indeed, on the first), I am convinced that nationalism needs to be tackled in this two-pronged way, and I hope to have helped clarify some of the thorny issues that impede our vision of this absorbing, disturbing, but seemingly inescapable feature of our modern world.

CHAPTER SIX

Conditions of an Unforced Consensus on Human Rights

Introduction

What would it mean to come to a genuine, unforced international consensus on human rights? I suppose it would be something like what Rawls describes in his *Political Liberalism* as an "overlapping consensus."[1] That is, different groups, countries, religious communities, and civilizations, although holding incompatible fundamental views on theology, metaphysics, human nature, and so on, would come to an agreement on certain norms that ought to govern human behavior. Each would have its own way of justifying this from out of its profound background conception. We would agree on the norms while disagreeing on why they were the right norms, and we would be content to live in this consensus, undisturbed by the differences of profound underlying belief.

The idea was already expressed in 1949 by Jacques Maritain: "I am quite certain that my way of justifying belief in the rights of man and the ideal of liberty, equality, fraternity is the only way with a firm foundation in truth. This does not prevent me from being in agreement on these practical convictions with people who are certain that their way of justifying them, entirely different from mine or opposed to mine, . . . is equally the only way founded upon truth."[2]

Is this kind of consensus possible? Perhaps because of my optimistic nature, I believe that it is. But we have to confess at the outset that it is not entirely clear around what the consensus would form, and we are only beginning to discern the obstacles we would have to overcome on the way there. I want to talk a little about both these issues here.

First, what would the consensus be on? One might have thought this was obvious: on human rights. That's what our original question was about, but there is an immediate obstacle that has often been pointed out. Rights talk is something that has roots in Western culture. Certain features of this talk have roots in Western history, and there only. This is not to say that something very like the underlying norms expressed in schedules of rights don't turn up elsewhere, but they are not expressed in this language. We can't assume without further examination that a future unforced world consensus could be formulated to the satisfaction of everyone in the language of rights. Maybe yes, maybe no. Or maybe partially yes, partially no, as we come to distinguish among the things that have been associated in the Western package.

This is not to say that we already have some adequate term for whatever universals we think we may discern between different cultures. Jack Donnelly speaks of "human dignity" as a universal value.[3] Onuma Yasuaki criticizes this expression, pointing out that "dignity" has itself been a favorite term in the Western philosophical stream that has elaborated human rights. He prefers to speak of the "pursuit of spiritual and material well-being" as the universal.[4] Where "dignity" might be too precise and culture-bound a term, "well-being" might be too vague and general. Perhaps we are incapable at this stage of formulating the universal values in play here. Perhaps we shall always be incapable of this. This wouldn't matter, because what we need to formulate for an overlapping consensus are certain norms of conduct. There does seem to be some basis for hoping that we can achieve at least some agreement on these norms. One can presumably find in all cultures condemnations of genocide, murder, torture, and slavery, as well as of, say, "disappearances" and the shooting of innocent demonstrators.[5] The deep underlying values supporting these common conclusions will, in the nature of the case, belong to the alternative, mutually incompatible justifications.

I have been distinguishing between norms of conduct and their underlying justification. The Western rights tradition in fact exists at both of these levels. On one plane, it is a legal tradition, legitimating certain kinds of legal actions and empowering certain kinds of people to make them. We could, and people sometimes do, consider this legal culture as the proper candidate for universalization, arguing that its adoption can be justified in more than one way. Then a legal culture entrenching rights would define the norms around which world consensus would supposedly crystallize.

Some people already have trouble with this, such as Lee Kwan Yew and those in East Asia who sympathize with him. They see something dangerously individualistic, fragmenting, dissolvent of community in this Western legal culture. (Of course, they have particularly in mind—or in their sights—the United States.)[6] In their criticism of Western procedures, they also seem to be attacking the underlying philosophy, which allegedly gives primacy to the individual, whereas supposedly a "Confucian" outlook would have a larger place for the community and the complex web of human relations in which each person stands.

The Western rights tradition also contains certain views on human nature, society, and the human good and carries some elements of an underlying justification. It might help the discussion to distinguish between these two levels, at least analytically, so that we can develop a more fine-grained picture of what our options are. Perhaps, in fact, the legal culture could "travel" better if it could be separated from some of its underlying justifications. Or perhaps the reverse is true, that the underlying picture of human life might look less frightening if it could find expression in a different legal culture. Or maybe neither of these simple solutions will work (this is my hunch), but modifications need to be made to both; however, distinguishing the levels still helps, because the modifications are different on each level.

In any case, a good place to start the discussion would be to give a rapid portrait of the language of rights that has developed in the West and of the surrounding notions of human agency and the good. We could then proceed to identify certain centers of disagreement across cultures, and we might then see what, if anything, could be done to bridge these differences.

The Language of Rights

Many societies have held that it is good to ensure certain immunities or liberties to their members—or sometimes even to outsiders (think of the stringent laws of hospitality that hold in many traditional cultures). Everywhere it is wrong to take human life, at least under certain circumstances and for certain categories of persons. Wrong is the opposite of right, so this is relevant to our discussion.

A quite different sense of the word is invoked when we start to use the definite or indefinite articles, or to put it in the plural, and speak of "a right" or "rights," or when we start to attribute these to persons, and speak of "your rights" or "my rights." This is to introduce what has been called "subjective rights." Instead of saying that it is wrong to kill me, we begin to say that I have a right to life. The two formulations are not equivalent in all respects, because in the latter case the immunity or liberty is considered as it were the property of someone. It is no longer just an element of the law that stands over and between all of us equally.

That I have a right to life says more than that you shouldn't kill me. It gives me some control over this immunity. A right is something that in principle I can waive.[7] It is also something which I have a role in enforcing.

Some element of subjective right exists in all legal systems. The peculiarity of the West is that, first, the concept played a bigger role in European medieval societies than elsewhere in history, and, second, it was the basis of the rewriting of Natural Law theory that marked the seventeenth century. The older notion that human society stands under a Law of Nature, whose origin is the Creator, and that is thus beyond human will, became transposed. The fundamental law was reconceived as consisting of natural rights, attributed to individuals prior to society. At the origin of society stands a Contract, which takes people out of a State of Nature, and puts them under political authority, as a result of an act of consent on their part.

Subjective rights are not only crucial to the Western tradition; even more significant is the fact that they were projected onto Nature and formed the basis of a philosophical view of humans and their society, one that greatly privileges individuals' freedom and their right to consent to the arrangements under which they live. This view has become an important strand in Western democratic theory of the last three centuries.

The notion of (subjective) rights both serves to define certain legal powers and also provides the master image for a philosophy of human nature, of individuals and their societies. It operates both as legal norm and as underlying justification. Moreover, these two levels are not unconnected. The force of the underlying philosophy has brought about a steady promotion of the legal norm in our politico-legal systems so that it now occupies pride of place in a number of contemporary polities. Charters of rights are now entrenched in the constitutions of a number of countries, and also of the European Union. These are the bases of judicial review, whereby the ordinary legislation of different levels of government can be invalidated on the grounds of conflict with these fundamental rights.

The modern Western discourse of rights involves, on the one hand, a set of legal forms by which immunities and liberties are inscribed as rights, with certain consequences for the possibility of waiver and for the ways in which they can be secured—whether these immunities and liberties are among those from time to time granted by duly constituted authority or among those that are entrenched in fundamental law. On the other hand, it involves a philosophy of the person and of society, attributing great importance to the individual and making significant matters turn on his or her power of consent. In both these regards, it contrasts with many other cultures, including the premodern West, not because some of the same protections and immunities were not present, but because they had a quite different basis.[8]

When people protest against the Western rights model, they seem to have this whole package in their sights. We can therefore see how resistance to the Western discourse of rights might occur on more than one level. Some governments might resist the enforcement of even widely accepted norms because they have an agenda that involves violation of these norms (for example, the contemporary People's Republic of China). Others, however, are certainly ready, even eager to espouse some universal norms, but they are made uneasy by the underlying philosophy of the human person in society. This seems to give pride of place to autonomous individuals, determined to demand their rights, even (indeed especially) in the face of widespread social consensus. How does this fit with the Confucian emphasis on close personal relationships, not only as highly valued in themselves, but as a model for the wider society? Can people who imbibe the full Western human rights ethos, which reaches its highest expression in the lone courageous individual fighting against all the forces of social conformity for her rights, ever be good members of a "Confucian" society? How does this ethic of demanding what is due to us fit with the Theravada Buddhist search for selflessness, for self-giving and *dana* (generosity)?[9]

Taking the rights package as a whole is not necessarily wrong, because the philosophy is plainly part of what has motivated the great promotion enjoyed by this legal form. But the kinds of misgivings expressed in the previous paragraph, which cannot be easily dismissed, show the potential advantages of distinguishing the elements and loosening the connection between a legal culture of rights enforcement and the philosophical conceptions of human life that originally nourished it.

It might help to structure our thinking if we made a tripartite distinction. What we are looking for, in the end, is a world consensus on certain norms of conduct enforceable on governments. To be accepted in any given society, these would in each case have to repose on some widely acknowledged philosophical justification, and to be enforced, they would have to find expression in legal mechanisms. One way of putting our central question might be this: What variations can we imagine in philosophical justifications or in legal forms that would still be compatible with a meaningful universal consensus on what really matters to us, the enforceable norms?

Following this line of thinking, it might help to understand better just what exactly we might want to converge on in the world society of the future, as well as to measure our chances of getting there, if we imagine variations separately on the two levels. What I propose to do is look at a number of instances in which there seem to be obvious conflicts between the present language of human rights and one or more major contemporary cultures. The goal will be to try to imagine ways in which the conflict might be resolved and the essential norms involved in the human rights claim preserved, and this through some modification either of legal forms or of philosophy.

Alternative Legal Forms

I would like to look at four kinds of conflict. The first could be resolved by legal innovation, and I will briefly discuss this possibility, but it can best be tackled on the philosophical level. The other three involve the basic justification of human rights claims. In developing these, I will have to spell out much further the justificatory basis for Western thinking and practice about rights than I have in my rather sparse remarks about Natural Rights theory. I shall return to this later.

Let us take the kind of objection that I mentioned at the outset, that someone like Lee Kwan Yew might raise about Western rights practice and its alleged unsuitability for other societies, in particular East Asian ones. The basic notion is that this practice, obviously nourished by the underlying philosophy I described in the previous section, supposes that individuals are the possessors of rights and encourages them to act, to go out and aggressively seek to make good their rights. But this has a number of bad consequences. First of all, it focuses people on their rights, on what they can claim from society and others, rather than on their responsibilities, what they owe to the whole community or to its members. It encourages people to be self-regarding and leads to an atrophied sense of belonging. This in turn leads to a higher degree of social conflict, more and more many-sided, tending ultimately to a war of all against all. Social solidarity weakens, and the threat of violence increases.

This scenario seems rather overdrawn to some. However, it seems to have elements of truth to others, including to people within Western societies, which perhaps might make us doubt that we are on to a difference between civilizations here. In fact, there is a long tradition in the West warning against pure rights talk outside a context in which the political community has a strong positive value. This "communitarian" theorizing has taken on a new urgency today because of the experience of conflict and alienation and the fraying of solidarity in many Western democracies, notably but not only the United States. Does this mean that Lee Kwan Yew's formula might offer a solution to present-day America?

The absurdity of this suggestion brings us back to the genuine differences of culture that exist today. But if we follow through on the logic of the "communitarian" critique in the West, we can perhaps find a framework in which to consider these differences.

One of the key points in the critique of a too exclusive focus on rights is that this neglects the crucial importance of political trust. Dictatorships, as Tocqueville pointed out, try to destroy trust between citizens,[10] but free societies vitally depend on it. The price of freedom is a strong common commitment to the political formula that binds us, because without the commitment the formula would have to be aggressively enforced and this threatens freedom. What will very quickly dissolve the commitment for each and every one of us is the sense that others no longer share it or are willing to act on it. The common allegiance is nourished on trust.

This goes for a political regime centered on the retrieval of rights as much as for any other. The condition of our being able to go out and seek to enforce our own rights is that the system within which this is carried out retains the respect and allegiance of everybody. Once rights retrieval begins to eat into this, once it begins to create a sense of embattled grievance pitting group against group, undermining the sense of common allegiance and solidarity, the whole system of freewheeling rights enforcement is in danger.

The issue is not "individualism" as such. There are many forms of this, and some have grown up together with modern, democratic forms of political society. The danger is in any form of either individualism or group identity that undercuts or undermines the trust that we share a common allegiance as citizens of this polity.

I don't want to pursue here the conditions of political trust in Western democracies, at least not for its own sake,[11] but I want to use this requirement as a heuristic tool, in search of a point of consensus on human rights. One way of considering a claim, similar to that of Lee Kwan Yew, that the Western rights focus does not fit a certain cultural tradition would be to ask how certain fundamental liberties and immunities could be guaranteed in the society in question, consistent with the maintenance of political trust. This means, of course, that one will not consider satisfactory any solution that does not preserve these liberties and immunities while accepting whatever modifications in legal form one needs to generate a sense of common acceptance of the guaranteeing process in the society concerned.

In the concrete case of Lee Kwan Yew's Singapore, this would mean that his claim in its present form is hardly receivable. There is too much evidence of the stifling of dissent and of the cramping (to say the least) of the democratic political process in Singapore. However, this kind of claim should lead us to reflect further on how immunities of the kinds we seek in human rights declarations can best be preserved in "Confucian" societies.

Turning back to Western societies, we note that judges and the judicial process enjoy in general a great deal of prestige and respect.[12] In some countries, this respect is based on a long tradition in which some notion of fundamental law played an important part, and hence in which its guardians had a special place. Is there a way of connecting rights retrieval in other societies to offices and institutions that enjoy the highest moral prestige there?

Adverting to another tradition, we note that in Thailand at certain crucial junctures the immense moral prestige of the monarchy has been used to confer legitimacy on moves to end military violence and repression and return to constitutional rule. This was the case following the student demonstrations in October 1973, and again in the wake of the popular reactions against the seizure of power by General Suchinda Kraprayoon in May 1992. In both cases, a military junta responded with violence, only to find its position unsustainable and to be forced to give way to a civilian regime and renewed elections. In both these cases, King Bhumibhol played a critical role.[13] The king was able to play this role because of elements in the traditions that have contributed to the Thai conception of monarchy, some of which go way back. For example, the conception of the king as *dharmaraja,* in the tradition of Ashoka,[14] sees the ruler as charged with establishing dharma in the world.

It was perhaps crucial to the upheavals of 1973 and 1992 that a king with this kind of status played the part he did. The trouble is that the power of the royal office can also be used in the other direction, as happened in 1976 when right-wing groups used the slogan "Nation, King and Religion" as a rallying cry in order to attack democratic and radical leaders. The movement of reaction culminated in the October 1976 coup, which relegated the democratic constitution once again to the wastebasket.[15]

The issue arising from all this is the following: Can the immense power to create trust and consensus that resides in the Thai monarchy be in some way stabilized, regularized, and channeled in support of constitutional rule and the defense of certain human rights, such as those concerned with the security of the person? In Weberian terms, could the charisma here be "routinized" enough to impart a stable direction to it without being lost altogether? If a way could be found to draw on this royal charisma, together with the legitimacy enjoyed by certain individuals of proven "merit" who are invested with moral authority as in the Thai tradition, to enhance support for a democratic order respectful of those immunities and liberties we generally describe as human rights, the fact that it might deviate from the standard Western model of judicial review initiated by individuals should be accorded less importance than the fact that it protects human beings from violence and oppression. We would have in fact achieved convergence on the substance of human rights, in spite of differences in form.

Alternative Foundations

Suppose we take the "communitarian" arguments against Western rights discourse emanating from other societies at another level, not questioning so much the legal forms but expressing disagreement with the underlying philosophical justification. My example is again drawn from Thailand. This society has seen in the last century a number of attempts to formulate reformed interpretations of the majority religion, Theravada Buddhism. Some of these have sought a basis in this form of Buddhism for democracy and human rights. This raises a somewhat broader issue than the one I'm focusing on because it concerns an alternative foundation for both democracy and human rights. The job of attaining a consensus on human rights in today's world will probably be simplified, however, if we don't try—at least at first—to come to agreement about forms of government, but concentrate solely on human rights standards. I believe that the developments in Thai thinking described here illustrate what is involved in coming to an "overlapping consensus" on the narrower basis as well.

One main stream of reform consists of movements that (as they see it) attempt to purify Buddhism, to turn it away from a focus on ritual, on gaining merit and even worldly success through blessings and acts of piety, and to focus more on (what they see as) the original goal of enlightenment. The late Phutthathat (Buddhadasa) has been a major figure in this regard. This stream tries to return to what (it sees as) the original core of Buddhist teaching, about the unavoidability of suffering, the illusion of the self, and the goal of Nibbana. It attacks the "superstition" of those who seek potent amulets, the blessings of monks, and the like; it wants to separate the search for enlightenment from the seeking of merit through ritual; and it is very critical of the whole metaphysical structure of belief that has developed in mainstream Buddhism about heavens, hell, gods, and demons, which plays a large part in popular belief. It has been described by the Sri Lankan anthropologist Gananath Obeyesekere as a "protestant Buddhism."[16]

This stream seems to be producing new reflections on Buddhism as a basis for democratic society and human rights. Sulak Sivaraksa and Saneh Chamarik are among the leading figures whose writings reflect this. They and others in their milieu are highly active in social justice advocacy. They are concerned with alternative models of development, which would be more ecologically sound, concerned to put limits to growth, critical of "consumerism," and conducive to social equality. The Buddhist commitment lies behind all these goals. As Sulak explains it, the Buddhist commitment to nonviolence entails a nonpredatory stance toward the environment and calls also for the limitation of greed, one of the sources of anger and conflict.[17]

We can see here an agenda of universal well-being, but what specifically pushes to democracy, to ensuring that people take charge of their own lives rather than simply being the beneficiaries of benevolent rule? Two things seem to come together in this outlook to underpin a strong democratic commitment. The first is the notion, central to Buddhism, that ultimately each individual must take responsibility for his or her own enlightenment. The second is a new application of the doctrine of nonviolence, which is now seen to call for a respect for the autonomy of each person, demanding in effect a minimal use of coercion in human affairs. This carries us far from the politics of imposed order, decreed by the wise minority, which has long been the traditional background to various forms and phases of nondemocratic rule. It is also evident that this underpinning for democracy offers a strong support for human rights legislation, and that, indeed, is how it is understood by thinkers like Sulak.[18]

There is an outlook here that converges on a policy of defense of human rights and democratic development but that is rather different from the standard Western justifications of these. It isn't grounded on a doctrine of the dignity of human beings as something commanding respect. The injunction to respect comes rather as a consequence of the fundamental value of nonviolence, which also generates a whole host of other consequences (including the requirement for an ecologically responsible development and the need to set limits to growth). Human rights don't stand out, as they often do in the West, as a claim on their own, independent from the rest of our moral commitments, even sometimes in potential conflict with them.

This Buddhist conception provides an alternative way of linking together the agenda of human rights and that of democratic development. Whereas in the Western framework, these go together because they are both seen as corequirements of human dignity, and indeed, as two facets of liberty, a connection of a somewhat different kind is visible among Thai Buddhists of this reform persuasion. Their commitment to people-centered and ecologically sensitive development makes them strong allies of those communities of villagers who are resisting encroachment by the state and big business, fighting to defend their lands and forests. This means that they are heavily into what has been recognized as a crucial part of the agenda of democratization in Thailand—decentralization, and in particular the recovery of local community control over natural resources.[19] They form a significant part of the NGO community committed to this agenda. A rather different route has been traveled to a similar goal.

Other differences stand out. Because of its roots in a certain justice agenda, the politics of establishing rights in the West has often been surrounded with anger, indignation, the imperative to punish historic wrongdoing. From this

Buddhist perspective comes a caution against the politics of anger, itself the potential source of new forms of violence. My aim here is not to judge between these approaches but to point to these differences as the source of a potentially fruitful exchange within a (hopefully) emerging world consensus on the practice of human rights and democracy.

We can in fact see a convergence here on certain norms of action, however they may be entrenched in law. What is unfamiliar to the Western observer is the entire philosophical basis and its appropriate reference points, as well as the rhetorical source of its appeal. In the West, both democracy and human rights have been furthered by the steady advance of a kind of humanism that stressed that humans stood out from the rest of the cosmos, had a higher status and dignity than anything else. This has its origins in Christianity and certain strands of ancient thought, but the distance is greatly exacerbated by what Weber describes as the disenchantment of the world, the rejection of a view of the cosmos as a meaningful order. The human agent stands out even more starkly from a mechanistic universe. For Pascal, the human being is a mere reed, but of incomparably greater significance than what threatens to crush it, because it is a thinking reed. Kant echoes some of the same reflections in his discussion of the sublime in the third critique[20] and also defines human dignity in terms of the incomparably greater worth of human beings compared to the rest of the contents of the universe.[21]

The human rights doctrine based on this humanism stresses the incomparable importance of the human agent. It centers everything on him or her, makes his or her freedom and self-control a major value, something to be maximized. Consequently, in the Western mind, the defense of human rights seems indissolubly linked with this exaltation of human agency. It is because humans justifiably command all this respect and attention, at least in comparison to anything else, that their rights must be defended.

The Buddhist philosophy that I have been describing starts from a quite different place, the demand of *ahimsa* (nonviolence), and yet seems to ground many of the same norms. (Of course, there will also be differences in the norms grounded, which raises its own problems, but for the moment I just want to note the substantial overlap.) The gamut of Western philosophical emotions, the exaltation at human dignity, the emphasis on freedom as the highest value, the drama of age-old wrongs righted in valor, all the things that move us in seeing *Fidelio* well performed, seem out of place in this alternative setting. So do the models of heroism. The heroes of *ahimsa* are not forceful revolutionaries, not Cola di Rienzi or Garibaldi, and with the philosophy and the models, a whole rhetoric loses its basis.

This perhaps gives us an idea of what an unforced world consensus on human rights might look like: agreement on norms, yes, but a profound sense of difference, of unfamiliarity, in the ideals, the notions of human excellence, the rhetorical tropes and reference points by which these norms become objects of deep commitment for us. To the extent that we can only acknowledge agreement with people who share the whole package and are moved by the same heroes, the consensus will either never come or must be forced.

This is the situation at the outset, in any case, when consensus on some aspect of human rights has just been attained. Later a process can follow of mutual learning, moving toward a "fusion of horizons" in Gadamer's term, in which the moral universe of the other becomes less strange. Out of this will come further borrowings and the creation of new hybrid forms.

After all, something of this has already occurred with another stream of the philosophy of *ahimsa,* that of Gandhi. Gandhi's practices of nonviolent resistance have been borrowed and adapted in the West, for example, in the American civil rights movement under Martin Luther King. Beyond that, they have become part of a world repertory of political practices, invoked in Manila in 1988 and in Prague in 1989, to name just two examples.

Also worthy of remark is one other facet of this case that may be generalizable as well. An important part of the Western consciousness of human rights lies in the awareness of an historic achievement. Human rights define norms of respect for human beings, more radical and more exigent than have ever existed in the past. They offer in principle greater freedom, greater security from violence, from arbitrary treatment, from discrimination and oppression, than humans have enjoyed at least in most major civilizations in history. In a sense they involve taking the exceptional treatment accorded to privileged people in the past, and extending it to everyone. That is why so many of the landmarks of the historical development of rights were in their day instruments of elite privilege, starting with Magna Carta.

There is a curious convergence in this respect with the strand of Reform Buddhism I have been describing. Here too there is the awareness that very exigent demands are being made that go way beyond what the majority of ordinary believers recognize as required practice. Reform Buddhism is practiced by an elite, as has been the case with most of its analogues in history. But here too, in developing a doctrine of democracy and human rights, Reform Buddhists are proposing to extend what has hitherto been a minority practice and entrench it in society as a whole. Here again there is a consciousness of the universalization of the highest of traditional minority practice.

It is as though in spite of the difference in philosophy this universalization of an exigent standard, which human rights practice at its best involves, was recognized as a valid move and re-created within a different cultural, philosophical, and religious world. The hope for a world consensus is that this kind of move will be made repeatedly.

Hierarchy and Identity

This example drawn from Thailand provides one model for what the path to world consensus might look like—a convergence on certain norms from out of very different philosophical and spiritual backgrounds. The consensus at first doesn't need to be based on any deep mutual understanding of these respective backgrounds. Each may seem strange to the other, even though both recognize and value the practical agreement attained. Of course, this is not to say that there is no borrowing involved at all. Plainly, democracy and human rights practices originated somewhere and are now being creatively recaptured (perhaps in a significantly different variant) elsewhere, but a mutual understanding and appreciation of each other's spiritual basis for signing on to the common norms may be close to nonexistent.

This, however, is not a satisfactory end point. Some attempt at deeper understanding must follow or the gains in agreement will remain fragile, for at least two closely connected reasons. The first is that the agreement is never complete. We already saw that what we can call the *ahimsa* basis for rights connects to ecological concerns differently from the Western humanist basis, in that the place of anger, indignation, righteous condemnation, and punishment is different in the two outlooks. All this must lead to differences of practice, of the detailed schedule of rights, or at least of the priority ordering among them. In practice, these differences may not emerge in variant schedules of rights. They may be reflected in the way a given schedule is interpreted and applied in different societies. After all, entrenched charters have to be applied by courts, and the courts make their interpretations within the framework of the moral views prevalent in their society. Some, like the Canadian charter, specifically provide for this adaptive interpretation by calling on the courts to interpret the charter in the light of social requirements, including those of a democratic society.[22] The demands of a world consensus will often include our squaring these differences in practical contexts, our accommodating or coming to some compromise version that both sides can live with. These negotiations will be inordinately difficult unless each side can come to some more fine-grained understanding of what moves the other.

The second reason follows on from the first and is in a sense just another facet of it. The continued coexistence in a broad consensus that continually generates particular disagreements, which have in turn to be negotiated to renewed consensus, is impossible without mutual respect. If the sense is strong on each side that the spiritual basis of the other is ridiculous, false, inferior, unworthy, these attitudes cannot but sap the will to agree of those who hold these views while engendering anger and resentment among those who are thus depreciated. The only cure for contempt here is understanding.

This alone can replace the too-facile depreciatory stories about others with which groups often tend to shore up their own sense of rightness and superiority. Consequently, the bare consensus must strive to go on toward a fusion of horizons.

In this discussion I have analytically distinguished consensus from mutual understanding and have imagined that they occur sequentially as successive phases. This is certainly a schematic oversimplification, but perhaps not totally wrong in the Thai case I was examining. However, in other situations some degree of mutual understanding is an essential condition of getting to consensus. The two cannot simply occur successively, because the path to agreement lies through some degree of sympathetic mutual comprehension.

I want to look now at another difference that seems to be of this latter type. To lay it out here, I will have to describe more fully another facet of the Western philosophical background of rights, which can hit a wall of incomprehension once one crosses the boundary to other cultures. This is the Western concern for equality, in the form of nondiscrimination. Existing charters of rights in the Western world are no longer concerned only with ensuring certain liberties and immunities to individuals. To an important degree, they also serve to counter various forms of discrimination. This represents a shift in the center of gravity of rights talk over the last centuries. One could argue that the central importance of nondiscrimination enters American judicial review with the Fourteenth Amendment, in the aftermath of the Civil War. Since then nondiscrimination provisions have been an important and growing part of schedules of rights both in the United States and elsewhere.

This connection is perhaps not surprising, although it took a long time to come to fruition. In a sense, the notion of equality was closely linked from the beginning to that of Natural Right, in contradistinction to the place of subjective rights in medieval systems of law, which were also those of certain estates or privileged individuals. Once right inheres in nature, then it is hard in the long run to deny it to anyone. The connection to equality is the stronger because of the thrust of modern humanism mentioned earlier, which defines itself against the view that we are embedded in a meaningful cosmic order. This latter has been a background against which various forms of human differentiation could appear natural, unchallengeable—be they social, racial, or sexual. The differences in human society, or gender roles, could be understood to reflect differentiations in the order of things and to correspond to differences in the cosmos, as with Plato's myth of the metals. This has been a very common form of thinking in almost all human societies.[23]

The destruction of this order has allowed for a process of unmasking existing social and gender differences as merely socially constructed, as without basis in the nature of things, as revocable and hence ultimately without justification. The process of working this out has been long, and we are not yet at the end, but it has been hard to resist in Western civilization in the last two centuries.

This aspect of Western rights talk is often very hard to export because it encounters societies in which certain social differences are still considered very meaningful, and they are seen in turn as intrinsically linked to certain practices that in Western societies are now regarded as discriminatory. However hard these sticking points may be for a Westerner to grasp in detail, it is not difficult to understand the general shape of the conflict, particularly because we in the West are far from having worked out how to combine gender equality with our conflicted ideas of gender difference.

To take this issue of gender equality as our example, we can readily understand that a certain way of framing the difference, however oppressive it may be in practice, also serves as the reference point for deeply felt human identities. The rejection of the framework can be felt as the utter denial of the basis of identity, and this not just for the favored gender, but also for the oppressed one. The gender definitions of a culture are interwoven with, among other things, its love stories, both those people tell and those they live.[24] Throwing off a traditional identity can be an act of liberation, but more than just liberation is involved here; without an alternative sense of identity, the loss of the traditional one is disorienting and potentially unbearable.

The whole shape of the change that could allow for an unforced consensus on human rights here includes a redefinition of identity, perhaps building on transformed traditional reference points in such a way as to allow for a recognition of an operative equality between the sexes. This can be a tall order, something we should have no trouble appreciating in the West because we have yet to complete our own redefinitions in this regard. This identity redefinition will be the easier to effect the more it can be presented as being in continuity with the most important traditions and reference points, properly understood. Correspondingly, it gets maximally difficult when it comes across as a brutal break with the past involving a condemnation and rejection of it. To some extent, which of these two scenarios gets enacted depends on developments internal to the society, but the relation with the outside world, and particularly the West, can also be determining.

The more the outside portrayal, or attempt at influence, comes across as a blanket condemnation of or contempt for the tradition, the more the dynamic of a "fundamentalist" resistance to all redefinition tends to get in train, and the harder it will be to find unforced consensus. This is a self-reinforcing dynamic, in which perceived external condemnation helps to feed extreme reaction, which calls down further condemnation, and hence further reaction, in a vicious spiral. The world is already drearily familiar with this dynamic in the unhealthy relation between the West and great parts of the Islamic world in our time.

In a sense, therefore, the road to consensus in relation to this difference is the opposite from the one mentioned earlier. There, the convergence on norms between Western humanism and reform Buddhism might be seen as preceding a phase in which they come better to understand and appreciate and learn from each other. In the field of gender discrimination, it may well be that the order would be better reversed, that is, that the path to consensus passes through greater sympathetic understanding of the situation of each party by the other. In this respect, the West with its own hugely unresolved issues about equality and difference is often more of a menace than a help.

The Polyvalence of Tradition

Before concluding, I want to look at another difference, which resembles in different respects both of the preceding. That is, it is certainly one in which the dynamic of mutual miscomprehension and condemnation is driving us away from consensus, but it also has potentialities like the Thai case, in that we can see how a quite different spiritual or theological basis might be found for a convergence on norms. I am thinking of the difference between international human rights standards and certain facets of the *Shari‘a,* recently discussed in so illuminating a fashion by Ahmed An-Na’im.[25] Certain punishments prescribed by the *Shari‘a,* such as amputation of the hand for theft or stoning for adultery, appear excessive and cruel in the light of standards prevalent in other countries.

It is worthwhile developing here, as I have in the other cases, the facet of Western philosophical thought and sensibility which has given particular force to this condemnation. This can best be shown through an example. When we read the opening pages of Michel Foucault's *Surveiller et Punir,* we are struck by its riveting description of the torture, execution, and dismemberment of Damien, the attempted assassin of Louis XV in the mid-eighteenth century.[26] We cannot but be aware of the cultural change that we have gone through since the Enlightenment.[27] We are much more concerned about pain and suffering than were our forebears; we shrink more from the infliction of gratuitous suffering. It would be hard to imagine people today taking their children to such a spectacle, at least openly and without some sense of unease and shame.

What has changed? We can distinguish two factors, one positive and one negative. On the positive side, we see pain and suffering and gratuitously inflicted death in a new light because of the immense cultural revolution that has been taking place in modernity, which I have called elsewhere "the affirmation of ordinary life."[28] What I was trying to gesture at with this term is the momentous cultural and spiritual change of the early modern period, which dethroned the supposedly higher activities of contemplation and the citizen life, and put the center of gravity of goodness in ordinary living, production, and the family. It belongs to this spiritual outlook that our first concern ought to be to increase life, relieve suffering, foster prosperity. Concern above all for the "good life" smacked of pride, of self-absorption. Beyond that, it was inherently inegalitarian, because the alleged "higher" activities could only be carried out by an elite minority, whereas leading rightly one's ordinary life was open to everyone. This is a moral temper to which it seems obvious that our major concern must be our dealings with others, in justice and benevolence, and these dealings must be on a level of equality. This affirmation, which constitutes a major component of our modern ethical outlook, was originally inspired by a mode of Christian piety. It exalted practical agape, and was polemically directed against the pride, elitism, and one might say self-absorption of those who believed in "higher" activities or spiritualities.

We can easily see how much this development is interwoven with the rise of the humanism that stands behind the Western discourse of human rights. They converge on the concern for equality, and also for the security of the person against burdens, dangers, and suffering imposed from outside.

But this is not the whole story. There is also a negative change; something has been cast off. It is not as though our ancestors would have simply thought the level of pain irrelevant, providing no reason at all to desist from some course of action involving torture and wounds. For us, the relief of suffering has become a supreme value, but it was always an important consideration. It is rather that, in cases like that of Damien, the negative significance of pain was subordinated to other, weightier, considerations. If it is necessary that punishment in a sense undo the evil of the crime, restore the balance—what is implicit in the whole notion of the criminal making *amende honorable*—then the very horror of regicide calls for a kind of theatre of the horrible as the medium in which this undoing can take place. In this context, pain takes on a different significance; there has to be lots of it to do the trick. A principle of minimizing pain is trumped.

Thus, we relate doubly to our forebears of two centuries ago. We have new reasons to minimize suffering, but we also lack a reason to override the minimizing of suffering. We no longer have the whole outlook—linked as it was to the cosmos as meaningful order—that made sense of the necessity of undoing the crime, restoring the breached order of things, in and through the punishment of the criminal.

In general, contemporaries in the West are so little aware of the positive change they have gone through—they tend anachronistically to think that people must always have felt this way—that they generally believe that the negative change is the crucial one that explains our difference from our predecessors. With this in mind, they look at the *Shari'a* punishments as the simple result of premodern illusions, in the same category in which they now place the ancien régime execution scenarios. With this dismissive condemnation, the stage is set for the dynamic I described earlier, in which contemptuous denunciation leads to "fundamentalist" reaffirmations, which in turn provoke even more strident denunciations, and so on.

What gets lost in this struggle is what An-Na'im shows so clearly, the possibilities of reinterpretation and reappropriation that the tradition itself contains. What also becomes invisible is what could be the motor of this change, analogous to the role played by the cultural revolution affirming ordinary life in the West. What this or these could be is not easy for an outsider to determine, but the striking Islamic theme of the mercy and compassion of God, reinvoked at the beginning of almost every sura of the Qur'an, might be the locus of a creative theological development. This might help toward a convergence in this domain, in which case we might see a consensus among those of very different spiritual backgrounds, analogous to the Thai Buddhist views I discussed earlier.

Conclusion

I started this chapter with the basic notion that an unforced world consensus on human rights would be something like a Rawlsian "overlapping consensus," in which convergent norms would be justified in very different underlying spiritual and philosophical outlooks. I then argued that these norms have to be distinguished and analytically separated not just from the background justifications, but also from the legal forms that give them force. These two could vary with good reason from society to society, even though the norms we crucially want to preserve remain constant. We need, in other words, a threefold distinction: norms, legal forms, and background justifications, which each have to be distinguished from the others.

I then looked at four examples of differences. These by no means exhaust the field, though each is important in the present international exchange on human rights. One of these dealt with the issue of variations in legal forms. In the other three, I tried to discuss issues around the convergence on norms out of different philosophical and spiritual backgrounds.

Two important facets of these convergences emerged. In one way, they involve the meeting of very different minds, worlds apart in their premises, uniting only in the immediate practical conclusions. From another side, it is clear that consensus requires that this extreme distance be closed, that we come better to understand each other in our differences, that we learn to recognize what is great and admirable in our different spiritual traditions. In some cases, this kind of mutual understanding can come after convergence, but in others it seems almost to be a condition of it.

An obstacle in the path to this mutual understanding comes from the inability of many Westerners to see their culture as one among many. An example of this difficulty was visible in the last difference discussed. To an extent, Westerners see their human rights doctrine as arising simply out of the falling away of previous countervailing ideas—such as the punishment scenarios of the ancien régime—that have now been discredited to leave the field free for the preoccupations with human life, freedom, the avoidance of suffering. To this extent, they will tend to think that the path to convergence requires that others too cast off their traditional ideas, that they even reject their religious heritage, and become "unmarked" moderns like us. Only if we in the West can recapture a more adequate view of our own history can we learn to understand better the spiritual ideas that have been interwoven in our development and hence be prepared to understand sympathetically the spiritual paths of others toward the converging goal.[29] Contrary to what many people think, world convergence will come not through a loss or denial of traditions all around, but rather by creative reimmersions of different groups, each in their own spiritual heritage, traveling different routes to the same goal.

CHAPTER SEVEN

Democratic Exclusion
(and Its Remedies?)

DEMOCRACY, particularly liberal democracy, is a great philosophy of in-clusion. Rule of the people, by the people, for the people; and where "people" is supposed to mean (unlike in earlier days) everybody—without the unspoken restrictions of yesteryear: peasants, women, slaves, etc.—this offers the prospect of the most inclusive politics of human history.

And yet, there is also something in the dynamic of democracy which pushes to exclusion. This was allowed full rein in earlier forms of this regime, as among the ancient poleis and republics; but today it is a great cause of malaise. I want in this chapter first to explore this dynamic, and then to look at various ways of compensating for it, or minimizing it.

I

What makes the thrust to exclusion? We might put it this way: what makes democracy inclusive is that it is the government of *all* the people; what makes for exclusion is that it is the *government* of all the people. The exclusion is a by-product of something else: the need, in self-governing societies, of a high degree of cohesion. Democratic states need something like a common identity.

We can see why as soon as we ponder what is involved in self-government, what is implied in the basic mode of legitimation of these states, that they are founded on popular sovereignty. Now for the people to be sovereign, it needs to form an entity and have a personality.

The revolutions which ushered in regimes of popular sovereignty transferred the ruling power from a king onto a "nation" or a "people." In the process, they invent a new kind of collective agency. These terms existed before, but the thing they now indicate, this new kind of agency, was something unprecedented, at least in the immediate context of early modern Europe. Thus the notion of "people" could certainly be applied to the ensemble of subjects of the kingdom, or to the non-élite strata of society, but prior to the turnover it hadn't indicated an entity which could decide and act together, to whom one could attribute a *will*.

Why does this new kind of entity need a strong form of cohesion? Isn't this notion of popular sovereignty simply that of majority will, more or less restrained by the respect of liberty and rights? But this kind of decision rule can be adopted by all sorts of bodies, even those which are the loosest aggregations. Supposing during a public lecture, some people feel the heat oppressive and ask that the windows be opened; others demur. One might easily decide this by a show of hands, and those present would accept this as legitimate. And yet the audience of the lecture might be the most disparate congeries of individuals, unknown to one another, without mutual concern, just brought together by that event.

This example shows by contrast what democratic societies need. It seems at once intuitively clear that they have to be bonded more powerfully than this chance grouping. But how can we understand this necessity?

One way to see it is to push a bit farther the logic of popular sovereignty. It not only recommends a certain class of decision procedures—those which are grounded ultimately on the majority (with restrictions)—but also offers a particular justification. Under a regime of popular sovereignty we are free, in a way we are not under an absolute monarch, or an entrenched aristocracy, for instance.

Now supposing we see this from the standpoint of some individual. Let's say I am outvoted on some important issue. I am forced to abide by a rule I am opposed to. My will is not being done. Why should I consider myself free? Does it matter that I am overridden by the majority of my fellow citizens, as against the decisions of a monarch? Why should that be decisive? We can even imagine that a potential monarch, waiting to return to power in a coup, agrees with me on this question, against the majority. Wouldn't I then be freer after the counterrevolution? After all, my will on this matter would then be put into effect.

We can recognize that this kind of question is not a merely theoretical one. It is rarely put on behalf of individuals, but it regularly arises on behalf of subgroups, for example, national minorities, who see themselves as oppressed. Perhaps no answer can satisfy them. Whatever one says, they cannot see themselves as part of this larger sovereign people. And therefore they see its rule over them as illegitimate, and this according to the logic of popular sovereignty itself.

We see here the inner link between popular sovereignty and the idea of the people as a collective agency, in some stronger sense than our lecture audience above. This agency is something you can be included by without really belonging to, which makes no sense for a member of the audience. We can see the nature of this belonging if we ask what is the answer we can give to those who are outvoted and are tempted by the argument above.

Of course, some extreme philosophical individualists believe that there is no valid answer, that appeals to some greater collective is just so much humbug to get contrary voters to accept voluntary servitude. But without deciding this ultimate philosophical issue, we can ask: what is the feature of our "imagined communities" by which people very often do readily accept that they are free under a democratic regime, even where their will is overridden on important issues?

The answer they accept runs something like this: you, like the rest of us, are free just in virtue of the fact that we are ruling ourselves in common, and not being ruled by some agency which need take no account of us. Your freedom consists in your having a guaranteed voice in the sovereign, that you can be heard and have some part in making the decision. You enjoy this freedom in virtue of a law which enfranchises all of us, and so we enjoy this together. Your freedom is realized and defended by this law, and this is so whether or not you win or lose in any particular decision. This law defines a community, of those whose freedom it realizes/defends together. It defines a collective agency, a people, whose acting together by the law preserves their freedom.

Such is the answer, valid or not, that people have come to accept in democratic societies. We can see right away that it involves their accepting a kind of belonging much stronger than the people in the lecture hall. It is an ongoing collective agency, one the membership in which realizes something very important, a kind of freedom. Insofar as this good is crucial to their identity, they thus identify strongly with this agency, and hence also feel a bond with their co-participants in this agency. It is only an appeal to this kind of membership which can answer the challenge of our imagined individual above, who is pondering whether to support the monarch's (or general's) coup in the name of his freedom.

The crucial point here is that, whoever is ultimately right philosophically, it is only insofar as people accept some such answer that the legitimacy principle of popular sovereignty can work to secure their consent. The principle only is effective via this appeal to a strong collective agency. If the identification with this is rejected, the rule of this government seems illegitimate in the eyes of the rejecters, as we see in countless cases with disaffected national minorities. Rule by the people, all right; but we can't accept rule by this lot, because we aren't part of their people. This is the inner link between democracy and strong common agency. It follows the logic of the legitimacy principle which underlies democratic regimes. They fail to generate this identity at their peril.

This last example points to an important modulation of the appeal to popular sovereignty. In the version I just gave above the appeal was to what we might call "republican freedom." It is the one inspired by ancient republics, and which was invoked in the American and French Revolutions. But very soon after, the same appeal began to take on a nationalist form. The attempts to spread the principles of the French Revolution through the force of French arms created a reaction in Germany, Italy, and elsewhere, the sense of not being part of or represented by that sovereign people in the name of which the Revolution was being made and defended. It came to be accepted in many circles that a sovereign people, in order to have the unity needed for collective agency, had already to have an antecedent unity, or culture, history, or (more often in Europe) language. And so behind the political nation, there had to stand a preexisting cultural (sometimes ethnic) nation.

Nationalism, in this sense, was born out of democracy, as a (benign or malign) growth. In early nineteenth-century Europe, as peoples struggled for emancipation from multinational despotic empires, joined in the Holy Alliance, there seemed to be no opposition between nationalism and democracy. For a Mazzini, they were perfectly converging goals.[1] Only later on do certain forms of nationalism throw off the allegiance to human rights and democracy, in the name of self-assertion.

But even before this stage, nationalism gives another modulation to popular sovereignty. The answer to the objector above: something essential to your identity is bound up in our common laws, now refers not just to republican freedom, but also to something of the order of cultural identity. What is defended and realized in the national state is not just your freedom as a human being; this state also guarantees the expression of a common cultural identity.

We can speak therefore of a "republican" variant and a "national" variant of the appeal to popular sovereignty, though in practice the two often run together, and often lie undistinguished in the rhetoric and imaginary of democratic societies.

And in fact, even the original "republican" pre-nationalist revolutions, the American and the French, have seen a kind of nationalism develop in the societies which issued from them. The point of these revolutions was the universal good of freedom, whatever the mental exclusions which the revolutionaries in fact accepted, even cherished. But their patriotic allegiance was to the particular historical project of realizing freedom, in America, in France. The very universalism became the basis of a fierce national pride, in the "last, best hope for mankind," in the republic which was bearer of "the rights of man." That's why freedom, at least in the French case, could become a project of conquest, with the fateful results in reactive nationalism elsewhere that I mentioned above.

And so we have a new kind of collective agency, with which its members identify as the realization/bulwark of their freedom, and/or the locus of their national/cultural expression. Of course, in premodern societies, too, people often "identified" with the regime, with sacred kings, or with hierarchical orders. They were often willing subjects. But in the democratic age we identify as free agents. That is why the notion of popular will plays a crucial role in the legitimating idea.[2]

This means that the modern democratic state has generally accepted common purposes, or reference points, the features whereby it can lay claim to being the bulwark of freedom and locus of expression of its citizens. Whether or not these claims are actually founded, the state must be so imagined by its citizens if it is to be legitimate.

So a question can arise for the modern state for which there is no analogue in most premodern forms: What/whom is this state for? Whose freedom? Whose expression? The question seems to make no sense applied to, say, the Austrian or Turkish empires—unless one answered the "whom for?" question by referring to the Habsburg or Ottoman dynasties; and this would hardly give you their legitimating ideas.

This is the sense in which a modern state has what I want to call a political identity, defined as the generally accepted answer to the "what/whom for?" question. This is distinct from the identities of its members, that is, the reference points, many and varied, which for each of these defines what is important in their lives. There better be some overlap, of course, if these members are to feel strongly identified with the state; but the identities of individuals and constituent groups will generally be richer and more complex, as well as often being quite different from each other.[3]

The recent constitutional struggles in Canada provide a good example of political identity as a source of contention. No one in Quebec doubts that its own "what for?" question must be answered in part by something like "to promote and protect Quebec's distinct character," paraphrasing the wording of the Meech Lake amendment. The major point at issue was whether Canada could take this goal as a component of its own answer to this question. The rejection of Meech was widely read in Quebec as a negative answer to this question, and this predictably gave an immense lift to the Independentist movement. But it wasn't enough to carry it over the top.

The close connection between popular sovereignty, strong cohesion, and political identity can also be shown in another way: the people is supposed to rule; this means that the members of this "people" make up a decision-making unit, a body which takes joint decisions. Moreover, it is supposed to take its decisions through a consensus, or at least a majority, of agents who are deemed equal and autonomous. It is not "democratic" for some citizens to be under the control of others. It might facilitate decision-making, but it is not democratically legitimate.

In addition, to form a decision-making unit of the type demanded here, it is not enough for a vote to record the fully formed opinions of all the members. These units must not only decide together, but deliberate together. A democratic state is constantly facing new questions, and in addition aspires to form a consensus on the questions that it has to decide, and not merely to reflect the outcome of diffuse opinions. However, a joint decision emerging from joint deliberation does not merely require everybody to vote according to his or her opinion. It is also necessary that each person's opinion should have been able to take shape or be reformed in the light of discussion, that is to say by exchange with others.

This necessarily implies a degree of cohesion. To some extent, the members must know one another, listen to one another, and understand one another. If they are not acquainted, or if they cannot really understand one another, how can they engage in joint deliberation? This is a matter which concerns the very conditions of legitimacy of democratic states.

If, for example, a subgroup of the "nation" considers that it is not being listened to by the rest, or that they are unable to understand its point of view, it will immediately consider itself excluded from joint deliberation. Popular sovereignty demands that we should live under laws which derive from such deliberation. Anyone who is excluded can have no part in the decisions which emerge, and these consequently lose their legitimacy for the excluded. A subgroup which is not listened to is in some respects excluded from the "national," but by this same token, it is no longer bound by the will of that nation.

For it to function legitimately, a people must thus be so constituted that its members are capable of listening to one another, and effectively do so; or at least the people should come close enough to that condition to ward off possible challenges to its democratic legitimacy from subgroups. In practice, more than that is normally required. It is not enough nowadays for us to be able to listen to one another. Our states aim to last, so we want an assurance that we shall continue to be able to listen to one another in the future. This demands a certain reciprocal commitment. In practice a nation can ensure the stability of its legitimacy only if its members are strongly committed to one another by means of their common allegiance to the political community. Moreover, it is the shared consciousness of this commitment which creates confidence in the various subgroups that they will indeed be heard, despite the possible causes for suspicion that are implicit in the differences between these subgroups.

In other words, a modern democratic state demands a "people" with a strong collective identity. Democracy obliges us to show much more solidarity and much more commitment to one another in our joint political project than was demanded by the hierarchical and authoritarian societies of yesteryears. In the good old days of the Austro-Hungarian Empire, the Polish peasant in Galicia could be altogether oblivious of the Hungarian country squire, the bourgeois of Prague, or the Viennese worker, without this in the slightest threatening the stability of the state. On the contrary. This condition of things only becomes untenable when ideas about popular government start to circulate. This is the moment when subgroups which will not, or cannot, be bound together, start to demand their own states. This is the era of nationalism, of the breakup of empires.

I have been discussing the political necessity of a strong common identity for modern democratic states in terms of the requirement of forming a people, a deliberative unit. But this is also evident in a number of other ways. Thinkers in the civic humanist tradition, from Aristotle through to Arendt, have noted that free societies require a higher level of commitment and participation than do despotic or authoritarian ones. Citizens have to do for themselves, as it were, what otherwise the rulers do for them. But this will only happen if these citizens feel a strong bond of identification with their political community, and hence with those who share with them in this.

From another angle again, because these societies require strong commitment to do the common work, and because a situation in which some carried the burdens of participation and others just enjoyed the benefits would be intolerable, free societies require a high level of mutual trust. In other words, they are extremely vulnerable to mistrust on the part of some citizens in relation to others, that the latter are not really assuming their commitments—for example, that others are not paying their taxes, or are cheating on welfare, or as employers are benefiting from a good labor market without assuming any of the social costs. This kind of mistrust creates extreme tension, and threatens to unravel the whole skein of the mores of commitment which democratic societies need to operate. A continuing and constantly renewed mutual commitment is an essential basis for taking the measures needed to renew this trust.

The relation between nation and state is often considered from a unilateral point of view, as if it were always the nation which sought to provide itself with a state. But there is also the opposite process. In order to remain viable, states sometimes seek to create a feeling of common belonging. This is an important theme in the history of Canada, for example. To form a state, in the democratic era, a society is forced to undertake the difficult and never-to-be-completed task of defining its collective identity.

2

So there is a need for common identity. How does this generate exclusion? In a host of possible ways, which we can see illustrated in different circumstances.

The most tragic of these circumstances is also the most obvious, where a group which cannot be assimilated to the reigning cohesion is brutally extruded—what we have come today to call "ethnic cleansing."

But there are other cases where it doesn't come to such drastic expedients, but where exclusion works all the same against those whose difference threatens the dominant identity. I want to class forced inclusion as a kind of exclusion, which might seem a logical sleight of hand. Thus the Hungarian national movement in the nineteenth century tried forcefully to assimilate Slovaks and Romanians; the Turks are reluctant to concede that there is a Kurdish minority in their eastern borderlands. This may not seem to constitute exclusion to the minority, but in another clear sense, it amounts to this. It is saying in effect: as you are, or consider yourselves to be, you have no place here; that's why we are going to make you over.

Or exclusion may take the form of chicanery, as in the old apartheid South Africa, where millions of blacks were denied citizenship, on the grounds that they were really citizens of "homelands" external to the state.

All these modes of exclusion are motivated by the threat that others represent to the dominant political identity. But this threat depends on the fact that popular sovereignty is the regnant legitimacy idea of our time. It is hard to sustain a frankly hierarchical society, in which groups are ranged in tiers, with some overtly marked as inferior or subject, as with the millet system of the Ottoman Empire.

Hence the paradox that earlier conquering people were quite happy to coexist with vast numbers of subjects which were very different from them. The more, the better. The early Muslim conquerors of the Ommeyad empire not only did not press for conversion of their Christian subjects; they even mildly discouraged it. Within the bounds of this unequal disposition, earlier empires very often had a very good record of "multicultural" tolerance and coexistence. Famous cases come down to us, like that of the Mughals under Akbar, which seem strikingly enlightened and humane, compared with much of what goes on today in that part of the world and elsewhere.

It is no accident that the twentieth century is the age of ethnic cleansing, starting with the Balkan Wars, extending in that area through the aftermath of World War I, and then reaching epic proportions in World War II, and still continuing—to speak only of Europe.

The democratic age poses new obstacles to coexistence, because it opens a new set of issues which may deeply divide people, those concerning the political identity of the state. In many parts of the Indian subcontinent, for instance, Hindus and Muslims coexisted in conditions of civility, even with a certain degree of syncretism, where later they would fight bitterly. The explanations often given for what happened include the British attempt to divide and rule, or even the British mania for census figures, which first made an issue of who was a majority where.

These factors may have their importance, but clearly what makes them vital is the surrounding situation, in which political identity becomes an issue. As the movement grows to throw off the alien, multinational empire and set up a democratic state, the question arises of its political identity: Will it simply be that of the majority? Are we heading for Hindu Raj? Muslims ask for reassurance. Gandhi's and Nehru's proposals for a pan-Indian identity do not satisfy Jinnah. Suspicion grows; demands are made for guarantees, and ultimately for separation.

Each side is mobilized to see the other as a threat to its political identity. This fear can then sometimes be transposed, through mechanisms we have yet to understand, into a threat to life; to which the response is savagery and counter-savagery, and we descend the spiral which has become terribly familiar. Census figures can then be charged with ominous significance, but only because in the age of democracy, being in the majority has decisive importance.

Secondly, there is the phenomenon we can sometimes see in immigrant societies with a high degree of historic ethnic unity. The sense of common bond and of common commitment has been for so long bound up with the common language, culture, history, ancestry, and so on, that it is difficult to adjust to a situation where the citizen body includes large numbers of people of other origins. People feel a certain discomfort with this situation, and this can be reflected in a number of ways.

In one kind of case, the homogeneous society is reluctant to concede citizenship to the outsiders. Germany is the best known example of this, with its third-generation Turkish "Gastarbeiter," whose only fluent language may be German, whose only familiar home is in Frankfurt, but who are still resident aliens.

But there are subtler, and more ambivalent, ways in which this discomfort can play out. Perhaps the outsiders automatically acquire citizenship after a standard period of waiting. There even may be an official policy of integrating them, widely agreed on by the members of the "old stock" population. But these are still so used to functioning politically among themselves that they find it difficult to adjust. Perhaps they don't quite know how to adjust yet and new reflexes are difficult to find. For instance, policy questions are discussed among themselves, in their electronic media and newspapers, as though immigrants were not a party to the debate. They discuss, for instance, how to gain the best advantage for their society of the new arrivals, or how to avoid certain possible negative consequences, but the newcomers are spoken of as "them," as though they weren't potential partners in the debate.

You will have guessed that the example I'm thinking of here is my native Quebec. I don't mean to exaggerate the phenomenon. It is changing, and I have great hopes that it will go on improving. It took time to learn the reflexes of inclusion, but they are being learned. Moreover, the problem is somewhat worse among extreme nationalists; it's not a universal phenomenon. It's worse among them, because nationalists cherish a dream, that of independence, which virtually no one not a "Québécois de souche" shares, for understandable psychological-historical reasons. It's only natural that this strand of the Quebec ideological spectrum should have more difficulty opening itself to outsiders, as was evident in the catastrophic speech of our ex-Premier after the last referendum, and some of the recent reactions to "reasonable accommodation."

This example helps to illustrate just what is at stake here. I don't want to claim that democracy unfailingly leads to exclusion. That would be a counsel of despair, and the situation is far from desperate. I also want to say, as the slogan above indicated, that there is a drive in modern democracy toward inclusion, in the fact that government should be by *all* the people. But my point is that alongside this, there is a standing temptation to exclusion, which arises from the fact that democracies work well when people know each other, trust each other, and feel a sense of commitment toward each other.

The coming of new kinds of people into the country, or into active citizenship, poses a challenge. The exact content of the mutual understanding, the bases of the mutual trust, and the shape of the mutual commitment, all have to be redefined, reinvented. This is not easy, and there is an understandable temptation to fall back on the old ways, and deny the problem; either by straight exclusion from citizenship (as in Germany), or by the perpetuation of "us and them" ways of talking, thinking, and doing politics.

And the temptation is the stronger, in that for a transition period, the traditional society may have to forgo certain advantages that came from the tighter cohesion of yore. Quebec clearly illustrates this. During the agonizing attempts by the government to cut back the galloping budget deficits in the late

1990s, the Premier organized summits of decision-makers from business, labor, and other segments of society. Not only the fact that this seemed worth trying, but the atmosphere of consensus, at least the earnest striving toward an agreement, reflected the extremely tightly knit nature of Quebec society as it has come down to us. The decision-makers still are disproportionately drawn from old stock Quebeckers, quite naturally at this stage of development. The operation might not be as easy to repeat twenty years from now.

So much for historically ethnically homogeneous societies. But we have analogous phenomena in mixed societies. Think of the history of the United States, how successive waves of immigrants were perceived by many Americans of longer standing as a threat to democracy and the American way of life. This was first of all the fate of the Irish from the 1840s. Then immigrants from south and eastern Europe were looked askance at in the last decades of the century. And of course, a long-established population, blacks, when they were given citizen rights for the first time after the Civil War, were in effect excluded from voting through lots of the Old South, until civil rights legislation redressed this exclusion.

Some of this was blind prejudice. But not all. In fact, the early Irish, and later European immigrants, could not integrate at once into American WASP political culture. The new immigrants often formed "vote banks" for bosses and machines in the cities; and this was strongly resented and opposed by Progressives and others, concerned for what they understood to be citizen democracy.

Here again, a transition was successfully navigated, and a new democracy emerged, in which a fairly high level of mutual understanding, trust, and commitment (alas, with the tragic exception, still, of the black-white divide) was re-created—although arguably at the price of the fading of the early ideals of a citizen republic and the triumph of the "procedural republic," in Michael Sandel's language.[4] But the temptation to exclusion was very strong for a time, and some of it was motivated by the commitment to democracy itself.

Thirdly, the cases I've been looking at are characterized by the arrival from abroad, or the entry into active citizenship, of new people, who have not shared the ethnic-linguistic culture, or else the political culture. But exclusion can also operate along another axis. Just because of the importance of cohesion, and of a common understanding of political culture, democracies have sometimes attempted to force their citizens into a single mold. The "Jacobin" tradition of the French Republic provides the best-known example of this.

Here the strategy is, from the very beginning, to make people over in a rigorous and uncompromising way. Common understanding is reached, and supposedly forever maintained, by a clear definition of what politics is about, and what citizenship entails, and these together define the primary allegiance of citizens. This complex is then vigorously defended against all comers, ideological enemies, slackers, and, when the case arises, immigrants.

The exclusion operates here, not in the first place against certain people already defined as outsiders, but against other ways of being. This formula forbids other ways of living modern citizenship; it castigates as unpatriotic a way of living which would not subordinate other facets of identity to citizenship. In the particular case of France, for instance, a certain solution to the problem of religion in public life was adopted by radical republicans, one of extrusion; and they have had immense difficulty even imagining that there might be other ways to safeguard the neutrality and comprehensiveness of the French state. Hence the overreaction to Muslim adolescents wearing the headscarf in school.

But the strength of this formula is that it managed for a long time to avoid or at least minimize the other kind of exclusion, that of new arrivals. It still surprises Frenchmen, and others, when they learn from Gérard Noiriel that one French person in four today has at least one grandparent born outside the country.[5] France in this century has been an immigrant country without thinking of itself as such. The policy of assimilation has hit a barrier with recent waves of Maghrébains, but it worked totally with the Italians, Poles, Czechs, who came between the wars. These people were never offered the choice, and became indistinguishable from "les Français de souche."

It has been argued that another dimension of this kind of inner exclusion has operated along gender lines—and this not only in Jacobin societies but in all liberal democracies, where without exception women received voting rights later than men. The argument is that the style of politics, the modes and tone of public debate, and the like, have been set by a political society which was exclusively male and that this has still to be modified to include women. If one looks at the behavior of some of our male-dominated legislatures at question time, resembling, as they sometimes do, a boisterous boys' school at recreation, it is clear that there is some truth to this point. The culture of politics could not fully include women without changing somewhat, even though we may be uncertain just how.

3

I hope I have made somewhat clear what I mean by the dynamic of exclusion in democracy. We might describe it as a temptation to exclude, beyond that which people may feel because of narrow sympathies or historic prejudice; a temptation which arises from the requirement of democratic rule itself for a high degree of mutual understanding, trust, and commitment. This can make it hard to integrate outsiders, and tempt us to draw a line around the original community. But it can also tempt us to what I have called "inner exclusion," the creation of a common identity around a rigid formula of politics and citizenship, which refuses to accommodate any alternatives, and imperiously demands the subordination of other aspects of citizens' identities.

It is clear that these two modes are not mutually exclusive. Societies based on inner exclusion may come to turn away outsiders as well, as the strength of the Front National, alas, so well illustrates; while societies whose main historical challenge has been the integration of outsiders may have recourse to inner exclusion in an attempt to create some unity amid all the diversity.

The present drama of English Canada (or Canada outside Quebec) illustrates this only too well. Partly because of a sense of fragmentation which some Canadians feel in face of the rapid diversification of Canada's population, partly because this sense of fragmentation is often intensified rather than diminished by Quebec's affirmation of difference, partly because of age-old Canadian angst about national identity in face of the traditional seeming security on this score of the United States, attitudes have become steadily more rigid in English Canada toward any possible accommodation of Quebec's difference during the last ten years. Canada's tragedy is that, at the moment where it is becoming more and more necessary to do something about Quebec's status in the federation, it is also becoming politically less and less possible to do anything meaningful.

Quite specifically, there is a growing rigidity around the political formula, visible, for instance, in the insistence that all provinces must be treated identically, a subsumption of this uniformity under the principle of citizen equality. This kind of uniformity is, in fact, very foreign to our history. It is very doubtful if the federation could ever have got going if we had tried to operate like this in the past. But it comes forward now, because it seems to many the only way to re-create trust and common understanding between diverse regions, some of whom bear a grudge against others. This rigidity will make it difficult not only to accommodate Quebec, but also to make space for aboriginal groups who are calling for new modes of self-rule.

Now the obvious fact about our era is that, first, the challenge of the new arrival is becoming generalized and multiplied in all democratic societies. The scope and rate of international migration is making all societies increasingly "multicultural." Second, the response to this challenge of the "Jacobin" sort, a rigorous assimilation to a formula involving fairly intense inner exclusion, is becoming less and less sustainable.

This last point is not easy to explain, but it seems to me an undeniable fact. There has been a subtle switch in mind-set in our civilization, probably coinciding with the 1960s. The idea that one ought to suppress one's difference for the sake of fitting in to a dominant mold, defined as the established way in one's society, has been considerably eroded. Feminists, cultural minorities, homosexuals, religious groups, all demand that the reigning formula be modified to accommodate them, rather than the other way around.

At the same time, possibly connected to this first change but certainly with its own roots, has come another. This is an equally subtle change, and hard to pin down. But migrants no longer feel the imperative to assimilate in the same way. One must not misidentify the switch. Most of them want to assimilate substantively to the societies they have entered; and they certainly want to be accepted as full members. But they frequently want now to do it at their own pace, and in their own way, and in the process, they reserve the right to alter the society even as they assimilate to it.

The case of Hispanics in the United States is very telling in this regard. It's not that they don't want to become Anglophone Americans. They see obvious advantages in doing so, and they have no intention of depriving themselves of these. But they frequently demand schools and services in Spanish, because they want to make this process as painless as they can for themselves, and because they welcome such retention of their original culture as may fall out of this process. And something like this is obviously on the cards. They will all eventually learn English, but they will also alter somewhat the going sense of what it means to be an American, even as earlier waves of immigrants had. The difference between the earlier waves and the Hispanics is that the Hispanics seem to be operating now with the sense of their eventual role in co-determining the culture, rather than this arising only retrospectively, as with earlier immigrants.

The difference between the earlier near-total success of France in assimilating East Europeans and others (who ever thought of Yves Montand as Italian?) and the present great difficulty with Maghrébains, while it reflects a whole lot of other factors—for example, greater cultural-religious difference and the collapse of full employment—nevertheless must also reflect, I believe, the new attitude among migrants. The earlier sense of unalloyed gratitude toward the new countries of refuge and opportunity, which seemed to make any demand to recognize difference quite unjustified and out of place, has been replaced by something harder to define. One is almost tempted to say, by something resembling the old doctrine which is central to many religions, that the earth has been given to the human species in common. A given space doesn't just unqualifiedly belong to the people born in it, so it isn't simply theirs to give. In return for entry, one is not morally bound to accept just any condition that others impose.

Two new features arise from this shift. First, the notion I attributed to Hispanics in the United States has become widespread, namely, the idea that the culture they are joining is something in continual evolution, and that they have a chance to codetermine its future. This, instead of a simple one-way assimilation, is more and more becoming the (often unspoken) understanding behind the act of migration.

Secondly, we have an intensification of a long-established phenomenon, which now seems fully "normal," that is, where certain immigrant groups still function morally, culturally, and politically as a "diaspora" in relation to their home country. This has been going on for a long time—think, for instance, of the "Polonia" in all the countries of exile. But whereas it was frowned on, or looked askance at, by many people in the receiving society, or where toleration for it depended on sympathy for the cause of the home country (the Poles were lucky in this respect), whereas people muttered darkly in the past about "double allegiances," I believe now that this kind of behavior is coming to be seen as normal. Of course, there are still extreme variants of it which arouse strong opposition, as when terrorists use the receiving countries as a base for their operations: but that is because these manifestations shock the dominant political ethic, and not because of the intense involvement in the country of origin. It is becoming more and more normal and unchallenged to think of oneself and be thought of as, say, a Canadian in good standing, while being heavily involved in the fate of some country of origin.

4

The upshot of the above discussion could be expressed this way: democracies are in a standing dilemma. They need strong cohesion around a political identity, and precisely this provides a strong temptation to exclude those who can't or won't fit easily into the identity which the majority feels comfortable with, or believes alone can hold them together. And yet exclusion, besides being profoundly morally objectionable, also goes against the legitimacy idea of popular sovereignty, which is to realize the government of *all* the people. The need to form a people as a collective agent runs against the demand for inclusion of all who have a legitimate claim on citizenship.

This is the source of the malady. The remedies are a lot harder to find. I believe that an important first step is to recognize the dilemma. For this allows us to see that it can very often only be dealt with by struggling toward a creative redefinition of our political identity. The dilemma after all arises because some often historically hallowed definition cannot accommodate all who have a moral claim to citizenship. And yet the reaction to this is all too often to render the original identity even more absolute and unchallengeable, as though it somehow belonged essentially to a certain people with its territory and history that it be organized under this and no other identity.

This appeal to the origins can occur in both "republican" and "national" registers. In the first case, the particular features of our republican constitution are made absolute and sacrosanct, in face of all evidence that they may be impeding the search for a new common ground. Thus there is a certain "Jacobin" fundamentalism which comes to the surface in France, in reaction to certain demands to accommodate the growing Muslim minority. The wearing of headscarves in school by Muslim teenagers is judged to infringe the principles of "laïcite," as laid down in the French republican tradition. The general principle of state neutrality, indispensable in a modern diverse democracy, is metaphysically fused with a particular historical way of realizing it, and the latter is rendered as nonnegotiable as the former.

As a panic reaction, this is understandable even if disastrous. Faced with the unfamiliar and disturbing, one reaches for the age-old sources of common identity. But the reaction is facilitated by the belief that this original constitution was meant to resolve the issue of political identity once and for all, that somehow it precluded in advance any need for illegitimate exclusion.

This amounts to a denial that the potential for the dilemma is built into democracy itself. It cannot be conjured once and for all by the ideal constitutional settlement. Even if this perfectly suits the population at the time of founding (and what constitution ever has?), the shifts in personal identity over time, through migration and moral or cultural change, can bring the established political identity out of true with the people who are supposed to live within it. This kind of fundamentalism attempts to deny history.

We are more familiar with this kind of reaching back to sources when it occurs in the national register; and its destructive consequences are more immediately evident there. The claim is that a certain territory belongs as of right to a certain historical ethnic, or cultural, or linguistic, or religious identity, regardless of what other people are living there, even if they've been there for centuries. And so Hungarian nationalists laid claim to the lands of the Crown of St. Stephen in the nineteenth century, and the Bharatiya Janata Party (BJP) feels it can and must impose a "Hindutva" identity on all the immense diversity of India today. Even more gruesome examples of the working out of this kind of claim have been visible in recent years in the territory of the former Yugoslavia.

The reflex of many people in liberal societies to this kind of thing is to blame "nationalism" and not democracy. But this is to take too quick a way with it. To start with, "nationalism" has many senses. The original idea—for instance, in its Herderian form—was a liberating one, and highly consonant with democracy. We do not have to force ourselves into an artificial homogeneity in order to live together in peace. We can recognize different "national" (Volk) identities, even give them political expression, because each in this act of recognition acknowledges that it is not universal, that it has to coexist with others which are equally legitimate. Herderian nationalism is a universalist idea, all Völker are equally worthy of respect; this principle can be used (and was so used by Herder) to defend Slavic people against German encroachment, as well as to defend German culture against the hegemonic claims of French. You do not have to accept French as a universal language in order to live in freedom with guaranteed rights. The political identity under which you live can reflect you, too. This demand allows of an impeccably democratic justification.

What this pushes us toward is the idea which I believe is the key to facing the dilemma of exclusion creatively, the idea of sharing identity space. Political identities have to be worked out, negotiated, creatively compromised between peoples who have to or want to live together under the same political roof (and this coexistence is always grounded in some mixture of necessity and choice). Moreover, these solutions are never meant to last forever, but have to be discovered/invented anew by succeeding generations.

The idea of nationalism which creates bitter trouble is that defined by Gellner: the "political principle, which holds that the political and national unit should be congruent."[6] According to this idea, the problem of how to share identity space can be solved by giving each nation its territory, on which it can erect its sovereign state. The utopian, even absurd nature of the proposal immediately strikes the eye. Quite apart from the thousands of groups which can claim the status of "nation," even giving each its parcel of land would still leave each pocket handkerchief state with national minorities, so inextricably mixed are the world's peoples. The utopian scheme could only be carried through by massive ethnic cleansing.

It is clear that this idea will "work" only by making certain nations more equal than others. These are to get their states, and the rest are to live in their shadow as minorities, if they are allowed to live at all. This idea of nationalism can only be applied by negating its own universalist ethical basis.

It is this distorted idea which justifies the claim by historical national identities to monopoly control over "their" territory. In the worst cases, this ends in a Yugoslav scenario. In the best cases, as with the Parti Québécois, and the more liberal wing of the BJP, minorities are to be guaranteed their rights, but the idea of sharing identity space, actually negotiating some compromise political identity with them, is vigorously rejected.

Just as with "republican" forms of constitutionalism above, the unreal idea of a definitive solution to the problem of democratic coexistence is blinding people to the effective situation on the ground in almost all democratic states. The hope is once again to arrest history, to fix it in some original moment when our people attached themselves to this territory. And similarly, what offers itself as a solution to the democratic dilemma can only exacerbate it to the point of bitter conflict.

But the belief that the problem here is "nationalism" sans phrase can accredit another utopian solution, that of a political identity grounded purely in "republican" elements, without any reference to national or cultural identities.

In face of the prospect of having to bring together so many differences of culture, origin, political experience, and identity, the temptation is natural to define the common understanding more and more in terms of "liberalism," rather than by reference to the identities of citizens. The focus should be totally on individual rights and democratic and legal procedures, rather than on the historical-cultural reference points, or the ideas of the good life by which citizens define their own identities. In short, the temptation is to go for what Sandel calls the "procedural republic."

Already this has been evident in the Canadian case. I mentioned above that there has been a tendency in English Canada, in face of growing cultural diversity, to make certain aspects of the political culture central to the national identity. The main element which has been chosen for this has, not surprisingly, been the Charter of Rights, introduced into the Constitution by the 1982 Act. The underlying idea is that, whatever other differences distinguish us, as Canadians we can share a certain schedule of rights, and certain procedures for enforcing them.

What does the procedural republic have going for it? A number of things, some of them tendencies in our philosophical tradition. I have discussed this elsewhere,[7] but I think we can both see and understand the drift away from an ethics of the good life toward an ethics based on something else, allegedly less contentious, and easier to carry general agreement. This partly explains the popularity of both utilitarianism and Kantian-derived deontological theories. Both manage to abstract from issues of what life is more worthy, more admirable, more human, and to fall back on what seems more solid ground. In one case, we count all the preferences, regardless of the supposed quality of the goals sought. In the other, we can abstract from the preferences, and focus on the rights of the preferring agent.

The act of abstraction here benefits from three important considerations. First, in an age of (at least menacing, if not actual) scepticism about moral views, it retreats from the terrain where the arguments seem the most dependent on our interpretations, the most contentious and incapable of winning universal ascent; whereas we can presumably all agree that, other things being equal, it is better to let people have what they want, or to respect their freedom to choose. Second, this refusal to adopt a particular view of the good life leaves it to the individual to make the choice, and hence it fits with the anti-paternalism of the modern age. It enshrines a kind of freedom.

Third, in face of the tremendous differences of outlook in modern society, utilitarianism and Kantian deontology seem to promise a way of deciding the issues we face in common without having to espouse the views of some against others.

Now the first two considerations are based on philosophical arguments—about what can and cannot be known and proved, and about the nature of freedom, respectively. They have been much discussed, debated, and often refuted by philosophers. But the third is a political argument. Regardless of who is ultimately right in the battle between procedural ethics and those of the good life, we could conceivably be convinced on political grounds that the best political formula for democratic government of a complex society was a kind of neutral liberalism. And this is where the argument has mainly gone today. The shift between Rawls I and Rawls II is a clear example of this. His theory of justice is now presented as "political, not metaphysical." This shift perhaps comes in part from the difficulties that the purely philosophical arguments run into. But it also corresponds to the universal perception that diversity is a more important and crucial dimension of contemporary society. This comes, as I argued above, partly from the actual growth in diversity in the population, through, say, international migration; and partly from the growing demand that age-old diversities be taken seriously, put forward, for instance, by feminists.

So the issue now could be: what conceptions of freedom, of equality, of fairness, and of the basis for social coexistence are—not right in the abstract, but feasible for modern democratic societies? How can people live together in difference, granted that this will be in a democratic regime, under conditions of fairness and equality?

The procedural republic starts right off with a big advantage. If in your understanding of the citizen's roles and rights, you abstract from any view of the good life, then you avoid endorsing the views of some at the expense of others. Moreover, you find an immediate common terrain on which all can gather. Respect me, and accord me rights, just in virtue of my being a citizen, not in virtue of my character, outlook, or the ends I espouse, not to speak of my gender, race, sexual orientation, et cetera.

Now no one in their right mind today would deny that this is an important dimension of any liberal society. The right to vote, for instance, is indeed accorded unconditionally; or on condition of certain bases of citizenship, put certainly in a way which is blind to differences of the range just quoted. The question we have to ask is whether this can be the *only* basis for living together in a democratic state, whether this is the valid approach in *all* contexts, whether our liberalism approaches perfection the more we can treat people in ways which abstract from what they stand for and others do not.

It may appear that whatever other reasons there might be for treating people this way, at least it facilitates our coming together, and feeling ourselves to be part of a common enterprise. What we do all have in common is that we make choices, opt for some things rather than others, want to be helped and not hindered in pursuing the ends that flow from these options. So an enterprise that promises to further everyone's plan, on some fair basis, seems to be the ideal common ground. Indeed, some people find it hard to imagine what else could be.

But this retreat to the procedural is no solution to the democratic dilemma. On the contrary, it very often itself contributes to activating it. We can readily see this in two ways.

First, the condition of a viable political identity is that people must actually be able to relate to it, to find themselves reflected in it. But in some cases, the preservation of an historical cultural identity is so important to a certain group that suppressing all mention of it in our answer to the "what for?" question cannot but alienate that group. The protection and promotion of its "distinct society" cannot but figure in the common identity of Quebec as a political entity, whether in the Canadian federation or outside. Refusing all mention of this in the canonical definitions of the Canadian identity can only increase the feeling of many Quebeckers that they have no place in the federation. This is not a solution to the conundrum of a common Canadian political identity; it is rather the source of the greatest contemporary threat to it.

Second, the procedural route supposes that we can uncontroversially distinguish neutral procedures from substantive goals. But it is in fact very difficult to devise a procedure which is seen as neutral by everyone. The point about procedures, or characters of rights, or distributive principles, is that they are meant not to enter into the knotty terrain of substantive difference in ways of life. But there is no way in practice of ensuring that this will be so.

The case of the Muslim teenagers wearing the headscarf in school in France is eloquent in this regard. "Laïcité" is supposedly a neutral principle, not favoring one religion or worldview over another. On this basis, the headscarves were refused, but other French girls often wear, for example, a cross around their necks, and this was unchallenged. In a "secular" society, this is presumably often just a "decoration." The presumption is valid enough, but the religious "indivisibility" of the cross reflects France as a "post-Christian" society, following centuries of Christian culture. How can one expect to convince Muslims that this combination of rulings is neutral?

The mistake here is to believe that there can be some decision whose neutrality is guaranteed by its emerging from some principle or procedure. This breeds the illusion that there is no need to negotiate the place of these symbols, and hence to confront the actual substantive differences of religious allegiance in the public sphere. But no procedure can dispense with the need to share identity space.

Something similar holds of the American case. What is meant to be a procedural move, neutral between all parties, the separation of church and state, turns out to be open to different interpretations, and some of these are seen as very far from neutral by some of the important actors in the society. The school prayer dispute is a case in point. One could argue that insistence on a procedural solution—in this case a winner-take-all constitutional adjudication—is exactly what will maximally inflame the division; which indeed, it seems to have done.

Moreover, as against a political solution, based on negotiation and compromise between competing demands, this provides no opportunity for people on each side to look into the substance of the other's case. Worse, by having their demand declared unconstitutional, the losers' program is delegitimated in a way which has deep resonance in American society. Not only can we not give you what you want, but you are primitive and un-American to want it.

In short, I would argue that the current American Kulturkampf has been exacerbated rather than reconciled by the heavy recourse in that polity to judicial resolution on the basis of the Constitution.

5

My argument here has been that a full understanding of the dilemma of democratic exclusion shows that there is no alternative to what I have called sharing identity space. This means negotiating a commonly acceptable, even compromised political identity between the different personal or group identities which want to / have to live in the polity. Some things will, of course, have to be nonnegotiable, that is, the basic principles of republican constitutions— democracy itself and human rights, among them. But this firmness has to be accompanied by a recognition that these principles can be realized in a number of different ways, and can never be applied neutrally without some confronting of the substantive religious-ethnic-cultural differences in societies. Historic identities cannot be just abstracted from. But nor can their claims to monopoly status be received. There are no exclusive claims to a given territory by historic right.

What this means in practice is beyond the ambit of this essay. Solutions have to be tailored to particular situations. But some of the political mechanisms of this sharing are already well-known, for example, various brands of federalism, as well as the design of forms of special status for minority societies, such as we see today in Scotland and Catalonia, for instance. But many other modalities remain to be devised for the still more diverse democratic societies of the twenty-first century.

In the meantime, it will have helped, I believe, if we can perceive more clearly and starkly the nature of our democratic dilemma, since the hold of unreal and ahistorical solutions over our minds and imagination is still crippling our efforts to deal with the growing conflicts which arise from it.

CHAPTER EIGHT

Religious Mobilizations

FOR THOSE WHO SEE secularism as part of modernity, and modernity as
fundamentally progress, the last few decades have been painful and bewil-
dering. Powerful political mobilizations that appear to center on religion seem
to betoken a return of what had already been safely relegated to the past. Religion seemed to be wreaking a terrible revenge for its previous marginalization,
not only in the world at large but even in the most powerful Western liberal
democracy, the United States. Liberals spoke darkly of a relapse into the medieval, into irrationality.

There is some truth in this picture. The notion of revenge here does point to
the way in which these religious mobilizations are reactive, at times feeding on
a previous process of secularization perceived as a threat. But in general, this
common view suffers from a defective understanding of both modernity and
secularization. There is not one thing, called "religion," which previously receded
and is now coming back, like some raging tsunami. What we call secularization
is a process that deeply destabilized and marginalized earlier forms of religion;
but, partly as a consequence of this, new forms have arisen. The forms that are
now "returning" in strength are thoroughly modern, and we cannot understand
either them or modernity if we ignore this.

Ironically, the most obvious site of novelty lies in what are called, in the
rough and rather confused language of media commentary, "fundamentalisms." These are usually so called because they see themselves as harking back
to earlier, purer forms of religion, beyond the recent compromises of modern-

ism. So Protestant fundamentalism sees itself as returning to the purity of the Reformation *sola scriptum* (by scripture alone), which in turn saw itself as a return to primitive Christianity. Influential Islamicist Sayyid Qutb proposes to return to the principles alive in the first polity established by the Prophet and his companions. The irony and pathos here lie in the fact that precisely these attempts to return to purer forms are the sites of the most startling innovations; what is more, they feed on those innovations that are usually seen as quintessentially modern.

Thus the notion of literal biblical inerrancy, with its clear distinction from and hostility to the figurative, is plainly part of the culture that has developed around modern positivistic science. Evolutionary theory has to be opposed by "creation science." Augustine, one of the great reference figures for Western Protestantism, would be bewildered by this discourse, recognizing as he did many levels of meaning in the biblical text. Protestant fundamentalists deviate from age-old Christian orthodoxy precisely in their wholesale acceptance of this modern positivist literalism, all the while loudly proclaiming their fidelity to the original pure form of Christianity.

In this essay, I want to explore some of these contemporary forms of religion, which are modern partly in that they involve what we can call *mobilization*. What do I mean by mobilization here? One obvious facet of its meaning is that it designates a process whereby people are persuaded, pushed, dragooned, or bullied into new forms of social and religious association. This generally means that they are induced through the actions of governments, church hierarchies, or other elites not only to adopt new structures but also, to some extent, to alter their social imaginaries and sense of legitimacy, as well as their sense of what is crucially important in their lives or society. Described in this way, mobilization was already taking place during the English Reformation and the French Counter-Reformation of the seventeenth century. But these changes were taking place within a wider social context, that of the political kingdom and church, which were seen not as the products of mobilization but, on the contrary, as already there, the unchanging and unchangeable backdrop of all legitimacy.

But in an age of mobilization, this backdrop is no longer there. It becomes clearer and clearer that whatever political, social, and ecclesial structures we desire must be mobilized into existence. This eventually becomes evident even to "reactionaries," whose paradigms are found in the ancien régime. They are often forced to act on this understanding before they can bring themselves to recognize it. But sooner or later, their discourse changes, and the features of the old order that they want to reinstate become forms to be established— eternally valid, perhaps, because willed by God or in conformity with Nature, but still an ideal yet to be realized and not already there. As this understanding dawns across the political and ecclesial spectrum, we enter the age of mobilization.

The ancien régime model interwove church and state, and it presented us as living in a hierarchical order that had divine endorsement. In societies of this type the presence of God was unavoidable; authority itself was bound up with the divine, and various invocations of God were inseparable from public life. But there was more than one form of this in our past. Between the sixteenth and the nineteenth centuries, we moved from that original model, which was alive in the Middle Ages and in a number of non-Western cultures, to another, very different one. It is this second one that defines what I want to call the "mobilization type."

The earlier, ancien régime form was connected to what one might call an "enchanted world." This is obviously borrowing from Max Weber and introducing the antonym to his term "disenchanted." In an enchanted world, there is a strong contrast between the sacred and the profane. By the sacred, I mean certain places (such as churches), certain agents (such as priests), certain times (such as high feasts), and certain actions (such as saying the Mass) in which the divine or the holy is present. In comparison to these, other places, people, times, and actions may count as profane.

In an enchanted world, there is an obvious way in which God can be present in society: in the locus of the sacred. Political society can be closely connected to these sacred forms and can itself be thought to exist on a higher plane. Ernst Kantorowicz tells us that one of the first uses of the term "mystical body" in European history referred to the French kingdom.[1] The king himself could be one of the links between the planes, represented respectively by the king's mortal and undying bodies.

In other words, in these earlier societies, the kingdom existed not only in ordinary, secular time, in which a strong transitivity rule held, but also in higher times. There are, of course, different kinds of higher times—Platonist eternity, where there is a level in which we are beyond the flux altogether; God's eternity as understood in the Christian tradition, as a kind of gathering of time together; and various times of origins, in Mircea Eliade's sense.

Now, with advancing disenchantment (especially in Protestant societies), another model took shape, with relation to both the cosmos and the polity. In this, the notion of design was crucial. As this model manifested itself in regard to the cosmos, there was a shift from the enchanted world to a cosmos conceived in conformity with post-Newtonian science, in which there is absolutely no question of higher meanings being expressed in the universe around us. But there is still, with someone like Newton himself, for instance, a strong sense that the universe declares the glory of God. This is evident in its design, its beauty, its regularity, but also in its having evidently been shaped to conduce to the welfare of God's creatures, particularly ourselves, the superior creatures who cap it all off. Now the presence of God no longer lies in the sacred, because this category fades in a disenchanted world. But he can be thought to be no less powerfully present through his design.

This presence of God in the cosmos is matched by another idea: his presence in the polity. Here an analogous change takes place. The divine isn't present in a king who straddles the planes. But it can be present to the extent that we build a society that plainly follows God's design. This can be supplemented with an idea of moral order that is seen as established by God, in the way invoked, for example, in the American Declaration of Independence: men have been created equal and have been endowed by their creator with certain inalienable rights.

The idea of moral order that is expressed in this declaration, and which has since become dominant in our world, is what I have been calling the modern moral order. It is quite different from the orders that preceded it, because it starts from individuals and doesn't see them as set a priori within a hierarchical order outside of which they wouldn't be fully human agents. Its members are not agents who are essentially embedded in a society that in turn reflects and connects with the cosmos but, rather, disembedded individuals who come to associate together. The design underlying the association is that each, in pursuing his or her own purposes in life, acts in mutual benefit with others. It calls for a society structured for mutual benefit, in which each respects the rights of others and which offers them mutual help of certain kinds. The most influential early articulator of this formula is John Locke, but the basic conception of such an order of mutual service has come down to us through a series of variants, including more radical ones such as those presented by Rousseau and Marx.[2]

But in the earlier days, when the plan was understood as providential and the order seen as natural law, which is the same as the law of God, building a society that fulfills these requirements was seen as fulfilling the design of God. To live in such a society was to live in one where God was present—not at all in the way that belonged to the enchanted world, through the sacred, but because that society was following his design. God is present as the designer of the way we live. We see ourselves, to quote a famous phrase, as "one nation under God."

In taking the United States as a paradigm case of this new idea of order, I am following Robert Bellah's tremendously fertile idea of an American "civil religion."[3] Of course, the concept is understandably and rightly contested today because some of the conditions of this religion are now being challenged, but there is no doubt that Bellah has captured something essential about American society, both at its inception and for about two centuries thereafter.

The fundamental idea that America had a vocation to carry out God's purposes, which alone makes sense of the passages Bellah quotes (for instance, Kennedy's inaugural address and Lincoln's second inaugural address) and which can seem strange and threatening to many unbelievers in America today, has to be understood in relation to this conception of order involving free, rights-bearing individuals. This was what was invoked in the Declaration of Independence, which appealed to "the Laws of Nature and of Nature's God." The rightness of these laws, for both deists and theists, was grounded in their being part of the providential design. What the activism of the American revolutionaries added to this was a view of history as the theater in which this design was to be progressively realized, and of their own society as the place where this realization was to be consummated—what Lincoln would later refer to as "the last best hope on earth." It was this notion of themselves as fulfilling divine purposes that, along with the biblical culture of Protestant America, facilitated the analogy with ancient Israel that often recurred in early American official rhetoric.[4]

The confusion today arises from the fact that there is both continuity and discontinuity. What continues is the importance of some form of the modern idea of moral order. It is this that gives the sense that Americans are still operating on the same principles as the country's founders. The rift comes from the fact that what makes this order the right one is, for many (though not, by any means, for all), no longer God's Providence; the order is grounded in nature alone, or in some concept of civilization, or even in supposedly unchallengeable a priori principles, often inspired by Kant. Thus some Americans want to rescue the Constitution from God, whereas others, with deeper historical roots, see this as doing violence to it: hence the contemporary American Kulturkampf.

I will call this kind of link between religion and the state "neo-Durkheimian,"[5] contrasting it, on the one hand, to the paleo-Durkheimian mode of baroque Catholic societies and, on the other, to more recent societal forms in which the spiritual dimension of existence is quite unhooked from the political. The "paleo" phase corresponds to a situation in which a sense of the ontic dependence of the state on God and higher times is still alive, even though it may be weakened by disenchantment and an instrumental spirit; whereas in "neo" societies, God is present because it is his design around which society is organized. It is this which we concur on as the identifying common description of our society and what we could call its political identity.

If we look at this Anglophone trajectory, we can see that, unlike the baroque one, where the church almost inevitably generated counterforces, it can sustain a high level of religious belief and practice. Resentment at the power of elites and estrangement from their spiritual style can find expression in another mode of Christian life and worship. Popular groups can find and live by their own spiritual style, as the "enthusiastic" Methodists did in eighteenth-century England, the Baptists did in the rural United States, and the Evangelicals and the Pentecostalists are doing today in Latin America, Africa, and Asia. Alienation from a Northeast dominated by genteel Episcopalians and Presbyterians can take the form of passionate, born-again Evangelicalism in the South and West.

At the same time, belief is sustained by the neo-Durkheimian identification with the state. Over a long period, for many English, Christianity of a certain Protestant variety was identified with certain moral standards, often summed up using the word *decency*,[6] and England was thought to be the preeminent carrier of this variety on the world scene. This complex of beliefs and norms was what we could call the "established synthesis," and, for many people, was central to the creation of English patriotism. Many Protestant Americans, and latterly some Catholic ones, have thought that the United States has a providential mission to spread liberal democracy among the rest of humankind.

In this neo-Durkheimian form, religious belonging is central to political identity. But the religious dimension also figures in what we might call the civilizational identity, the sense people have that the basic order by which they live, even imperfectly, is good and (usually) is superior to the ways of life of outsiders, be they "barbarians," "savages," or (in more polite contemporary language) "less developed" peoples.

In fact, most of the time, we relate to the order established in our civilization the way people have always related to their most fundamental sense of order: we have a sense of security in believing that order actually exists in our world, and we also have a sense of our own superiority and goodness deriving from the confidence that we participate in it and uphold it. This means that we can react with great insecurity when we see that our order can be breached from outside, as at the World Trade Center, but also that we are even more shaken when we feel that it might be undermined from within, or that we might be betraying it. In the latter case, it is not only our security that is threatened, it is also our sense of our own integrity and goodness. To see this questioned is profoundly unsettling, threatening ultimately our ability to act.

This is why, in earlier times, we see people lashing out at such moments of threat in scapegoating violence against "the enemy within." In other words, they meet the threat to their security by dealing with the threat to their group's integrity, deflecting the threatening features onto scapegoats. In earlier periods of Latin Christendom, Jews and witches were cast in this unenviable role. The evidence that we are still tempted to turn to similar mechanisms in our so-called enlightened age is unsettling. But it would not be the first such paradox in history if a doctrine of peaceful universalism were invoked to mobilize scapegoating violence.[7]

The point I want to make about British and later American patriotism, based as it was at first on the sense of fulfilling God's design, is that national identity was based on a self-ascribed preeminence in realizing a certain civilizational superiority. The superiority may have ultimately been understood as that of Christendom over infidel religions, but within Christendom, Britain and America stood at the cutting edge.

This sense of superiority was, of course, originally religious. It goes without saying that in Christendom the sense of civilizational order was inseparable from Christianity. But what this meant evolved over time; and here too we must make a distinction between premodern and modern forms. Reformation, in both its Catholic and Protestant variants, involved a strong moralization— that is, the Christian faith was identified with a more stringent code of order and self-restraint.

We can see many examples of this link between Reformation and moral stringency, but the most impressive connection is visible in what are loosely called "evangelical" modes of revival, which were widespread in Britain and America from the end of the eighteenth century.[8] At their most intense, these centered on certain central doctrines of the Reformation: our sinful condition and the need for conversion, turning to God in faith, which would open us to his grace. The stress was often on this conversion as a personal act, undertaken for oneself, rather than as a disposition inhering in the group; and it was often taken, dramatically, under the press of powerful emotions and in public.

Here was a powerful transformation perspective, in the terms of my earlier discussion: defined, on the one side, by a deep, potentially overpowering sense of sin and imperfection and, on the other, by an overwhelming feeling of the love of God and its power to heal—amazing grace. As in the earlier Reformation, this new empowerment was meant to yield fruit in an ordered life. And order and disorder were conceived in terms that were very understandable given the common predicament of many at that time who were often struggling to find their feet in a more and more market-driven economy, where survival often depended on adaptation to new conditions such as migration and new work disciplines outside of traditional social forms. The danger was of sinking into forms of behavior that were idle, irresponsible, undisciplined, and wasteful. And behind these lay the lure of traditional modes of recreation and conviviality that could immure you in such dysfunctional forms—traditions such as, in the first place, drink and the tavern. This is why temperance was one of the central goals of evangelical cultures, in a way that sounds totally excessive to many contemporary ears. We are perhaps sobered (if that's the word), however, when we learn how much of a curse drink could be; for instance, in the United States in the 1820s, the liquor consumption per capita was four times what it is today.[9]

Along with drink (also aiding and abetting it) were other favored activities: cruel sports, gambling, sexual promiscuity. This understanding of disorder targeted certain long-standing male forms of conviviality outside the family. The new understanding of order was family-centered, and it often involved identifying the male as the source of potential disruption and the female as victim and guardian of this ordered domestic space. Callum Brown even speaks here of a "demonization" of male qualities, and a "feminization of piety."[10] Order required the male to be a family man and a good provider, and this required that he become educated, disciplined, and a hard worker. Sobriety, industry, and discipline were the principal virtues. Education and self-help were highly valued qualities. By attaining these, the man acquired a certain dignity, that of a free, self-governing agent. The goal could be captured in two terms: on the one hand, the respectability that went with an ordered life has been much stressed; but, along with this, we should place free agency and the dignity of the citizen. Evangelicalism was basically an antihierarchical force, thus part of the drive for democracy.

This connection of salvation and sanctity with a certain moral order in our lives reminds us of the Reformation, of which evangelicalism is in a sense a reprise, in different circumstances and with an even more central emphasis on personal commitment. We can also look in the other direction and note how this movement carries on in our day, not so much in its home terrain of Britain and the United States (though it is still very strong in the latter) but in Latin America, Africa, and Asia.[11] In these places we can note the same connection between accepting salvation and putting a certain kind of order in one's life, so that men in Latin America become more family centered, deserting certain kinds of male conviviality that stress machismo and becoming sober and good providers. Indeed, we might even extend the comparison to include non-Christian movements like the Nation of Islam in the United States.[12]

Quite naturally, then, the modern sense of civilizational order is closely bound up with a stringent moral code. Our order is dependent on our maintaining this code, rather than in our fidelity to certain rituals or our maintaining a certain spiritual stance, as is the case with other links between religion and civilization.

Thus in the beleaguered and embattled Catholic churches of Europe, in the aftermath of the French Revolution, the sense was strong that they offered the only possible bulwark of civilizational order. The claim was frequently made by the church in France, and accepted by many in the possessing classes, that Catholicism was the only defense against the destructive disorders of revolution, whose return was a constant menace. But the idea was not just that only the church could persuade people to obey due authority, it was also that the very basis of morality and social and family life would crumble away without the constant and patient work of dedicated clergy. As the Curé d'Ars himself once put it: "Laissez une paroisse vingt ans sans prêtre, on y adorera des bêtes" ("Leave a parish twenty years, and they'll be adoring beasts").[13]

Here was a strongly clericalist form of the doctrine; but without this nuance, there were analogies to views held across the Channel by Evangelicals, and indeed many others, to the effect that basic morality could not long survive the demise of religion. A common view among churchgoers was, as Jeffrey Cox put it, that "society would fall apart without morality, morality was impossible without religion, and religion would disappear without the churches."[14] To quote from the Duke of Devonshire in a speech to supporters of the South London Church Fund:

> Can you imagine for one moment what England would have been like today without those churches and all that those churches mean? . . . Certainly it would not have been safe to walk the streets. All respect, decency, all those things which tend to make modern civilization what it is would not have been in existence. You can imagine what we should have had to pay for our police, for lunatic asylums, for criminal asylums. . . . The charges would have been increased hundredfold if it had not been for the work the church has done and is doing today.[15]

The Duke was perhaps mainly referring to the churches' philanthropic work in this speech, but this was plainly part of a more fundamental point about the moral bases of civilizational order.

In most Christian sentiment of this age, the issue was not the one many believers might raise today: whether one should restrict one's goals to a purely human fulfillment or open a transcendent perspective to something more than this. In the dominant outlook, then, this first option didn't exist. Unless one reached out to something beyond, to God and salvation through Jesus Christ, the conditions of even the most basic human fulfillment would crumble in immorality and disorder. This view is still defended in some circles today, but a century ago it was standard and hegemonic among Christian believers.

Now this religio-moral link can and does undergo a secularization as the sense of civilizational superiority becomes detached from Providence and attributed to race, or enlightenment, or even some combination of the two. But the point of identifying here this sense of order is that it provides another niche, as it were, in which God can be present in our lives, or in our social imaginary—as the author not just of the design that defines our political identity, but also of the design that defines civilizational order.

But why distinguish them, when they so obviously go together in the paradigm case of the United States? Because they don't always fit together in this way but can operate separately. It is a notion absolutely crucial to much of Christian apologetics, from the French Revolution onward, that the Christian faith is essential to the maintenance of civilizational order, whether this is defined in terms of the modern moral order or in terms of an earlier hierarchical complementarity. This is the very staple of counterrevolutionary thought as it flows from the pen, for instance, of Joseph de Maistre. But one can hear something similar today, in a quite neo-Durkheimian context, from some parts of the religious Right in the United States. The doctrine is that our order is not stable unless based on an explicit recognition that we are following God's plan. So much for the belief involved.

But this belief issues in a social imaginary that either our order is now stable, because we are following God's plan, or our order is threatened, because we are deviating from the plan. This sense of the presence (or the threatened absence) of God in our world, as the designer and guarantor of the civilizational order, can be very present, even where it is not linked with a sense that our nation singles itself out by its preeminence in realizing his order. It may be relatively unhooked from our political identity. At the risk of calling attention to my personal standpoint, I will say that the self-arrogation of such a vanguard position is more likely (at least over the long run) among hegemonic powers. It's more difficult to think that you are at the cutting edge of human history if you come from Norway, or Belgium, or Canada. But people in these smaller nations can still have a sense of God as the basis of their civilizational order.

But it may also work the other way around. God may be central to our political identity without this identity being essential to the broader social order. Thus, in the course of modern history, confessional allegiances have come to be woven into the sense of identity of certain ethnic, national, class, or regional groups.

We can discern here one application of a pattern that is central to what we might call the age of mobilization. The modern citizen social imaginary contrasts with various premodern forms in that these latter forms reflect an embedded understanding of human life. In relation to an ancien régime kingdom, we are seen as already defined (and having been so since time out of mind) as subjects of the king; or, placed even more exactly, as serfs of a lord, who holds from a duke, who holds from the king; or, alternatively, as bourgeois of this city; or as members of this cathedral chapter, which is under this bishop, who relates to both pope and king; and so on. Our relation to the whole is mediated. The modern citizen imaginary, on the other hand, sees us all as coming together to form this political entity, to which we all relate in the same way, as equal members. This entity has to be (or had to be, if it's already up and running) constructed. However much various modern ideologies, like nationalism, may convince us that we were always members of people X (even though our ancestors didn't fully realize it and were even forced or induced to speak people Y's language), and however much this gives us the vocation to construct our own state, X-land, nevertheless this state has (or had) to be constructed. People need to be convinced that they were really Xs, and not Ys.

Two related ideas are crucial to this self-understanding. The first is that realizing who we really are (Xs) requires mobilization. We had to be brought to act together to erect our state: rebel against the Ys, or appeal to the League of Nations, and so forth. And the second is that this mobilization is inseparable from a (re)definition of identity: we have to define ourselves, saliently, even sometimes primarily, as Xs, and not as a host of other things that we also are or could be (Catholic-Uniates, or members of a certain village, or just peasants).

These new entities—citizen states or other products of mobilization—are ordered around certain common poles of identity; let's call them political identities. This doesn't have to be focused around a linguistically defined nation, of course (though it often has been in the West). The pole of identity can be a religious confession, it can be certain principles of government (as in revolutionary France and the United States), it can be historical links, and so on.

This allows us to see the U.S. case as one example of a widespread feature of the modern world, in the age of mobilization. Political identities can also be woven around religious or confessional definitions. Britain and the United States are powerful, independent nations. But the confessional kind of identification often happens with marginal or oppressed populations. The Polish and Irish Catholic identities are well-known cases in point. The erstwhile French Canadian case is another.

The link here between group and confession is not of the ancien régime type that we saw in counterrevolutionary France, even though the same Catholic Church is involved. The throne and the altar can't be allied, because the throne is alien—not just when it is Lutheran, Anglican, or Orthodox, but even when or where it is Catholic (as in Vienna). Resentment toward elites becomes marginal to the extent that these elites lose power and privilege. But the sense of national domination and oppression, the sense of virtue in suffering and struggle, is deeply interwoven with religious belief and allegiance—even to the point of such rhetorical excesses as the depiction of Poland as Christ crucified among the nations. The result is what I'm calling a neo-Durkheimian effect, where the senses of belonging to group and confession are fused, and the moral issues of the group's history tend to be coded in religious categories. (The rival language for oppressed people was always that of the French Revolution, which had its moments in each of the subaltern nations mentioned here: the United Irish, Papineau's rebellion in 1837, Dabrowski's legion; but in each case, the Catholic coding later took the upper hand.)

My neo-Durkheimian category can even be expanded to include a founding of political identity on an anti-religious philosophical stance, such as we saw with the long-standing republican French identity. The long-standing *guerre franco-française,* the French ideological civil war, was in this sense fought between two neo-Durkheimian identities. These then contrast with other kinds of political identities, those founded on a supposed linguistic-historical nation, for instance, or on a certain constitutional order.

This last, French case shows that neo-Durkheimian identity mobilization extends well beyond established nations, or even wannabe nations, like Poland or Ireland. There are also cases of confessional mobilization that aims at political impact, even where this is purely defensive and can't hope to result in independent nationhood, as with Catholics in Germany during the Kulturkampf or Dutch pillarization.

Now this phenomenon, religiously defined political-identity mobilization, obviously has a tremendous present and (I fear) future in our world. I want to return to this in a later section of this essay. But for the moment, I want to point out that, where this phenomenon takes hold, a potential decline in belief and practice is retarded or fails to occur. This easily gives rise to a misunderstanding in the climate of contemporary sociology with its rather secular mind-set. Once again, as with Evangelicalism or the Anglophone nations mentioned above, we may be tempted to say of these situations that religion is performing an "integrating function," or, in Bruce's language, a function of "cultural defense."[16] The slide is easy to the thesis that religious belief is the dependent variable here, its integrative function being the explanatory factor.

But I think it would be less distortive to say that the religious language is the one in which people find it meaningful to code their strong moral and political experience, either of oppression or of successful state building around certain moral principles. The point of citing the different predicaments of the Polish or Irish peasants and workers, on one hand, and their Spanish or French counterparts, on the other, is that the former offered inducements and little resistance to coding in a Catholic language, whereas for the latter, life in a baroque regime generates experiences that are strong deterrents to doing so.

I have been identifying in the preceding pages, either centrally or peripherally, various religious forms that are "modern," in the sense that they figure prominently in what I've been calling the age of mobilization; in some cases they make sense only within this age. I want to mention three of these forms.

1. First, there is a phenomenon that I touched on only glancingly in the previous discussion, when I spoke of evangelical revivals. These are paradigmatic examples of movements that weave together the meeting of spiritual and devotional aspirations with personal and often collective

empowerment. These are familiar in the Protestant world, but there are analogous forms elsewhere: for instance, the various movements of the Catholic Action network and Catholic prayer and devotion, as well as the Nation of Islam among African Americans. Other examples could be cited in other religious milieus. Let's call these modes of empowering devotion.

2. Then, there are the interweavings of religious or confessional belonging with political identities: the neo-Durkheimian phenomenon.

3. Finally, there are the various ways in which religious or confessional faith becomes connected, via a strong moral code, to our sense of civilizational order and the sense of security or superiority that connects to this. Let us call this the civilizational connection.

These can be happily intertwined, as in Anglophone Protestantism over many centuries, or they can exist quite separately from each other, as with various evangelical or Catholic movements in the global south (where Christians are in a minority), which are modes of (1) unconnected to (2) or (3); or in Catholic or Polish nationalism, where (2) exists without any necessary linkage to (1) or (3). And (3) notoriously can exist alone among beleaguered elites, who sense that their society is going to the dogs. Or (2) and (3) can be alloyed without (1), as with nineteenth-century German *Kulturprotestantismus.*

At the outset of this essay, I mentioned the highly conflictual "return of religion" that secular liberals have been noting with alarm in recent decades. My point was that the religion that underlies these conflicts was not really returning, because the forms that powered the challenge to secular hegemony were in fact relatively new and belonged to the modern age. Can the three forms I have just identified help us to understand these conflicts?

Let's take the battle that is most on the minds of American liberals, and to some extent those in other Western countries: the culture wars of the United States. From a European perspective these seem to be a peculiarly American phenomenon. Indeed, educated, cultivated Europeans are extremely uncomfortable with any overt manifestations of either strong nationalism or religious sentiment. The contrast to the United States in this regard has often been remarked upon. It might help to take up here one of the most debated issues in the field of secularization theory, that of the American exception—or, if one likes, as seen from a broader perspective, the European exception. Put either way, we are faced with a strong, even if not uniform, pattern of decline in European societies and virtually nothing of the sort in the United States. How can this difference be explained?

Various attempts have been made to do so. For instance, Bruce attributes the strength of religion in America partly to the immigrant context. Immigrants needed to group together with those of similar origins in order to ease their transition into American society. The rallying point was often a shared religion, and the main agency was often a church.[17]

If we take the United Kingdom as representative of Europe, another important factor in explaining the contrast may have been the hierarchical nature of British society. British elites, and particularly the intelligentsia, have been living in a fractured culture since the eighteenth century; the saliency of unbelief may have been lower in certain periods of strong piety, but it was always there. Something similar may also have been true of the American intelligentsia, but the position it occupied in U.S. society was very different. In deferential British society, the pattern of elite life has a prestige that it largely lacks in the United States. This means that elite unbelief can both more effectively resist conforming and also more readily provide models for people at other levels. There are parallels with other European societies, which all, in this respect, contrast with the United States.[18]

But perhaps the most important factors explaining the transatlantic difference may be susceptible to formulation in the terms I have been developing here. From this point of view there are three facets to the American exception. I have been speaking of the undermining of social matrices that have hitherto kept large numbers of people within the churches, or at least within the faith. But what has been undermined is different in the two cases. The heart of the American exception is that this society is the only one that from the beginning (if we leave aside the countries of the old British Commonwealth) was entirely within the neo-Durkheimian mold. All European societies had some element of the ancien régime or the paleo-Durkheimian, perhaps more vestigial than real, like the rituals surrounding even constitutional monarchies, but often important enough—such as the presence of (at least would-be) state churches or of rural communities with their *religion du terroir* (local forms of religion). The proportions of paleo- and neo-Durkheimian elements are very different as we move from Spain to Britain or Sweden, but all European states contain some mix of the two, whereas American religious life was entirely in the age of mobilization.

This means that, in varying degrees, some of the dynamics arising from ancien régime structures will take place in all the Old World societies. One of these dynamics is the reaction against a state church in the context of an inegalitarian society, where the temptation to align established religion with power and privilege is almost irresistible. This cannot fail to produce anticlerical reactions, which can easily turn, given the availability of exclusive humanist options since the eighteenth century, into militant unbelief, which is then available to canalize the full force of popular discontent with established clergy. We see this dynamic played out in France, Spain, and even, to some extent, Prussia. In

Britain, on the other hand, we saw that much popular anticlericalism found expression in nonconformity. But even here an alternative stream was there from the beginning, in figures like Tom Paine and William Godwin, whereas such ideas didn't have the same impact in the early history of the United States. The imprint of an impressive array of deists among the founders, most notably Thomas Jefferson, seems to have been largely effaced by the Second Great Awakening.

The other important dynamic in these cases is that the perturbing effect on religious belief of destabilization, which is affecting both ancien régime forms and mobilization forms at one and the same time, is obviously greater than a challenge addressed to neo-Durkheimian structures alone. If peasants being turned into Frenchmen can be rescued from unbelief only by modes of neo-Durkheimian mobilization, then the undermining of these modes has a much more profoundly destabilizing effect on belief, or at least practice. In a society, on the other hand, where the move to the age of mobilization has been completed without any significant lessening of belief, the effect of undermining the previously dominant modes of this mobilization will obviously be much less.

This is one facet of the American exception. A second is perhaps this: the actual undermining of neo-Durkheimian modes has been far less severe in America than it has elsewhere. In particular, the constitutional-moral patriotism, what I called earlier the reigning synthesis between nation, morality, and religion, which was very similar in Britain and the United States, was nevertheless much less strong in Britain; indeed, it was much more strongly contested. This was particularly so in the aftermath of the First World War, which was much more traumatic for British society than for American society. The challenge to civilization in Britain that this cataclysm represented was certainly lived by many as a challenge to their faith, as I argued earlier. The strong sense generated by a neo-Durkheimian effect that everyone shares a certain moral or spiritual coding, and that this is how we must understand our strong collective moral experience, thus faded more rapidly in Britain and weakened the code, whereas in the American case, many people felt and have gone on feeling that you can show your Americanness by joining a church. In this respect, following the above argument, other European societies are similar to Britain and have gone through the same historical experiences, with similar results.[19]

Against this argument has to be set the triple attack that the family-religion-patriotism complex of the 1950s suffered in the era of civil rights, Vietnam, and the expressive revolution. Was this not the analogue in the American case to the First World War for the British? Perhaps, but plainly not everyone sees it this way. Indeed, the different reactions to this era seem to underlie the culture wars of contemporary U.S. politics. It seems that that fusion of faith, family values, and patriotism is still extremely important to one half of American so-ciety, and that they are dismayed to see it challenged, both in its central values (for example, the fight over abortion or gay marriage) and in the link between their faith and the polity (fights over school prayer, the phrase "under God," and the like).

In addition, lots of Americans, even those who are not on the Right, still feel quite at home with the idea of the United States as being "one nation under God." Those made uncomfortable by this identity are vocal and domi-nant in universities and (some) media but are not all that numerous. And be-sides, groups of non-Christian and non-Jewish immigrants, who might be thought natural allies of those who want to resist a biblical coding of the Ameri-can identity, are themselves anxious to be co-opted into a suitably widened variation of it. Imams are now alongside priests and rabbis at public prayers, and this panreligious unity surfaces especially at moments of crisis or disaster, as after 9/11.

Now this is partly the result of the sheer difference in numbers of people who adhere to some religion in the United States, as against Europe. But it has also to do with the respective attitudes toward national identity. Europe in the second half of the twentieth century has been full of reticence about its former senses of nationhood, and the events of the first half of this century explain why. The European Union is built on the attempt to go beyond the earlier forms, in the full consciousness of how destructive they have been. The full-throated assertions of the older self-exalting nationalisms are now reserved for the radical Right, which is felt by everyone else to represent a pestilence, a pos-sibly deadly disease, and which in turn is anti-European. War, even righteous war, as an expression of the superiority of the national project, makes most Eu-ropeans profoundly uneasy.

Quite different is the attitude of the United States. This may be partly be-cause Americans have fewer skeletons in the family closet to confront than do their European cousins. But I think the answer is simpler than that. It is easier to be unreservedly confident in your own rightness when you are the hege-monic power. The skeletons are there, but they can be resolutely ignored, in spite of the efforts of a gallant band of scholars who are engaged in the "history wars." Most Germans have to cringe when they are reminded of the First World War slogan *Gott mit uns* (God is with us)—and about the Second World War, the less said, the better. But most Americans have few doubts about whose side God is on. In this context, the traditional neo-Durkheimian defini-tion is far easier to live with.

So in terms of my discussion a few paragraphs back, the traditional Ameri-can synthesis—of civil religion, a strong neo-Durkheimian identity originally based around a nondenominational Christianity, and a strong connection to civilizational order—is still in a hot phase, unlike its British counterpart. The original civil religion gradually extended beyond its Protestant base, but it has now come to a stage where, while the link to civilizational order remains strong, the connection to religion is now challenged by a broad range of secularists and liberal believers. Issues like the banning of school prayer, abortion, and, more recently, homosexual marriage become highly charged. I spoke above of a culture war, but another analogy might be *la guerre franco-française,* two strongly opposed ideological codings of the same nation's identity, in a context where nationalism (not to say great power chauvinism) remains powerful. This is the recipe for bitter struggles.[20]

Perhaps a control case can be found in the societies of the old British Commonwealth: Canada, Australia, New Zealand. Like the United States, and (almost) from the beginning, they have been in the age of mobilization. But their faith-related neo-Durkheimian definitions haven't fared as well. Either they lived in a British identity, which has since decayed in the mother country as well as the ex-colony, or (as in the case of Quebec) they have undergone a turnover that much more resembles the European model. But above all, they are not hegemonic powers; one case, Canada, is constantly reminded of this fact by its proximity to the nation that is. So it is not surprising to find the figures for religious belief and practice somewhat between European and U.S. ones. It is also not surprising that the issue of gay marriage, while it has been upsetting for Conservatives in Canada as well, has not awakened the same degree of heat and indignation in Canada as in its neighbor to the south.

There is a third way of stating the American exception, which overlaps in some respects with the two points above. The United States since the early nineteenth century has been a home of religious freedom, expressed in a very American way: that is, it has been a country of religious choice. People move, form new denominations, join ones that they weren't brought up in, break away from existing ones, and so on. Their whole religious culture was in some way prepared for the age of authenticity, even before this became a facet of mass culture in the latter part of the twentieth century. This whole shift was therefore much less destabilizing. We have just to think of the contrast with Germany and France, where the new cults deeply disturb people. Even French atheists are a trifle horrified when religion doesn't take the standard Catholic form that they love to hate. It is harder to see the discontinuity in America, and indeed, the discontinuity was, in a sense, less, since the culture of authenticity was, before the 1960s, present everywhere among cultured elites, and the educated were a much larger proportion of the U.S. population even before the postwar expansion of universities.

When all is said and done, however, I have to admit that this list of factors, while probably valid, doesn't satisfy as an answer to the question of why the gamut of options that spiritual seekers choose among is so much more tilted toward the believing end in the United States than in Europe. This is one of the big unresolved issues of the secularization debate.

But in relation to the question being considered here, how to understand the intensity of the (partly) religion-inspired conflict, it is the second factor that seems decisive, that is, the continuing strength of a neo-Durkheimian identity, linking a nondenominational theism to the national project via a strong conception of religio-moral civilizational order. Or, one might say it is both the strength and the weakness of that identity. It once was hegemonic—even relatively skeptical elites felt they had to acknowledge it—but, in the latter half of the twentieth century, another liberal consensus arose which interpreted the political ethic defining the American way (freedom, rights, democracy) as calling for neutrality, not just between denominations, but between belief and unbelief. This has become strong enough to challenge the original theistically anchored identity but not enough to displace it. The result is a bitter struggle between two definitions of the national identity, each of which considers the other to be a betrayal. For liberals, the religious Right is guilty of transgressing the core American principle of the separation of church and state; the religious Right, in turn, cannot accept this accusation because they distinguish separating church from state and separating state from (nondenominational) religion. They see liberals as betraying the original and essential anchoring of the American project in the supremacy of God and the moral code ("family values").

As is often the case in this kind of struggle, and as one saw in France in the nineteenth century, the result is a kind of bunching of issues into packages: to be on one or the other side is to have an obligatory position on gun control, redistributive taxation, wilderness protection, gas-guzzling vehicles, and the like. In a less ideologically heated environment, people might pick and choose a combination of stands on these issues that made sense to them in the light of the considerations valid for each one. But the pressure of the ideological battle tends to drive these (one might think, more rational) crosscutting stands to the margins. People feel they have to vote their package. So the actual facts in some issue area—say, the war in Iraq—become irrelevant; one votes the package, by focusing on issues that are most powerfully emblematic of it (like "morals" or "family values").

The worrying thing is that the polarization seems to be intensifying. Erstwhile crosscutters, like the former liberal Republicans, have become an endangered species, as we can see in the fate of the Bush dynasty as it swings from liberal Northeast Republicans to raging Texas ideologues in two generations. The rest of the world looks on, alarmed and despondent, as a new macho-militarist unilateralism becomes an integral part of one of the packages—the one that is now winning out. American culture wars now endanger the planet.

Is this a "return of religion"? Well, it certainly represents a reaction of some believers to the drift of the contemporary world: the sexual revolution, the age of authenticity, the rise of the new liberal definition of the American way. But, first, this is not the reaction of believers as such: there are many people of faith on the liberal side. Second, the virulence of the conflict comes from the intrication of religion in a tripartite neo-Durkheimian identity, uniting faith, morals, and nation—something that is rather recent, and, one might add, something that is, from a faith point of view, perhaps highly questionable.

Part III

THEMES FROM *A SECULAR AGE*

CHAPTER NINE

A Catholic Modernity?

I WANT TO SAY first how deeply honored I am to have been chosen as this
year's recipient of the Marianist Award. I am very grateful to the University
of Dayton, not only for their recognition of my work but also for this chance
to raise with you today some issues that have been at the center of my concern
for decades. They have been reflected in my philosophical work, but not in the
same form as I raise them this afternoon, because of the nature of philosophical discourse (as I see it, anyway), which has to try to persuade honest thinkers
of any and all metaphysical or theological commitments. I am very glad of the
chance to open out with you some of the questions that surround the notion of
a Catholic modernity.

I

My title could have been reversed; I could have called this talk "A Modern
Catholicism?" But such is the force of this adjective *modern* in our culture that
one might immediately get the sense that the object of my search was a new,
better, higher Catholicism, meant to replace all those outmoded varieties that
clutter up our past. But to search for this would be to chase a chimera, a mon-
ster that cannot exist in the nature of things.

It cannot exist because of what "catholicism" means, at least to me. So
I'll start by saying a word about that. "Go ye and teach all nations." How to

understand this injunction? The easy way, the one in which it has all too often been taken, has been to take the global worldview of us who are Christians and strive to make over other nations and cultures to fit it. But this violates one of the basic demands of Catholicism. I want to take the original word *katholou* in two related senses, comprising both universality and wholeness; one might say universality through wholeness.

Redemption happens through Incarnation, the weaving of God's life into human lives, but these human lives are different, plural, irreducible to each other. Redemption-Incarnation brings reconciliation, a kind of oneness. This is the oneness of diverse beings who come to see that they cannot attain wholeness alone, that their complementarity is essential, rather than of beings who come to accept that they are ultimately identical. Or perhaps we might put it: complementarity and identity will both be part of our ultimate oneness. Our great historical temptation has been to forget the complementarity, to go straight for the sameness, making as many people as possible into "good Catholics"—and in the process failing of catholicity: failing of catholicity, because failing wholeness; unity bought at the price of suppressing something of the diversity in the humanity that God created; unity of the part masquerading as the whole. It is universality without wholeness, and so not true Catholicism.

This unity-across-difference, as against unity-through-identity, seems the only possibility for us, not just because of the diversity among humans, starting with the difference between men and women and ramifying outward. It's not just that the human material, with which God's life is to be interwoven, imposes this formula as a kind of second-best solution to sameness. Nor is it just because any unity between humans and God would have to be one across (immense) difference. But it seems that the life of God itself, understood as trinitarian, is already a oneness of this kind. Human diversity is part of the way in which we are made in the image of God.

So a Catholic principle, if I can put it in this perhaps overrigid way, is no widening of the faith without an increase in the variety of devotions and spiritualities and liturgical forms and responses to Incarnation. This is a demand which we in the Catholic Church have often failed to respect but which we have also often tried to live up to; I'm thinking, for instance, of the great Jesuit missions in China and India at the beginning of the modern era.

The advantage for us moderns is that, living in the wake of so many varied forms of Christian life, we have this vast field of spiritualities already there before us with which to compensate for our own narrowness, to remind us of all that we need to complement our own partiality, on our road to wholeness—which is why I'm chary of the possible resonance of "a modern Catholicism," with the potential echoes of triumphalism and self-sufficiency residing in the adjective (added to those which have often enough resided in the noun!).

The point is not to be a "modern Catholic," if by this we (perhaps semiconsciously and surreptitiously) begin to see ourselves as the ultimate "compleat Catholics," summing up and going beyond our less advantaged ancestors (a powerful connotation that hangs over the word *modern* in much contemporary use).[1] Rather, the point is, taking our modern civilization for another of those great cultural forms that have come and gone in human history, to see what it means to be a Christian here, to find our authentic voice in the eventual Catholic chorus, to try to do for our time and place what Matteo Ricci was striving to do four centuries ago in China.

I realize how strange, even outlandish, it seems to take Matteo Ricci and the great Jesuit experiment in China as our model here. It seems impossible to take this kind of stance toward our time, for two opposite reasons. First, we are too close to it. This is still, in many respects, a Christian civilization; at least, it is a society with many churchgoers. How can we start from the outsider's standpoint that was inevitably Ricci's?

But second, immediately after we say this, we are reminded of all those facets of modern thought and culture that strive to define Christian faith as the other, as what needs to be overcome and set firmly in the past, if enlightenment, liberalism, humanism is to flourish. With this in mind, it's not hard to feel like an outsider. But just for this reason, the Ricci project can seem totally inappropriate. He faced another civilization, one built largely in ignorance of the Judeo-Christian revelation, so the question could arise how to adapt this latter to these new addresses. But to see modernity under its non-Christian aspect is generally to see it as anti-Christian, as deliberately excluding the Christian kerygma. And how can you adapt your message to its negation?

So the Ricci project in relation to our own time looks strange for two seemingly incompatible reasons. On one hand, we feel already at home here, in this civilization which has issued from Christendom, so what do we need to strive further to understand? On the other hand, whatever is foreign to Christianity seems to involve a rejection of it, so how can we envisage accommodating? Put in other terms, the Ricci project involves the difficult task of making new discriminations: what in the culture represents a valid human difference, and what is incompatible with Christian faith? The celebrated debate about the Chinese rites turned on this issue. But it seems that, for modernity, things are already neatly sorted out: whatever is in continuity with our past is legitimate Christian culture, and the novel, secularist twist to things is simply incompatible. No further inquiry seems necessary.

Now I think that this double reaction, which we are easily tempted to go along with, is quite wrong. The view I'd like to defend, if I can put it in a nutshell, is that in modern, secularist culture there are mingled together both authentic developments of the Gospel, of an incarnational mode of life, and also a closing off to God that negates the Gospel. The notion is that modern culture, in breaking with the structures and beliefs of Christendom, also carried certain facets of Christian life further than they ever were taken or could have been taken within Christendom. In relation to the earlier forms of Christian culture, we have to face the humbling realization that the breakout was a necessary condition of the development.

For instance, modern liberal political culture is characterized by an affirmation of universal human rights—to life, freedom, citizenship, self-realization—which are seen as radically unconditional; that is, they are not dependent on such things as gender, cultural belonging, civilizational development, or religious allegiance, which always limited them in the past. As long as we were living within the terms of Christendom—that is, of a civilization where the structures, institutions, and culture were all supposed to reflect the Christian nature of the society (even in the nondenominational form in which this was understood in the early United States)—we could never have attained this radical unconditionality. It is difficult for a "Christian" society, in this sense, to accept full equality of rights for atheists, for people of a quite alien religion, or for those who violate what seems to be the Christian moral code (e.g., homosexuals).

This is not because having Christian faith as such makes you narrow or intolerant, as many militant unbelievers say. We have our share of bigots and zealots, to be sure, but we are far from alone in this. The record of certain forms of militant atheism in this century is far from reassuring. No, the impossibility I was arguing for doesn't lie in Christian faith itself but in the project of Christendom: the attempt to marry the faith with a form of culture and a mode of society. There is something noble in the attempt; indeed, it is inspired by the very logic of Incarnation I mentioned previously, whereby it strives to be interwoven more and more in human life. But as a project to be realized in history, it is ultimately doomed to frustration and even threatens to turn into its opposite.

That's because human society in history inevitably involves coercion (as political society, at least, but also in other ways); it involves the pressure of conformity; it involves inescapably some confiscation of the highest ideals for narrow interests, and a host of other imperfections. There can never be a total fusion of the faith and any particular society, and the attempt to achieve it is dangerous for the faith. Something of this kind has been recognized from the beginning of Christianity in the distinction between church and state. The various constructions of Christendom since then could be seen unkindly as attempts post-Constantine to bring Christianity closer to other, prevalent forms of religion, where the sacred was bound up with and supported the political order. A lot more can be said for the project of Christendom than this unfavorable judgment allows. Nevertheless, this project at its best sails very close to the wind and is in constant danger of turning into a parodic denial of itself.

Thus, to say that the fullness of rights culture couldn't have come about under Christendom is not to point to a special weakness of Christian faith. Indeed, the attempt to put some secular philosophy in the place of the faith—Jacobinism, Marxism—has scarcely led to better results (in some cases, spectacularly worse). This culture has flourished where the casing of Christendom has been broken open and where no other single philosophy has taken its place, but the public sphere has remained the locus of competing ultimate visions.

I also make no assumption that modern rights culture is perfectly all right as it is. On the contrary, it has lots of problems. I hope to come to some of these later. But for all its drawbacks, it has produced something quite remarkable: the attempt to call political power to book against a yardstick of fundamental human requirements, universally applied. As the present pope has amply testified, it is impossible for the Christian conscience not to be moved by this.

This example illustrates the thesis I'm trying to argue here. Somewhere along the line of the last centuries, the Christian faith was attacked from within Christendom and dethroned. In some cases, it was gradually dethroned without being frontally attacked (largely in Protestant countries); but this displacement also often meant sidelining, rendering the faith irrelevant to great segments of modern life. In other cases, the confrontation was bitter, even violent; the dethroning followed long and vigorous attack (e.g., in France, in Spain, that is, largely in Catholic countries). In neither case is the development particularly comforting for Christian faith. Yet we have to agree that it was this process that made possible what we now recognize as a great advance in the practical penetration of the Gospel in human life.

Where does this leave us? Well, it's a humbling experience, but also a liberating one. The humbling side is that we are reminded by our more aggressive secularist colleagues: "It's lucky that the show is no longer being run by you card-carrying Christians, or we'd be back with the Inquisition." The liberating side comes when we recognize the truth in this (however exaggerated the formulation) and draw the appropriate conclusions. This kind of freedom, so much the fruit of the Gospel, we have only when nobody (that is, no particular outlook) is running the show. So a vote of thanks to Voltaire and others for (not necessarily wittingly) showing us this and for allowing us to live the Gospel in a purer way, free of that continual and often bloody forcing of conscience which was the sin and blight of all those "Christian" centuries. The

Gospel was always meant to stand out, unencumbered by arms. We have now been able to return a little closer to this ideal—with a little help from our enemies.

Does acknowledging our debt mean that we have to fall silent? Not at all. This freedom, which is prized by so many different people for different reasons, also has its Christian meaning. It is, for instance, the freedom to come to God on one's own or, otherwise put, moved only by the Holy Spirit, whose barely audible voice will often be heard better when the loudspeakers of armed authority are silent.

That is true, but it may well be that Christians will feel reticent about articulating this meaning, lest they be seen as trying to take over again by giving the (authoritative) meaning. Here they may be doing a disservice to this freedom, and this for a reason they are far from alone in seeing but which they are often more likely to discern than their secularist compatriots.

The very fact that freedom has been well served by a situation in which no view is in charge—that it has therefore gained from the relative weakening of Christianity and from the absence of any other strong, transcendental outlook—can be seen to accredit the view that human life is better off without transcendental vision altogether. The development of modern freedom is then identified with the rise of an exclusive humanism—that is, one based exclusively on a notion of human flourishing, which recognizes no valid aim beyond this. The strong sense that continually arises that there is something more, that human life aims beyond itself, is stamped as an illusion and judged to be dangerous because the peaceful coexistence of people in freedom has already been identified as the fruit of waning transcendental visions.

To a Christian, this outlook seems stifling. Do we really have to pay this price—a kind of spiritual lobotomy—to enjoy modern freedom? Well, no one can deny that religion generates dangerous passions, but that is far from being the whole story. Exclusive humanism also carries great dangers, which remain very underexplored in modern thought.

2

I want to look at some of these dangers here. In doing so, I will be offering my own interpretation of modern life and sensibilities. All this is very much open to contestation, but we urgently need new perspectives in this domain—as it were, Ricci readings of modernity.

The first danger that threatens an exclusive humanism, which wipes out the transcendent beyond life, is that it provokes as reaction an immanent negation of life. Let me try to explain this a little better.

I have been speaking of the transcendent as being "beyond life." In doing this, I am trying to get at something that is essential not only in Christianity but also in a number of other faiths—for instance, in Buddhism. A fundamental idea enters these faiths in very different forms, an idea one might try to grasp in the claim that life isn't the whole story.

One way to take this expression is that it means something like: life goes on after death, there is a continuation, our lives don't totally end in our deaths. I don't mean to deny what is affirmed on this reading, but I want to take the expression here in a somewhat different (though undoubtedly related) sense.

What I mean is something more like: the point of things isn't exhausted by life, the fullness of life, even the goodness of life. This is not meant to be just a repudiation of egoism, the idea that the fullness of my life (and perhaps those of people I love) should be my only concern. Let us agree with John Stuart Mill that a full life must involve striving for the benefit of humankind. Then acknowledging the transcendent means seeing a point beyond that.

One form of this is the insight that we can find in suffering and death—not merely negation, the undoing of fullness and life, but also a place to affirm something that matters beyond life, on which life itself originally draws. The last clause seems to bring us back into the focus on life. It may be readily understandable, even within the purview of an exclusive humanism, how one could accept suffering and death in order to give life to others. On a certain view, that, too, has been part of the fullness of life. Acknowledging the transcendent involves something more. What matters beyond life doesn't matter just because it sustains life; otherwise, it wouldn't be "beyond life" in the meaning of the act. (For Christians, God wills human flourishing, but "thy will be done" doesn't reduce to "let human beings flourish.")

This is the way of putting it that goes most against the grain of contemporary Western civilization. There are other ways of framing it. One that goes back to the very beginning of Christianity is a redefinition of the term *life* to incorporate what I'm calling "beyond life": for instance, the New Testament evocations of "eternal life" and John 10:10, "abundant life."

Or we could put it a third way: acknowledging the transcendent means being called to a change of identity. Buddhism gives us an obvious reason to talk this way. The change here is quite radical, from self to "no self" *(anatta)*. But Christian faith can be seen in the same terms: as calling for a radical decentering of the self, in relation with God ("Thy will be done."). In the language of Abbé Henri Bremond in his magnificent study of French seventeenth-century spiritualities,[2] we can speak of "theocentrism." This way of putting it brings out a similar point to my first way, in that most conceptions of a flourishing life assume a stable identity, the self for whom flourishing can be defined.

So acknowledging the transcendent means aiming beyond life or opening yourself to a change in identity. But if you do this, where do you stand in regard to human flourishing? There is much division, confusion, and uncertainty about this. Historic religions have, in fact, combined concern for flourishing and transcendence in their normal practice. It has even been the rule that the supreme achievements of those who went beyond life have served to nourish the fullness of life of those who remain on this side of the barrier. Thus, prayers at the tombs of martyrs brought long life, health, and a whole host of good things for the Christian faithful; something of the same is true for the tombs of certain saints in Muslim lands, and in Theravada Buddhism, for example, the dedication of monks is turned, through blessings, amulets, and the like, to all the ordinary purposes of flourishing among the laity.

Over against this, there have recurrently been reformers in all religions who have considered this symbiotic, complementary relation between renunciation and flourishing to be a travesty. They insist on returning religion to its purity, and posit the goals of renunciation on their own as goals for everyone, disintricated from the pursuit of flourishing. Some are even moved to denigrate the latter pursuit altogether, to declare it unimportant or an obstacle to sanctity.

But this extreme stance runs athwart a very central thrust in some religions. Christianity and Buddhism will be my examples here. Renouncing—aiming beyond life—not only takes you away but also brings you back to flourishing. In Christian terms, if renunciation decenters you in relation with God, God's will is that humans flourish, and so you are taken back to an affirmation of this flourishing, which is biblically called *agape*. In Buddhist terms, enlightenment doesn't just turn you from the world; it also opens the floodgates of *metta* (loving kindness) and *karuna* (compassion). There is the Theravada concept of the Paccekabuddha, concerned only for his own salvation, but he is ranked below the highest Buddha, who acts for the liberation of all beings.

Thus, outside the stance that accepts the complementary symbiosis of renunciation and flourishing, and beyond the stance of purity, there is a third, which I could call the stance of agape/*karuna*.

Enough has been said to bring out the conflict between modern culture and the transcendent. In fact, a powerful constitutive strand of modern Western spirituality is involved in an affirmation of life. It is perhaps evident in the contemporary concern to preserve life, to bring prosperity, and to reduce suffering worldwide, which is, I believe, without precedent in history.

This arises historically out of what I have called elsewhere "the affirmation of ordinary life."[3] What I was trying to gesture at with this term is the cultural revolution of the early modern period, which dethroned the supposedly higher activities of contemplation and the citizen life and put the center of gravity of goodness in ordinary living, production, and the family. It belongs to this spiritual outlook that our first concern ought to be to increase life, relieve suffering, and foster prosperity. Concern above all for the "good life" smacked of pride, of self-absorption. Beyond that, it was inherently inegalitarian because the alleged "higher" activities could be carried out only by an elite minority, whereas rightly leading one's ordinary life was open to everyone. This is a moral temper to which it seems obvious that our major concern must be our dealings with others, injustice, and benevolence and that these dealings must be on a level of equality.

This affirmation, which constitutes a major component of our modern ethical outlook, was originally inspired by a mode of Christian piety. It exalted practical agape and was polemically directed against the pride, elitism, and, one might say, self-absorption of those who believed in "higher" activities or spiritualities.

Consider the Reformers' attack on the supposedly higher vocations of the monastic life. These vocations were meant to mark out elite paths of superior dedication but were, in fact, deviations into pride and self-delusion. The really holy life for the Christian was within ordinary life itself, living in work and household in a Christian and worshipful manner.

There was an earthly—one might say earthy—critique of the allegedly higher here, which was then transposed and used as a secular critique of Christianity and, indeed, religion in general. Something of the same rhetorical stance adopted by Reformers against monks and nuns is taken up by secularists and unbelievers against Christian faith itself. This allegedly scorns the real, sensual, earthly human good for some purely imaginary higher end, the pursuit of which can lead only to the frustration of the real, earthly good and to suffering, mortification, repression, and so on. The motivations of those who espouse this higher path are thus, indeed, suspect. Pride, elitism, and the desire to dominate play a part in this story, too, along with fear and timidity (also present in the earlier Reformers' story, but less prominent).

In this critique, of course, religion is identified with the second, purist stance or else with a combination of this and the first "symbiotic" (usually labeled superstitious) stance. The third, the stance of agape/*karuna,* becomes invisible. That is because a transformed variant of it has, in fact, been assumed by the secularist critic.

Now one mustn't exaggerate. This outlook on religion is far from universal in our society. One might think that this is particularly true in the United States, with the high rates here of religious belief and practice. Yet, I want to claim that this whole way of understanding things has penetrated far more deeply and widely than simply card-carrying, village atheist–style secularists, that it also shapes the outlook of many people who see themselves as believers.

What do I mean by "this way of understanding"? Well, it is a climate of thought, a horizon of assumptions, more than a doctrine. That means that there will be some distortion in my attempt to lay it out in a set of propositions. But I'm going to do that anyway because there is no other way of characterizing it that I know.

Spelled out in propositions, it would read something like this: (1) that for us life, flourishing, and driving back the frontiers of death and suffering are of supreme value; (2) that this wasn't always so; it wasn't so for our ancestors, or for people in other earlier civilizations; (3) that one of the things that stopped it from being so in the past was precisely a sense, inculcated by religion, that there were higher goals; and (4) that we have arrived at (1) by a critique and overcoming of (this kind of) religion.

We live in something analogous to a postrevolutionary climate. Revolutions generate the sense that they have won a great victory and identify the adversary in the previous régime. A postrevolutionary climate is extremely sensitive to anything that smacks of the ancien régime and sees backsliding even in relatively innocent concessions to generalized human preferences. Thus Puritans saw the return of popery in any rituals, and Bolsheviks compulsively addressed people as "Comrade," proscribing the ordinary appellations "Mister" and "Miss."

I would argue that a milder but very pervasive version of this kind of climate is widespread in our culture. To speak of aiming beyond life is to appear to undermine the supreme concern with life of our humanitarian, "civilized" world. It is to try to reverse the revolution and bring back the bad old order of priorities, in which life and happiness could be sacrificed on the altars of renunciation. Hence, even believers are often induced to redefine their faith in such a way as not to challenge the primacy of life.

My claim is that this climate, often unaccompanied by any formulated awareness of the underlying reasons, pervades our culture. It emerges, for instance, in the widespread inability to give any human meaning to suffering and death, other than as dangers and enemies to be avoided or combated. This inability is not just the failing of certain individuals; it is entrenched in many of our institutions and practices—for instance, the practice of medicine, which has great trouble understanding its own limits or conceiving of some natural term to human life.[4]

What gets lost, as always, in this postrevolutionary climate is the crucial nuance. Challenging the primacy can mean two things. It can mean trying to displace the saving of life and the avoidance of suffering from their rank as central concerns of policy, or it can mean making the claim, or at least opening the way for the insight, that more than life matters. These two are evidently not the same. It is not even true, as people might plausibly believe, that they are causally linked in the sense that making the second challenge "softens us up" and makes the first challenge easier. Indeed, I want to claim (and did in the concluding chapter of *Sources*) that the reverse is the case: that clinging to the primacy of life in the second (let's call this the "metaphysical") sense is making it harder for us to affirm it wholeheartedly in the first (or practical) sense.

But I don't want to pursue this claim right now. I return to it later. The thesis I'm presenting here is that it is by virtue of its postrevolutionary climate that Western modernity is very inhospitable to the transcendent. This, of course, runs contrary to the mainline Enlightenment story, according to which religion has become less credible, thanks to the advance of science. There is, of course, something in this, but it isn't, in my view, the main story. More, to the extent that it is true—that is, that people interpret science and religion as being at loggerheads—it is often because of an already felt incompatibility at the moral level. It is this deeper level that I have been trying to explore here.

In other words, to oversimplify again, in Western modernity the obstacles to belief are primarily moral and spiritual, rather than epistemic. I am talking about the driving force here, rather than what is said in arguments in justification of unbelief.

3

But I am in danger in wandering from the main line of my argument. I have been painting a portrait of our age in order to be able to suggest that exclusive humanism has provoked, as it were, a revolt from within. Before I do this, let us pause to notice how in the secularist affirmation of ordinary life, just as with the positing of universal and unconditional rights, an undeniable prolongation of the Gospel has been perplexingly linked with a denial of transcendence.

We live in an extraordinary moral culture, measured against the norm of human history, in which suffering and death, through famine, flood, earthquake, pestilence, or war, can awaken worldwide movements of sympathy and practical solidarity. Granted, of course, this is made possible by modern media and modes of transportation, not to mention surpluses. These shouldn't blind us to the importance of the cultural-moral change. The same media and means of transport don't awaken the same response everywhere; it is disproportionately strong in ex-Latin Christendom.

Let us grant also the distortions produced by media hype and the media gazer's short attention span, the way dramatic pictures produce the strongest response, often relegating even needier cases to a zone of neglect from which only the cameras of CNN can rescue them. Nevertheless, the phenomenon is remarkable and, for the Christian conscience, inspiring. The age of Hiroshima and Auschwitz has also produced Amnesty International and Médecins sans Frontières.

The Christian roots of all this run deep. There was the extraordinary missionary effort of the Counter-Reformation church, taken up later by the Protestant denominations. Then there were the mass-mobilization campaigns of the early nineteenth century: the antislavery movement in England, largely inspired and led by evangelicals; the parallel abolitionist movement in the United States, also largely Christian inspired. Then this habit of mobilizing for the redress of injustice and the relief of suffering worldwide becomes part of our political culture. Somewhere along the road, this culture ceases to be simply Christian-inspired—although people of deep Christian faith continue to be important in today's movements. Moreover, it needed this breach with the culture of Christendom, as I argued before in connection with human rights, for the impulse of solidarity to transcend the frontier of Christendom itself.

So we see a phenomenon, of which the Christian conscience cannot but say "flesh of my flesh, and bone of my bone" and which is paradoxically often seen by some of its most dedicated carriers as conditional on a denial of the transcendent. We return again to the point our argument was at some time ago, in which the Christian conscience experiences a mixture of humility and unease: the humility in realizing that the break with Christendom was necessary for this great extension of Gospel-inspired actions; the unease in the sense that the denial of transcendence places this action under threat.

This brings us back to the main line of the argument. One such threat is what I am calling the immanent revolt. Of course, this is not something that can be demonstrated beyond doubt to those who don't see it, yet, from another perspective, it is just terribly obvious. I am going to offer a perspectival reading, and in the end we have to ask ourselves which perspective makes the most sense of human life.

Exclusive humanism closes the transcendent window, as though there were nothing beyond—more, as though it weren't a crying need of the human heart to open that window, gaze, and then go beyond; as though feeling this need were the result of a mistake, an erroneous worldview, bad conditioning, or, worse, some pathology. Two radically different perspectives on the human condition: who is right?

Well, who can make more sense of the life all of us are living? If we are right, then human beings have an ineradicable bent to respond to something beyond life. Denying this stifles. But then, even for those who accept the metaphysical primacy of life, this outlook will itself seem imprisoning.

Now there is a feature of modern culture that fits this perspective. This is the revolt from within unbelief, as it were, against the primacy of life—not now in the name of something beyond but really more just from a sense of being confined, diminished by the acknowledgment of this primacy. This has been an important stream in our culture, something woven into the inspiration of poets and writers—for example, Baudelaire (but was he entirely an unbeliever?) and Mallarmé. The most influential proponent of this kind of view is undoubtedly Nietzsche, and it is significant that the most important antihumanist thinkers of our time—for example, Foucault, Derrida, and, behind them, Bataille—all draw heavily on Nietzsche.

Nietzsche, of course, rebelled against the idea that our highest goal is to preserve and increase life, to prevent suffering. He rejects this both metaphysically and practically. He rejects the egalitarianism underlying this whole affirmation of ordinary life. But his rebellion is, in a sense, also internal. Life itself can push to cruelty, to domination, to exclusion, and, indeed, does so in its moments of most exuberant affirmation.

So this move remains within the modern affirmation of life, in a sense. There is nothing higher than the movement of life itself (the Will to Power). But it chafes at the benevolence, the universalism, the harmony, the order. It wants to rehabilitate destruction and chaos, the infliction of suffering and exploitation, as part of the life to be affirmed. Life properly understood also affirms death and destruction. To pretend otherwise is to try to restrict it, tame it, hem it in, deprive it of its highest manifestations, which are precisely what makes it something you can say yes to.

A religion of life that would proscribe death dealing, the infliction of suffering, is confining and demeaning. Nietzsche thinks of himself as having taken up some of the legacy of pre-Platonic and pre-Christian warrior ethics and their exaltation of courage, greatness, elite excellence. Modern life-affirming humanism breeds pusillanimity. This accusation frequently occurs in the culture of counter-Enlightenment.

Of course, one of the fruits of this counterculture was Fascism—to which Nietzsche's influence was not entirely foreign, however true and valid is Walter Kaufman's refutation of the simple myth of Nietzsche as a proto-Nazi. But in spite of this, the fascination with death and violence recurs, for example, in the interest in Bataille, shared by Derrida and Foucault. James Miller's book on Foucault shows the depths of this rebellion against "humanism" as a stifling, confining space one has to break out of.[5]

My point here is not to score off neo-Nietzscheanism as some kind of antechamber to Fascism. A secular humanist might want to do this, but my perspective is rather different. I see these connections as another manifestation of our (human) inability to be content simply with an affirmation of life.

The Nietzschean understanding of enhanced life, which can fully affirm itself, also in a sense takes us beyond life, and in this it is analogous with other, religious, notions of enhanced life (like the New Testament's "eternal life"). But it takes us beyond by incorporating a fascination with the negation of life, with death and suffering. It doesn't acknowledge some supreme good beyond life and, in that sense, sees itself rightly as utterly antithetical to religion.

I am tempted to speculate further and suggest that the perennial human susceptibility to be fascinated by death and violence is at base a manifestation of our nature as *homo religiosus*. From the point of view of someone who acknowledges transcendence, it is one of the places this aspiration beyond most easily goes when it fails to take us there. This doesn't mean that religion and violence are simply alternatives. To the contrary, it has meant that most historical religion has been deeply intricated with violence, from human sacrifice to intercommunal massacres. Most historical religion remains only very imperfectly oriented to the beyond. The religious affinities of the cult of violence in its different forms are indeed palpable.

What it might mean, however, is that the only way to escape fully the draw toward violence lies somewhere in the turn to transcendence—that is, through the full-hearted love of some good beyond life. A thesis of this kind has been put forward by René Girard, for whose work I have a great deal of sympathy, although I don't agree on the centrality he gives to the scapegoat phenomenon.[6]

On the perspective I'm developing here, no position can be set aside as simply devoid of insight. We could think of modern culture as the scene of a three-cornered, perhaps ultimately a four-cornered, battle. There are secular humanists, there are neo-Nietzscheans, and there are those who acknowledge some good beyond life. Any pair can gang up against the third on some important issue. Neo-Nietzscheans and secular humanists together condemn religion and reject any good beyond life. But neo-Nietzscheans and acknowledgers of transcendence are together in their absence of surprise at the continued disappointments of secular humanism, and together also in the sense that its vision of life lacks a dimension. In a third lineup, secular humanists and believers come together in defending an idea of the human good against the anti-humanism of Nietzsche's heirs.

A fourth party can be introduced to this field if we take account of the fact that the acknowledgers of transcendence are divided. Some think that the whole move to secular humanism was just a mistake, which needs to be undone. We need to return to an earlier view of things. Others, among whom I place myself, think that the practical primacy of life has been a great gain for humankind and that there is some truth in the "revolutionary" story: this gain was, in fact, unlikely to come about without some breach with established religion. (We might even be tempted to say that modern unbelief is providential, but that might be too provocative a way of putting it.) But we nevertheless think that the metaphysical primacy of life is wrong and stifling and that its continued dominance puts in danger the practical primacy.

I have rather complicated the scene in the last paragraphs. Nevertheless, the simple lines sketched earlier still stand out, I believe. Both secular humanists and anti-humanists concur in the revolutionary story; that is, they see us as having been liberated from the illusion of a good beyond life and thus enabled to affirm ourselves. This may take the form of an Enlightenment endorsement of benevolence and justice, or it may be the charter for the full affirmation of the Will to Power—or "the free play of the signifier," the aesthetics of the self, or whatever the current version is. But it remains within the same postrevolutionary climate. For those fully within this climate, Transcendence becomes all but invisible.

4

The previous picture of modern culture, seen from one perspective, suggests a way in which the denial of transcendence can put in danger the most valuable gains of modernity, here the primacy of rights and the affirmation of life. This is, I repeat, one perspective among others; the issue is whether it makes more sense of what has been happening over the last two centuries than that of an exclusive, secular humanism. It seems very much to me that it does so.

I now want to take up this danger from another angle. I spoke before about an immanent revolt against the affirmation of life. Nietzsche has become an important figure in the articulation of this, a counterbelief to the modern philanthropy that strives to increase life and relieve suffering. But Nietzsche also articulated something equally disquieting: an acid account of the sources of this modern philanthropy, of the mainsprings of this compassion and sympathy that powers the impressive enterprises of modern solidarity.

Nietzsche's "genealogy" of modern universalism, of the concern for the relief of suffering, of "pity," will probably not convince any people who have the highest examples of Christian agape or Buddhist *karuna* before their eyes. But the question remains very much open as to whether this unflattering portrait doesn't capture the possible fate of a culture that has aimed higher than its moral sources can sustain.

This is the issue I raised very briefly in the last chapter of *Sources*. The more impressed one is with this colossal extension of a Gospel ethic to a universal solidarity, to a concern for human beings on the other side of the globe whom we shall never meet or need as companions or compatriots—or, because that is not the ultimate difficult challenge, the more impressed we are at the sense of justice we can still feel for people we do have contact with and tend to dislike or despise, or at a willingness to help people who often seem to be the cause of their own suffering—the more we contemplate all this, the more surprise we can feel at people who generate the motivation to engage in these enterprises of solidarity, international philanthropy, or the modern welfare state or, to bring out the negative side, the less surprised we are when the motivation to keep these people going flags, as we see in the present hardening of feeling against the impoverished and disfavored in Western democracies.

We could put the matter this way: our age makes higher demands for solidarity and benevolence on people today than ever before. Never before have people been asked to stretch out so far, so consistently, so systematically, so as a matter of course, to the stranger outside the gates. A similar point can be made, if we look at the other dimension of the affirmation of ordinary life, that concerned with universal justice. Here, too, we are asked to maintain standards of equality that cover wider and wider classes of people, bridge more and more kinds of difference, impinge more and more in our lives. How do we manage to do it?

Perhaps we don't manage all that well, and the interesting and important question might run: how could we manage to do it? But at least to get close to the answer to this, we should ask: how do we do as well as we do, which, after all, at first sight seems in these domains of solidarity and justice much better than in previous ages?

1. Performance to these standards has become part of what we understand as a decent, civilized human life. We live up to them to the extent that we do because we would be somewhat ashamed of ourselves if we didn't. They have become part of our self-image, our sense of our own worth. Alongside this, we feel a sense of satisfaction and superiority when we contemplate others—our ancestors or contemporary illiberal societies—who didn't or don't recognize them.

But we sense immediately how fragile this is as a motivation. It makes our philanthropy vulnerable to the shifting fashion of media attention and the various modes of feel-good hype. We throw ourselves into the cause of the month, raise funds for this famine, petition the government to intervene in that grisly civil war, and then forget all about it next month, when it drops off the CNN screen. A solidarity ultimately driven by the giver's own sense of moral superiority is a whimsical and fickle thing. We are far, in fact, from the universality and unconditionality which our moral outlook prescribes.

We might envisage getting beyond this by a more exigent sense of our own moral worth, one that would require more consistency, a certain independence from fashion, and careful, informed attention to the real needs. This is part of what people working in nongovernmental organizations in the field must feel, who correspondingly look down on us TV-image-driven givers, as we do on the lesser breeds who don't respond to this type of campaign at all.

2. But the most exigent, lofty sense of self-worth has limitations. I feel worthy in helping people, in giving without stint. But what is worthy about helping people? It's obvious; as humans, they have a certain dignity. My feelings of self-worth connect intellectually and emotionally with my sense of the worth of human beings. Here is where modern secular humanism is tempted to congratulate itself. In replacing the low and demeaning picture of human beings as depraved, inveterate sinners and in articulating the potential of human beings for goodness and greatness, humanism not only has given us the courage to act for reform but also explains why this philanthropic action is so immensely worthwhile. The higher the human potential, the greater the enterprise of realizing it and the more the carriers of this potential are worthy of our help in achieving it.

However, philanthropy and solidarity driven by a lofty humanism, just as that which was driven often by high religious ideals, has a Janus face. On one side, in the abstract, one is inspired to act. On the other, faced with the immense disappointments of actual human performance and with the myriad ways in which real, concrete human beings fall short of, ignore, parody, and betray this magnificent potential, one experiences a growing sense of anger and futility. Are these people really worthy objects of all these efforts? Perhaps in the face of all this stupid recalcitrance, it would not be a betrayal of human worth, or one's self-worth, to abandon them—or perhaps the best that can be done for them is to force them to shape up.

Before the reality of human shortcomings, philanthropy—the love of the human—can gradually come to be invested with contempt, hatred, aggression. The action is broken off or, worse, continues but is invested now with these new feelings, becoming progressively more coercive and inhumane. The history of despotic socialism (i.e., twentieth-century communism) is replete with this tragic turn, brilliantly foreseen by Dostoyevsky more than a hundred years ago ("Starting from unlimited freedom, I arrived at unlimited despotism")[7] and then repeated again and again with a fatal regularity, through one-party régimes on a macro level, to a host of "helping" institutions on a micro level from orphanages to boarding schools for aboriginals.

The ultimate stop on the line was reached by Elena Ceauşescu in her last recorded statement before her murder by the successor régime: that the Romanian people have shown themselves unworthy of the immense, untiring efforts of her husband on their behalf.

The tragic irony is that the higher the sense of potential, the more grievously do real people fall short and the more severe the turnaround that is inspired by the disappointment. A lofty humanism posits high standards of self-worth and a magnificent goal to strive toward. It inspires enterprises of great moment. But by this very token it encourages force, despotism, tutelage, ultimately contempt, and a certain ruthlessness in shaping refractory human material—oddly enough, the same horrors that Enlightenment critique picked up in societies and institutions dominated by religion, and for the same causes.

The difference of belief here is not crucial. Wherever action for high ideals is not tempered, controlled, and ultimately engulfed in an unconditional love of the beneficiaries, this ugly dialectic risks repetition. And, of course, just holding the appropriate religious beliefs is no guarantee that this will be so.

3. A third pattern of motivation, which we have seen repeatedly, this time occurs in the register of justice rather than benevolence. We have seen it with Jacobins and Bolsheviks and today with the politically correct Left and the so-called Christian Right. We fight against injustices that cry out to heaven for vengeance. We are moved by a flaming indignation against these: racism, oppression, sexism, or leftist attacks on the family or Christian faith. This indignation comes to be fueled by hatred for those who support and connive with these injustices, which, in turn, is fed by our sense of superiority that we are not like these instruments and accomplices of evil. Soon, we are blinded to the havoc we wreak around us. Our picture of the world has safely located all evil outside us. The very energy and hatred with which we combat evil prove its exteriority to us. We must never relent but, on the contrary, double our energy, vie with each other in indignation and denunciation.

Another tragic irony nests here. The stronger the sense of (often correctly identified) injustice, the more powerfully this pattern can become entrenched. We become centers of hatred, generators of new modes of injustice on a greater scale, but we started with the most exquisite sense of wrong, the greatest passion for justice and equality and peace.

A Buddhist friend of mine from Thailand briefly visited the German Greens. He confessed to utter bewilderment. He thought he understood the goals of the party: peace between human beings and a stance of respect and friendship by humans toward nature. What astonished him was all the anger, the tone of denunciation and hatred toward the established parties. These people didn't seem to see that the first step toward their goal would have to involve stilling the anger and aggression in themselves. He couldn't understand what they were up to.

The blindness is typical of modern exclusive secular humanism. This modern humanism prides itself on having released energy for philanthropy and reform; by getting rid of "original sin," of a lowly and demeaning picture of human nature, it encourages us to reach high. Of course, there is some truth in this, but it is also terribly partial and terribly naive because it has never faced the questions I have been raising here: what can power this great effort at philanthropic reform? This humanism leaves us with our own high sense of self-worth to keep us from backsliding, a high notion of human worth to inspire us forward, and a flaming indignation against wrong and oppression to energize us. It cannot appreciate how problematic all of these are, how easily they can slide into something trivial, ugly, or downright dangerous and destructive.

A Nietzschean genealogist can have a field day here. Nothing gave Nietzsche greater satisfaction than showing how morality or spirituality is really powered by its direct opposite—for example, that the Christian aspiration to love is really motivated by the hatred of the weak for the strong. Whatever one thinks of this judgment on Christianity, it is clear that modern humanism is full of potential for such disconcerting reversals: from dedication to others to self-indulgent, feel-good responses, from a lofty sense of human dignity to control powered by contempt and hatred, from absolute freedom to absolute despotism, from a flaming desire to help the oppressed to an incandescent hatred for all those who stand in the way. And the higher the flight, the farther the potential fall.

Perhaps, after all, it's safer to have small goals rather than great expectations and to be somewhat cynical about human potentiality from the start. This is undoubtedly so, but then one also risks not having the motivation to undertake great acts of solidarity and to combat great injustices. In the end, the question becomes a maximum one: how to have the greatest degree of philanthropic action with the minimum hope in mankind. A figure like Dr. Rieu in Camus's *La Peste* stands as a possible solution to this problem. But that is fiction. What is possible in real life?

I said earlier that just having appropriate beliefs is no solution to these dilemmas, and the transformation of high ideals into brutal practice was demonstrated lavishly in Christendom, well before modern humanism came on the scene. So is there a way out?

This cannot be a matter of guarantee, only of faith. But it is clear that Christian spirituality points to one. It can be described in two ways: either as a love or compassion that is unconditional—that is, not based on what you the recipient have made of yourself—or as one based on what you are most profoundly, a being in the image of God. They obviously amount to the same thing. In either case, the love is not conditional on the worth realized in you just as an individual or even in what is realizable in you alone. That's because being made in the image of God, as a feature of each human being, is not something that can be characterized just by reference to this being alone. Our being in the image of God is also our standing among others in the stream of love, which is that facet of God's life we try to grasp, very inadequately, in speaking of the Trinity.

Now, it makes a whole lot of difference whether you think this kind of love is a possibility for us humans. I think it is, but only to the extent that we open ourselves to God, which means, in fact, overstepping the limits set in theory by exclusive humanisms. If one does believe that, then one has something very important to say to modern times, something that addresses the fragility of what all of us, believers and unbelievers alike, most value in these times.

Can we try to take stock of the first leg of our strange Ricci-like journey into the present? The trip is obviously not complete. We have just looked at some facets of modernity: the espousal of universal and unconditional rights, the affirmation of life, universal justice and benevolence. Important as these are, there are plainly others—for instance, freedom and the ethic of authenticity,[8] to mention just two. Nor have I had time to examine other dark features of modernity, such as its drive toward instrumental reason and control. But I think an examination of these other facets would show a similar pattern. So I'd like to try to define this more closely.

In a sense, our journey was a flop. Imitating Ricci would involve taking ourselves a distance from our time, feeling as strange in it as he felt as he was arriving in China. But what we saw as children of Christendom was, first, something terribly familiar—certain intimations of the Gospel, carried to unprecedented lengths—and second, a flat negation of our faith, exclusive humanism. But still, like Ricci, we were bewildered. We had to struggle to make a discernment, as he did. He wanted to distinguish between those things in the new culture that came from the natural knowledge we all have of God and thus should be affirmed and extended, on one hand, and those practices that were distortions and would have to be changed, on the other. Similarly, we are challenged to a difficult discernment, trying to see what in modern culture reflects its furthering of the Gospel, and what its refusal of the transcendent.

The point of my Ricci image is that this is not easy. The best way to try to achieve it is to take at least some relative distance, in history if not in geography. The danger is that we will not be sufficiently bewildered, that we think we have it all figured out from the start and know what to affirm and what to deny. We then can enter smoothly into the mainstream of a debate that is already going on in our society about the nature and value of modernity. As I have indicated,[9] this debate tends to become polarized between "boosters" and "knockers," who either condemn or affirm modernity en bloc, thus missing what is really at stake here, which is how to rescue admirable ideals from sliding into demeaning modes of realization.

From the Christian point of view, the corresponding error is to fall into one of two untenable positions: either we pick certain fruits of modernity, like human rights, and take them on board but then condemn the whole movement of thought and practice that underlies them, in particular the breakout from

Christendom (in earlier variants, even the fruits were condemned), or, in reaction to this first position, we feel we have to go all the way with the boosters of modernity and become fellow travelers of exclusive humanism.

Better, I would argue, after initial (and, let's face it, still continuing) bewilderment, we would gradually find our voice from within the achievements of modernity, measure the humbling degree to which some of the most impressive extensions of a Gospel ethic depended on a breakaway from Christendom, and from within these gains try to make clearer to ourselves and others the tremendous dangers that arise in them. It is perhaps not an accident that the history of the twentieth century can be read either in a perspective of progress or in one of mounting horror. Perhaps it is not contingent that it is the century both of Auschwitz and Hiroshima and of Amnesty International and Médecins sans Frontières. As with Ricci, the Gospel message to this time and society has to respond both to what in it already reflects the life of God and to the doors that have been closed against this life. And in the end, it is no easier for us than it was for Ricci to discern both correctly, even if for opposite reasons. Between us twentieth-century Catholics, we have our own variants of the Chinese rites controversy. Let us pray that we do better this time.

CHAPTER TEN

Notes on the Sources of Violence:
Perennial and Modern

1. The Enigma of Violence

What I want to focus on here is not violence in all its aspects, which include things like domestic violence, criminal violence, and the like. What concerns me is categorical violence, exercised against whole categories of others, people therefore that one may never have known or been in any contact with. I'm thinking of the violence wrought against a scapegoat minority, or phenomena like ethnic cleansing or genocide. And, needless to say, the events of September 11, 2001, come very much to mind.

The fact that these recur so frequently in our "civilized" century is deeply troubling. How can we explain this recurrence? Is it a mere "survival," a "throw-back" to earlier times? What is deeply disturbing about this violence is not just that it occurs at all, that people can be motivated to kill whole categories of others, often on patently irrational grounds, but also (i) that this violence is frequently "excessive," spreading beyond its original target to englobe more victims, or involving atrocities, mutilations; and (ii) that it can involve some language of purification, as one sees with a term like "ethnic cleansing"; while (iii) it can also include a ritual element. These latter two features remind us sometimes of modes of violence which belong to sacrifice in primitive religions, and this can enhance the sense of a "throwback."

Can we understand violence in biological terms, or must we have recourse to the metabiological? I am using "meta-" here in one of the original senses of its use in "metaphysical," what is after or beyond the physical. What is "meta" in "metabiological" in this sense? We could put it this way: the biological is what we share with other animals, that we need food, shelter, sex; and other things that we alone seek, but which serve needs analogous to those of other animals, like clothes for warmth. We enter the realm of the metabiological when we come to needs like that for meaning. Here we can no longer spell out what is involved in biological terms, those with animal analogues, nor state what kinds of things will answer this need, like a sense of purpose, of the importance or value of a certain kind of life, or the like.

We can have sociobiological accounts of both sex and violence. We can imagine that our ancestors had to develop propensities for fighting and, if necessary, killing outsiders to their clans, or otherwise they would not have survived; just as we have such accounts of man-woman pair-bonding, which allowed more offspring to survive. Perhaps we might think that this explains phenomena of today, like nationalist mobilizations to war, which justify ruthless attacks on the enemy; or the importance of love and marriage in all human societies. That our evolutionary history has contributed something to who we are today must in some sense be true. The issue about sociobiology is just how much it explains.

Even sociobiologists must be aware that we have created elaborate metabiological matrices around both love and war; that we have notions about real, profound love; or about war for a just cause. The issue is: do these matrices of self-understanding explain anything important about our behavior in these domains? In particular, these matrices are cultural; they vary between societies. Is it important to understand the variations in order to grasp why we do what we do, or are the main features of our actions in these domains adequately accounted for in terms of our common evolutionary inheritance?

No one would want to deny that these varying cultural matrices are crucial to understanding the moral and religious outlooks of different societies. Perhaps we have to go to the metabiological level in order to understand the ways in which each culture struggles to control the powerful, disruptive forces of sex and violence. But these forces themselves could perhaps be understood in purely biological terms. This way of dividing up the field goes easily along with notions of categorical violence as a "throwback"; culture evolves, and brings higher and higher standards of moral behavior. We now live with and partly by notions of human rights which are incomparably more demanding than those of previous civilizations; but the old drives lurk there still, waiting for certain conditions which will allow them to break out. We can even add a Freudian twist to this take on things: the advance of civilization brings with it ever more stringent standards which place an ever heavier interdict on violent behavior. Previous outlets, like Carnival, riots, public and ritualized executions, bullfights, fox hunting, and other things we now consider barbarous, have all fallen under interdict. This adds to the sense of release and the surge of excitement which accompanies outbreaks of categorical violence, when they are at last permitted.

Within this explanatory division of labor, we could think of explaining the violence itself on a purely biological level, as something that presumably remains the same in human life, even as culture "advances." We note that men, even more frequently young men, are usually the perpetrators, and that can point us to a hormonal explanation. Does it all come down to testosterone? But this seems radically insufficient. It's not that body chemistry is not a crucial factor, but that it never operates alone in human life, only through the meanings that things have for us. The hormonal explanation doesn't tell us why people are susceptible to certain meanings. It could at best explain just the brute fact of violence, whenever we're crossed, for instance; like: why men are violent in relationships, more than women. But even that is questionable, because of findings, like those of James Gilligan, that humiliation is an important causal factor in individual violence.[1]

And when we come to categorical violence, we see that metabiological factors often play a decisive role. Yes, young men are often drawn to it; but we also see that they are all the more drawn when they are unemployed, just hanging around, see no meaningful future for themselves, as in the refugee camps of Palestine. It is the matrices of meaning that their lives are embedded in which offer them the sense of vibrant purpose, which can galvanize them and give significance to their lives. Moreover, it is these matrices which designate who is compatriot, and who is the enemy.

And then there is what I called above, a bit euphemistically, the "excess" which often accompanies this violence. This can give to its perpetrators a "high," which both allows and tempts us beyond all permissible limits. As a perceptive observer puts in a recent book:

> The god-like empowerment over other human lives and the drug of war combine, like the ecstasy of erotic love, to let our senses command our bodies. Killing unleashes within us dark undercurrents that see us desecrate and whip ourselves into greater orgies of destruction. The dead, treated with respect in peacetime, are abused in wartime. They become pieces of performance art. Corpses were impaled in Bosnia on the side of barn doors, decapitated, or draped like discarded clothing over fences. They were dumped into rivers, burned alive in homes, herded into warehouses and shot and mutilated, or left on the roadside. Children could pass them on the street, gape at them and walk on.[2]

We are tempted to explain this kind of outbreak of barbarity in the way this term suggests, as throwbacks to earlier, less civilized times. This is, I believe, a dangerous illusion. But even if it were true, this wouldn't mean that the archaic here is to be explained in terms of biology and not of culture.

We might be tempted to explain the high here, the wild abandon, by the fact that these underlying drives are severely reined in, and even repressed in modern civilization, which makes for the high energy of sudden release when we can let go. And this view may be strengthened when we note how the release of violence can also be a kind of aphrodisiac, unchaining sexual desire, and giving the perpetrators an erotic aura.[3]

But even when we go back to "barbaric" times, prior to the heavy interdictions of modern civilization, we find that these two drives were from the earliest times interwoven with metabiological meaning. Sexuality was connected to the sacred, through rituals like sacred marriage, or temple prostitution. Categorical violence, in the form of war, goes deep in human history. Keegan argues that at first it too was largely ritualized.[4] This limited the damage. (The irony is that "progress" has meant greater destruction, because of "rational" action.) And then there is the rich and varied history of human sacrifice.

So not only our struggles to control unchained sexual desire and violence need to be understood in metabiological terms; these "drives" themselves have to be grasped through the matrices of meaning which give them shape in our lives.

My aim here will be to try to identify some of these meanings. Excess, purification, ritual seem to point back to "primitive" history, religious history, indeed, "primitive" religion. Are these phenomena then mere "throwbacks"?

Yes and no. There is a continuity with this old history; but it is more like a re-edition of an old story in a new version; or the transfer of old melodies to a new register.

2. The Metaphysical Meanings of Violence

How to understand the higher significance, the metaphysical meanings of violence?

As far back as we can look, we see that religion often involves sacrifice, in some fashion or other. We need to give up something; it can be to placate God, or to feed God, or to get His favor. But this demand can also be spiritualized or moralized: we are radically imperfect, below what God wants. So we need to sacrifice the bad parts; or sacrifice something in punishment for the bad parts.

The sense of unworthiness is playing an important role here. But humans have also always been under threat from destructive forces. There are fierce hurricanes, earthquakes, famines, floods. And then also in human affairs, there are wildly destructive people and actions: invasions, sackings, conquests, massacres. Or perhaps we feel the menace of ultimate entropy.

It may be that these are given a meaning by being subsumed into the terrible demands of baleful fate, which is ours in virtue of what we owe to the gods, or of our imperfections. This account fits the Nietzschean idea that we want to give a meaning to suffering in order to make it bearable. But we could also see it the other way around: the sense of lack, of our falling short, is the primitive factor, and we need to give a shape to it. Not: first suffering, then we look for a meaning; so suffering becomes punishment; but: first deserving punishment (or the sense of falling short), so we look for certain modes of suffering to give a shape to all this or a sense of how we can make it up. So our punishment becomes identified with this suffering. In this way, even natural destructive forces come to be seen as wild and full of a spirit of destruction.

Religion can thus mean that we identify with these demands/fates. So we see destruction as also divine, as with Kali-Shiva. And when you can bring yourself to identify with it, you are renouncing all the things which get destroyed, purifying yourself. Wild destruction is given a meaning and a purpose. In a sense it is domesticated, becomes less fearful in one way, even as it acquires part of the terror of the numinous.

This, of course, involves submitting to an external, higher will, purpose, or demand; it requires decentering. But there is also a way of dealing with violence and destruction, and the terrible fears they arouse in us, which gives us a sense of power, of being in control. It is a central part of the warrior ethic. We face down the fear of destruction; we accept the possibility of violent death. We even see ourselves as in advance already claimed by death: we are "dead men on leave." Think of the symbolism in naming a regiment after the death's head: the "Totenkopf" battalion of the Prussian army.

Then we live in the element of violence, but like kings, unafraid, as agents of pure action, dealing death; we are the rulers of death. What was terrifying before is now exciting, exhilarating; we're on a high. It gives a sense to our lives. This is what it means to transcend. In the words of Sudhir Kakar, commenting on his interviews with leaders of the communal riots in Hyderabad: "The excitement of violence becomes the biggest confirmation that one is physically still alive, a confirmation of one's very existence."[5] We are back to the "god-like empowerment" of which Hedges speaks in the earlier quote.

We can see in all warrior cultures how this willingness to risk life is a source of dignity; it is a crucial basis of honor. Those who flinch are dishonored (the basis of the dueling code). We see this reflected in Hegel's Master-Slave dialectic: each side in the duel to the death wishes to prove that they have set themselves above mere life.[6]

Honor in turn intensifies the drive to vendetta. We lose face unless we pay back fully in kind what has been inflicted on us.[7]

Hence one way of dealing with the terror stills the turbulence of violence, either depriving it of its numinous power, or identifying it with some higher such power, which is ultimately benign. The other keeps the numinous force of violence, but reverses the field of fear; what previously made us cower now exhilarates; we now live by it, transcend normal limits through it. This is what animates battle rage, berserker fury, which makes possible feats of arms undreamt of in our everyday mode.

There are also ways of combining these two responses, as in some cultures with human sacrifice. On one hand, we submit to the God to whom we offer our blood, but the sacrificers also become agents of violence; they do it instead of just submitting to it; they wade in blood and gore, but now with sacred intent. Because it combines the two strategies for dealing with this terror, there is nothing more satisfying than a sacred massacre. René Girard has explored this terrain, where religion and violence meet, in a series of pathbreaking works.[8]

Girard sees sacred violence as that of a people finding unanimity again in an attack on a victim. This heals the rifts of mimetic rivalry which otherwise threaten to tear them apart. This is part of the mechanism of sacred violence. But there seem also to be other dimensions: there are

a. the offering of some part of our goods to God, in order to conserve the rest; like Aztec sacrifices to the God of the corn. The numinous dimension enters here with the sense of being fed by the God, spirit, totem, or whatever; then there is the sense that we need to be worthy of this, or to win favor for this. We need to give, and this has to cost us. So sacrifice.

b. the raising of violence to the level of the sacred; making it a way of participating in the power of God; participating in the divine destruction. So we purify ourselves of what seems evil, or merely self-absorbed, in our aggression. This may play a part in ritual sacrifice; but also in the Girardian mechanism of expelling the scapegoat.

c. But then this latter expelling violence also purifies, because it is a way of affirming its presupposition, namely, that that which is expelled, or the enemy, concentrates all evil in itself. It is no longer in us, but outside us.

3. Purity and Contrast

But how does this get focused? How do some people become targets?

We find one account in (1) the mechanism of sacrifice, as described by René Girard. First there is mimetic rivalry, which threatens to dissolve our society; then we forge a unity out of everyone-minus-one, the victim; and this restores the general peace, but at the expense of the person sacrificed. But this is not necessarily extensionally equivalent to (2) the scapegoat mechanism. Here there is a catharsis, expelling evil; with the corollary, that what has been expelled concentrates all evil in itself. Again we give vent to a holy rage. (2) also shores up unity, but against another danger, the sense that the order which binds us is suffering corruption, breakdown, loss of solidity, or of a really firm allegiance.

(3) This sense of our solidity can also be achieved by focusing on an external enemy. The opposition can be expressed in war. But there can also be mimetic rivalry between societies, short of war, as with nineteenth-century imperialism.

How do we understand (2) above? Why do we want to purify or expel evil? And how do people become candidates for the scapegoat role? Who becomes the Outsider?

We define ourselves in terms of our beliefs, ethic, ideal order, or way of life. We need something like this, because we can't just live with chaos: evil, violence, wrong, destruction, desert, meaninglessness. We saw this above, in our manner of dealing with destructive forces.

But we also cope by holding evil to be outside. Seeing oneself as evil, or in moral chaos, disables, paralyzes. We can't admit it, or else we reverse the field and say something like "evil be thou my good," or we go "beyond good and evil," like Nietzsche.

To see the evil or disorder as external, we need a contrast case. The role has been played by "barbarians" and "savages." Of course the contrast case can be distant, people with whom there is no real contact. The contrast helps define us; but also defines evil, failing, lapse, as outside; at least we're not savages, barbarians, Nazis, Stalinists, robbers, murderers, child molesters, et cetera.

Where there is no contact, this can be relatively harmless; although it can license terrible cruelty on contact. Think of the Conquista, the slave trade, the way that they released the joys of aggression.

But then there are also cases where the outsider, the contrast case, can be seen as a vital threat. One way this can happen is that the enemy can be within.

a. This can be because we're tempted, as with some homophobia or myths of the sexual potency of outsiders.

b. Or else the order is under some kind of strain. Then the Girardian scapegoat mechanism defines the outsiders as operating inside; they are polluters. This is typical, for instance, of medieval European anti-Semitism. This kind of thing happened frequently in the enchanted world. The witchcraft craze, another striking example, came at the boundary between the two ages, as disenchantment was under way.

Of course, (a) and (b) can combine.

c. But also the boundary may tend to erode. Emancipation, and the end of the enchanted age, undermined the old sense of a boundary around Christendom.

All these factors came together in the late nineteenth and early twentieth centuries to create a terrible new anti-Semitism. This was motivated by envy, and a felt threat to order which seeks a scapegoat, but at the same time there was also an eroding of the boundary. Because of emancipation, the Jews were no longer outsiders in the same sense, so that the "enemy" was within. This culminated in Nazism, which brought together a renewed warrior ethic, reversing the field of fear and taboo, and mobilized a scapegoat attack, complete with the mythology of expelling evil: holy rage, sacred massacre.

4. Sacred Killing

We can perhaps understand the scapegoat mechanism as a convergence point between two formations: One is the response of assuring ourselves that we are good/ordered by identifying a contrast case from which we separate ourselves. We draw the line between us. This can be expressed in terms of purity/pollution, the self-affirming contrast. The second is the strength and spiritual force which comes from identifying with numinous violence, the violence of the gods—identifying actively, in some form of sacred massacre. We can have the self-affirming contrast without the sacred massacre: for example, the Indian caste system. But when they come together, the result is peculiarly powerful.

This sacred killing powered by the contrast comes in two major forms, if this rather oversimplified grid can be imposed on a host of complex phenomena. There is the scapegoat mechanism as such, where we turn on, kill, or expel an outsider (contrast case) who is within, who has eroded the boundary. And then there is the crusade, where we go to war with a contrast case outside. The latter, in addition to fusing together numinous violence and purity, also realizes another powerful synthesis: it bonds the warrior stance, as lord of death, with the higher cause of numinous violence. So it both gathers all this potentially centrifugal violence into a higher unity, but it also gives the warrior self-affirmation a higher meaning and purpose. The Crusades are a paradigm case, a "solution" to the grinding conflict between Christian faith and the aristocratic-warrior way of life of the rulers of medieval society; to the perpetual battle of the Church to impose a "peace of God" on an unruly and bellicose nobility.

What is involved in identifying with numinous violence? This doesn't mean necessarily identifying with the good. In the pre-axial period, the gods were both benign and malign—some mainly one, some mainly the other, most often both. "Benign" here is measured in relation to ordinary human flourishing: life, health, prosperity, many descendants. We have often to trick and propitiate these higher beings (hence the importance of the "trickster" figure). But the axial revolution tended to place the Divine on the side of the ultimate good; while at the same time redefining this as something which goes beyond what is understood as ordinary human flourishing: Nirvana, Eternal Life.

Some forms of the axial transformation bring God closer to a conception of morality; some code which is justified and made sense of in terms of this higher Good, as with Plato. We also see this with the God invoked by the Prophets, who frequently enjoins us to forget sacrifice, and succor the widows and orphans.

In an important sense, the modern disengaged rational and secular world goes even farther in this direction.

Morality rationalizes. That is, the code is based on some conception of what the good or right is, related to human well-being. This brings with it some notion of responsibility. We punish wrong-doers. We move away from the ambivalences of early religion; where the sacred brought both boon and danger; where we can worship the victim of the sacrifice afterwards.

In the Christian context, identifying with divine violence became identifying with the (of course, righteous) wrath of God. And so we persecute heretics. Also witchcraft trials participate formally in this logic, however based on murderous fantasies.

The modern moral order, and the disenchanted, rationalized world, should put an end to all this. There is no place for the Wrath of God; and even among believers there has been a "Decline of Hell."

But as we see with anti-Semitism, the modern moral order can also intensify evil. Of course, we could argue that this may just be a transition: see the situation of Jews in the contemporary United States and in much of the Western world.

But moralizing may make things worse; and the question arises whether we don't invent new murderous fantasies in the enlightened, disenchanted world. How "dated" is this violence, precisely the "excess"?

Note how in the modern world, the original sacrifice of victims, who are both sacred and dangerous, sources of trouble and of healing, is broken apart. This yields (a) the scapegoat who is entirely wrong, evil, as in witchcraft and anti-Semitism; and (b) the purely righteous sacrifice: the brave young men fallen in battle, an idea ultimately derived from Christianity.[9]

Let's now look at some of the modes of this transition to new forms of categorical violence.

5. Patria o (y) Muerte

First the democratic republic. We are citizens together, ruling as a people. A certain narration is inseparable from this. We can see how often this narrative is violent. It speaks of the violence done to us, and our good counter-violence. This latter often bears the name of Revolution. Well, we might say, here is no myth; that's history; we had to fight. Violence was done to us. True. But does that explain the whole thing?

Let's look at the French Revolution, and its ultimate filiation with the (Castrist) slogan "Patria o muerte." This is a tradition which englobes the Jacobins, then the Bolsheviks.

But first of all we should examine the link between democracy and violence: the Terror.

What is the Terror? Not just violence against enemies. There were real enemies, inner and outer. But beyond what can be explained by these there was first (i) the fabrication of enemies, who didn't need to be seen as such. All those who disagree are seen as traitors, as irremediably hostile, to be eliminated; these included all people of certain classes, regardless of their actual stance. The violence therefore escalates. A similar extension of hostility to whole categories explains the genocidal policy in la Vendée. Then we see (ii) the discourse surrounding this; it is a discourse of purification: getting rid of impurities, poisons. This goes along with a language of virtue, of the purity of Republic. Then third, there was (iii) the quasi-ritual element: public executions.

The Terror can be understood in two perspectives. First, it is a hangover, a continuation. Its source was the culture of popular rebellion in the ancien régime. The people in cities could rise against abuses such as engrossing *(accaparer)*, price gouging, when the price of corn rose steeply. These actions reflected a strong community code, what Edward Thompson has called the "moral economy."[10] The sense was that when things go wrong, someone is to blame. The people could not accept that the impersonal mechanisms of new political economy were the problem. They had to find a villain, either the *accapareur* or perhaps some corrupt royal official. And having identified the evildoer, they exercised a kind of violence against him, going all the way from purely symbolic acts, like burning in effigy, through the destruction of property, to terrible forms of execution. This punishment, whatever it was, was seen as a kind of retribution/purification.[11]

There is no doubt that this popular culture was pushing the Assembly and Convention throughout the early years of the Revolution. Particularly traumatic for the political élites of the Constituent Assembly and the Convention were the frightening popular massacres of September 1792. There seemed no other recourse but to attempt to canalize this violence; simply suppressing it seemed out of the question. As Danton put it a year later in the autumn of 1793: "Soyons terribles pour dispenser le peuple de l'être" ("Let us practice terror, so that the people don't have to"). This in turn created a climate in which the temptation inevitably arose to win every factional struggle by mobilizing this mass sentiment against one's adversaries; but this meant turning the factional struggle into a fight for life. It was a Hobbesian world, in which attack was sometimes the only form of defense, and the attempt to stop the spiral of killings could be fatal, as Danton learned to his cost.

The second perspective stresses the ideology of virtue and purity. This was clearest with Robespierre. For Robespierre, the key to a republican form of government was virtue, defined in a somewhat traditional way as "l'amour exclusif des lois de la patrie." But this in turn was given a Rousseauian gloss: virtue exists when love of self and love of one's country are fused together in one. "L'âme de la République, c'est la vertu, c'est l'amour de la patrie, le dévouement magnanime qui confond tous les intérêts dans l'intérêt général," as he put it in a speech of 1792.[12] In the face of this ideal, all those who fail to rise to these heights, all the "lâches égoïstes," are enemies of the Republic. From this it is just a further step to conclude that the new form can only really come into being when they have been somehow removed from the scene. For "l'esclave de l'avarice ou de l'ambition pourrait-il immoler son idole à la patrie?" This removal would constitute a purification. The high goal thus sought would justify the most stringent means for it would finally "remplir les voeux de la nature, accomplir les destinées de l'humanité, tenir les promesses de la philosophie, absoudre la Providence du long règne du crime de la tyrannie" ("fulfill the aims of nature, accomplish the destiny of humanity, fulfill the promises of philosophy, absolve Providence of the long crime-filled reign of tyranny"; from a speech of February 5, 1794).[13] And in fact, the paroxysm of Terror in June–July 1794 was based on this idea of killing to purify, to bring about reign of virtue.

This philosophy had certain disquieting parallels to the outlook underlying popular revolt. First, all evils were attributable to evildoing. There was no question of explaining certain of the ills of the new society by impersonal factors, deep divergences of interest, or effects of scale. If things were going wrong, there had to be a "plot." The constant reference to a "complot aristocratique" was what united this popular culture and the Jacobin discourse. And the link between the two was forged by agitators like Marat, who kept the public in a state of febrile vigilance against hidden enemies. It followed, second, that those responsible for our misfortunes were actuated by ill will; they were vicious and incorrigible. The Republic of virtue could come about only through their purgation. Eliminating them was a purification of society.

Now in fact I want to argue that both these perspectives are right. The parties of the revolutionary élite were forced into the politics of the Terror by popular pressure and the irresistible temptation that this provided to win over their adversaries through an alliance with the mobilized sections. This in turn gave a place to the Jacobin discourse that it would never have gained on its own, in a struggle with other ideological tendencies unaffected by the pressure from below. But the result of all this was the re-editing of new forms of purificatory violence at the heart of "rational" modernity. The Jacobins tried to channel popular revolt, but they also tried to rationalize and purify it. It would be justified not just by a traditional morality, but by a rational outlook on virtue, moreover, one which promised to lift the condition of humankind to a new plane. By the same token, the victims were to be selected by rational criteria, not just by the instinct of the mob. And the new liturgy of purification was "clean" and scientific, the swift and surgical death by guillotine, as against the cruel play of symbolism of the vengeful crowd, which mixed elements of Carnival hilarity with those of gruesome spectacle. The old melody of scapegoat stigma and purification was replayed in a new register of rational morality. One can argue that the Bolsheviks later followed a similar path.

We feel a paradox here: the ideal is a republic of perfect equality, justice, peace; the most ordered and peaceful regime in history. So how can it treat humanity as an impurity to be purged? Robespierre incarnates the paradox. He voted against the death penalty during the debates of the Constituent Assembly which were designing the future constitution. These two sides of the Revolution have to be brought together. The very idea of high moral purity involved in the true republic means that those who knowingly, willfully refuse it must be truly evil. They are incomprehensible (as real evil is); they are not really human; they are to be likened to animals. (This latter idea was, indeed, built into the Natural Law doctrine, as articulated, say, by Locke, who says that those who violate it may be treated like lions and tigers.) And so finally, those who stand in the way are total enemies, irrevocable enemies, to be simply eliminated.

So royalists and foreigners are enemies. And the enemies of the Republic are "immondices" and "rebuts de l'humanité."[14]

Thus unity was achieved through the purgation of inner enemies (using the scapegoat mechanism). But we can also attain this unity and purity through the defeat of external enemies (through a crusade). These two can be linked. Indeed, it became possible to appease the mechanisms of inner purgation through the common cause of the fight with the Coalition. This is what the Directory was trying to do. Napoleon realized this at its fullest. The Sacred War, the crusade, was the spreading of the Revolution to Europe. But this also subsumes the warrior culture of the ancien régime; and the value of glory on the battlefield was now democratized with the career open to talents.

We can see analogous meanings in the American Civil War. For the abolitionists, one had to purge the evil of slavery. Civil war allowed them to make the inner purge an external one. But we also see the idea of having to atone for sin being invoked in Lincoln's second inaugural address.

The Revolution overcame its inner divisions by a sublimation of the temptation to inner purgation through the glorification of external war/crusade. This is what makes the cult of sacrifice, of the noble dead, so central to the new republican identity. We see a parallel sublimation in Republican historiography. This attempts partly or largely to exculpate Robespierre because of "circumstances," that is, the fight against enemies: the Coalition and La Vendée, passing over in silence what is really troubling in the Terror: our three elements of excess, purification, ritual.

Part of the legacy of this revolution in modern democracy is that the very heart of much patriotism, what gives it a higher dimension, what bonds us to something great, noble, unbreakable, is the memory of the people united in (holy) war. We can't break with the dead; we must keep faith with them, who have sacrificed their lives for us. So "sacrifice" again; and "tombs," and the "sacred." We are bound by the dead. (Benedict Anderson has written very tellingly on this.) This democratization of the cult of dead warrior heroes is consecrated in the tombs of the Unknown Soldier.

This can partly account for the ease with which modern, rational, "civilized" Europe sleepwalked into the hecatomb of the First World War; and thus incurred the massive destabilization which followed for Western civilization.

This seems connected to the democratic state. But it also mutates into nationalism.

6. Nations and Cleansing

The Republic supposes a new agency: the people or nation. The nation can be conceived as a previously existing cultural/linguistic entity. The nation is different from other nations, but this difference is unlike that between what we formerly understood as religious communities or civilizations. The nation is supposedly one among equal others. This notion of one among others even survives the metastasis of fascism, minus the recognition of equality. But the idea still is that this way is only for us. What is jettisoned is the universalism.

The nation is founded on "will," like the Republic. But this in turn appeals to "identity."

The modern horizon is described in terms of the contemporary notion of "identity." Identities, unlike the fixed horizons in which premoderns moved, are (a) one among many, and (b) they need to be defined, further determined. On the individual level, (b) holds because of the ethic of authenticity, the idea that each human being, or each group, has their own way of being human. On the social level, (b) holds largely because of the sense that either (i) we have never really had our moment, our identity has been suppressed by some intolerant majority or some rapacious empire; and/or (ii) as history changes, we have to redefine ourselves to continue our authentic form of life. We have to tell our story in a way which culminates in today's identity. Hence comes all the bad "invented" history of which Hobsbawm speaks.[15]

Identity goes together with recognition. The new horizon has to be defined; and so a lack of recognition can derail us at a very profound level. The more powerful and more successful have a unique power; their gaze can disturb, devastate, hamper the identity definition of those less secure—and the more so in that we are frequently divided about what our identity consists in.

Now given that a nation, an identity, is one among others, why doesn't this solve the problem? Can we not all learn to tolerate each other? This may be hard because following "our" way, and being able to do so, becomes all the more important in our age. It's our way of being human in the modern world. And this may be destabilized from outside by a lack of recognition or a crass misrecognition.

But the tensions are also intensified by democracy, or sovereignty based on popular will, which requires a political identity. We have to be on our own, in order to live out our way; and we can't be challenged by others who might want to dispute its legitimacy.

This tension is increased by our attachment to a specific territory, which is an essential feature of the modern state. Our identity becomes linked to this land. The peculiar nature of modern identities is that, although they are always the result of creative redefinition, they are also linked to a given, be it language, or tradition, but also soil, and sometimes also religion, as a historic marker.[16]

In this context, others become an identity threat. This is a form of the threat to the integrity of our social order, discussed earlier, and which has been occurring since time out of mind. But this is of a new kind, and in an unprecedented context. The context is that of popular sovereignty (PopSov), which may make it impossible to live with a minority as a safe, subordinate population, for instance, as dhimmis were under the Caliphate. They are a legitimacy challenge, hence an identity threat. Under the principle of PopSov, the political identity of a state must be ultimately decided by the people. But if we include this minority in our "people," they may easily vote to change our political identity; if we exclude them, then we deny them one of the recognized rights of modernity, that of citizenship in a sovereign people. In either case, they may want to dismember our territory. So we have to assimilate them, or else when they remain refractory, we are tempted to ethnically cleanse them. This is why the twentieth century has been both the age of rising democracy, and the heyday of ethnic cleansing. This is not a mere coincidence.[17]

We feel an analogous painful paradox to the one that arises around the Terror. Since the enframing idea of modern nationalism is that each people is one among others, that everybody has a right to be, how can we exclude others like this, much less kill them? Because by being here, they are aggressors. Here's where the benign context itself turns malignant. The benign context is that every people has the right to their identity. Where something goes wrong, and this picture can't be carried out, it is because there is some aggression by some against others; some are depriving others. We can't live our identity fully on "our" territory; so we're being prevented by those who stand in our way. They are the aggressors. Hence we are victims.

The framework of equal peoples is the basis for the universal appeal to the victim scenario today. This is a remarkable fact about our age. Where my identity is being blocked, this must be because I am being unfairly put upon—unfair, in the light of the ideal order of equal coexisting identities. We are victims, underdogs.

We can see how the modern moral order intensifies the conflict by moralizing it. Take the bad old days where we faced aggressive outsiders—say, in the Balkans, where Christians faced Muslims. The Muslims are our traditional enemies, Turks. On top of that they have embraced an incomprehensibly perverse form of religion. On both these grounds, it is "normal" that they attack us and we defend ourselves. It is part of the order of things; they can't do other than attack, under either description. No hard feelings, in a sense.

But now in the modern universalist moral understanding, they are equal participants in the same moral order, which they have violated, while we are innocent. They are in something of the category that a renegade from our side might have been under the old dispensation. They have read themselves out of the protections of the order. They are bad, evil; they have the worst coming to them. And fighting them is a way of giving expression to our innocence. Modern morality gives the cachet to the victim scenario.

There is a double moralization here: first, rights are violated; second, democracy or PopSov itself is more highly moralized; it requires self-responsible action; it calls forth duty *(Pflicht)*.

Modern moralizing ups the ante; it gives group hatred a new charge of holy rage. Hence Communists, who can wipe out kulaks. And now this is transposed to certain older rivalries with different peoples in the Balkans.

So we hate these people as aggressors. Take the Muslims in India, in the eyes of the Bharatiya Janata Party (BJP): We can burn down their mosque, because it's taken to be a fruit of aggression. Among less sophisticated members of the party the discourse becomes very crude: Muslims don't belong here; send them to Pakistan. So the framework of PopSov and coexisting equal peoples can generate its own grounds for hate and even killing. This is our paradox. Note how much even the Nazis took over this framework, negating the universal order, of course, but inheriting a particular identity. They then played extensively on the sense of grievance. Germany was unfairly blamed for the war; before that, unfairly denied its place in the sun. Hitler railed against the "Diktat" of Versailles. He invoked the "stab in the back." Let us purge the traitorous elements, invoking Holy Anger.

The logic is: We have been unfairly treated, so we can strike out. This is invoked by most terrorist movements today. We see lots of it today in Palestine, and not just on one side.

Note the terrible alchemy: how does an identity threat become a mortal threat? A minority can be an identity threat by just being there. So this is turned first into an act of aggression. But wanting to wipe us out as a political identity is close to wanting to wipe us out tout court. It just needs some believable atrocity stories. But there are always men, often young, who are ready to act out aggression, violence, as discussed above. So atrocities are committed. Some group cleanses village A; then a counter-group cleanses village B. Then we have believable atrocity stories to tell on both sides. The mechanisms of vendetta take over. What is tragic here is the terrible destruction of trust, even where people have lived together for years and intermarried. And then it spirals downward.

This must also be put in the context where elites are trying to recruit the masses to their concern with nation or identity. Provoking massacre can further this enterprise.

And so we have Bosnia in the 1990s; or the Punjab in 1947. But the recent history of the Punjab, where the killing between Sikhs and Hindus seems to have come to an end, shows that this terrible dialectic is not irresistible. Sometimes the fabric of cross-community relations can win out over the attempts to destroy it by massacre.

What I'm suggesting here is that nationalist violence can be put in the broader category of violence generated by the threat surrounding modern collective identities. In this context, we can see the analogies with movements like Al Qaeda, where the sense of threat is mobilized around not a nation, or a language, but an idealized Islam, supposedly undermined or attacked by "Jews and Christians," or by America. And it is understandable that in what we often class a "nationalist" movement, the main marker of difference can be a "religious" one, as with the BJP in India.

The move of modern history has been toward a wider and wider recruitment of people into such identities, from out of earlier, more local, identifications, focusing often on kinship systems, clans or tribes. These early identities are often defined by "networks," where people stand in a dense web of relations, linked to many people but in a different fashion to each one; as in a kinship system, where I am related to one person as father, another as son, another as cross cousin, and so forth. In contrast, modern political identities are "categorial": they bind people together in virtue of their falling together under a category, like Serb, or American, or Hindu, where we all relate in a uniform way to a whole.[18]

This movement seems to be accelerating. A host of factors are drawing people away from the earlier network identities; not only the efforts of élites to mobilize them, but also migration, or the effects of globalization, either through the spread of media, or by undermining older ways in which we make our living. Migration can mean being mixed with unfamiliar others, not knowing how they will react, being unable to reconstitute the older way of life. Loss of the older forms of making a living can undermine our dignity, our identity, induce a sense of loss and helplessness. The decay of the old often brings disorientation, or feelings of humiliation and lowered self-worth.

In these circumstances, a new categorial identity can offer people something very precious: not only a direction, an orientation, but also a sense of (collective) agency. We are no longer just to suffer a sense of helplessness before dimly understood global forces, but we are to be mobilized against named and identified ills. It is not surprising, in the light of what was said above about scapegoating and holy wars, that these ills are often attributed to a source in an enemy, who wants to destroy us and whom we must combat. We should measure how overwhelming the temptation can be to go along with this kind of (often murderous) mobilization, where it comes across as the only way to recover orientation, dignity, agency.[19]

Violence around categorial identities is one of the most pressing dangers of the coming century. It could literally destroy our world.

7. Morally Driven Hate/Exclusion

I have been dealing with what we all recognize as the terrible cases of group violence. But along with this, we have in the modern world highly peaceful societies, where the level of everyday violence is quite low. Indeed, in some of these societies, the level is very much lower than in earlier epochs. Compare France under the ancien régime and the France of today, for instance. So modern civilization presents the paradoxical spectacle of societies which in their "normal" internal operation, sometimes through long periods, are more pacific than any others in history, while at moments at their boundaries, so to speak, they wage hugely destructive wars, which can then in certain circumstances engulf them; and on occasion they can even fall prey to civil wars. If we just look at the long periods of internal peace, we can nourish the hope that modern civilization will tame war and violence, which is one of the great aspirations of liberalism. If we think of the terrible destruction of modern war and ethnic cleansing, we are plunged in gloom.

But how does it work when it works? Our civilization is built on an idea of order, between equal rights-bearing individuals, whose action should be directed to mutually enriching and mutually enhancing forms of self-realization. This is not just an idea but something that has become entrenched in the institutions and practices, political and economic, in the social imaginary, and in the disciplined training of modern subjects. As an established order, it does a great part of the time succeed in keeping us in line, and preventing the worst of mutual violence and threats; though we sense how fragile this order can be, and in particular how much depends on the inclusion of masses of people within the mutually enhancing mechanisms of the economy and welfare state.

But even when it works at its best, the modern order can secrete various forms of contempt and exclusion, which replicate some of the motives which break out in violence in less restrained contexts. In earlier sections, I was dealing with the survival of full-blooded violence, sometimes highly ritualized, always with a purificatory element. But there is also subviolent hatred, even where violence is contained. Let's look at some of these.

Look at another facet of the modern moral order: Many of the disciplines which constitute it, as well as the intellectual outlook which it inculcates, call for an objectifying, disengaged stance; one that seems consonant with a "scientific" perspective. This justifies itself for a host of reasons, but not least because it separates us from the wild, and metaphysical-religious sense of the numinous power of violence and sexuality. It thus should preserve us from going along with holy anger. And it also allows us to see calmly and coolly what needs to be done. We can become calm, collected, clear-seeing agents of healing, of reform, of betterment.

Objectification easily goes along with the therapeutic stance. When we come to treat our problem cases, we are not dealing with evil, but with different kinds of pathology, which we have to heal. We seem at the antipodes of Robespierre, with his pervasive moralization. But the therapeutic perspective justifies us in dealing with these people as charges, patients. Evil has a certain dignity, that of deep investment in a distorted vision of the good. Pathology is just incapacity. This is the source of a potentially paradoxical deviation, in which a benign stance turns malign.

This deviation can also be seen from another side. The disengaged stance is also a distancing strategy. Thinking of these people as sick, pathological, needing therapy, makes them other, not real interlocutors, not really embodying alternative possibilities which can draw us, tempt us. So there is an analogue here to the earlier mode of identifying the outsider as a contrast case, as another species, as savages. They exist in another space, behind a turn in the road, where they aren't our interlocutors.

But their not being real interlocutors, fully responsible beings, also can mean that you can treat them roughly, even perhaps that you have to. You want to make them shape up. We don't need to be too tender with them. See how the politically correct in the United States treat those classed as "homophobes" or "misogynists." We can use shaming as an instrument of coercion, or compulsory re-education, or worse.

The benignity of exculpation can become the malignity of rough, contemptuous treatment. But perhaps also something worse is happening. Perhaps that holy anger is recurring here. So one distancing strategy can become the cover for another, much older one. Dostoyevsky has given a penetrating depiction of this turn, for instance, in *The Possessed*. Disengagement can become partly a sham, a comedy we play with/on ourselves.

The two kinds of hate, identity-driven and liberally-morally driven (or Jacobin- or Bolshevik-moral driven), can combine: for example, in the crusade of our civilization against Milošević's Serbia. My invoking this example does not mean that I think the policy was wrong. That is another and very difficult and complex issue. But right or wrong, we should be clear about the kinds of feeling mobilized behind it in our societies. And some of these are troubling.

In a quite different, one might say even opposite way, this distancing, disengaged stance encouraged by the modern moral order can generate violence, as a reaction to it. There is an attempt in our modern liberal world to work directly against the mechanisms I have been describing in the previous sections, to take all the numinous out of violence, and make life tame and ordered. This means also leveling down the hero. From almost the beginning this has provoked a reaction to what is seen as a leveling down of life, a denial of heroism and greatness. The denial of violence is also that of warrior dignity, and this has seemed to many too high a price to pay. Perhaps the most influential figure who has given voice to this reaction, and in one of the most radical forms, is Friedrich Nietzsche. His influence is ubiquitous in the higher culture of the last century. And this kind of reaction has also erupted onto the political scene, with Fascism. It goes on today without benefit of either high culture or Fascist ideology in outbreaks of violence, by, for example, skinheads.[20]

8. Le Souci de la Victime

The defeat of the Nazis left room for another powerful narrative. This is what Girard has called "le souci de la victime" (the concern for the victim).[21] This shows the tremendous force of the New Testament in our culture. But this impact is also captured and deflected.

There is a narrative of the modern world, like and parallel to that of the growth of freedom, democracy, which sees us as redressing all the historical wrongs and inequalities. We rescue and recognize all the victims. But this is connected to the moralism of meting out punishment to perpetrators, victimizers. Which justifies wreaking punishment/vengeance on them. So another powerful engine of destruction is born; and an equally paradoxical one.

The concern for the victim is, in Girard's view, a crucial feature of the modern world. How to understand this? Partly in terms of the modern moral order; but this is not sufficient. This provides the standard of equality and mutual respect, against which victims are identified. But there is something more in le souci de la victime.

This is the idea that we move toward the ultimate order through the unmasking of hidden victimizations, which are covered up, denied, and have to be denounced. So it is part of the dynamic theory of how we move toward the order, not prescribed by the order itself—which was, after all, originally used for the justification of the established structures, or what underlay these structures, the proper constitution of power, as, for instance, with Locke.

This concern is a more direct borrowing from Christianity. The Gospel involves a reversal, showing the victim to be innocent; it points toward the raising up of victims, of the despised and rejected. Various religious reforms involve taking this idea of reversal farther. The Reformation itself is one such. As also is modern humanism, which defends ordinary human life against persecution in the name of "higher" modes of spirituality.

So this élan becomes part of the ethic of our time, the political ethic. Joined to a view of history, this yields a transfigured version of the modern moral order as eschatological idea.

This becomes, on one hand, a great force for battling against injustices. But it also becomes a way of drawing lines, denouncing enemies, the evil ones.

Hence comes the powerful cachet of victimhood. This would have been very surprising to our ancestors living by the warrior ethic; no Greek warrior would insist that he was the oppressed serf. Friedrich Nietzsche would be doubly horrified. Why this cachet? Because my being the victim means that you are the victimizer. I am pure. Claiming victimhood is an assertion of our purity; we are all right. Moreover, our cause is good, so we can fight, inflict a violence which is righteous: a holy violence. Hence we have a right to do terrible things, which others haven't. Here is the logic of modern terrorism. Even the Nazis made use of a proto-form of this. I have suffered terribly at the hands of others; *therefore* I can wreak mayhem.

All this depends on the external placing of evil, thus on good/evil. Now according to the outlook of modern disengaged objectification, we are not supposed to believe in evil. But this is subverted by the fact that the very definition of ourselves as people of good will seems to require that we see the others as evil. So we show our goodness in fighting against the bad guys.

Even for the greatest disenchanters, evil has to return to their picture, because they have a sense of themselves as actuated by a pure, good will, and have to see somewhere their opponent, pure evil. So there are new myths of evil, which are not admitted to be such theoretically. They have to fit the myths of good will. These are Rousseauian: we are all good au fond. So whence comes evil? Bad upbringing, perhaps, or from being abused. But this reduces the agents of bad to victims themselves, people who have become incapacitated. The therapeutic perspective dominates. Somewhere we need to find an object to expel, one which concentrates evil. At first, this can just be the "system," as remarked by David Martin.[22] But the search for evil needs in the end wills. So it alights on those who support the system. These are the really evil people, the real victimizers, even though they may be hiding this from themselves; they may not realize it; they may think the system totally "normal"; even so, perhaps especially so, they are the evil ones. They can be treated as pure enemies.

9. Vanquishing Violence

Does all this tell us anything about how to lessen violence or how to get rid of it? Have we a hope of doing this?

Let us consider first what I will call the Kant hypothesis, although he wasn't the only person to hold it. This is the view that ordered, democratic societies will become less violent; won't go to war with each other, and presumably won't suffer civil wars. There is some truth to this, as we saw in Section 7. Modern disciplined order has had some effect. But the peace is fragile, for a host of reasons; partly because there are certain success conditions of economic order; partly because of tensions of exclusion and rivalry, which remain sub-violent, but generate hostility. And then there is the problem that some societies have great trouble acceding to the category of ordered democratic polities.

So any program to overcome violence must contain at least two objectives: (1) to build such ordered democratic polities; (2) to try to make their benefits spread as wide as possible, for example, by preventing the formation of desperate, excluded groups; particularly young men.

But this program seems radically incomplete, in face of the carryover or better re-editing of older forms of scapegoating, and holy war, to our day. Can we do something to fight these? Is there a third element to our program?

One answer might be: let us note the metaphysical/religious roots of this categorial, purificatory violence. So how do we get rid of it? It is religious, or, at least, metaphysical, and so we will get rid of it only by totally overcoming the religious dimension in our existence. The problem up to now is that many of the main builders of a supposedly secular republic, the Lenins and the Robespierres, have not really liberated themselves from this incubus as they thought they had.

But it seems clear from the phenomena reviewed above that just proposing some nonreligious theory, like modern humanism, doesn't really do the trick. The religious forms seem to reconstitute themselves. So we would have to fight for a real, thoroughgoing disenchantment, a total escape from religion. How do we do this? Is this really possible?

This suggests another answer: all the above shows that the religious dimension is inescapable. Perhaps there is only the choice between good and bad religion. Now there is good religion. For instance, there is Girard's take on the Old and New Testaments, as the source for a counter-story to the scapegoat narrative, which shows the victim to be innocent. And we can say something analogous about the Buddha, for instance.

Thus we can point to the Gospel picture of a Christian counter-violence: a transformation of the energy which usually goes into scapegoat purification; transformation which reaches to overcome the fear of violence not by becoming lord of it, by directing it as an annihilating force against evil, but which aims, rather, to overcome fear by offering oneself to it; responding with love and forgiveness, thereby tapping a source of goodness and healing.

But an analogous point to the one just made about humanism can be made about these religious positions. Just adopting some religion, even in principle a "good" one, doesn't do the trick. Christianity is responsible for le souci de la victime in the modern world. But we see how this can be colonized by the religion of purification of scapegoats. Do we want to protest that this is a secularized variant? Then how about the long, dreary, and terrible history of Christian anti-Semitism? Seen in a Girardian light, this is a straight betrayal of the Gospel; a 180-degree reversal. So just believing in these "good" religions doesn't overcome the danger.

Both sides have the virus, and must fight against it.

Where does this leave us in our search for a third kind of measure in our program? We noticed a pattern in the paradoxical reversals above. The goodness which inhabits our goal, or our vision of order, is somehow undone when it comes to struggling to realize it. Robespierre's republic without a death penalty somehow energizes a program of escalating butchery; and similar things can be said for the Herderian order of nations coexisting in diversity, or the goal of rescuing all victims. The paradox is that the very goodness of the goal defines us, its builders and defenders, as good, and hence opens the way to our grounding our self-integrity on a contrast case who must be as evil as we are virtuous. The higher the morality, the more vicious the hatred and hence destruction we can, indeed, must, wreak. When the crusade comes to its fullness in the moralism of the modern world, even the last vestiges of chivalric respect for an enemy, as in the days of Saladin and Richard Coeur de Lion, have disappeared. There is nothing left but the grim, relentless struggle against evil.

There is no general remedy against this self-righteous reconstitution of the categorizations of violence, the lines drawn between the good and evil ones which permit the most terrible atrocities. But there can be moves, always within a given context, whereby someone renounces the right conferred by suffering, the right of the innocent to punish the guilty, of the victim to purge the victimizer. The move is the very opposite of the instinctive defense of our righteousness. It is a move which can be called forgiveness, but at a deeper level, it is based on a recognition of common, flawed humanity.

In Dostoyevsky's *Possessed,* the slogan of the scientistic revolutionaries who would remake the world is "no-one is to blame." That is the slogan of the disengaged stance to reality, of the therapeutic outlook. What this slogan hides is another stance which projects the blame entirely on the enemy, giving ourselves the power to act that comes from total righteousness. Opposed to this is the insight that Dostoyevsky's potentially redemptive characters struggle to reach: "we are all to blame." It is this restoration of a common ground which defines the kind of move I am talking about. It opens a new footing of co-responsibility to the erstwhile enemy.

It is best to see this in an example. And a very remarkable one stands in our recent history. I'm thinking of Nelson Mandela. There was great political wisdom there. Because following the only too understandable path of revenge would have made it impossible to build a new, democratic society. It is this reflection which has pushed many leaders after periods of civil war in history to offer amnesties. But there was more than that here. Amnesties have the flaw that they usually involve suppressing the truth or at least consciousness of the terrible wrongs that have been done, which therefore fester in the body politic. Mandela's answer was the Truth and Reconciliation Commission, one which is meant to bring terrible deeds to light, but not necessarily in a context of retribution. Moreover, the deeds to be brought to light were not only those of the former ruling side. Here is the new ground of co-responsibility which this Commission offered.

No one knows whether this will ultimately work. A move like this goes against the utterly understandable desire for revenge by those who have suffered, as well as all the reflexes of self-righteousness. But without this, and even more without the extraordinary stance of Mandela from his first release from prison, what I have called his renunciation of the rights of victimhood, the new South Africa might never have even begun to emerge from the temptations to civil war which threatened and are not yet quite stilled.[23]

There are other examples in this whole field of transitions from despotic and often murderous régimes, inseparable from the spread of democracy. The Polish case also comes to mind, and the strong advice of people like Adam Michnik to forego the satisfactions of retribution in the name of building a new society. The Dalai Lama's response to Chinese oppression in Tibet offers another striking case.

It is in moves of this kind that we need to seek the third element in our program. They follow neither of the lines suggested above, in that, although they clearly derive a lot from the religious traditions involved, they are not necessarily the fruit of a personal religious faith. But however motivated, their power lies not in suppressing the madness of violent categorization, but in transfiguring it in the name of a new kind of common world.

10. Coda: Religion and Violence

What does all this tell us about the relation of violence and religion? Is religion the main instigator of categorical violence? Well, it would certainly appear that since the very beginning of human culture, religion and violence have been closely interwoven. And there certainly are cases today where the connection holds.

But on the other hand, when we examine more closely some of what we might call the religious uses of violence, in particular its appeal to scapegoat mechanisms, and the self-affirmation of our purity by identifying all evil with the enemy outside (or provisionally within, but who therefore needs to be expelled), we find that all this can easily survive the rejection of religion, and recurs in ideological-political forms which are resolutely lay, even atheist. Moreover, it recurs in them with a kind of false good conscience, an unawareness of repeating an old and execrable pattern, just because of the easy assumption that all that belonged to the old days of religion, and therefore can't be happening in our enlightened age.

But more than this, if religion has from the beginning been bound up with violence, the nature of the involvement has changed. In archaic, pre-axial forms, ritual in war or sacrifice consecrates violence; it relates violence to the sacred, and gives a kind of numinous depth to killing and the excitements and inebriation of killing, just as it does through other rituals for sexual desire and union.

With the coming of "higher," post-axial religions, this kind of numinous endorsement is more and more withdrawn. We move toward a point where, in some religions, violence has no more place at all in the sanctified life, or its analogues. This is true of Christianity, of Buddhism; and we find in Hinduism a steady spread of the demands of *ahimsa,* so that even jatis who were previously allowed and expected to kill animals now try to rise through abandoning these practices.

But nevertheless, as we have seen, various forms of sanctified and purifying violence recur. We get a phenomenon like the Crusades. This is profoundly at odds with the spirit of Christianity, which early medieval bishops were aware of on one level, when they tried to restrain noble bellicosity, and proclaim truces of God. But they were nevertheless induced to preach support for the Crusades by falling back into scapegoat mode: the infidel was the servant of darkness, and therefore deserved the most utter hostility, in the name of the Prince of Peace.

There remained nonetheless a profound ambivalence. These holy campaigns were supposed to act under stricter rules than existed in ordinary war; clergy were not themselves supposed to take up arms. But basically, we have the mold in which Robespierre will later fit. An enemy of the death penalty once the Republic is established, he is willing to wade through blood to set it up in all its purity. The illusion is that one can separate before and after, within and without. Purity will reign within and during the Kingdom/Republic, but savagery will rule our relations to what is without or before this realm of peace.

Post-axial religions often suffer from a profound bad faith, even hypocrisy. But in this, they are not alone. They have been followed by some of the militant secular ideologies in this, as well as that hybrid phenomenon of our day, confessionally defined nationalisms (e.g., the BJP's Hindutva and George Bush's nation bringing liberty to the world, following God's will for humanity).

But these higher religions and ideologies want to use violence to affirm their own purity, while depriving it altogether of the numinous depth that archaic and earlier forms endowed it with. Violence is ugly and savage, but it must nevertheless be used by noble and dedicated warriors. We are constantly repressing one half of what we deep down know about the world of war and violence; and we are constantly being surprised when confronted by the savagery of our own valiant soldiers, be it in My Lai or Abu Ghraib.

The modern world, religious and secular, suffers from a deep rift in its self-understanding, an ideological blindness of massive proportions; something which is brilliantly anatomized by Chris Hedges in his harrowing book.[24]

CHAPTER ELEVEN

The Future of the Religious Past

A S I START to write this essay, I have great misgivings. Predicting the future is an extremely foolish enterprise. Historians and social scientists know this well, and refrain from it entirely. And although philosophers haven't got much of a reputation for accuracy to lose, it still seems somewhat foolhardy.

But I still my fears by telling myself that what I'm actually going to do is give an account of the vectors of religious development up to the present (itself a high-risk, accident-prone enterprise), from which some very tentative guesses might be made about their continuation or alteration in the future. In short, I'm going to lay out some pieces of my "grand narrative." I do not share the postmodern aversion to grand narratives; this is because I think that we all operate with our own (perhaps confused) version and that the best way to deal with this is to be as clear as we can about the one we're relying on, while being as open as possible to objections to and criticisms of it.

I'm going to rely on my narrative to suggest a set of categories of religious life—belief, devotion, ritual, community, and so on—whose present and future condition, developments, transformations we can then assess.

Before I start, let me make one more disclaimer. My narrative is for the most part about only one civilization: the "West," aka Europe and its extensions, earlier known as "Latin Christendom." There will be some reference to a wider frame in order to set the developments in this civilization in context. And then I will make some tentative remarks about possible parallels with / differences from other parts of the world. But the main story line I will be leaning on is the "Western" one.

I

One of the main vectors over the last six or seven centuries in this civilization has been a steadily increasing emphasis on a religion of personal commitment and devotion, over against forms centered on collective ritual. We can see this in the growth of a more Christocentric religion in the High Middle Ages. It is further evident both in devotional movements and associations, like the Brethren of the Common Life in the fifteenth century, and in the demands made by Church hierarchies and leaders on their members. An early example of the latter is the decision of the Lateran Council in 1215 to require all the faithful to confess to a priest and be shriven, so as to receive communion at least once a year.

From that point on, the pressure to adopt a more personal, committed, inward form of religion continues, through the preaching of the mendicant friars and others, through the devotional movements mentioned above, reaching a new stage with the Reformation. The point of declaring that salvation comes through faith was radically to devalue ritual and external practice in favor of inward adherence to Christ as Savior. It was not just that external ritual was of no effect, but that relying on it was tantamount to a presumption that we could control God. The Reformation also tended to delegitimate the distinction between fully committed believers and other, less devoted ones. As against a view of the church in which people operating at many different "speeds" coexisted with religious "virtuosi," to use Max Weber's term, on one end, and ordinary intermittent practitioners, on the other, all Christians were expected to be fully committed.

This movement toward the personal, committed, and inward didn't exist only in the Protestant churches. There is a parallel development in the Counter-Reformation, with the spread of different devotional movements and attempts to regulate the lives of the laity according to more and more stringent models of practice. The clergy were reformed; their training was upgraded; they were expected to reach out and demand a higher level of personal practice from their flocks. A striking figure illustrates this whole movement: in the history of Catholic France, the moment at which the level of practice, as measured by baptisms and Easter Communions, reaches its highest has been estimated to fall around 1870.[1] This is well after the anticlericalism of the Revolution and its attempts at de-Christianization, after a definite movement toward unbelief has set in among the educated classes. In spite of this incipient loss, the apogee of practice comes this late because it stands at the end of a long process in which ordinary believers have been preached at, organized, sometimes bullied into patterns of practice that reflect more personal commitment.

They have been pressed, we might be tempted to say, into "taking their religion seriously." To take my religion seriously is to take it personally, more devotionally, inwardly, more committedly. Just taking part in external rituals, those which don't require the kind of personal engagement that, for example, auricular confession, with its self-examination and promises of amendment, entails, is devalued in this understanding. This isn't what religion is "really about."

Now, a striking feature of the Western march toward secularity is that it has been interwoven from the start with this drive toward personal religion, as has frequently been remarked.[2] The connections are multiple. It is not just that the falling off of religious belief and practice has forced a greater degree of reflection and commitment on those who remain. This has perhaps been evident in more recent times. It is much more that the drive to personal religion has itself been part of the impetus toward different facets of secularization. It was this drive, for instance, that powerfully contributed to the disenchantment of the world of spirits and higher forces in which our ancestors lived. The Reformation and Counter-Reformation repressed first magical practices and then those facets of traditional Christian sacramental ritual that they began to deem magical: for Calvinists, this even included the Mass. Later, at the time of the early American republic, a separation of church and state was brought about, mainly to give space for, and avoid the contamination of, personal religion, which itself had been given a further impetus through the Great Awakening.

We might identify two closely connected vectors here: toward personal commitment and toward the repression of what came to be understood as "magical" elements in religion: practices that suppose and draw upon various intra-cosmic spirits, good or bad, and higher powers inhering in things (e.g., relics). I want to use the word *disenchantment* for this movement of repression. This is a narrower sense than the word often bears, for it is frequently synonymous with the sidelining of religion as such, but it has some warrant in the original Weberian term, *Entzauberung*.

I want now to place this double vector (commitment-disenchantment) in an even deeper and broader historical context, the rise and forward march of what Jaspers called "axial" religions and spiritualities. The whole sweep, as it continues up to and into Western modernity, can be seen as a great disembedding of the merely human, and even of the human individual. The full scale of this millennial change becomes clearer if we focus first on some features of the religious life of earlier, smaller-scale societies, insofar as we can trace this. There must have been a phase in which all humans lived in such small-scale societies, even though much of the life of this epoch can only be guessed at.

If we focus on what I will call "early religion" (which covers partly what Robert Bellah, for example, calls "archaic religion"),[3] we note how profoundly these forms of life "embed" the agent. They do so in three crucial ways.

First, socially: in Paleolithic, and even certain Neolithic, tribal societies, religious life is inseparably linked with social life. The primary agency of important religious action—invoking, praying to, sacrificing to, or propitiating gods or spirits, coming close to these powers, getting healing or protection from them, divining under their guidance, and so on—involved the social group as a whole, or some more specialized agency recognized as acting for the group. In early religion, we primarily relate to God as a society.

We see both aspects of this in, for example, ritual sacrifices among the Dinka, as they were described a half century ago by Godfrey Lienhardt. On the one hand, the major agents of the sacrifice, the "masters of the fishing spear," are in a sense "functionaries," acting for the whole society, while on the other, the whole community becomes involved, repeats the invocations of the masters, until everyone's attention is focused and concentrated on the single ritual action. It is at the climax "that those attending the ceremony are most palpably members of a single undifferentiated body." This participation often takes the form of possession by the divinity being invoked.[4]

Nor is this just the way things happen to be in a certain community. This collective action is essential for the efficacy of the ritual. You can't mount a powerful invocation of the divinities like this on your own in the Dinka world. This "importance of corporate action by a community of which the individual is really and traditionally a member is the reason for the fear which individual Dinka feel when they suffer misfortune away from home and kin."[5]

This kind of collective ritual action, where the principal agents are acting on behalf of a community, which also in its own way becomes involved in the action, seems to figure virtually everywhere in early religion and continues in some ways up till our day. Certainly it goes on occupying an important place as long as people live in an "enchanted" world—a world of spirits and forces, prior to what I am calling "disenchantment." The medieval ceremony of "beating the bounds" of the agricultural village, for instance, involved the whole parish and could only be effective as a collective act of this whole.

This embedding in social ritual usually carries with it another feature. Just because the most important religious action was that of the collective, and because it often required that certain functionaries—priests, shamans, medicine men, diviners, chiefs, and so on—fill crucial roles in the action, the social order in which these roles were defined tended to be sacrosanct. This is, of course, the aspect of religious life that was most centrally identified and pilloried by the radical Enlightenment. The crime laid bare here was the entrenchment of forms of inequality, domination, and exploitation through their identification with the untouchable, sacred structure of things. Hence the longing to see the day "when the last king had been strangled in the entrails of the last priest." But this identification is in fact very old and goes back to a time when many of the later, more egregious, and vicious forms of inequality had not yet been developed, before there were kings and hierarchies of priests.[6]

Behind the issue of inequality and justice lies something deeper, which touches what we would call today the "identity" of the human beings in those earlier societies. Just because their most important actions were the doings of whole groups (tribe, clan, subtribe, lineage), articulated in a certain way (the actions were led by chiefs, shamans, masters of the fishing spear), they couldn't conceive themselves as potentially disconnected from this social matrix. It would probably never even occur to them to try.

What I'm calling "social embeddedness" is thus partly an identity thing. From the standpoint of the individual's sense of self, it means the inability to imagine oneself outside a certain matrix. But it also can be understood as a social reality, and here it refers to the way we together imagine our social existence, for instance, that our most important actions are those of the whole society, which must be structured in a certain way to carry them out. And we can see that it is growing up in a world where this kind of social imaginary reign sets the limits to our sense of self.

Embedding in society also brings with it an embedding in the cosmos. In early religion, the spirits and forces with whom we are dealing are in numerous ways intricated in the world. We can see examples of this aplenty if we refer back to the enchanted world of our medieval ancestors: although the God they worshipped transcended the world, they nevertheless also had to do with intracosmic spirits, and they dealt with causal powers that were embedded in things: relics, sacred places, and the like. In early religion, even the high gods are often identified with certain features of the world, and where the phenomenon that has come to be called "totemism" exists, we can even say that some feature of the world, an animal or plant species, for instance, is central to the identity of a group.[7] It may even be that a particular geographical terrain is essential to our religious life. Certain places are sacred. Or the layout of the land speaks to us of the original disposition of things in sacred time. We relate to the ancestors and to this higher time through this landscape.[8]

This is something that we, products of the vector toward the personal, the committed, the inward, have trouble understanding. In Latin Christendom, movement along this vector tended more and more to privilege belief, as against unthinking practice. "Secular" people have inherited this emphasis and often propound an "ethics of belief,"[9] where it can be seen as a sin against science or epistemic decency to believe in God. So we tend to think of our differences from our remote forbears in terms of different *beliefs,* whereas there is something much more puzzling involved. It is clear that for our forbears, and for many people in the world today who live in a similar religious world, the presence of spirits and of different forms of possession is no more a matter of (optional, voluntarily embraced) belief than is for me the presence of this computer and its keyboard at the tips of my fingers. Like my ancestors, I confront a great deal in the inner workings of this computer that I don't understand (almost everything, in fact) and about which I could be induced by experts to accept various theories. But the encounter with a computer is not a matter of "belief." It's a basic feature of my experience.

So it must have been for Celestine, interviewed by Birgit Meyer,[10] who "walked home from Aventile with her mother, accompanied by a stranger dressed in a white northern gown." When asked afterward, her mother denied having seen the man. He turned out to be the Akan spirit Sowlui, and Celestine was pressed into his service. In Celestine's world, perhaps the identification of the man with this spirit might be called a "belief," in that it came after the experience in an attempt to explain what it was all about. But the man accompanying her was just something that happened to her, a fact of her world.

We have great trouble getting our minds around this, and we rapidly reach for intra-psychic explanations, in terms of delusions, projections, and the like. But one thing that seems clear is that the whole situation of the self in experience is subtly but importantly different in these worlds and in ours. We make a sharp distinction between inner and outer, what is in the "mind" and what is out there in the world. Whatever has to do with thought, purpose, human meaning, has to be in the mind, rather than in the world. Some chemical can cause hormonal change and thus alter the psyche. There can be an aphrodisiac, but not a love potion, that is, a chemical that determines the human/moral meaning of the experience it enables. A phial of liquid can cure a specific disease, but there can't be phials like those brought back from pilgrimage at Canterbury, which contained a miniscule drop of the blood of Thomas à Becket, which could cure anything and which could even make us better people—that is, the liquid was the locus not of certain specific chemical properties but of a generalized beneficence.

Modern Westerners have a clear boundary between mind and world, even mind and body. Moral and other meanings are "in the mind." They cannot reside outside, and thus the boundary is firm. But formerly it was not so. Let us take a well-known example of influence inhering in an inanimate substance, as this was understood in earlier times. Consider melancholy: black bile was not the cause of melancholy; it embodied, it *was,* melancholy. The emotional life was porous here; it didn't simply exist in an inner mental space.

Our vulnerability to the evil, the inwardly destructive, extended to more than just spirits that are malevolent. It went beyond them to things that have no wills but are nevertheless redolent with evil meanings.

See the contrast. A modern is feeling depressed, melancholy. He is told: it's just your body chemistry, you're hungry, or there is a hormone malfunction, or whatever. Straightway he feels relieved. He can take a distance from this feeling, which is ipso facto declared not justified. Things don't really have this meaning; it just feels this way, which is the result of a causal action utterly unrelated to the meanings of things. This step of disengagement depends on our modern mind/body distinction, and the relegation of the physical to being "just" a contingent cause of the psychic.

A premodern may not be helped by learning that his mood comes from black bile, because this doesn't permit a distancing. Black bile *is* melancholy. Now he just knows that he's in the grips of the real thing.

Here is the contrast between the modern, bounded self—I want to say the "buffered" self—and the "porous" self of the earlier, enchanted world. What difference does this make?

It is a very different existential condition. The last example about melancholy and its causes illustrates this well. For the modern, buffered self, it is possible to take a distance from, to disengage from, everything outside the mind. My ultimate purposes arise within me, the crucial meanings of things are defined in my responses to them. These purposes and meanings may be vulnerable to manipulation in various ways, including the use of chemicals; but this can in principle be met with a counter-manipulation: I avoid distressing or tempting experiences, I don't shoot up the wrong substances, and so on.

This is not to say that the buffered understanding necessitates taking this stance. It is just that it allows it as a possibility, whereas the porous one does not. By definition, for the porous self, the sources of its most powerful and important emotions are outside the "mind"; better put, the very notion that there is a clear boundary, allowing us to define an inner base area, grounded in which we can disengage from the rest, has no sense.

As a bounded self I can see the boundary as a buffer, such that the things beyond don't need to "get to me," to use the contemporary expression. That's the sense in my use of the term *buffered* here. This self can see itself as invulnerable, as master of the meanings of things for it.

These two descriptions get at, respectively, the two important facets of this contrast. First, the porous self is vulnerable: to spirits, demons, cosmic forces. And along with this go certain fears, which can grip it in certain circumstances. The buffered self has been taken out of the world of this kind of fear: for instance, the kind of thing vividly portrayed in some of the paintings of Bosch.

True, something analogous can take its place. These images can also be seen as coded manifestations of inner depths, repressed thoughts and feelings. But the point is that, in this quite transformed understanding of self and world, we define these as inner, and naturally, we deal with them very differently. And, indeed, an important part of the treatment is designed to make disengagement possible.

Perhaps the clearest sign of the transformation in our world is that today many people look back to the world of the porous self with nostalgia, as though the creation of a thick emotional boundary between us and the cosmos were now lived as a loss. The aim is to try to recover some measure of this lost feeling. So people go to movies about the uncanny in order to experience a frisson. Our peasant ancestors would have thought us insane. You can't get a frisson from what is really in fact terrifying you.

The second facet is that the buffered self can form the ambition of disengaging from whatever is beyond the boundary and of giving its own autonomous order to its life. The absence of fear can be not just enjoyed but seen as an opportunity for self-control or self-direction.

The boundary between agents and forces is fuzzy in the enchanted world, and the boundary between mind and world is porous, as we see in the way that charged objects can influence us. I have just been speaking about the moral influence of substances, like black bile. But a similar point can be made about the relation to spirits. The porousness of the boundary emerges here in the various kinds of "possession," all the way from a full takeover of a person, as with a medium, to various kinds of domination by, or partial fusion with a spirit or God.[11] Here again, the boundary between self and other is fuzzy, porous. And this has to be seen as a fact of *experience,* not a matter of "theory" or "belief."

Besides this relation to society and the cosmos, we can see in early religion a third form of embedding in existing reality. This is what makes the most striking contrast with what we tend to think of as the "higher" religions. What people ask for when they invoke or placate divinities and powers is prosperity, health, long life, fertility; what they ask to be preserved from is disease, dearth, sterility, premature death. There is a certain understanding of human flourishing here that we can immediately understand and that, however much we might want to add to it, seems to us quite "natural." What there isn't, and what seems central to the later, "higher" religions, is the idea that we have to question radically this ordinary understanding, that we are called in some way to go beyond it.

This is not to say that human flourishing is the end sought by all things. The divine may also have other purposes, some of which have a harmful impact. There is a sense in which, for early religions, the divine is never simply well disposed toward us. The gods (or some of them) may also be in certain ways indifferent; or there may also be hostility, or jealousy, or anger, which we must deflect. Although benevolence, in principle, may have the upper hand, this process may have to be helped along by propitiation or even by the action of "trickster" figures. But through all this, what remains true is that divinity's benign purposes are defined in terms of ordinary human flourishing. Again, there may be capacities that some people can attain, that go way beyond the ordinary human ones, which, say, prophets or shamans have. But these in the end subserve well-being as ordinarily understood.

By contrast, with Christianity or Buddhism, for instance, there is a notion of our good that goes beyond human flourishing, that we may gain even while failing utterly on the scales of human flourishing, even *through* such a failing (like dying young on a cross), or that involves leaving the field of flourishing altogether (ending the cycle of rebirth). The paradox of Christianity, in relation to early religion, is that it seems to assert the unconditional benevolence of God toward humans—there is none of the ambivalence of early divinity in this respect—and yet it redefines our ends so as to take us beyond flourishing.

In this respect, early religion has something in common with modern exclusive humanism, and this has been felt and expressed in the sympathy of many modern, post-Enlightenment people for "paganism." "Pagan self-assertion," thought John Stuart Mill, was as valid as "Christian self-denial," if not more so.[12] (This is related to, but not quite the same as, the sympathy felt for "polytheism.") What makes modern humanism unprecedented, of course, is the idea that this flourishing involves no relation to anything higher.

Now, as earlier mentions suggest, I have been speaking of "early religion" to contrast what many people have called "postaxial" religions.[13] The reference is to what Karl Jaspers called the "axial age,"[14] the extraordinary period in the last millennium b.c.e. when various "higher" forms of religion appeared seemingly independently in different civilizations, marked by such founding figures as Confucius, Gautama, Socrates, and the Hebrew prophets.

The surprising feature of the axial religions, compared with what went before, what would in other words have made them hard to predict beforehand, is that they initiate a break in all three dimensions of embeddedness: social order, cosmos, human good. Not in all cases and all at once. Perhaps in some ways Buddhism is the most far-reaching, because it radically undercuts the second dimension: the order of the world itself is called into question, because the wheel of rebirth means suffering. In Christianity, there is something analogous: our world is disordered and must be made anew. But some postaxial outlooks keep the sense of relation to an ordered cosmos, as we see in very different ways with Confucius and Plato. They mark a distinction, however, between this and the actual, highly imperfect social order, so that the close link to the cosmos through collective religious life is made problematic.

Perhaps most fundamental of all is the revisionary stance toward the human good in axial religions. More or less radically, they all call into question the received, seemingly unquestionable understandings of human flourishing, and hence inevitably also the structures of society and the features of the cosmos through which this flourishing was supposedly achieved.

We might try to put the contrast in this way: unlike postaxial religion, early religion involved an acceptance of the order of things, in the three dimensions I have been discussing. In a remarkable series of articles on Australian Aboriginal religion, W. E. H. Stanner speaks of "the mood of assent" that is central to this spirituality. Aboriginals have not set up the "kind of quarrel with life" that springs from the various postaxial religious initiatives.[15] The contrast is in some ways easy to miss, because Aboriginal mythology, in relating the way in which the order of things came to be in the Dream Time—the original time out of time, which is also "everywhen"—contains a number of stories of catastrophe, brought on by trickery, deceit, and violence, from which human life recouped and reemerged, but in an impaired and divided fashion, so that there remains the intrinsic connection between life and suffering, and unity is inseparable from division. Now this may seem reminiscent of other stories of a Fall, including that related in Genesis. But in contrast to what Christianity has made of this, for the Aboriginals the imperative to "follow up" the Dreaming, to recover through ritual and insight their contact with the order of the original time, relates to this riven and impaired dispensation, in which good and evil are interwoven. There is no question of reparation of the original rift, or of a compensation, or of making good the original loss. What is more, ritual and the wisdom that goes with it can even bring them to accept the inexorable and "celebrate joyously what could not be changed."[16] The original catastrophe doesn't separate or alienate us from the sacred or Higher, as in the Genesis story; rather, it contributes to shaping the sacred order we are trying to "follow up."[17]

Now, axial religion didn't do away with early religious life. In many ways, features of this continued in modified form to define majority religious life for centuries. Modifications arose, of course, not just from the axial formulations but also from the growth of large-scale, more differentiated, often urban-centered societies, with more hierarchical organization and embryonic state structures. Indeed, it has been argued that these, too, played a part in the process of disembedding, because the very existence of state power entails some attempt to control and shape religious life and the social structures it requires, and hence undercuts the sense of intangibility surrounding this life and these structures.[18] I think there is a lot to this thesis, and, indeed, I invoke something like it later on. But for the moment I want to focus on the significance of the axial period.

This doesn't at once totally change the religious life of whole societies. But it does open new possibilities of disembedded religion: seeking a relation to the divine or the Higher, which severely revises notions of flourishing or even exceeds them, and can be carried through by individuals on their own and/or in new kinds of sociality, uncoupled from the established sacred order. So monks, Bhikkus, sanyassi, devotees of some avatar or God, strike out on their own, and from this spring unprecedented modes of sociality: initiation groups, sects of devotees, the sangha, monastic orders, and so on.

In all these cases, there is some kind of hiatus, difference, or even break in relation to the religious life of the larger society. This may itself be to some extent differentiated, with different strata or castes or classes, and a new religious outlook may lodge in one of them. But very often a new devotion may cut across all of these, particularly where there is a break in the third dimension, with a "higher" idea of the human good.

There is inevitably a tension here, but there often is also an attempt to secure the unity of the whole, to recover some sense of complementarity between different religious forms. So those who are fully dedicated to the "higher" forms, while on the one hand can be seen as a standing reproach to those who remain in the earlier forms, supplicating the powers for human flourishing, nevertheless can, on the other hand, also be seen as in a relationship of mutual help with them. The laity feed the monks, and by this they earn "merit," which can be understood as taking them a little farther along the "higher" road, but also serves to protect them from the dangers of life and to increase their health, prosperity, and fertility.

So strong is the pull toward complementarity that even in those cases where a "higher" religion took over the whole society, as we see with Buddhism, Christianity, and Islam—so that there is supposedly nothing left to contrast with—the difference between dedicated minorities of religious "virtuosi" (to use Max Weber's term) and the mass religion of the social sacred, still largely oriented to flourishing, survived or reconstituted itself, with the same combination of strain, on the one hand, and hierarchical complementarity, on the other.

From our modern perspective, with 20:20 hindsight, it appears as though the axial spiritualities were prevented from producing their full disembedding effect because they were, so to speak, hemmed in by the force of the majority religious life, which remained firmly in the old mold. They did bring about a certain form of religious individualism, but this was what Louis Dumont calls the charter for "the individual outside the world": that is, it was the way of life of elite minorities, and it was in some ways marginal to, or in some tension with, the "world," meaning not just the cosmos, which is ordered in relation to the Higher or the Sacred, but also society, which is ordered in relation to both the cosmos and the sacred.[19] This "world" was still a matrix of embeddedness, and it still provided the inescapable framework for social life, including that of the individuals who tried to turn their backs on it, insofar as they remained in some sense within its reach.

What had yet to happen was for this matrix to be itself transformed, to be made over according to some of the principles of axial spirituality, so that the "world" itself would come to be seen as constituted by individuals. This would be the charter for "the individual in the world," in Dumont's terms, the agent who in his ordinary "worldly" life sees himself as primordially an individual, that is, the human agent of Western modernity.

Now, I believe this project of transformation has been carried out in Latin Christendom. The vectors of commitment and disenchantment came about through a series of attempts at reform. The goal was to make over the lives of Christians, and also their social order, in a thoroughgoing way so as to make them conform to the demands of the Gospel. I am talking not of a particular, revolutionary moment but of a long, ascending series of attempts to establish a Christian order, in which the Reformation is a key phase. These attempts show a progressive impatience with older modes of postaxial religion, in which certain collective, ritualistic forms of earlier religions existed in uneasy coexistence with the demands of individual devotion and ethical reform, which came from the "higher" revelations. In Latin Christendom, the attempt was to recover and impose on everyone a more individually committed and Christocentric religion of devotion and action, and to repress or even abolish older, supposedly "magical" or "superstitious" forms of collective ritual practice. Social life was to be purged of its connection to an enchanted cosmos, and all vestiges removed of the old complementarities, between spiritual and temporal, between life devoted to God and life in the "world," between order and the chaos on which it draws.

This project was thoroughly disembedding just by virtue of its form or mode of operation: the disciplined remaking of behavior and social forms through objectification and an instrumental stance. But its ends were also intrinsically concerned to disembed. This is clear with the drive to disenchantment, which destroys the second dimension of embeddedness, but we can also see it in the Christian context. In one way, Christianity here operates like any axial spirituality; indeed, it operates in conjunction with another such, namely, Stoicism. But there also were specifically Christian modes. The New Testament is full of calls to leave or relativize solidarities of family, clan, society, to be part of the Kingdom. We see this seriously reflected in the way certain Protestant churches operated, where one was not simply a member by virtue of birth but had to join by answering a personal call. This in turn helped give force to a conception of society as founded on a covenant, and hence as ultimately constituted by the decision of free individuals.

This is a relatively obvious filiation. But my thesis is that the effect of the Christian, or Christian-Stoic, attempt to remake society in bringing about the modern "individual in the world" was much more pervasive and multitracked. It helped to nudge first the moral, then the social imaginary in the direction of modern individualism. I believe that this is what we see emerging in the new conception of moral order of seventeenth-century natural law theory. This was heavily indebted to Stoicism, and its originators were arguably the Netherlands neo-Stoics Justus Lipsius and Hugo Grotius. But this was a Christianized Stoicism, and a modern one, in the sense that it gave a crucial place to a willed remaking of human society.

We could say that both buffered identity and the project of reform contributed to disembedding. Embeddedness, as I said above, is both a matter of identity—the contextual limits to the imagination of the self—and of the social imaginary: the ways we are able to think or imagine the whole of society. But the new buffered identity, with its insistence on personal devotion and discipline, increased distance from, disidentification with, even hostility to, the older forms of collective ritual and belonging, while the drive to reform came to envisage their abolition. Both in their sense of self and in their project for society, the disciplined elites moved toward a conception of the social world as constituted by individuals.

So to the two linked vectors of personal commitment and disenchantment we can add two more, also closely related, those of the movement to reform and of disembedding, or the rise of modern individualism. These are connected to a fifth, which I think is one of the basic features of modern secularity, if not the basic one.

What do we mean when we speak of Western modernity as "secular"? There are all sorts of ways of describing it: separation of religion from public life, decline of religious belief and practice. While one cannot avoid touching on these, my main interest here lies in another facet of our age: belief in God or in the transcendent in any form is contested; it is an option among many; it is therefore fragile, for some people in some milieus very difficult, even "weird." Five hundred years ago in our civilization, it wasn't so. Unbelief was off the map for most people, close to inconceivable. But that description also applies to the whole of human history outside the modern West.

What had to happen for this kind of secular climate to come about? First, there had to develop a culture that marks a clear division between the "natural" and the "supernatural," and second, it had to come to seem possible to live entirely within the natural. The first was something to strive for, but the second came about at first quite inadvertently.

Very briefly, I believe that it came about as the by-product of the series of actions in the vector I have called reform. The attempt was to make individuals and their society over so as to conform to the demands of the Gospel. Allied with a neo-Stoic outlook, this became the charter for a series of attempts to establish new forms of social order, drawing on new disciplines (Foucault enters the story here), which helped to reduce violence and disorder, and to create populations of relatively pacific and productive artisans and peasants, who were more and more induced/forced into the new forms of devotional practice and moral behavior, be this in Protestant England, Holland, the American colonies, Counter-Reformation France, or the Germany of the *Polizeistaat* ("police state").

My hypothesis is that this new creation of a civilized, "polite" order succeeded beyond what its first originators could have hoped for, and that this in turn led to a new reading of what a Christian order might be, one that was seen more and more in "immanent" terms (polite, civilized order *is* Christian order). This version of Christianity was shorn of much of its "transcendent" content, and was thus open to a new departure, in which the understanding of good order (what I call the "modern moral order") could be embraced outside of the original theological, providential framework, and in certain cases even against it (as with Voltaire, Gibbon, and, in another way, Hume).

Disbelief in God arises in close symbiosis with this belief in a moral order of rights-bearing individuals, who are destined (by God or Nature) to act for mutual benefit, an order that thus rejects the earlier honor ethic, which exalted the warrior, as it also tends to occlude any transcendent horizon. (We see one good formulation of this notion of order in Locke's *Second Treatise.*) This understanding of order has profoundly shaped the forms of social imaginary that dominate in the modern West: the market economy, the public sphere, the sovereign "people."[20]

In other words, the crucial change here could be described as the possibility of living within a purely immanent order; that is, the possibility of really conceiving/imagining ourselves within such an order, one that could be accounted for on its own terms, and thus that leaves belief in the transcendent as a kind of "optional extra"—something it had never been before in any human society. This presupposed the clear separation between natural and supernatural as a necessary condition, but it needed more than that. A social order sustained by a social imaginary having that purely immanent character had to develop; we see it arising, for instance, in the modern forms of the public sphere, the market economy, and the citizen state.

I want to continue a little further laying out features of the narrative I propose, because they are necessary to the categories I want to put forward for understanding our present and future. It is all too easy to see the modern citizen state as in its very nature an implicit rejection of transcendence. This is easier if we focus too exclusively on the great, climactic event of the French Revolution. Sovereignty comes from the people, not from the king; but the king's sovereignty comes from above, from God; so democracy is already an implicit rejection of God. This, of course, can easily fit into a rival master narrative that I want to reject, one in which secularity, defined as the falling off of belief and practice, is generated in a linear way by the conditions of modern life.

On the contrary, what strikes me is the way these conditions steadily destabilize earlier forms, which in turn leads to a "recomposition" of religious life, to use Danièle Hervieu-Léger's expression.[21] The form of divine presence in the French monarchy, which was deeply interwoven with the enchanted world (e.g., the king's two bodies, the power to cure scrofula), was indeed a casualty of the French Revolution. When Charles X in 1825 tried to have the full, original liturgy of Coronation at Rheims Cathedral, it all fell terribly flat. This was perhaps the final gasp of Bourbon nostalgia.

But with advancing disenchantment, especially in Protestant societies, another model of divine presence took shape, with relation to both the cosmos and the polity. In this the notion of design was crucial. To take the cosmos, there was a shift from the enchanted world to a cosmos conceived in conformity with post-Newtonian science, in which there is absolutely no question of higher meanings being *expressed* in the universe around us. But there is still, with someone like Newton himself, for instance, a strong sense that the universe declares the glory of God. This is evident in its design, its beauty, its regularity, but also in its having evidently been shaped in a way conducive to the welfare of God's creatures, particularly of ourselves, the superior creatures who cap it all off. Now the presence of God no longer lies in the sacred, because this category fades in a disenchanted world. But He can be thought to be no less powerfully present through His design.

This presence of God in the cosmos is matched by another idea: His presence in the polity. Here an analogous change takes place. The divine isn't there in a king who straddles the planes. But it can be present to the extent that we build a society that plainly follows God's design. This can be filled in with an idea of moral order seen as established by God, in the way invoked, for instance, in the American Declaration of Independence: men have been created equal and have been endowed by their creator with certain inalienable rights.

The idea of moral order that is expressed in this declaration and that has since become dominant in our world is what I have been calling the modern moral order. It is quite different from the orders that preceded it because it starts from individuals and doesn't see these as set a priori within a hierarchical order, outside of which they wouldn't be fully human agents. Its members are not agents who are essentially embedded in a society that reflects and connects with the cosmos, but rather disembedded individuals who come to associate together. The design underlying the association is that each, in pursuing his or her own purposes in life, acts to benefit others mutually. It calls for a society structured for mutual benefit, in which each respects the rights of others, and offers them mutual help of certain kinds. The most influential early articulator of this formula is John Locke, but the basic conception of such an order of mutual service has come down to us through a series of variants, including more radical ones, such as those presented by Rousseau and Marx.

In the earlier days, when the plan was understood as providential and the order seen as natural law, which is the same as the law of God, building a society that fulfills these requirements was seen as fulfilling the design of God. To live in such a society was to live in one where God was present, not at all in the way that belonged to the enchanted world, through the sacred, but by following His design. God is present as the designer of the way we live. We see ourselves, to quote a famous phrase, as "one people under God."

In thus taking the United States as a paradigm case of this new idea of order, I am following Robert Bellah's tremendously fertile idea of an American "civil religion." Of course, the concept is understandably and rightly contested today, because some of the conditions of this religion are now being challenged, but there is no doubt that Bellah has captured something essential about American society, both at its inception and for about two centuries thereafter.

The fundamental idea, that America had a vocation to carry out God's purposes, which alone makes sense of the passages Bellah quotes, for instance, from Kennedy's inaugural address, and even more from Lincoln's second inaugural, and which can seem strange and threatening to many unbelievers in America today, has to be understood in relation to this conception of an order of free, rights-bearing individuals. This was what was invoked in the Declaration of Independence, which appealed to "the Laws of Nature and of Nature's God." The rightness of these laws, for both Deists and theists, was grounded in their being part of the providential design. What the activism of the American Revolutionaries added to this was a view of history as the theater in which this design was to be progressively realized and of their own society as the place where this realization was to be consummated—what Lincoln would later refer to as "the last best hope on earth." It was this notion of themselves as fulfilling divine purposes that, along with the biblical culture of Protestant America, facilitated the analogy with ancient Israel that often recurs in American official rhetoric of the early days.[22]

The confusion today arises from the fact that there is both continuity and discontinuity. What continues is the importance of some form of the modern idea of moral order. This gives the sense that Americans are still operating on the same principles as the Founders. The rift comes from the fact that what makes this order the right one is, for many though not by any means for all, no longer God's Providence; the order is grounded in nature alone, or in some concept of civilization, or even in supposedly unchallengeable a priori principles, often inspired by Kant. Thus some Americans want to rescue the Constitution from God, whereas others see this as doing violence to it. Hence the contemporary American Kulturkampf.

The young American republic is one paradigm of this new kind of relation of polity to God (not *the* paradigm, as many Americans are tempted to believe). This is the relation that I have called "neo-Durkheimian."[23] We can discern here a pattern that is central to what we might call the age of mobilization. The modern citizen social imaginary contrasts various premodern forms in that these reflect an "embedded" understanding of human life. In an ancien régime kingdom, we would have been seen as already, since time out of mind, defined as subjects of the king and, indeed, placed more exactly, as serfs of this lord, who holds from a duke, who holds from the king; or as bourgeois of this city, who holds its charter from the ruler; or as members of this cathedral chapter, which is under this bishop, who relates to both pope and king; and so on. Our relation to the whole would be mediated. The modern citizen imaginary, by contrast, sees us all as coming together to form a political entity, to which we all relate in the same way, as equal members. This entity has to be (or had to be, if it's already up and running) constructed. However much various modern ideologies, like nationalism, may convince us that we were always, since time out of mind, members of the X people (even though our ancestors didn't fully realize it and even were forced/induced to speak the Y's language), and however much this gives us the vocation to construct our own state, X-land, this state nevertheless has (had) to be constructed. People need(ed) to be convinced that they were really Xs and not Ys (Ukrainians and not Poles).

Two related features are crucial to this self-understanding. The first is that realizing who we really are (Xs) requires (required) mobilization. We had to be brought to act together to erect our state: rebel against the Ys, appeal to the League of Nations, or whatever. The second is that this mobilization is inseparable from a (re)definition of identity: we have to define ourselves, saliently, even sometimes primarily, as Xs and not as a host of other things that we also are or could be (Poles, or Catholic-Uniates, or just members of this village, or just peasants, and so forth).

These new entities—citizen states or other products of mobilization—are ordered around certain common poles of identity; let's call them "political identities." This doesn't have to be a linguistically defined nation, of course (though it often has been in the West). It can be a religious confession; it can be certain principles of government (Revolutionary France and the United States); it can be historical links; and so on.

This allows us to see the U.S. case as one example of a widespread feature of the modern world in the age of mobilization. Political identities can be woven around religious or confessional definitions. Thus, in the course of modern history, confessional allegiances have come to be woven into the sense of identity of certain ethnic, national, class, or regional groups. Britain and the United States are powerful, independent nations. But this kind of identification often happens with marginal or oppressed populations. Polish and Irish Catholic identities are well-known cases in point. The erstwhile French-Canadian one is another.

The link here between group and confession is not of the ancien régime type that we saw in counter-Revolutionary France, even though the same Catholic Church is involved. Throne and altar can't be allied, because the throne is alien, not just when it is Lutheran, Anglican, or Orthodox, but even where it is Catholic (as in Vienna). Resentment of elites becomes marginal to the extent that these elites lose power and privilege. But the sense of national domination and oppression, the sense of virtue in suffering and struggle, is deeply interwoven with religious belief and allegiance—even to the point of such rhetorical excesses as the depiction of Poland as "Christ crucified among the nations." The result is what I'm calling a "neo-Durkheimian" effect, where the senses of belonging to group and confession are fused, and the moral issues of the group's history tend to be coded in religious categories. (The rival language for oppressed people was always that of the French Revolution. This had its moments in each of the subaltern nations mentioned here: the United Irish, Papineau's rebellion in 1837, Dabrowski's legion; but in each case, the Catholic coding later took the upper hand.)

My neo-Durkheimian category can even be expanded to include a founding of political identity on an anti-religious philosophical stance, as we saw with the long-standing "republican" French identity. The long-standing *guerre franco-française,* the battle between republicans and Catholic monarchists, was in this sense fought between two neo-Durkheimian identities. These then contrast with other kinds of political identities, those founded on a supposed linguistic-historical nation, for instance, or on a certain constitutional order.

This last French case shows that neo-Durkheimian identity mobilization extends well beyond established nations or even wannabe nations, like Poland or Ireland. There are also cases of confessional mobilization that aim to have political impact, even where this is purely defensive and can't hope to issue in independent nationhood, as with Catholics in Germany during the Kulturkampf, and Dutch pillarization.

Now this phenomenon, religiously defined political identity mobilization, obviously has a tremendous present and (I fear) future in our world. We are almost at a point where my narratively based categorization should tip over into a discussion of the contemporary world. I certainly want to undertake this, but I crave the reader's patience, because I want to draw some other categories from our history, including those that arise from the decay of the neo-Durkheimian forms.

Before discussing these, I want to turn to another feature of the age of mobilization, the intrication of religion and morality or religion and civilization. As a lead-in to this, we should look at the way in which mobilization began to alter the structure of churches.

David Martin, in a number of insightful works,[24] has developed an interesting account of the "Protestant," more particularly "Anglophone," path of historical development. This comes about in societies in which the reigning forms of social imaginary center more and more on the order of mutual benefit, and the ancien régime order is seen as distant and somewhat abhorrent, in short, "Papist."

In keeping with this outlook, it seems more and more evident in these cultures that valid religious adherence can only be voluntary. Forcing it has less and less legitimacy. And so popular alienation from elite-dominated religion can take the form of new voluntary associations, rather different from the earlier churches. The prototype of these is Wesleyan Methodists. But the real explosion in such free churches occurred in the United States at the end of the eighteenth century, and it transformed the face of American religion.

With the Methodists, we have something new, neither a church nor a sect but a proto-form of what we now call a "denomination." A "church" in this Troeltschian sense claims to gather within it all members of society; like the Catholic Church, it sees its vocation as being the church for everyone. Some of the main Reformation churches had the same aspiration and often managed to take with them into dissidence whole societies, for instance, in Germany, Scandinavia, and initially England as well.

The denomination clearly belongs to the age of mobilization. It is not a divinely established body (though in another sense the broader "church" may be seen as such), but something that we must create—not just at our whim, but to fulfill the plan of God. In this, it resembles the new republic as providentially conceived in its civil religion. There is an affinity between the two, and each strengthened the other. That is, the voluntaristic dimension of the Great Awakening in the mid-eighteenth century obviously prepared the way for the revolutionary break of 1776, and in turn, the ethos of self-governing "independence" in the new republic meant that the Second Awakening in the early nineteenth century involved an even greater profusion of denominational initiatives than before.[25]

Now, it is clear that this kind of spontaneously created affinity group offered unique advantages when migration, social change, or class conflict rendered older, more inclusive churches in one way or another alien and forbidding for non-elites. Methodism was certainly not devised in order to accommodate class division; Wesley himself clove to the most unshakeable Tory convictions about social order and even condemned the American Revolution, in which so many of his transatlantic followers enthusiastically participated. Later, the main Methodist connections in England tried to damp worker militancy against employers (although they were ready to mobilize both sides of industry against Tory landowners).

Nevertheless, whatever the original idea of the Founders, the form was there, ready to give shape and expression to the religious aspirations and insights of some group, whether defined by class, by locality (such as mining villages in Northern England), by region (like Wales), by region plus ideological affinity (e.g., the splits between northern and southern Methodists and Baptists in the United States), or even by race (again, the U.S. case). Now, in societies where the model of one big, society-wide church, in continuity with the original divine foundation, dominated the imagination (i.e., Catholic societies but also some Lutheran ones, and even, to a lesser degree, some Calvinist ones, such as Scotland), finding a creative solution to non-elite alienation within the compass of Christian faith was extremely difficult (but not impossible, as we shall see in certain examples below). But where the voluntarist culture of mobilization was already part of religious self-understanding, new faith initiatives could more easily arise. The denominational imaginary made possible a flexibility unknown in most Continental societies.[26]

A number of different initiatives in fact took place, but the most impressive class was made up of what are loosely called "evangelical" modes of revival, which were widespread in Britain and America from the end of the eighteenth century on.[27] At their most intense, these centered on certain central doctrines of the Reformation: our sinful condition and the need for conversion, for a turning to God in faith, which would open us to His grace. The stress was often on this conversion as a personal act, undertaken for oneself, rather than as a disposition inhering in the group; and it was often taken, dramatically, under the press of powerful emotions, and in public.

Here was a powerful transformational perspective, defined on one side by a deep, potentially overpowering sense of sin and imperfection, and, on the other, by an overwhelming feeling of the love of God and its power to heal—in a word, of "amazing grace." As in the earlier Reformation, this new empowerment was meant to yield fruit in an ordered life. And order and disorder were conceived in terms which were very understandable in the existing predicament of the popular strata of the time, where people often struggled to find their bearings in a more and more market-driven economy, in which survival often depended upon adaptation to new conditions, migration, or adopting new work disciplines outside of traditional social forms. The danger was that of sinking into modes of behavior that were idle, irresponsible, undisciplined, and wasteful. And behind these lay the lure of traditional forms of recreation and conviviality, which could immure you in dysfunctional modes—in the first place, drink and the tavern. That is why temperance was one of the central goals of evangelical cultures, in a way that sounds totally excessive to many contemporary ears. We are perhaps sobered (it that's the word), however, when we learn how much of a curse drink could be; for instance, in the United States in the 1820s, liquor consumption per capita was four times what it is today.[28]

Along with drink, aiding and abetting it were other favored activities: cruel sports, gambling, and sexual promiscuity. This understanding of disorder targeted certain long-standing male forms of conviviality outside the family. The new understanding of order was family-centered and often involved identifying the male as the source of potential disruption and the female as victim and as guardian of this ordered domestic space. Callum Brown even speaks of a "demonization" of male qualities and a "feminization of piety."[29] Order required the male to be a family man and a good provider, which in turn required that he become educated, disciplined, and a hard worker. Sobriety, industry, and discipline were the principal virtues. Education and self-help were highly valued qualities. By attaining these, the man acquired a certain dignity, that of a free, self-governing agent. The goal could be captured in two terms: on the one hand, the "respectability" that went with an ordered life has been much stressed; but along with this, we should stress free agency, the dignity of the citizen. Evangelicalism was basically an antihierarchical force, part of the drive for democracy.

This connection of salvation and sanctity with a certain moral order in our lives reminds us of the first Reformation, of which evangelicalism is in a sense a reprise, in different circumstances and with an even more central emphasis on personal commitment. We can also look in the other direction and note how this movement carries on in our day, not so much in its home terrain in Britain and the United States (though it is still very strong in the latter), as nowadays in Latin America, Africa, and Asia.[30] And we can note the same connection between accepting salvation and putting a certain kind of order in one's life, so that men in Latin America become more family-centered, deserting certain kinds of male conviviality that stress machismo, becoming sober and good providers. Indeed, we might even extend the comparison to include non-Christian movements like the Nation of Islam in the United States.[31]

We can see that these movements have a powerful effect in "secular" history, that of enabling certain populations to become capable of functioning as productive, ordered agents in a new, nontraditional environment, be it nineteenth-century Manchester, twentieth-century São Paolo, or twenty-first-century Lagos. This gives rise to two reflections. First, will this tight identification of faith and a certain morality or order end up undercutting faith, as I have already argued it did among elites in the seventeenth and eighteenth centuries, and as it seems to have done in Britain in the twentieth? It does indeed seem that a faith that was originally connected with a sense of one's own powerlessness to bring order to one's life unaided, contrasted with the efficacy of grace to do this, will lose some of its relevance and convincing power if/when the required disciplines become second nature and, instead of feeling powerless, one feels in control of one's life. But however this may seem borne out by the long-term fate of earlier waves, we would be very foolish to predict what will happen to current waves of Pentecostalism in the Third World, not only because they have features of their own, unmatched by their predecessors, but because they are happening in a quite different social context, and our past experience concerns only the West.

Once again, I am running ahead of my argument. I have still further categories to bring out. The next flows directly from the above discussion of evangelical denominationalism. This was linked to powerful movements of moral reform, on the one hand, and it could be integrated into a neo-Durkheimian political identity, on the other, as in the United States. But these two links could themselves be inwardly connected. Political identity could itself be partly defined by high moral standards.

Over a long period, for many of the English, Christianity of a certain Protestant variety was identified with certain moral standards, often summed up in the word *decency,*[32] and England was thought to be the preeminent carrier of this on the world scene. This was what we could call the "established synthesis." For many, English patriotism was built around this complex of beliefs and norms. Many Protestant Americans, and later some Catholic ones, have thought that the United States has a providential mission to spread liberal democracy among the rest of humankind.

In this neo-Durkheimian form, religious belonging is central to political identity. But the religious dimension also figures in what we might call "civilizational" identity, the sense people have of the basic order by which they live, even imperfectly, as good and (usually) as superior to the ways of life of outsiders, be they "barbarians," "savages," or (in the more polite contemporary language) "less developed" peoples.

In fact, most of the time we relate to the order established in our "civilization" the way people have always related to their most fundamental sense of order; we have both a sense of security in believing that it is really in effect in our world and also a sense of our own superiority and goodness deriving from the confidence that we participate in it and uphold it. This means that we can react with great insecurity when we see that it can be breached from the outside, as at the World Trade Center, but also that we are even more shaken when we feel that it might be undermined from within, or that we might be betraying it. Then not only our security is threatened, but also our sense of our own integrity and goodness. To see this questioned is profoundly unsettling, ultimately threatening our ability to act.

That is why, in earlier times, we see people lashing out at such moments of threat, scapegoating violence against "the enemy within," meeting the threat to our security by finessing that to our integrity, deflecting it onto the scapegoats. In earlier periods of Latin Christendom, Jews and witches were cast in this unenviable role. The evidence that we are still tempted to have recourse to similar mechanisms in our "enlightened" age is unsettling. But it would not be the first such paradox in history if a doctrine of peaceful universalism were invoked to mobilize scapegoating violence.[33]

The point I want to make about British and later American patriotism, based as it was at first on the sense of fulfilling God's design, is that national identity was based on a self-ascribed preeminence in realizing a certain civilizational superiority. The superiority may have ultimately been understood as that of "Christendom" over infidel religions, but within Christendom, Britain/America stood at the cutting edge.

This sense of superiority, originally religious in essence, can and does undergo a "secularization" as the sense of civilizational superiority becomes detached from Providence and attributed to race, or enlightenment, or even some combination of the two. But the point of identifying this sense of order is that it provides another niche, as it were, in which God can be present in our lives, or in our social imaginary—the author not just of the design that defines our political identity but also of the design that defines civilizational order.

But why distinguish the two when they so obviously go together, as in the paradigm case of the United States? Because they don't always fit together in this way, but can operate separately. It is absolutely crucial to much Christian apologetics from the French Revolution onward that the Christian faith is essential to the maintenance of civilizational order, whether this is defined in terms of the modern moral order or in terms of the earlier hierarchical complementarity. This is the very staple of counterrevolutionary thought, as it flows from the pen, for instance, of Joseph de Maistre. But one can hear something similar today, in a quite neo-Durkheimian context, from some parts of the religious Right in the United States. The doctrine is that our order is not stable unless based on an explicit recognition that we are following God's plan. So much for the belief involved.

But this can issue in a social imaginary: that our order is now stable, because we are following God's plan; or that our order is threatened, because we are deviating from the plan. This sense of the presence or the threatened absence of God in our world, as the designer/guarantor of the civilizational order, can be very present, even where it is not linked with a sense that our nation singles itself out by its preeminence in realizing God's order. It may be relatively unhooked from our political identity.

Think of the Catholic recovery in France after the Restoration and of Catholic reactions in Germany to the Kulturkampf. These were, of course, phenomena of mobilization. They had to be; there was no other way to achieve their ends. And in some cases, they were animated by their own definition of national identity, as with Royalism in France. But even in this case, and frequently where there was no such overall proposal for the nation, as in Germany, they showed an acute sense of the church as essential to civilizational order. This was even the basis of the strange alliance, in so many ways against nature, between the positivist Maurras and right-wing Catholics in France, up to the papal condemnation of Action Française in 1926. And a great many of the conversions to Catholicism in the nineteenth and early twentieth centuries were inspired by, or at least interwoven with, this sense that the Church was a bulwark of order in a world threatened with moral and social disintegration.[34]

There were, in the end, strong analogies between evangelicalism and reconstituted postrevolutionary Catholicism, for all the differences. We should mention, first of all, new or renewed forms of spirituality, with a strong emotional appeal: conversion to a loving God, on one side, and devotions such as the Sacred Heart and that mobilized around the life and example of Thérèse de Lisieux, on the other. It would be a mistake to focus, as perhaps our sociological sensibility invites us to do, simply on the "functional" features of these faith forms, their providing people with the skills and disciplines they needed to operate in their changed circumstances. All may share a certain liturgy and ethos. But various people will feel the need for some special, stronger, more focused, concentrated, and/or disciplined form of devotion, prayer, meditation, or dedication. It may be that they confront a crisis or a tough period in their lives, and they need to concentrate their spiritual resources to meet it. It may be that they feel their lives are too shallow or unfocused, or all over the place; they need a stronger center, a point of concentration. It may be just that they feel the need to give some expression, some vent, to powerful feelings of gratitude, to acknowledge and rejoice in the gifts of God.

These forms of spirituality on both the Protestant and the Catholic sides were combined with attempts to inculcate the new ethos and disciplines necessary to function in a changed economy and society. The battle against drunkenness was also waged by priests in Irish parishes, at the same time as Nonconformity was campaigning for temperance.[35] On both sides, attempts to set up the necessary organs of economic survival, such as friendly societies and credit unions, were often linked with churches.

The various successful forms of faith in the age of mobilization combine these two strands; not only ethical/disciplinary, in which all (or most) partake, but also a series of special devotions, services, modes of prayer, and so on, for those who from time to time feel the need for some special form of dedication. These arise from individual choices, though they often are carried out in groups. They can be indefinitely varied and allow new forms to be created. A principal site of these on the Protestant side is, of course, the revival. On the Catholic side, we have novenas, retreats, special devotions (as to the Sacred Heart), pilgrimages, the steps of the Oratoire Saint-Joseph, and forms of service to priests, parish, and the like. Saint Thérèse de Lisieux was an important trailblazer in this kind of devotion.

These special forms were often gendered: Sacred Heart for the women, whereas the men would either opt out altogether from this dimension or else do something "active," like running Catholic trade unions.

I have been identifying three forms of religious life arising in the age of mobilization:

1. There are movements that weave together spiritual and devotional aspirations with personal and often collective empowerment, as in evangelical revivals and various movements of Catholic action, as well as Catholic prayer and devotion. Let's call these modes of empowering devotion.
2. Then there are interweavings of religious or confessional belonging with political identities—the neo-Durkheimian phenomenon.
3. Then there are the various ways in which religious or confessional faith becomes connected to our sense of civilizational order and the sense of security and/or superiority that connects to this. Let's call this the civilizational connection.

These can be happily intertwined, as in Anglophone Protestantism over many centuries; or they can exist quite separately from each other, as with various evangelical or Catholic movements in the non(majority) Christian South, which are modes of (1) unconnected to (2) or (3), or in Catholic or Polish nationalism, where (2) exists without (1) or (3). And (3) notoriously can exist alone among beleaguered elites, who sense that their society is going to the dogs. Or (2) and (3) can be alloyed without (1), as in the nineteenth-century German *Kulturprotestantismus*.

But the major points of tension in the contemporary West come from a further stage of our story, the dramatic collapse in large parts of Western society in the last third of the twentieth century of (2) and (3), in societies where they had been strongly established.

Let's call this the age of authenticity. It appears that something has happened in the last half century, perhaps even less, which has profoundly altered the conditions of belief in our societies.

I believe, along with many others, that our North Atlantic civilization has been undergoing a cultural revolution in recent decades. The 1960s perhaps provide the hinge moment, at least symbolically. It is, on the one hand, an individuating revolution, which may sound strange, because our modern age was already based on a certain individualism. But this has shifted onto a new axis, without deserting the others. As well as moral/spiritual and instrumental individualisms, we now have a widespread "expressive" individualism. This is, of course, not totally new. Expressivism was an invention of the Romantic period in the late eighteenth century. Intellectual and artistic elites searched for an authentic way of living or expressing themselves throughout the nineteenth century. What is new is that this kind of self-orientation seems to have become a mass phenomenon.

Its most obvious external manifestation has perhaps been the consumer revolution. With postwar affluence and the diffusion of what many had considered luxuries before came a new concentration on private space and the means to fill it, which began distending the relations of previously close-knit working-class or peasant communities, even of extended families.[36] Modes of mutual help dropped off, perhaps partly because of the receding of dire necessity. People concentrated more on their own lives and those of their nuclear families. They moved to new towns or suburbs, lived more on their own, tried to make a life out of the ever-growing gamut of new goods and services on offer, from washing machines to packaged holidays, and the freer individual lifestyles they facilitated. The "pursuit of happiness" took on a new, more immediate meaning, with a growing range of easily available means. And in this newly individuated space, the customer was encouraged more and more to express her taste, to furnish her space according to her own needs and affinities, as only the rich had been able to do in previous eras.

Of course, the "pursuit of (individual) happiness" has been integral to liberalism since the American Revolution, which enshrined it as one of a trinity of basic rights. But in the first century of the American republic, it was inscribed within certain taken-for-granted boundaries. First, there was the citizen ethic, centered on the good of self-rule, which Americans were meant to live up to. Beyond this, there were certain basic demands of sexual morality, of what later would be called "family values," as well as the values of hard work and productivity, which gave a framework to the pursuit of individual good. To move outside of these was not so much to seek one's happiness as to head toward perdition. There seemed, therefore, nothing contrary to the three basic rights enshrined by the Declaration of Independence in society's striving to inculcate, even in certain cases (e.g., sexual morality) to enforce these norms. European societies were perhaps less keen than the Americans to enforce various modes of social conformity, but their code was, if anything, even more restrictive.

The erosion of these limits on individual fulfillment has been in some cases gradual, with oscillations forward and backward, but with an unmistakable general tendency over the long run. Michael Sandel has noted how the concern for the citizen ethic was much more prominent in the first century of American history. Brandeis could argue the antitrust case at the beginning of the century partly on the ground that large combines erode "the moral and civic capacities that equip workers to think like citizens."[37] But as the twentieth century advanced, such considerations increasingly took a backseat. Courts became more concerned to defend the "privacy" of the individual.

It is really in the period after the Second World War that the limits on the pursuit of individual happiness have been most clearly set aside, particularly in sexual matters, but also in other domains as well. The U.S. Supreme Court decisions invoking privacy, and thereby restricting the range of the criminal law, provide a clear example. Something similar happens with the revisions of the Canadian Criminal Code under Trudeau, which expressed his principle that "the State has no business in the bedrooms of the nation." Michel Winock notes the change in *mentalités* in France during the 1970s. "The lifting of censorship, the 'liberalization of mores' . . . became law" with the legalization of abortion, divorce reform, the authorization of pornographic films, and so on.[38] This evolution takes place in virtually all Atlantic societies.

The heart of this revolution lies in sexual mores. This was a long time a-building, as the previous paragraph indicates, but the development took place earlier among cultural elites. In the 1960s, it was generalized to all classes. This is obviously a profound shift. The relativization of chastity and monogamy, the affirmation of homosexuality as a legitimate option, all these have a tremendous impact on churches, whose stance in recent centuries has laid so much stress on these issues and where piety has often been identified with a very stringent sexual code. I shall return to this shortly.

Here I want to concentrate on what is relevant to our purposes, which we could describe as the imagined place of the sacred, in the widest sense. Drawing an ideal type of this new social imaginary of expressive individualism, we could say that it is quite non-Durkheimian.

Under the ancien régime or "paleo-Durkheimian" dispensation, my connection to the sacred entailed my belonging to a church, in principle coextensive with society, although in fact there were perhaps tolerated outsiders and as yet undisciplined heretics. The neo-Durkheimian dispensation saw me enter the denomination of my choice, but that in turn connected me to a broader, more elusive "church" and, more importantly, to a political entity with a providential role to play. In both these cases, there was a link between adhering to God and belonging to the state—hence my epithet *Durkheimian.*

The neo-Durkheimian mode could involve an important step toward the individual and the right of choice. In societies with the appropriate kind of religious structures, one joined a denomination because it seemed right to do so. Indeed, it now comes to seem that there is no way of being in the "church" except through such a choice. Where under paleo-Durkheimian rules one could—and did—demand that people be forcibly integrated, be rightly connected with God against their will, this now often makes no sense. Coercion comes to seem not only wrong, but absurd and thus obscene. We saw an important watershed in the development of this consciousness in the reaction of educated Europe to the revocation of the Edict of Nantes. Even the Pope thought it was a mistake.

The expressivist outlook takes this a stage farther. The religious life or practice that I become part of must not only be my choice, but it must speak to me, it must make sense in terms of my spiritual development as I understand this. This takes us farther. The choice of denomination was understood to take place within a fixed cadre, say, that of the Apostles' Creed, the faith of the broader "church." Within this framework of belief, I choose the church in which I feel most comfortable. But if the focus is now going to be on my spiritual path, thus on what insights come to me in the subtler languages that I find meaningful, then maintaining this or any other framework becomes increasingly difficult.

But this means that my place in the broader "church" may not be that relevant for me, and along with this, my place in a "people under God" or other such political agency with a providential role. In the new expressivist dispensation, there is no necessary embedding of our link to the sacred in any particular broader framework, whether "church" or state.

This is why the developments of recent decades in France have been so destabilizing for both sides of the old *guerre franco-française.* Not only did the church see a sharp drop in adherence, but young people began to drop out of the rival Jacobin and/or Communist worldviews as well. In keeping with the dynamic of baroque, paleo-Durkheimian clericalism, the struggle threw up a kind of humanism that aspired in its own way to be a kind of national "church," that of the Republic and its principles, the framework within which people would hold their different metaphysical and (if they insisted) religious views. The Republic played a kind of neo-Durkheimian dispensation against the paleo-Durkheimianism of the clerical monarchists. This tradition even took over the term *sacred* for itself. (Think of *l'union sacrée,* of *la main sacrilège,* which killed Marat and others. This usage obviously facilitated Durkheim's theoretical use of the term to overarch both ancien régime and Republic.) It is not surprising that both Catholicism and this brand of republicanism undergo defections in the new, post-Durkheimian dispensation of expressive individualism.

This changes utterly the ways in which ideals of order used to be interwoven with the polemic between belief and unbelief. What has changed to make this much less the case is not only that we have achieved a broad consensus on our ideal of moral order. It is also that, in our post-Durkheimian dispensation, the "sacred," either religious or *laïque,* has become uncoupled from our political allegiance. It was the rivalry between two such kinds of global allegiance that animated the *guerre franco-française.* It was also this older dispensation that could send masses of men into the trenches to fight for their country in 1914 and keep them there, with few desertions and rare instances of mutiny, for over four years.[39]

I speak of this in the past tense, because in many of the countries that were the prime belligerents in this war the new dispensation has probably made this kind of thing impossible. But it is also clear that the geographic area for which this holds true is limited. Down in the Balkans, not that much has changed since the wars that broke out in 1911. And we should not be too sanguine in believing that the change is irreversible even in the core North Atlantic societies.

But for the moment, Western societies seem to have passed a crucial watershed. While in the original paleo-Durkheimian dispensation people could easily feel that they had to obey the command to abandon their own religious instincts, because these, being at variance with orthodoxy, must be heretical or at least inferior; while those inhabiting a neo-Durkheimian world felt that their choice had to conform to the overall framework of the "church" or favored nation, so that even Unitarians and ethical societies presented themselves as denominations with services and sermons on Sunday; in the post-Durkheimian age many people are uncomprehending in face of the demand to conform. Just as in the neo-Durkheimian world joining a church you don't believe in seems not just wrong, but absurd, contradictory, so in the post-Durkheimian age seems the idea of adhering to a spirituality that doesn't present itself as your path, the one that moves and inspires you. For many people today, to set aside their own path in order to conform to some external authority just doesn't seem comprehensible as a form of spiritual life.[40] The injunction is, in the words of a speaker at a New Age festival: "Only accept what rings true to your own inner Self." [41]

Paleo-, neo-, and *post-Durkheimian* describe ideal types. My claim is not that any of these provides a total description, but that our Western history has moved through these dispensations, and that the last has come to color our age more and more.

That the new dispensation doesn't provide the whole story is readily evident from struggles in contemporary society. In a sense, part of what drove the Moral Majority and motivates the Christian Right in the United States is an aspiration to reestablish something of the fractured neo-Durkheimian understanding that used to define the nation, where being American would once more have a connection with theism, with being "one people under God," or at least with the ethic that was interwoven with this. Similarly, much of the leadership of the Catholic Church, led by the Vatican, is trying to resist the challenge to monolithic authority implicit in the new expressivist understanding of spirituality. And the Catholic Church in the United States frequently lines up with the Christian Right in attempts to reestablish earlier versions of the moral consensus that enjoyed neo-Durkheimian religious grounding.[42] For all these groups, the idea remains strong that there is a link between Christian faith and civilizational order. But the embattled nature of these attempts shows how we have slid out of the old dispensation. This shift goes a long way to explain the conditions of belief in our day.

The last paragraph takes us into a new terrain. The expressive revolution has undermined not only neo-Durkheimian identities but also the link between Christian faith and civilizational order. A leading feature of many of the religious forms of the age of mobilization described above was their strong sense of an ordered life, along with their attempts to aid, persuade, or pressure their members into realizing this. As I indicated above, it was perhaps inevitable, as the new disciplines became internalized, that this disciplining function would be less valued, that some of the rigid measures earlier seen as essential, such as absolute temperance or total Sabbath observance, would appear irksome to the descendants of those who had put them in place. There was always a certain resistance to evangelicals, on the alleged grounds that they were puritans, spoil sports, sowers of division. Fictional characters like Dickens's Melchisedech Howler and Jabez Fireworks as well as George Eliot's Bulstrode, express some of this hostility, and there were sometimes criticisms of Methodists, with their insistence on temperance and banning village sports, as disrupting convivial community culture and setting people against each other.[43] A more general reaction set in toward the end of the nineteenth century against evangelical morality as dessicating, repressing freedom and self-development, imposing uniformity, denying beauty, and the like. Writers like Shaw, Ibsen, and Nietzsche articulated this very powerfully, and something of this is expressed in J. S. Mill's famous statement that "pagan self-assertion is better than Christian self-denial."[44] For his part, Arnold bemoaned the lack of cultivation of the Nonconformist middle class. And the culture of

Bloomsbury can be seen as formed partly in reaction to this whole religious climate.

All this was intensified by the cultural revolution of the 1960s, not only in that more people were swept into a stance in opposition to much of the religious ethic but also in that the new sexual mores were even more strongly at odds with it. A tripartite connection had in the past seemed to many absolutely unquestionable: between Christian faith and an ethic of discipline and self-control, even of abnegation, on the one hand; and between this ethic and civilizational order, on the other. But as I described above, the second link has come to seem less and less credible to more and more people. The pursuit of happiness has come to seem not only not to need a restrictive sexual ethic and the disciplines of deferred gratification but actually to demand their transgression in the name of self-fulfillment. The people who feel this most strongly are, of course, precisely those for whom many of these disciplines have become second nature, not needing a strong ethical/spiritual backing to maintain themselves. To the surprise of many Weberian sociologists of my generation, the children of the 1960s and 1970s managed to relax many of the traditional disciplines in their personal lives while keeping them in their work life. This is not necessarily easy to manage; some people can't make it. There are, moreover, whole milieus where the disciplines are still too new and distant from their way of life for this kind of picking and choosing to be possible. As David Martin puts it, in describing the advance of Pentecostalism in the global South:

> In the developed world the permissions and releases can be pursued by quite large numbers of people while ignoring the economic disciplines, at least for a quite extended period of licence, but in the developing world the economic disciplines cannot be evaded. Though in the developed world you can accept the disciplines in your working life and ignore them elsewhere, in the developing world your disciplines must govern your whole life, or you fall by the wayside—or fall into crime.[45]

This feat of selective assumption of disciplines, which supposes a long, often multigenerational interiorization, is a crucial facilitating condition of the new stance, even though the expressive revolution provided the reason to transgress the old boundaries. At other times and places, such principled transgression seems insane, almost suicidal.

Where the link between disciplines and civilizational order is broken, but that between Christian faith and the disciplines remains unchallenged, expressivism and the conjoined sexual revolution have alienated many people from the churches, on two counts. First, those who have gone along with the current changes find themselves profoundly at odds with the sexual ethic that churches have been propounding. Second, their sense of following their own path is offended by what they experience as the "authoritarian" approach of churches, laying down the law without waiting for a reply.

Churches find it hard to talk to people in this mind-set. Talking to them is not a matter of simply agreeing with what they say. There has been too much hype, Utopian illusion, and reacting to old taboos in the sexual revolution for this to make sense. And indeed, forty years on, this is more and more evident to lots of young people. (Which is not to say that churches don't also have something to learn from this whole transition.)[46]

But just as, in the face of any responsible agent, those who claim to possess some wisdom have an obligation to explain it persuasively, starting from where their interlocutor is, so it is here. The attachment to a rigid code, as well as the sense of being an embattled band of the faithful, that developed through the defensive postures of the last two centuries makes it almost impossible to find language here.

The break has been profound. As Callum Brown has shown for the evangelical case, the ethical stance was predicated on an idea of women as wanting a stable family life, which was constantly endangered by male temptation—to drinking, gambling, infidelity. We see similar ideas propounded on the Catholic side. This way of defining the issues was not without basis in the past, when women feared the consequences for themselves and their children of male irresponsibility and even violence, and it is not without basis in many milieus in the present, especially in the global South, as David Martin has pointed out.[47]

We connect up here with a profound development, evident across the confessional divide over the last two or three centuries, which has been called the "feminization" of Christianity, about which Callum Brown speaks in his interesting recent book.[48] It obviously has something to do with the close symbiosis established between Christian faith and the ethic of "family values" and disciplined work, which has downgraded if not been directed against military and combative modes of life, as well as forms of male sociability—drinking, gambling, sport—which took men outside the arenas of both work and home. This has not just been an issue for churches; we can see the conflict—and the ambivalence—reflected in the whole society, with the development of the ideal of "polite" society, based on commerce in the eighteenth century. Even some of the intellectual figures who defined and welcomed this new development, such as Adam Smith or Adam Ferguson, expressed their misgivings about it. It might lead to an atrophy of the martial virtues necessary to the self-governing citizen. Others feared an "effeminization" of the male.[49] Feminization of the culture went parallel to feminization of the faith

In the Christian context, this was reflected, as well as further entrenched, by a relative drop in male practice as against female. "The men are leaving" is the unanimous lament of priests in the Ain Department in the nineteenth century, particularly in the latter half.[50] This absence often reflects a sense of male pride and dignity, which is seen as incompatible with a too unbridled devotion; there is something "womanish" about this kind of dedication. This sense was connected to, fed, and was fed by a certain mistrust of clerical power: on the one hand, the priest (whose habit resembled that of a woman) had perhaps too much power over wives and daughters; but on the other hand, that was no bad thing, because he taught them chastity and fidelity, and offered security to the male head of the household. At the same time, however good for women, this acceptance of clerical leadership was incompatible with the independence that was a crucial part of male dignity. Obviously, this attitude could give a point of purchase for the philosophical anti-clericalism of the Republican.[51]

The present sexual revolution in the West has challenged the whole picture of male and female on which this understanding of civilizational order reposed.[52] It has brought with it a gamut of feminist positions, and in some of these women demand for themselves the right to sexual exploration and unfettered fulfillment that was previously thought central to male desire. This totally undercuts the conceptual base of the hitherto dominant ethic. In a line from a 1970 Church of Scotland report on the issue: "It is the promiscuous girl who is the real problem here."[53]

Of course, not everybody agrees with this account of female desire. But it shows a new uncertainty about the forms of women's identity—matched by corresponding uncertainty among men. It is not possible to address the question of sexual ethics without engaging with these issues.

2

At last I come to our present situation and those elements of it that we might expect to continue into our future. I want to take this in two stages: first, the situation in the "West," and then later some speculations about possible analogies to phenomena elsewhere in the world.

Clearly, the three phenomena I mentioned above are prominent parts of our present/future: (1) modes of empowering devotion; (2) the neo-Durkheimian phenomenon; and (3) religion as the basis for moral/civilizational order. But a salient feature of the West today is the tension, even conflict, between one or more of these, and the slide toward expressive individualism and an ethic of authenticity. I want to look at several features of our Western situation; let's first take up this tension.

THE GENERATIONS FORMED by the cultural revolution of the 1960s are in some respects deeply alienated from a strong traditional model of Christian faith in the West. We have already seen how they are refractory to the sexual disciplines that were part of the good Christian life as understood, for instance, in the nineteenth-century evangelical revivals in English-speaking countries. Indeed, the contemporary swing goes beyond just repudiating these very high standards. Even the limitations that were generally accepted among traditional peasant communities, which clerical minorities thought were terribly lax and which they were always trying to get to shape up, have been set aside by large numbers of people in our society today. The clergy used to frown on premarital sex, for instance, and were concerned when couples who came to be married were already expecting a child. But the same peasant communities, although they thought it quite normal to try things out beforehand, particularly to be sure that they could have children, accepted that it was mandatory to confirm their union by a ceremony. Those who tried to step outside these limits were brought back into line by strong social pressure, charivaris, or "rough music."[54]

But we have clearly stepped way beyond these limits today. Not only do people experiment widely before settling down in a stable couple, but they also form couples without ever marrying; in addition, they form, then break, then re-form these relationships. Our peasant ancestors also engaged in a kind of "serial monogamy," but in their cases the earlier unions were always broken by death, while in ours it is divorce (or, in the case of unmarried partners, just moving out) that ends them.[55]

There is something deeply at odds here with all forms of sexual ethic—be it folk tradition or Christian doctrine—that saw the stability of marriage as essential to social order. But there is more than this. Christians did see their faith as essential to civilizational order, but this was not the only source of the sexual ethic that has dominated modern Western Christianity. There were also strong images of spirituality that enshrined particular images of sexual purity. We can see these developing in the early modern period. John Bossy has argued that, in the medieval understanding of the seven deadly sins, the sins of the spirit (pride, envy, anger) were seen as more grievous than those of the flesh (gluttony, lechery, sloth; avarice could be put in either column). But during the Catholic Reformation concupiscence as the crucial obstacle to sanctity came to be emphasized more and more.[56]

What was perhaps ancient was to see sexual ethics through a prism of pollution and purity. "Hence the ban on marriage during Lent and at other seasons, the doctrine that sexual acts between the married were always venially sinful, the purification of women after childbirth, the peculiar preoccupation with sexuality among priests."[57] The modern age seems to have spiritualized the underlying notion of purity and made it the principal gateway (or its opposite, the principal obstacle) in our approach to God.

In the terms I have been using in this study, we can think of the Catholic Reformation, especially in France, as an attempt to inculcate a deep, personal devotion to God (through Christ or Mary) in (potentially) everyone, an attempt, moreover, that was to be carried out mainly through the agency of the clergy, who would preach, persuade, cajole, or push their charges toward this new, higher orientation and away from the traditional, community-based, preaxial forms of the sacred. If we posit this as the goal, we can think of various ways in which one might try to encompass it. A heavy emphasis might be put on certain examples of sanctity, in the hope of awakening a desire to follow them. Or the major thrust might be to frighten people into shaping up, at least minimally. Of course, both of these paths were tried, but the overwhelming weight fell on the negative one. This was, indeed, part of the whole process of reform starting in the High Middle Ages. Jean Delumeau has spoken of "the pastoralia of fear."[58]

Perhaps we might just take this as a given, particularly as the tradition goes so far back before the modern period. But we can perhaps also see it as inseparable from the reforming enterprise itself. If the aim is not just to make certain forms of spirituality shine forth and draw as many people as possible to them but really to make everybody over (or everybody who is not heading for damnation), then perhaps the only way you can ever hope to produce this kind of mass movement is by leaning heavily on threat and fear. This is certainly the pattern set up very early on in the process of reform, in the preaching mission of wandering friars starting in the thirteenth century.

The irony is that, where clerical leadership really managed to transform a community, it was through the personal holiness of the incumbent and not through his parading the horrors of Hell. A particularly striking case is that of the saintly life and persevering ministry of the Curé d'Ars. But you can't expect a Jean Vianney in every parish. If the goal is to move everyone, even through spiritually unimpressive agents, then fear is your best bet.

To quote a mission preacher at the time of the Restoration in France:

Soon the hour of your death will sound; continue the web of your disorders; sink yourselves deeper in the mire of your shameful passions; insult by the impiety of your heart Him who judges even the just. Soon you will fall under the pitiless blows of death, and the measure of your iniquities will be that of the fearful torments which will then be inflicted upon you.[59]

Once one goes this route, something else follows. The threat has to attach to very clearly defined failures. Do this, or else (damnation will follow). The "this" also has to be clearly definable. Of course, there were periods, particularly in the Calvinist theological context, in which it had to remain ultimately uncertain whether anyone had really been chosen by God. But as Weber pointed out, this is an unlivable predicament, and very soon certain signs of election crystallize, whatever the lack of theological warrant. In the context of the

Catholic Reformation, the relevant standards are not signs of election but minimal conformity to the demands of God: the avoidance of mortal sin, or at least doing whatever is necessary to have these sins remitted.

What emerges from all this is what we might call "moralism," that is, the crucial importance given to a certain code in our spiritual lives. We should all come closer to God, but a crucial stage on this road has to be the minimal conformity to the code. Without this, you aren't even at the starting line, as it were, of this crucial journey. You are not in the game at all. This is perhaps not an outlook that squares easily with a reading of the New Testament, but it nevertheless achieved a kind of hegemony across broad reaches of the Christian church in the modern era.

This outlook ends up putting all the emphasis on what we should do, and/or what we should believe, to the detriment of spiritual growth. Sister Elisabeth Germain, analyzing a representative catechism in wide use in the nineteenth century, concludes that "Morality takes precedence over everything, and religion becomes its servant. Faith and the sacraments are no longer understood as the basis of the moral life, but as duties to be carried out, as truths that we must believe, and as means to help us fulfill these moral obligations."[60]

Now one can have clerically driven reform, powered by fear of damnation, and hence moralism, and the code around which this crystallizes can nevertheless take different forms. The central issues could be questions of charity versus aggression, anger, and vengeance; or a central vector could be the issue of sexual purity. Again, both are present, but with a surprisingly strong emphasis on the sexual. We saw above that, in a sense, the emphasis shifted in this direction with the Catholic Reformation. It is not that sins of aggression, violence, or injustice were neglected. On the contrary. It is just that the code, the definition of what it is to get to the starting line, was extremely rigid about sexual matters. There were mortal sins in the other dimensions as well—for instance, murder—and there were many in the domain of church rules (e.g., skipping Mass); but you could go quite far in being unjust and hard-hearted in your dealings with subordinates and others without incurring the automatic exclusion you would incur through sexual license. Sexual deviation and not listening to the church seemed to be the major domains where automatic excluders lurked. Sexual purity, along with obedience, was therefore given extraordinary salience.

Hence the tremendously (as it seems to us) disproportionate fuss that clergy made in nineteenth-century France about banning dancing, cleaning up folk festivals, and the like. (There are analogues, of course, among evangelicals in Protestant countries.) Young people were refused communion or absolution unless they gave these up altogether. The concern with this issue appears at certain moments obsessive.

I can't pretend to be able to explain this; but perhaps a couple of considerations can put it in context. The first is the pacification of modern society that was one of the chief fruits of reform, the fact that the level of everyday violence not related to wars, that caused by brigands, feuds, rebellions, clan rivalries, and the like, declined between the fifteenth and the nineteenth centuries. As violence and anger became less overwhelming realities of life, attention could shift toward purity. The second is the obvious remark that sexual abstinence was a central fact of life for a celibate clergy. It is perhaps not surprising that they made a lot of it.

But there is certainly more to it than these two factors can account for. We have to explain the growing concentration on sexual purity over many centuries and its perhaps dialectical relation with the increasing focus in modernity on sexual relations as a domain of personal fulfillment—all that Foucault was getting at when he spoke, provocatively and paradoxically, of "sexuality" as a modern invention. We have to take into account, for instance, the nineteenth-century obsession with onanism, the concern for sexual "perversion," in the Catholic context with "disorderly" or "unnatural" practices,[61] which led in some countries to legislation against homosexuality.

In any case, it was clearly fated that this combination of clerical reform from the top, moralism, and repression of sexual life would come into conflict with the developing modernity that I have been describing. Emphasis on individual responsibility and freedom would eventually run athwart the claims of clerical control. And the post-Romantic reactions against the disciplines of modernity, the attempts to rehabilitate the body and the life of feeling, would eventually fuel a reaction against sexual repression.

These tensions were already evident before the mid-twentieth century. I mentioned above the decline in male religious practice, in relation to female practice, starting in the late eighteenth century. One common explanation I mentioned there invokes images of male pride and dignity. But we might also come at the same phenomenon from another direction, stressing that this more rigid sexual code frontally attacked certain male practices, particularly the rowdy lifestyle of young men. Perhaps more profoundly, it seems that the combination of sexual repression and clerical control, as it was felt in the practice of confession, drove men away. Clerical control went against their sense of independence, and this became doubly intolerable when the control took the form of opening up the most reserved and intimate facet of their lives. Hence the immense resistance to confession, in just about any period, and the attempt to confess, if one had to, not to one's own curé, but to a visiting priest on mission to whom one was unknown. As Delumeau put it, "the main reason for voluntary silence in the confessional was shame about admitting to sexual sins." Eventually, this tension drove men out of the confessional; as Gibson describes the sequel in the nineteenth century, "unable to take communion, and angry at the prying of the clergy, they increasingly abandoned the Church."[62]

The repellent effect of this complex is clearly at its maximum in the age of authenticity, in a widespread popular culture in which individual self-realization and sexual fulfillment are interwoven. The irony is that this alienation took place just when so many of the features of the reform-clerical complex were called into question at Vatican II. Unquestionably, clericalism, moralism, and the primacy of fear were largely repudiated. Other elements of the complex were less clearly addressed. It's not clear that the full negative consequences of the drive to reform itself, with its constant attempt to purge popular religion of its "unchristian" elements, were properly understood. Certain attempts at reform in Latin America, post–Vatican II and in its spirit, like those around "liberation theology," seem to have repeated the old pattern of "clerical dechristianization," depreciating and banning popular cults, and alienating many of the faithful, some of whom—ironically—have turned to Protestant churches in the region, who have a greater place for the miraculous and the festive than the progressive "liberators" had.[63] A strange turn of events, which would surprise Calvin, were he to return! As for the issue of sexual morality, attempts to review this, in the question of birth control, were abandoned in a fit of clerical nerves about the "authority" of the Church.

In fact, the present position of the Vatican seems to want to retain the most rigid moralism in the sexual field, relaxing nothing of the rules, with the result that people with "irregular" sexual lives are (supposed to be) automatically denied the sacraments, while as-yet-unconvicted mafiosi, not to speak of unrepentant latifundistas in the Third World and Roman aristocrats with enough clout to wangle an annulment, find no bar.

But however incomplete and hesitantly followed the turnings taken at Vatican II, the present position of the Vatican has clearly relativized the old reform-clerical complex. It has opened a field in which you don't have to be deeply read in the history of the Church to see that the dominant spiritual fashion of recent centuries is no longer unquestionably normative. Which is not to say that this whole spirituality, aspiring to a full devotion to God and fueled by abnegation and a strong image of sexual purity, is to be condemned in turn. This would be a clerical-reform way of dealing with the reform-clerical complex! It is clear that there have been and are today celibate vocations that are spiritually fertile, and many of these turn centrally on aspirations to sexual abstinence and purity. It would just repeat the mistake of the Protestant reformers to turn around and depreciate these. The fateful feature of reform-clericalism, which erects such a barrier between the Church and contemporary society, is not its animating spirituality; our world is, if anything, drowned in exalted images of sexual fulfillment and needs to hear about paths of renunciation. The deviation was to make this take on sexuality mandatory for everyone, through a moralistic code that made a certain kind of purity a base condition for relating to God through the sacraments. What Vatican rule makers and secularist ideologies unite in not being able to see is that there are more ways of being a Catholic Christian than either have yet imagined. And yet this shouldn't be so hard to grasp. Even during those centuries when the reform-clerical outlook dominated pastoral policy, there were always other paths present, represented sometimes by the most prominent figures, including (to remain with the French Catholic Reformation) Saint François de Sales and Fénelon, not to speak of Pascal, who, though he gave comfort to the fearmongers, offered an incomparably deeper vision.

But as long as this monolithic image dominates the scene, the Christian message as the Catholic Church attempts to make it its vehicle will not be easy to hear in wide zones of the age of authenticity. But then these are not very hospitable to a narrow secularism, either.

Of course, this tension is not specific to the Catholic Church. We see it in the Anglican communion and in some Protestant churches in the virtual civil war over homosexual marriage and the acceptance of homosexual clergy, and it plays its role in the "culture wars" that bedevil politics in the United States.

So THE DOMINANT religious forms of the age of mobilization have been destabilized by the current cultural revolution, even as those of the ancien régime were by the onset of the age of mobilization. The forms of the last two centuries have taken a double whammy: on one side, an undermining of churches connected to strong national or minority identities; on the other, an estrangement from much of the ethic and style of authority of these same churches.

What are the consequences? First, one that everybody will welcome: a breaking down of barriers between different religious groups, a deconstruction of ghetto walls where such existed, as Michael Hornsby-Smith reports for the English Catholic Church after Vatican II.[64] And, of course, the effects of this are even more palpable in what were previously denominationally partitioned societies, like Holland.

But the flip side of this is a decline. The measurable, external results are as we might expect: first, in many countries, including Britain, France, the United States, and Australia, a rise in the number of those who state themselves to be atheists, to be agnostics, or to have no religion.[65] Beyond this, the gamut of intermediate positions greatly widens: many people drop out of active practice while still declaring that they belong to some confession, or believe in God. In another dimension, the gamut of beliefs in something beyond widens, with fewer declaring belief in a personal God while more hold to something like an impersonal force.[66] In other words, a wider range of people express religious beliefs that move outside Christian orthodoxy. Following in this line is the growth of non-Christian religions, particularly those originating in the Orient, and the proliferation of New Age modes of practice, of views that bridge the humanist/spiritual boundary, of practices that link spirituality and therapy. On top of this, more and more people adopt what would earlier have been seen as untenable positions: for example, they consider themselves Catholic while not accepting many crucial dogmas, or they combine Christianity with Buddhism, or they pray while not being certain they believe. This is not to say that people didn't occupy positions like this in the past, just that now it seems to be easier to be upfront about it. In reaction to all this, Christian faith is in the process of redefining and recomposing itself in various ways, from Vatican II to the charismatic movements. All this represents the consequence of expressivist culture as it affects our world. It has created a quite new predicament.[67]

Danièle Hervieu-Léger speaks of a "decoupling of belief and practice," of a "disembedding of belief, belonging, and identitary reference." Grace Davie speaks of "believing without belonging." The tight normative link between a certain religious identity, the belief in certain theological propositions, and a standard practice no longer holds for great numbers of people. Many of these are engaged in assembling their own personal outlook, through a kind of "bricolage," but there are also some widespread patterns that run athwart the traditional constellations: not only declaring some faith in God and identifying with a church without actually attending its services ("believing without belonging"), but also a Scandinavian pattern of identifying with the national church, which one attends only for crucial rites of passage, while professing widespread skepticism about its theology. The tight connection between national identity, a certain ecclesial tradition, strong common beliefs, and a sense of civilizational order, which was standard for the age of mobilization, has given way, weakening crucially the hold of theology. But whereas in other countries this has also meant a decline in identification with the church, that connection seems strong in Scandinavian countries, though deprived of its original theological connotations. The churches are seen, one might say, as a crucial element in historical-cultural identity. This pattern can also be found in other European countries, but in the Nordic nations it seems dominant.[68]

What lies behind these figures and trends? We cannot understand our present situation through a single ideal type, but if we understand ourselves to be moving away from an age of mobilization and more into an age of authenticity, then we can see this whole move as in a sense a retreat of Christendom. I mean by "Christendom" a civilization where society and culture are profoundly informed by Christian faith. This retreat is a shattering development, if we think of the way, until quite recently, Christian churches conceived their task. If we take just the Catholic Church (and there were analogues with the interdenominational "church" in pluralist Protestant societies), its goal was to provide a common religious home for the whole society. We can think in the French case of the seventeenth-century Catholic Reformation, trying to win back ground lost to the Reformed Church, as well as to penetrate segments of rural society that had never been properly Christianized; then, in the nineteenth century, the Church tried again to make up the ravages of the Revolution; the goal of Action Catholique in the early twentieth century was to missionize the milieus that had slipped away. But it is clear today that this ambition cannot be realized.

Our societies in the West will forever remain historically informed by Christianity. I will return below to some of the significance of this. What I mean by "the retreat of Christendom" is that it will be less and less common for people to be drawn into or kept within a faith by some strong political or group identity, or by the sense that they are sustaining a socially essential ethic. There will obviously still be lots of both of these things: at the very least, group identity may be important for immigrants, particularly of recent provenance—and even more among non-Christians, say, Muslims or Hindus, who feel their difference from the established majority religion. And there will certainly remain a core of people who are both members and regular attenders of churches, larger or smaller from country to country (vast in the United States, miniscule in Sweden).

There is another reason that assures the continuing importance of neo-Durkheimian identities. In some societies these are in a quasi-agonistic relation to the post-Durkheimian climate. Think, for instance, of the United States and certain demands of the Christian Right, for example, for school prayer. But these identities are perhaps even more in evidence among groups that feel suppressed or threatened (perhaps this is also the case with the Christian Right?), and often people of a certain ethnic or historical identity will look to gather around some religious marker. I mentioned the Poles and Irish earlier. These were peoples cast into the modern political form because they were mobilized to attain their independence or establish their integrity, in the context of being ruled from outside, sometimes with heavy oppression. They therefore took on the modern language and the modern conceptions of a political entity; they became in a modern sense peoples. And modern peoples, that is, collectivities that strive to be agents in history, need some understanding of what they're about, what I'm calling "political identity." In the two cases mentioned, being Catholic was an important part of that identity.

This phenomenon remains important in the modern world. From a faith perspective, one might be ambivalent about it, however, because there are a gamut of cases, from a deeply felt religious allegiance all the way to situations in which the religious marker is cynically manipulated in order to mobilize people. Think of Milošević or the Bharatiya Janata Party (BJP). But whatever one's ethical judgments, this is a powerful reality in today's world, and one that is not about to disappear. But in general, we can say that in modern societies not riven by ethnic-confessional differences (e.g., we're not talking about Northern Ireland), the recently dominant forms of the age of mobilization will not tend to hold their members.

If we don't accept the view that the human aspiration to religion will flag, and I do not, then where will access to the practice of and deeper engagement with religion lie? The answer is the various forms of spiritual practice to which each person is drawn in his or her own spiritual life. These may involve meditation, or some charitable work, or a study group, or a pilgrimage, or some special form of prayer, or a host of such things.

A range of such forms has always existed, of course, as optional extras, as it were, for those who are already and primarily embedded in ordinary church practice. But now it is frequently the reverse. First people are drawn to a pilgrimage, or a World Youth Day, or a meditation group, or a prayer circle; and then later, if they move along in the appropriate direction, they will find themselves embedded in ordinary practice. And there will be much movement between such forms of practice, and between the associated faiths.

It is often said of the contemporary search for the spiritual, very often through a kind of individualized bricolage, that it is excessively focused on self-fulfillment, on finding one's own path. This is often said in a tone of reproach or deprecation, in a negative comparison with earlier, mainstream forms of religious life. It would be absurd to deny that even the most caricatural portraits are often lived down to, as it were. But these hostile depictions miss something essential. Where a return to religion is not actuated by a strong group or political identity or by a felt need to defend or recover a civilizational order against threatened dissolution, what is the main motivation? In many cases today, it is a profound dissatisfaction with a life encased entirely in the immanent order. The sense is that this life is empty, flat, devoid of higher purpose.

This, of course, has been a widespread response to the world created by Western modernity over at least the last two centuries. We might borrow as its slogan the title of a song by the American singer Peggy Lee: "Is that all there is?" There has to be more to life than our current definitions of social and individual success define for us. This was always a factor in previous returns to religion, like the conversions to Catholicism in nineteenth- and early-twentieth-century France I mentioned above. But there it was interwoven with a neo-Durkheimian identity and, even more, with a project for restoring civilizational order. When these fall away, the search occurs for its own sake. It is a personal search, and can easily be coded in the language of authenticity: I am trying to find my path, or find myself. But this doesn't mean that it has to be self-enclosed, that it can't end up with a strong sense of the transcendent, or of devotion to something beyond the self.

This shows the error of confusing the post-Durkheimian dispensation with a trivialized and utterly privatized spirituality. Of course, there will exist lots of both. These are the dangers that attend our present predicament. A post-Durkheimian world means, as I said above, that our relation to the spiritual is being more and more unhooked from our relation to our political societies. But that by itself doesn't say anything about whether or how our relation to the sacred will be mediated by collective connections. A thoroughly post-Durkheimian society will be one in which our religious belonging would be unconnected from our national identity. It will almost certainly be one in which the gamut of such religious allegiances will be wide and varied. It will also almost certainly have lots of people who are following a religious life centered on personal experience in the sense that William James made famous.[69] But it doesn't follow that everyone, or even most people, will be doing this. Many people will find their spiritual home in churches, for instance, including the Catholic Church. In a post-Durkheimian world, this allegiance will be unhooked from that to a sacralized society (paleo-style) or some national identity (neo-style) or from the (now arrogant-sounding) claim to provide the indispensable matrix for the common civilizational order. If I am right above, the mode of access will be different; but it will still be a collective connection.

These connections, sacramental or through a common practice, are obviously still powerful in the modern world. We must avoid an easy error here: that of confusing the new place of religion in our personal and social lives, the framework of understanding that we should be following in our own spiritual sense, with the issue of what paths we will follow. The new framework has a strongly individualist component, but this will not necessarily mean that the content will be individuating. Many people will find themselves joining extremely powerful religious communities, because that's where many people's sense of the spiritual will lead them.

Of course, they won't necessarily sit as easily in these communities as their forbears did. In particular, a post-Durkheimian age may mean a much lower rate of intergenerational continuity of religious allegiance. But the strongly collective options will not lose adherents. Perhaps even the contrary trend might declare itself.

ONE REASON to take this idea seriously is the continuing importance of what we might call the "festive." I have been talking about the future of the relatively recent past—in the case of the culture of authenticity, only decades old. But here we are speaking of a more remote past, one that was repressed in the whole movement of reform. One by-product of the culture of authenticity might be a partial return of the repressed.

We saw that reform tended to suppress or downplay the elements of collective ritual and of magic, in favor of personal commitment, devotion, and moral discipline. This was more severe in Protestant than in Catholic countries, but the trend was general across the board. The Counter-Reformation in France, for instance, constantly attempted to change and reform those elements of popular religion of which the Church did not approve, and disapproval was particularly strong among the Jansenist clergy.

This was even true of the post-Restoration French Catholic Church. The nineteenth-century clergy were, of course, much more cautious. They saw how excess of reforming zeal could alienate whole populations from Catholicism, and they had felt on their own backs what this could mean in the Revolutionary period. They were much more tolerant of folk religion than were their predecessors, but nevertheless, they couldn't resist interfering.[70]

One of their most important targets was the "festive Christianism" of their flocks. It wasn't just that many of the festivals were around some dubious focus, for instance, a pilgrimage to a site of healing, where the rite seemed to have little to do with orthodox Christianity. It wasn't only that the state, using the powers of the Napoleonic Concordat, wanted to cut down on the number of feast days, in the name of greater productivity (in this, following a path already trodden by Protestant countries centuries earlier). What often troubled the clergy was the culture of the feast itself, which mixed some sacred ritual with a lot of very earthy eating, drinking, and dancing, often with unmentionable consequences for the sexual morality of young and old alike. They wanted to clean the feasts up, disengage their properly religious significance from the rather riotous community celebrations, and tone down the latter as much as possible. We connect up here with a long-standing vector of the centuries-long process of reform: visible, for instance, on both Catholic and Protestant sides in the suppression of the "excesses" of Carnival; visible also in the attempts to suppress rowdiness and drinking at the nineteenth-century statute fairs and village feasts in Lincolnshire, as described by Jim Obelkevich.[71]

Moreover, the very attempt of the clergy to make people over and raise their level of practice and morality meant that they were constantly pushing, reprimanding, demanding that some cabaret or dance hall be closed, that money be spent on a new church. Conflicts inevitably arose between priests and communities. At first these revolts were quite independent of any philosophical foundation. But through them a new outlook, denouncing clerical power and exalting the moral independence of the laity, could enter. As Maurice Agulhon puts it: "In order for the influence of free thinking to come fully into play, it was necessary first that the influence of the Church be weakened by reasons from within. . . . in the foremost rank of these was the birth of conflicts between the people and the clergy."[72] Of course, once the division had set in, the Church could defend itself only by mobilizing its own partisans. So its response to the crisis itself augmented the break, and helped to push along the dissolution of the earlier parish consensus. Religion is now not a community *mentalité,* but a partisan stance.[73]

With hindsight, the pathos of this self-defeating action shows that the Catholic Church was engaged in a mission impossible. This is of wider significance than just the contradictions of Pius IX and the ultramontane Church in the nineteenth century. In a way, it shows up the tensions in the whole project of reform. The strength of the rural parish was its collective ritual and its strong consensual notion of "human respect." But the whole drive of the reform movement, from the High Middle Ages through the Reformation and Counter-Reformation right up through evangelical renewal and the post-Restoration Church, was to make Christians with a strong personal and devotional commitment to God and the faith. But strong personal faith and all-powerful community consensus ultimately cannot exist together. If the aim is to encourage Christians in their strong devotional lives to come to frequent communion, then this must, in the end, mean that they break out of the restraining force of "human respect." In theory, any one of these conflicts on the ground could be resolved by a reversal of the local consensus, but in the long run it is impossible that it should always be this way. There can't be a Jean Vianney in every parish (and even he took decades to turn the village of Ars around).

But the nineteenth-century Catholic Church, much to the disgust of certain educated Catholic elites, didn't only take a negative stance toward popular religion. In an age of mobilization, it needed to canalize it. The new building of a mass movement around ultramontane Catholicism didn't just repress or sideline the old festive Christianity that had been so important in the *religions du terroir* of the parish community. It re-created its own versions. Already on the parish level, priests tried not so much to suppress popular feasts and pilgrimages as to gain control of them, redirect them, clean them up, as I described above. One common attempt was to shift the focus from local traditional sites to important regional centers of pilgrimage. As Ralph Gibson puts it, "the clergy tried to redirect the characteristic localism of popular religion in a more universalist direction."[74] In the course of the nineteenth century, there developed in France important national sites, tied to recent apparitions of the Virgin—at, for instance, La Salette, Lourdes, and Paray le Monial. By the end of the century, people were going to Lourdes every year in the hundreds of thousands, traveling in organized groups, mostly by train.

This was, on one level, a triumph of mobilization. It appears to be the ultimate success of the clergy's attempt to supplant local cults, jealously controlled by the parish community, with translocal ones, blessed by the hierarchy. But like all the other forms of Catholic mobilization, this one, too, was ambiguous. In fact, the apparitions of the Virgin start locally; she appears to peasants, shepherds. The hierarchy are at first wary, and anyway, they have to put these new claims to the test. The great translocal sites of Marian pilgrimage of the last two centuries, from Guadalupe to Medjugorje, all started as new departures in popular religion, and they took off because they spoke to masses of ordinary believers. The clergy can sometimes kill these movements, but they don't create them.[75]

The notion of the "festive" I'm invoking here has to be understood in a broad sense. It includes feasts and pilgrimages. It involves large numbers of people coming together outside of quotidian routine, whether the "outside" is geographic, as in the case of pilgrimage, or resides in the ritual of the feast, which breaks with the everyday order of things. We can recognize as another species of this genus the Carnivals of yore, which still survive in some form in Brazil, for instance. Moreover, this assembly is felt to put them in touch with the sacred, or at least some greater power. This may manifest itself in the form of healing, as at Lourdes. But even where it does not, the sense of tapping into something deeper or higher is present. That's why it is not stretching things to include Carnival in this category. If we follow Victor Turner's account,[76] this world "turned upside down" connects us again to the "communitas" dimension of our society, where beyond the hierarchical divisions of the established order, we are together as equal human beings.

I raise this because I believe that the festive, in this sense, is an important, continuing form of religious and quasi-religious life in our own day. It must be part of any description of the place of the spiritual in our society. We might think that these nineteenth-century Catholic forms didn't have any analogue on the Protestant side. But on a second look, this can be challenged. The revival meeting presents obvious analogues. And when we think of the explosion of Pentecostalism during the last century, now spreading to many parts of the world, we have all the more reason to see the festive as a crucial dimension of contemporary religious life.

People still seek those moments of fusion, which wrench us out of the everyday and put us in contact with something beyond ourselves. We see this in pilgrimages, in mass assemblies like World Youth Days, in one-off gatherings of people moved by some highly resonating event, like the funeral of Princess Diana, as well as in rock concerts, raves, and the like. What has all this got to do with religion? The relationship is complex. On the one hand, some of these events are unquestionably "religious," in the sense in which most people use this term, that is, oriented to something putatively transcendent (a pilgrimage to Medjugorje, or a World Youth Day). What has perhaps not sufficiently been remarked is the way in which this dimension of religion, which goes back to its earliest forms, well before the axial age, is still alive and well today, in spite of all attempts by reforming elites over many centuries to render our religious and/or moral lives more personal and inward, to disenchant the universe and downplay the collective.

In some respects, these forms are well adapted to the contemporary predicament. Hervieu-Léger points out how the traditional figure of the pilgrim can be given a new sense today, as young people travel in search of faith or meaning in their lives. The pilgrimage is also a quest. The example of Taizé is striking in this regard. An interconfessional Christian center in Burgundy, with at its core a community of monks, gathered around Roger Schütz, it draws thousands of young people from a great range of countries in the summer months, and tens of thousands to its international gatherings. The drawing power lies partly in the fact that they are received as searchers, that they can express themselves, without being "confronted with a normative system [*dispositif*] of belief, nor with a discourse of preconstituted meaning." Yet at the same time, the center is clearly rooted in Christianity, and in values of international understanding and reconciliation, whose religious roots are explored through Bible study and liturgy. This whole combination is what attracts young people, who want to meet their counterparts from other lands and explore Christian faith without any preconditions as to the outcome. As one visitor put it, "At Taizé, you are not given the answer before you have posed the question, and, moreover, it is up to each person to search for his or her answer."

Of course, the Taizé experience is not simply and totally in the category of the festive. There certainly is the departure from the everyday, and the contact with something greater, a sense of universal brotherhood, even if not always having its source in the fatherhood of God. But the sense of fusion is not always prominent. It is not, however, totally absent; a central part of the Taizé experience is singing together, chants especially designed by members of the community, each in his or her own language, a model and foretaste of the reconciliation sought between peoples and cultures. It is not surprising that Taizé should provide the template from which World Youth Days were developed, a form of Christian pilgrimage/assembly for the age of authenticity.[77]

But how about rock concerts and raves? In terms of our criterion, they are plainly "nonreligious," and yet they also sit uneasily in the secular, disenchanted world. Fusions in common action/feeling, which take us out of the everyday, they often generate the powerful phenomenological sense that we are in contact with something greater, however we ultimately want to explain or understand this. A disenchanted view of the world needs a theory to explain the continuing power of this kind of experience. Of course, such theories can be devised; some already have been: see, for example, those of Durkheim, Freud, Bataille. But it remains true that the state of mind of the participant is far removed from the disengaged, objectifying stance from which the alleged truth of the immanent, naturalistic worldview is supposed to be convincingly evident. It is not obvious a priori that the sense of something beyond, inherent in these fusions, can be ultimately explained (away) in naturalistic categories. The festive remains a niche in our world, where the (putatively) transcendent can erupt into our lives, however well we have organized them around immanent understandings of order.

If the retreat from Christendom offers one key to our situation in the West, if the connections between faith and national/group political identities and ways of life steadily weaken, this still leaves much that is enigmatic and difficult to understand. Many people have placed distance between themselves and their ancestral churches without altogether breaking off. They retain some of the beliefs of Christianity, for instance, and/or they retain some nominal tie with the church and still identify in some way with it: they will reply, say, to a poll by saying that they are Anglican or Catholic. Sociologists are forced to invent new terms, such as *believing without belonging,* or *diffusive Christianity,* to come to grips with this.[78]

Now something like this has always existed. That is, churches have always had around the core of orthodox, fully practicing believers a penumbra whose beliefs shade off into heterodoxy and/or whose practice is partial or fragmentary. We saw examples of this above in the "folk religion" of populations still living partly or largely within ancient régime forms. In fact, the term *diffusive Christianity* was coined for the unofficial popular religion of a more modern, but still not contemporary period, the late nineteenth and early twentieth centuries in the United Kingdom. John Wolffe, following Cox, tries to give a sense of one version of this outlook. He calls it

> a vague non-doctrinal kind of belief: God exists; Christ was a good man and an example to be followed; people should lead decent lives on charitable terms with their neighbors, and those who do so will go to Heaven when they die. Those who suffer in this world will receive compensation in the next. The churches were regarded with apathy rather than hostility: their social activities made some contribution to the community. Sunday School was felt to provide a necessary part of the upbringing of children, and the rites of passage required formal religious sanction. Association was maintained by attendance at certain annual and seasonal festivals, but weekly participation in worship was felt to be unnecessary and excessive. Women and children were more likely than men to be regularly involved, but this did not imply that adult males were hostile; merely—it can be surmised—that they tended to

see themselves as the main breadwinners, and felt that women should therefore represent the family's interests in the religious arena. The emphasis was
on the practical and the communal rather than on the theological and the
individual.[79]

Perhaps this kind of penumbra was bigger in 1900, and the core it surrounded
somewhat smaller, than at the high tide of the evangelical wave, around 1850.
But there has always been such a hinterland surrounding the central zones of
belief and practice in any large-membership church. Only small, committed
minorities, battling with their surroundings, have been able to maintain 100
percent commitment by 100 percent of their members. In earlier times, the
hinterland of lesser orthodoxy lay more in the dimension of folk religion, of
semimagical beliefs and practices surrounding the liturgy and festivals of the
church. Some of this survived even into the early twentieth century, as the
work of Sarah Williams attests, though the "diffusive Christianity" of 1900
was in its essentials different from the religious penumbra of earlier times. But
penumbra it was nonetheless. When one compares these different stages of
British Christianity, there is "some foundation for the judgment," Wolffe
opines, "that around 1900 the British people were, albeit in a diffuse and passive sense, closer to Christian orthodoxy than they had ever been in their
history."[80]

What, then, has happened since 1960? Well, clearly some of the penumbra
has been lost; people now stand clearly outside Christian belief, no longer
identifying with any church, and they were in the hinterland before (or their
parents were). Some of these people have consciously adopted some quite different outlook—materialist, for instance—or they may have adopted a non-
Christian religion. Some of this shift is reflected in the rise in numbers of those
who declare themselves to have no religion. But that still doesn't account for
the substantial number of those who declare themselves still to believe in God,
and/or to identify with some church, even though they stand at a much greater
distance from it than the "diffused" Christians of a century ago. Their views
are more heterodox, for instance (God is often conceived more like a life force),
and they no longer participate in many of the rites of passage, for example,
baptism and marriage. (In Britain, unlike Germany, religious funerals hold up
better than the other rites.)

In other words, the falling off or alienation from the Church and from some
aspects of orthodox Christianity has taken the form of what Grace Davie calls
"Christian nominalism." Committed secularism "remains the creed of a relatively small minority. . . . In terms of belief, nominalism rather than secularism is the residual category."[81]

How to understand this is as yet unclear. A great deal of ambivalence, of
different kinds, inhabits this distancing stance, which Davie calls "believing

without belonging." Is it merely a transitional phenomenon, as secularists hold? For some people, undoubtedly. But for all?

In some ways, this phenomenon can perhaps best be described in terms of past forms of Christian collective life. It stands at a distance from "diffusive Christianity," which itself stood at a certain distance from the models of totally committed practice. It is orbiting farther out from a star that is still a key reference point. In this way, the forms of the age of mobilization remain still alive at the margins of contemporary life. This becomes evident at certain moments, for instance, when people feel a desire to be connected to their past: to take the British case, at moments of royal ceremonial, such as the Jubilee and the funeral of the Queen Mum. Here it is as though the full force of the old neo-Durkheimian identity, linking Britishness to a certain form of Protestant Christianity, where oddly, the Anglican Church is allowed to perform ceremonies for everyone (even Catholics), lives again for a day. Our eccentric orbit, which normally carries us far into outer space, passes close to the original sun on those occasions. This is part of the significance, which I mentioned earlier, of the fact that our past is irrevocably within Christendom. A similar moment occurred in France recently, in the celebrations of the fifteen-hundredth anniversary of the baptism of Clovis. Various *laïque* figures grumbled, but the ceremonies went on regardless. History is hard to deny.

The other kind of occasion arises when disaster strikes, such as September 11, 2001, in the United States or the Hillsborough football tragedy in England in April 1989, where ninety-four people died, mostly Liverpool supporters. Grace Davie describes the ceremonies that followed in Liverpool.[82] A recent German case is the school massacre that occurred at Erfurt in April 2002. Here, in the former East Germany, where the level of practice has fallen lower than anywhere else in the world, there was a rush to churches, which are normally deserted. And, of course, there are events that combine both of the above, such as the mourning and funeral for Princess Di in 1997.

So it appears that the religious or spiritual identity of masses of people still remains defined by religious forms from which they normally keep themselves at a good distance. We still need some attempt to articulate this stance, to describe it from the inside, as it were, as Wolffe attempted for diffusive Christianity in the passage quoted above. There is perhaps also one other clue we can use here. It is, after all, a quite well-known stance to be holding oneself at some distance from a spiritual demand that one nevertheless acknowledges. The famous Augustinian statement, "Lord, make me chaste, but not yet," encapsulates some of this. But it is normally less dramatic; we all have important things to get on with in our lives, and we feel we can't give our full attention and effort to spiritual or moral demands that we hold in some sense valid, that we may admire others for giving themselves to more fully.

Our attachment to these comes in our not wanting to lose sight of them, our resistance to denying them or seeing them denigrated by others. This may be part of what lies behind people answering a survey by saying that they believe in God (or angels, or an afterlife), even though they don't, say, baptize their children or marry in a church, or perhaps do anything else that clearly reflects this belief. It would also explain why the same people may be very moved by actions of others that do manifest their relation to that spiritual source. People may retain an attachment to a perspective of transformation that they are not presently acting on; they may even find themselves losing sight of it from time to time. The reception, as it were, fades in and out, like a city FM station in the countryside. When they see or hear of people's lives that seem really to have been touched by these sources of transformation, they can be strongly moved. The broadcast is now loud and clear. They are moved, and curiously grateful. I remember the response to the life, and particularly the death, of Pope John XXIII. Something similar has happened with some of the actions of John Paul II. These reactions often went well beyond the borders of the Catholic Church. We are dealing with a phenomenon that is not confined to religion. A figure like Nelson Mandela has awakened the same kind of response of confirmation and gratitude.

Perhaps what we need here is a new concept that could capture the inner dynamic underlying this phenomenon. Grace Davie and Danièle Hervieu-Léger seem to have been working toward this in their writings. We might borrow from Davie the term *vicarious religion*.[83] What she is trying to capture is the relationship of people to a church from which they stand at a certain distance but which they nevertheless in some sense cherish, which they want to be there, partly as a holder of ancestral memory, partly as a resource against some future need (e.g., their need for a rite of passage, especially a funeral; or as a source of comfort and orientation in the face of some collective disaster).

In this case, we shouldn't perhaps speak simply of the loss of a neo-Durkheimian identity or connection to religion through our allegiance to civilizational order, but rather of a kind of mutation. The religious reference in our national identity (and/or sense of civilizational order) doesn't so much disappear as change, retreat to a certain distance. It remains powerful in memory, but also as a kind of reserve fund of spiritual force or consolation. It mutates from a "hot" to a "cold" form (with apologies to Marshall McLuhan). The hot form demands a strong, participating identity, and/or an acute sense of Christianity as the bulwark of moral order. The colder form allows a certain ambivalence about historical identity, as well as a certain degree of dissidence from the church's official morality (which these days will be strongest in the domain of sexual ethics).[84]

To take Britain as an example, the original hot form of the synthesis between being British, decent, and Christian was damaged in a number of ways in the twentieth century, perhaps most of all by the experience of the First World War. On the European scene in general, hot, militant nationalism has suffered a great loss of credit through both world wars. But these identities, both national and civilizational, have not just vanished. And the new, fledgling European identity, where it exists, unites these two dimensions; Europe is a supranational community, which is to be defined by certain "values." But the older identities take a new form, involving distance, passivity, and above all a certain queasiness in face of the assertions of their erstwhile "hot" variants.

Indeed, educated, cultivated Europeans are extremely uncomfortable with any overt manifestations of either strong nationalism or religious sentiment. The contrast with the United States in this regard has often been remarked upon. And it might help to take up here one of the most debated issues in the field of secularization theory, that of the "American exception"—or, if one likes, seen from a broader perspective, the "European exception." Put either way, we are faced with a strong even if not uniform pattern of decline in European societies, and virtually nothing of the sort in the United States. How can this difference be explained?

Various attempts have been made: for instance, Steve Bruce attributes the strength of religion in America partly to the immigrant context. Immigrants needed to group together with those of similar origins in order to ease their transition into American society. The rallying point was often a shared religion, and the main agency was often a church.[85]

As to possible other factors, one might be that constitutional-moral patriotism, what I called above the reigning synthesis between nation, morality, and religion, which was very similar in Britain and the United States, was nevertheless much less strong in Britain—indeed, it was much more strongly contested. This was particularly so in the aftermath of the First World War, which was much more traumatic for British than for American society. The challenge to civilization in Britain that this cataclysm represented was certainly lived by many as a challenge to their faith. The strong sense generated by a neo-Durkheimian effect, that everyone shares a certain moral or spiritual coding, that this is how you understand our strong collective moral experience, thus faded more rapidly in Britain, and weakened the code, whereas in the United States many people felt and have gone on feeling that you can show your Americanness by joining a church. In this respect, following the above argument, other European societies are similar to Britain, having gone through the same historical experiences, with similar results.[86]

Another important factor may have been the hierarchical nature of British society. British elites, particularly the intelligentsia, have been living in a fractured culture since the eighteenth century; the saliency of unbelief may have been lower in certain periods of strong piety, but it was always there. Something similar may also have been true of the American intelligentsia, but the position this occupied in its own society was very different. In deferential British society, the pattern of elite life has a prestige that it largely lacks in the United States. This means that elite unbelief can both more effectively resist conforming and also more readily provide models for people at other levels. Again, there are parallels with other European societies, which all in this respect contrast with the United States.[87]

But perhaps the most important factors explaining the transatlantic difference can be formulated in the terms I have been developing here. From this point of view, there are three facets to the American "exception." I have been speaking of the undermining of social matrices that have hitherto kept large numbers of people within the churches, or at least the faith. But what has been suffering the undermining has been different in the two cases. The heart of the American exception is that this society is the only one that from the beginning (if we leave aside the countries of the "old" British Commonwealth) was entirely within the neo-Durkheimian mold. All European societies had some element of the ancien régime or the paleo-Durkheimian, perhaps more vestigial than real, like the ritual surrounding even constitutional monarchies, but often important enough—such as the presence of (at least would-be) state churches, or of rural communities with their *religion du terroir*. The proportions of paleo- and neo- are very different as we move from Spain to Britain or Sweden, but all European states contain some mix of the two, whereas American religious life was entirely in the age of mobilization.

This means that in varying degrees some of the dynamic arising from ancien régime structures takes place in all Old World societies. One of these is the reaction against a state church in the context of an inegalitarian society, where the temptation to align established religion with power and privilege is almost irresistible. This cannot fail to produce anticlerical reactions, which can easily turn, given the availability of exclusively humanist options since the eighteenth century, into militant unbelief, which is then available to canalize the full force of popular discontent with established clergy. We see this dynamic played out in France and Spain, even to some extent in Prussia. In Britain, by contrast, much popular anticlericalism found expression in Nonconformity. But even here an alternative stream existed from the beginning, in figures like Tom Paine and William Godwin, whereas ideas of this sort didn't have the same impact in the early history of the United States. The imprint of an impressive array of Deists among the founders, most notably Jefferson, seems to have been largely effaced by the Second Great Awakening.

The other dynamic that is important in these cases is that the perturbing effect on religious belief of a shakeout that affects both ancien régime and mobilization forms at once is obviously greater than a challenge addressed to neo-Durkheimian structures alone. If peasants being turned into Frenchmen can only be rescued from unbelief by modes of neo-Durkheimian mobilization, then the undermining of the latter has a more profoundly destabilizing effect on belief, or at least practice. In a society, on the other hand, where the move to the age of mobilization has been completed without any significant falloff in belief, the effect of undermining the previously dominant modes of this mobilization will obviously be much less.

This is one facet of the American exception. A second is perhaps this: the actual undermining of neo-Durkheimian modes has been far less severe in America than it has elsewhere. Lots of Americans still feel quite at home with the idea of the United States as "one people under God." Those whom this identity makes uncomfortable are vocal and dominant in universities and (some) media but are not all that numerous. It is this standoff that makes possible the present American Kulturkampf. The "culture wars" are one offshoot of this but are misleading about its religious significance, since the polls on abortion or homosexuality are more evenly divided, or show a slight "liberal" majority. But the number of people who can make their peace with "one people under God" is much greater than the "conservative" numbers on such polls; it includes lots of "liberals." This is the more so in that groups of non-Christian and non-Jewish immigrants, who might be thought natural allies of those who want to resist a biblical coding of American identity, are themselves anxious to be co-opted into a suitably widened variation of it. Imams are now alongside priests and rabbis at public prayers, and this panreligious unity surfaces especially at moments of crisis or disaster, as after 9/11.

Now, this is partly the result of the sheer difference in numbers of people who adhere to some religion in the United States, as opposed to Europe. But it also has to do with the respective attitudes toward national identity. Europe in the second half of the twentieth century has been full of reticences about its erstwhile senses of nationhood, and the events of the first half of that century explain why. The European Union is built on the attempt to go beyond earlier forms, in the full consciousness of how destructive they have been. The full-throated assertion of the older, self-exalting nationalisms is now reserved for the radical Right, which is felt by everyone else to represent a pestilence, a possibly deadly disease, and which in turn is anti-European. War, even "righteous" war, as an expression of the superiority of the national project makes most Europeans profoundly uneasy.

Attitudes in the United States seem quite different. This may partly be because Americans have fewer skeletons in the family closet to confront than do their European cousins. But I think the answer is simpler. It is easier to be unreservedly confident in your own rightness when you are the hegemonic power. The skeletons are there, but they can be resolutely ignored, in spite of the efforts of a gallant band of scholars, who are engaged in the "history wars." Most Germans have to cringe when they are reminded of the First World War slogan "Gott mit uns" (God is with us)—and about the Second World War, the less said the better. But most Americans have few doubts about whose side God is on. In this context, the traditional neo-Durkheimian definition is far easier to live with.

So in terms of my discussion a few paragraphs back, the traditional American synthesis of "civil religion," a strong neo-Durkheimian identity, originally around a nondenominational Christianity, with a strong connection to civilizational order, is still in a "hot" phase, unlike its British counterpart. This goes some way to explaining the American culture wars. The original civil religion gradually moved wider than its Protestant base, but it has now come to a stage where, while the link to civilizational order remains strong, the connection to religion is now challenged by a broad range of secularists and liberal believers. Issues like the banning of school prayer, abortion, and, more recently, homosexual marriage become highly charged. I spoke above of a "Kulturkampf," but another analogy might be *la guerre franco-française*, two strongly opposed ideological codings of the same nation's identity, in a context where nationalism (not to say great-power chauvinism) remains powerful. This is a recipe for bitter struggles.[88]

Perhaps a "control case" can be found in the societies of the old British Commonwealth: Canada, Australia, New Zealand. Like the United States, and (almost) from the beginning, they have been in the age of mobilization. But their faith-related neo-Durkheimian definitions haven't fared as well. Either they lived a "British" identity, which has since decayed in the "mother country" as well as the ex-colony, or (as in the case of Quebec), they have undergone a turnover that more resembles the European model. But above all, they are not hegemonic powers; one case, Canada, is constantly reminded of this fact by its proximity to the nation that is. So it is not surprising to find the figures for religious belief/practice in these countries somewhere between European and U.S. ones. It is also not surprising that the issue of gay marriage, while it has been upsetting for Conservatives in Canada as well, has not awakened the same degree of heat and indignation in Canada as in its neighbor to the south.

There is a third way of stating the American exception, which overlaps in some respects with the two points above. The United States since the early nineteenth century has been home to religious freedom, expressed in a very American way: that is, it has been a country of religious choice. People move, form new denominations, join ones that they weren't brought up in, break away from existing ones, and so on. Their whole religious culture was in some ways prepared for the age of authenticity, even before this became a facet of mass culture in the latter part of the twentieth century. This whole shift was therefore much less destabilizing. We have just to think of the contrast with Germany and France, where the new "cults" deeply disturb people. Even French atheists are a trifle horrified when religion does not take the standard Catholic form that they love to hate. It is harder to see the discontinuity in America, and indeed it was in a sense less, since before the 1960s the culture of authenticity was everywhere present among cultured elites, and the educated were a much larger proportion of the U.S. population even before the postwar expansion of universities.

3

I want now to make a few hesitant comments about developments outside the West, or on a global scale. A problem that has been awaiting us here, and that we must acknowledge, is: What is the West, after all? What are its limits? I have tried to define it by its descent from Latin Christendom. But what about Latin America? Does Mexico belong to the West? And how about the Balkans? And the world of Greek/Russian Orthodoxy in Eastern Europe?

I don't think there is any way to resolve these issues. The boundaries are inherently fuzzy. But what these questions already make evident is that the future of the religious past may present itself quite differently in other civilizations. Japan, and in other ways China, went through the axial revolution in a very different way from the civilizations dominated by monotheism, let alone the West. Indeed, it has been claimed that Japanese culture has remained in some ways pre-axial.[89] Neither China nor the West comes even close to resembling Indian civilization, where postaxial reforms have taken a very different shape. Hinduism can indeed be related to, even considered as, a civilization, but not because this "religion" defines the shape of a moral-civilizational order, which it sustains and of which it is the bulwark, something that has often been claimed for both Christianity and Islam. In spite of certain nineteenth- and twentieth-century reform movements, influenced by European models, like the Brahmo Samaj, popular piety, replete with pre-axial elements, has not been seriously repressed and overhauled—despite the banning of certain practices such as suttee or the exclusion of Dalits from temples. Hinduism can indeed be seen as the basis of a civilization, but as its central inspiration, rather than as a moralistic bulwark against chaos and dissolution.

I can't even begin to cope with the immense diversity that a truly world perspective would open up. Here I will attempt only some comments on certain Western forms, which seem in some way to have become "globalized." I shall be looking at variants of the modes of empowering devotion, the neo-Durkheimian phenomenon, and religion as the basis for moral/civilizational order that I have been discussing.

NOT ALL FEATURES of Western individualism have "traveled," as it were, into other religious traditions. The stress on inwardness, for instance, may not have straddled the gap. And clearly, the conception of society as made up of rights-bearing individuals has not been everywhere accepted. But the importance of personal commitment and responsibility does seem to have been become an important part of some contemporary ways of being Islamic.

Some of these are characterized by their own adherents, or outsiders, as "Islamist." But there are also those who shun the label, wanting to stress that their interest lies not in politics or state power, but in the recovery of a genuine Islamic piety. This is true, for instance, of the currents within the Islamic revival in Egypt, of which Saba Mahmood has written.[90] It is true of the young preachers of the Tabligh in France. When Moussa Kömeçoglu contrasts the "enlightened and puritanical Islam" of these young preachers to the "routinized and traditionalist Islam" of their parents, he is pointing, I believe, to a similar shift to individual responsibility.[91] A study of contemporary Islamic coffeehouses in Turkey makes the point that they no longer rely on dress codes and spatial separation, but now have to appeal to inner conviction and self-formation. The "Cartesian dichotomy" of which its author speaks is close to this idea of personal responsibility, which can separate itself from all external forms.[92] This kind of individuation can sometimes have the effect of devaluing certain traditional forms of ritual or devotion as "un-Islamic"; Islamic reformers have frequently in our day not only wanted to return to the full rigors of the *Shari'a,* but also looked askance at various forms of devotion, which have sometimes gone under the general descriptive term *Sufi,* and have sometimes been targeted because they smack to much of an "enchanted" worldview, which the reformers want to put behind them.

But the shift can also have the effect of breaking people loose from network identities of various kinds—families, clans, villages—precisely the loci in which a "routinized and traditionalist Islam" is often practiced. The break with network identity means the ascendancy of a categorical identity, as Muslims, or real Muslims, and/or Muslims of a certain strict form of practice.[93] Of course, this identity was also in some sense theirs beforehand. The difference is that in many milieus Islam was something one belonged to *through* the collective practice of one's clan or village, whereas now one may be living one's religion against the grain of all this.

Now, this assumption of a categorical identity through one's own responsible commitment pitches one out into a kind of public space of a modern kind. By that I mean a space that is not defined by some preexisting action-transcendent structure, like a divinely established kingdom or caliphate, or a tribal law since time out of mind, or a sacred "theater state," or whatever; modern public space is, rather, self-consciously founded by the common action of those who appear in it. An association is formed by people becoming mobilized, or mobilizing themselves, coming together for certain purposes and interacting with a larger space, which may easily be indifferent or hostile to this common purpose. Indeed, if it is not to be indifferent or hostile, this space must itself be produced by mobilization and collective action, as with the rebellion that overturned the Shah and the creation of an Islamic Republic in Iran.

So we have a religious identity that fits clearly within a modern-type public space and presupposes a space of this kind. It requires individual commitment and thus often mobilization into associations, which is a standard feature of modern polities. It thus often proceeds through and makes heavy use of mass media of various kinds to sustain itself and grow. D. Eikelman has noted how much contemporary Islamic movements rely on the printed word, on their members acquiring conviction and commitment through reading, often becoming in this way inducted into polemics with what are defined as hostile ideas: for instance, those of Western secularism.[94] Some of the intellectual leaders of the Iranian Revolution defined their thought partly in relation to various French philosophers, whose thought is also widely read in the West. And everyone is aware of how much Ayatollah Khomeini's revolution depended on cassette recordings of his sermons.

Note that God can figure in public space, and very obtrusively, but this has a different meaning from many premodern forms. These were based on the sacred in a strong, localizable sense, what I have called the paleo-Durkheimian dispensation, like the divinely endorsed kingship of, say, ancien régime France. But there is also the neo-Durkheimian model, best illustrated in the West by the new American republic. God was present here, because the republic was seen as based on a providential design. There are analogies between this and today's Islamic republic, despite all the differences.

People often claim to see a paradox here, in that some of the movements that operate in modern public space themselves claim to be returning to a purer, early form of religion, the movements that tend to be called "fundamentalist" in the West. Of course, there is a paradox only if we accept some overly simple definitions of "modernity" and "religion" as frozen constellations based on opposing premises. Even the paradigm case of "fundamentalism" for Westerners, Protestant biblical literalism, not only makes use of the latest and most sophisticated media, but in many ways only makes sense within modern assumptions, such as a clear and exhaustive distinction of literal versus figurative, which would have been difficult to grasp in earlier Christian centuries.

But although there is no paradox, there can be strains. To be mobilized through an appeal to individual commitment, in what is often an indifferent or even hostile public space, requires a degree of responsibility that may clash with certain features of the code of conduct that reflects the new commitment. This is perhaps clearest in the case of women in Islamic movements, as much of the research of Nilüfer Göle and others has shown. Responsible commitment, in a movement based on mobilization, may require, for instance, one to take leadership positions, act as spokesperson, and the like. And this may conflict with the recessive role the code ascribes to women, who are meant to be anonymous or invisible in public space. The new identity is thus liable to strains, which are an important source of conflict and evolution.[95]

There are clearly certain analogues here with Western forms in the age of mobilization. But more precisely, we can see the development, not just in Islam, of what I called above neo-Durkheimian identities. Indeed, a host of factors, which we often gesture at with such portmanteau terms as *globalization* or *development,* are pushing more and more people into an age of mobilization.

The move of modern history has been toward a wider and wider recruitment of people into what I called above "categorical" identities, from out of earlier, more local identifications, focusing often on kinship systems, clans, or tribes. These early identities are often defined by "networks," where people stand in a dense web of relations, linked to many people but in a different fashion to each one; as in a kinship system, where I am related to one person as father, another as son, another as cousin, and so on. By contrast, modern political identities are "categorical"; they bind people together in virtue of their falling together under a category, like Serb, or American, or Hindu, where we all relate in a uniform way to a whole.[96]

This movement seems to be accelerating. Many factors are drawing people away from the earlier network identities: not only the efforts of elites to mobilize them but also migration or the effects of globalization, either through the spread of media or by undermining older ways in which we make our living. Migration can mean being mixed with unfamiliar others, not knowing how they will react, being unable to reconstitute the older way of life. Loss of the older forms of making a living can undermine our dignity, our identity, induce a sense of loss and helplessness. The decay of the old often brings disorientation, or feelings of humiliation and lowered self-worth.

In these circumstances, a new categorical identity can offer people something very precious: not only a direction, an orientation, but also a sense of (collective) agency. We are no longer just to suffer a sense of helplessness before dimly understood global forces, but we are to be mobilized against named and identified ills.

The fact that mobilization is often against something brings us to the aspect of these new developments that most strikes us in the West today: the way in which new identities can be turned to foster violence. And indeed, it is often noted that many of the most violent, or at least conflictual, have a religious basis.

This has led to a lot of loose talk about religion as a source for violence, which needs to be examined a lot more closely, precisely with an eye to the different kinds of religious involvements with political identities and civilizational norms that I have been analyzing in the preceding pages.

According to a view of things that has been widespread since the Enlightenment, the sources of hate, conflict, and persecution seem to lie deep in our religious heritage. Indeed, this penchant toward conflict and repression has been seen as particularly strong in the religions that issued from Jewish monotheism. Enlightenment thinkers, with the terrible history of the Crusades and the Inquisition in mind, saw Christianity as particularly culpable, although they often also saw Islam as equally bad, if not worse. In many ways, this outlook lingers on in liberal, secular circles in the West, in that there is deep suspicion of militant Christianity, and practically a demonization of Islam.

Blaming monotheism is not just a matter of prejudice. It is remarkable how, in the ancient world, Jews and later Christians were condemned by their neighbors as *atheioi* because they broke with the usual mores of mutual recognition of each other's divinities, fading into cross-worship and syncretism. They denied the very existence of other gods, or identified them with demons, and they strictly forbade their adherents to worship them. They set up a clear boundary, and guarded it zealously.

Christianity and Islam inherited this boundary from Judaism, but then added to it a vocation to proselytize, to extend their faith to the whole of mankind. This was the source of religious wars of conquest, often of forced conversions, particularly in Christian history, while the boundary was also defended internally against deviancy and apostasy was sternly punished.

We can build up a picture of a certain kind of religion as the source of group conflict, war, persecution, and enforced conformity. To this was often contrasted the more tolerant attitude of enlightened paganism (Gibbon), or the wisdom of Chinese civilization (an important Enlightenment topos), or, in recent centuries, the loose boundaries of Hinduism and the pacifism of Buddhism.

There is some truth in all this historically, but it's certainly not the whole truth about religion and hate in the twentieth century. Hinduism, in some sense, seems to be the rallying point of a superchauvinist political movement that has won partial power in India. Terrible violence has been committed in Sri Lanka in the name of Buddhism. Many people have seen in these events a betrayal of the religious traditions concerned,[97] but the implication of religion in violence seems undeniable. Is the persecutory virus of monotheism contagious?

I want to argue that things are not quite as they appear. In one sense, it is not exactly religion that is at the root of violence in many twentieth-century cases. Or, to put it differently, it gets involved through a quite different mechanism, which itself is not intrinsically tied to religion. Already certain notorious cases should alert us to this. They point to a different relation between devotion and violence.

In the bad old days of the Inquisition, for instance, allowing for the usual quota of time-servers and opportunists, the persecutors were often among the most devout and dedicated; they were fired by a holy zeal for the faith. But if one looks at Ulster these days, this is not the pattern one observes. The men of violence are more and more distinct from the really devout Catholics and Protestants, who are more frequently heard as brave voices for peace. The Reverend Ian Paisley, an extremist who is a man of the cloth, seems more and more an anachronistic survival. The killers are certainly full of some kind of zeal, to them no doubt holy, but not for the service of God.

Another striking case is that of the BJP and its parent organization, the Rashtriya Swayamsevak Sangh (RSS). In what sense, if at all, is this body defined by religious as opposed to secular goals? The assassins of Gandhi didn't reproach him for his devotion to God or the dharma (how could they?) but for returning their share of the gold stock of the old, undivided India to Pakistan and for opposing militarism. Their successors have now realized one of their long-standing ambitions and made India into a full-dress nuclear power. These are the goals of a certain kind of nationalism everywhere. What do they have to do with religion, and specifically Hinduism?

It is true that the BJP has, in recent years, singled itself out by a campaign to destroy a mosque in the birthplace of Rama and erect a temple on the site. Mobilization to this end has probably helped, on balance, its recent rise to power (although the destruction of the Babri Masjid also frightened a lot of Indians, and the party has played down this part of its program since). So the reality is complex. But when one looks at the goals of the core organization, the RSS, what strikes one is, rather, the exploitation, by an organization whose goals lie in the domain of secular power, of currents of popular devotion. In any case, it is clear here, as in Northern Ireland, that the most active in stirring this agitation are not necessarily among the most devout.

So what is happening here? I want to argue that much of the implication of religion in violence in our century is to be understood as the working out of what can be called identity struggles. These crystallize around definitions of one's own and the other's identities. But these definitions are not necessarily religious. On the contrary, they frequently turn on perceived nationality, language, tribe, or whatever. What drives these struggles is frequently very similar across the different modes of definition. That religion figures in the definition—as against language, say—often changes very little (not always, of course, as I will discuss below). In cases like Northern Ireland or the former Yugoslavia, one is tempted to say that originally religious differences have now hardened into an enmity between "nations," felt and lived as such. Atheists like Milošević will combat the Bosnians or Kosovo Albanians as a "Serb." God and the devotional life of the Orthodox Church don't figure in this conflict. What matters is the historical identity of the people, and here some monasteries and traditional sites of devotion are important markers of territory, but little more.

In other words, even when religion is a major source of definition in modern identity struggles, it tends to figure under a description (e.g., the historical tradition that defines "our" people) that displaces the center of attention from what has always been seen as the main point of religious devotion and practice: God, *moksha,* Nirvana. Which is what raises the legitimate question: Is the struggle "about" religion any more?

These struggles are occurring in a new, modern, structural context. The democratic age poses new obstacles to coexistence, because it opens a new set of issues that can deeply divide people, those concerning the political identity of the state. In many parts of the Indian subcontinent, for instance, Hindus and Muslims coexisted in conditions of civility, even with a certain degree of syncretism, where later they would fight bitterly. What happened? The explanations given often include the British attempt to divide and rule, or even the British mania for census figures, which first made an issue of who was a majority where.

These factors may have their importance, but clearly what makes them vital is the surrounding situation, in which political identity becomes an issue. As the movement grows to throw off the alien, multinational empire and to set up a democratic state, the question of its political identity arises. Will it simply be that of the majority? Are we heading for Hindu Raj? Muslims ask for reassurance. Gandhi's and Nehru's proposals for a pan-Indian identity don't satisfy Jinnah. Suspicion grows, as do demands for guarantees and ultimately separation.

Each side is mobilized to see the other as a threat to political identity. This fear can then sometimes be transposed, through mechanisms we have yet to understand, into a threat to life, to which the response is savagery and countersavagery, and we descend a spiral that has become terribly familiar. Census figures can then be charged with ominous significance, but only because in the age of democracy being in the majority has decisive importance.

Democracy thus underlies identity struggles, because the age of popular sovereignty opens a new kind of question, which I've been calling that of the political identity of the state. What/whom is the state for? And for any given answer, the question can arise for me/us, can I/we "identify with" this state? Do we see ourselves as reflected there? Can we see ourselves as part of the people this state is meant to reflect/promote?

These questions can be deeply felt, strongly contested, because they arise at the juncture between political identity and personal identity, meaning by the latter the reference points by which individuals and component groups define what is important in their lives. If it is important to me that I belong to a French-speaking community, then a state defined by its official language as English will hardly reflect me; if I am more than a pro forma Muslim, then a state defined by "Hindutva" cannot fully be mine; and so on. We are in the very heartland of modern nationalism.

But these "nationalist" issues are the more deeply fraught because the personal and group identities that vie for reflection are often themselves in the course of redefinition. This redefinition is often forced by circumstances, and at the same time can be extremely conflictual and unsettling. We can see the forces surrounding this process if we follow the serial rise of nationalisms in the modern world.

If we try to identify the source of the modern nationalist turn, the refusal—at first among elites—of incorporation by the metropolitan culture, we can see that it often takes the form of the need for difference. This is felt existentially as a challenge, not just as a matter of a valuable common good to be created but also viscerally as a matter of dignity, in which one's self-worth is engaged. This is what gives nationalism its emotive power. This is what places it so frequently in the register of pride and humiliation.

So nationalism can be said to be modern, because it's a response to a modern predicament. But the link is also more intimate. It has often been remarked that nationalism usually arises among "modernizing" elites. The link can be understood as more than accidental. One facet of nationalism, I have been arguing, is a response to a threat to dignity. But modernity has also transformed the conditions of dignity.

These could not but change in the move from hierarchical, "mediated" societies to "horizontal," direct-access ones. The concept of honor, which was in place in the earlier forms, was intrinsically hierarchical. It supposed "preferences," in Montesquieu's terms.[98] For me to have honor, I must have a status that not everyone shares, as is still the case with an "honors list" of awards today. Equal direct-access societies have developed the modern notion of "dignity." This is based on the opposite supposition, that all humans enjoy this equally. The term as used by Kant, for instance, designates what is supposed to be the appanage of all rational agents.[99] Philosophically, we may want to attribute this status to all, but politically the sense of equal dignity is really shared by people who belong to a functioning direct-access society together.[100] In this typically modern predicament, their dignity passes through their common categorical identity. My sense of my own worth can no longer be based mainly on my lineage, my clan. A goodly part of it will usually be invested in some other categorical identity.

But categorical identities can also be threatened, even humiliated. The more we are inducted into modern society, the more this is the form in which the question of dignity will pose itself for us. Nationalism is modern, because it is a typically modern way of responding to the threat represented by the advancing wave of modernization. Elites have always been susceptible to experiencing a dramatic loss of dignity in the face of conquering power. One way of responding is to fight back or to come to terms with the conquerors out of the same traditional identity and sense of honor. Another is to forge a new categorical identity to be the bearer of the sought-for dignity. It is (a subspecies of) this second reaction that we call nationalist. But it is essentially modern. The 1857 rebellion in India was in part an attempt to expunge this perennially possible loss of dignity in a premodern context. In this sense, it was not a nationalist movement, as the later Congress was.

The modern context of nationalism also turns its search for dignity outward. No human identity is purely inwardly formed. The other always plays some role. But it can be just as a foil, a contrast, a way of defining what we're not, for better or for worse. So the aboriginals of the newly "discovered" world figured for post-Columbian Europeans. The "savage," the other of civilization, provided a way for Europeans to define themselves both favorably (applying "civilized" to themselves in self-congratulation) and sometimes unfavorably (Europeans as corrupted in contrast to the "noble savage"). This kind of other reference requires no interaction. Indeed, the less interaction, the better, or else the stereotype may be resisted.

But the other can also play a role directly, where I need his or her recognition to be confident of my identity. This has been standard for our relation to our intimates, but it wasn't that important in relation to outsiders in the premodern period. Identities were defined by reference to the other but not out of the other's reactions. Where the latter becomes so, the way we interact is crucial. Perhaps we should correct this statement: because of the big part played by illusion, the way the interaction is seen by the parties is crucial. But the point is that the interaction is understood to be crucial by the identity bearers themselves.

I would like to argue that identities in the modern world are more and more formed in this direct relation to others, in a space of recognition. I can't argue the general case here,[101] but I hope that this is evident for modern nationalism. Modern nationalist politics is a species of identity politics. Indeed, the original species—that is, national struggles—is the site from which the model comes to be applied to feminism, to the struggles of cultural minorities, to the gay movement, and so on. The work of someone like Frantz Fanon,[102] which was written in the context of the anticolonial struggle but whose themes have been recuperated in other contexts, illustrates the connections. Strong national sentiment among elites usually arises in the first phase because an identity is threatened in its worth.

This identity is vulnerable to nonrecognition, at first by members of the dominant societies. Later, there has developed a world public scene, on which peoples see themselves as standing, on which they see themselves as rated, which rating matters to them. This world scene is dominated by a vocabulary of relative advance, even to the point of having to discover periodic neologisms in order to euphemize the distinctions. Hence what used to be called "backward" societies began to be called "underdeveloped" after the war. Then even this came to be seen as indelicate, and so we have the present partition: developed/developing. The backdrop of modern nationalism, that there is something to be caught up with, each society in its own way, is inscribed in this common language, which in turn animates the world public sphere.

Modern nationalism thus taps into something perennial. Conquest, or the threat of conquest, has never been good for one's sense of worth. But the whole context in which this nationalism arises, that of successive waves of (institutional) modernization, and the resultant challenge to difference, that of the growth of categorical identities, as well as the creation of a world public sphere as a space of recognition—this is quintessentially modern. We are very far from atavistic reactions and primal identities.

I have been attempting to give some of the background of modern identity struggles. These have a locus, which is frequently inescapable, in the modern state, which poses the question of political identity—What/whom is this polity for?—and the derivative question: Do I/we have a place here? These issues can be particularly charged, because they are the point at which the necessary redefinition of a traditional way of life can be carried out. Indeed, the very staking of a claim for "us" as a people demanding our own state, or calling for reflection in an existing state whose definition excludes us, this very move to peoplehood in the modern sense will often involve a redefinition of what "we" are. Thus the erstwhile dominant, conservative and clerical, definition of *la nation canadienne-française* was not meant to realize itself primarily in political institutions but rather in the conservation of a way of life in which the Church played the major role. The political strategy was to hold North American Anglophone-Protestant society at bay, both in its concentration on economic growth and in its tendency to enlarge the state's role in the management of certain social affairs, especially education and health matters. This required the jealous guarding of provincial autonomy, but also the self-denial of the provincial government, which refrained from itself entering the domains from which it was excluding the federal government. Quite a different self-definition underlies the present identity as "Québécois," which for some people at any rate motivates the demand for separate statehood.

Of course, this move involved a shift away from a religious self-definition. The last fifty years have seen a rapid laicization of Quebec society. But the earlier variant of nationalism also involved a controversial stance on what it meant to be a Catholic community in majority Protestant Canada and North America, as the long and bitter quarrel with Irish clergy testifies.

The point is that the resolution of issues of political identity—What kind of state will one settle for? Do we have a real choice? Can we strike out on our own? Should we accept assimilation?—goes along with the settling of the major issues of personal or group identity: Who are we really? What really matters to us? How does this relate to how we used to define what matters? What is the important continuity with our past that makes us = us? (For example, is it just speaking French in this territory for four centuries, or is it also being Catholic?)

These reassertions or redefinitions are particularly fraught, not just because they are anguishing, the point at which people may feel that there has been a loss of identity or a betrayal, but also because they are often lived in the register of dignity: the issue of whether the identity we end up with somehow will brand us as inferior, not up to the rest, as a group destined to be dominated, cast in the shade by others. This may indeed be how we are seen by powerful others, but the issue is how much this gets to us, how much we feel that only by changing ourselves in some direction ("modernizing" our economy, reforming some of our social practices, attaining statehood or autonomy) could we really refute this disparaging judgment and hold our heads high among the nations. And our plight is not made easier by the fact that one person's essential reform, by which dignity is recovered, is another person's utter betrayal.

Now, religion gets caught up in this process of struggle through redefinition. Sometimes the result is negative: the old faith is extruded or marginalized, as, for instance, in Jacobin-nationalist or leftist identities. But sometimes it seems to be revalorized. "Reformed" versions of an old religious tradition come forward as the way to embrace what is good in modernity, even rediscover these good things in a neglected part of our tradition (Brahmo Samaj, for instance). Or against these, the counterclaim is made that these reformed versions have abandoned what is essential, and new, more rigorous returns to the origins are proposed. But these latter efforts take place in a modern context, and very often while attempting to meet the demands of power, statehood, and economic and military viability, with full use of communications technology, which belong to this age. And so they are frequently less of a pure return to origins than they claim on the surface to be. The pathos of "fundamentalisms" is always a certain hybridity. Present-day Protestant biblical "fundamentalism" would have been unthinkable in the symbolic universe of medieval Catholicism, where everything was a sign; it presupposes the literal-mindedness of the modern scientific age. Earlier Christians lived in a world in which secular time was interwoven with various orders of higher time, various dimensions of eternity. From within this time sense, it may be hard to explain just what is at stake in the issue of whether "day" in Genesis literally means the twenty-four hours between sunset and sunset, let alone see why people should be concerned about it. Or, to take another example, the Iranian revolution and subsequent regime have been deeply marked by modern communications, modes of mass mobilization, and forms of state (a sort of attempt at a parliamentary theocracy).

Looked at from a certain angle, these movements can be seen as attempts to live the traditional faith to the full in contemporary conditions. The ultimate goal in each case is something that would be recognized as such across the history of the tradition in question—for instance, in the Muslim case, living the life of submission to God in the light of the Qur'an and hadith—even if some of the forms might seem strange and new. But to the extent that the struggle for reassertion/redefinition becomes entangled in identity struggles, a displacement comes about. Two other goals or issues begin to impinge, which may draw the enterprise out of the orbit of the religious tradition. These are the twin goals/issues of the power and the dignity of a certain "people." These may impose objectives that are more or less alien to the faith, not only as lived historically, but even in terms of what can be justified today.

Constituting a dominant people, especially one with the power to impose its will through weapons of mass destruction, has never been seen as a demand of Hindu piety. A case to the diametrically opposite effect would be easier to make, as Gandhi showed, and as his brutal elimination by the spiritual ancestors of the government in Delhi emphasizes. Nor has genocide been seen as a goal of orthodox Christianity, even allowing for the worst modes of perversion of the faith historically.

In many of its most flagrant cases, contemporary violence that seems "religious" in origin is quite alien to religion. We might want to protest that it is powered by something quite different. But this would also be too simple. It arises in certain basically modern forms where identity struggles that are constituted by and help constitute "peoples," groups struggling to define themselves and to attain political identity, incorporate religion as a historical marker. Sometimes where this is the case, the demands of piety have utterly disappeared or atrophied: for example, as with the "Serb" militants, the Irish Republican Army and Orange killers, and much of the leadership of the BJP. A less clear case is the BJP movement as a whole, in which undeniably powerful popular devotion is harnessed to a campaign for political domination, as with the agitation around the Rama temple in Ayodhya.

Even more mixed are various of the militant Muslim movements of our day. Many of these are undoubtedly powered by deeply felt conceptions of piety. But this doesn't mean that their form and course may not be deeply influenced by the context of identity struggle. It would be absurd to reduce Islamic integrism to a single mode of explanation; we are dealing with a complex, many-sided, overdetermined reality. I nevertheless would like to argue that its various manifestations have some features of the profile I have been outlining above. The sense of operating on a world scene, in the register of threatened dignity, is very much present, as is the overvehement rejection of the West (or its quintessence, America, the "great Satan"), and the tremendous sensitivity to criticism from this quarter, for all the protestations of hostility and indifference. Islamic societies are perhaps, if anything, more vulnerable to a threat to their self-esteem from the impact of superior power in that Islam's self-image was of the definitive revelation, destined to spread outward without check. The Islamic sense of Providence, if I may use this Christian expression, can cope with the status of conquerors, but tends to be bewildered by the experience of powerlessness and conquest.

Again, for all their protestations of faithfulness to the origins, this integrism is in some respects very modern, as I argued above. It mobilizes people in a modern fashion, in horizontal, direct-access movements; it thus has no problem using the "modern" institutional apparatus of elected legislatures, bureaucratic states, armies. While it would reject the doctrine of popular sovereignty in favor of a species of theocracy, it has also delegitimated all the traditional ruling strata. The Iranian revolution was carried out against the Shah. Those enjoying special authority are exclusively those who "rationally" merit this, granted the nature and goals of the state, namely, the experts in God's law. Not to mention the Ayatollah Khomeini's media-oriented abuse of Islamic judicial forms in issuing his fatwa against Salman Rushdie. And to what extent was the heinousness of Rushdie's "crime" greatly increased by the fact that he published his "blasphemies" in English and for a Western audience?

Again, we do not understand as fully as we might the tremendous emphasis laid on the dress and comportment of women in contemporary Islamic reform movements. Very often the demands seem to spin out of all relation to the Qur'an and tradition, as with the Taliban in Afghanistan. But we can trace the way in which women have become the "markers" for "modernism" and integrism. Atatürk insisted that women dress in Western fashion, that they walk in the streets and attend social functions, even dance with men. The traditional modes were stigmatized as "backward." Perhaps this has something to do with the extraordinary stress on rigorism in dress and contact imposed on women in many places today. These matters have become internationally recognized symbols of where one stands, ways of making a statement, of declaring one's rejection of Western modernity. The struggle in international public space may be dictating what happens here more than the weight of the *Shariʿa,* or hallowed modes of piety.[103]

Perhaps the most striking case has come to world prominence with the attack on the World Trade Center of September 11, 2001. The network known as al-Qaeda, headed by Osama bin Laden, has pushed even farther a development already evident in certain Islamist "terrorist" movements; this involves using the concept of jihad and the status of shahid to legitimate a form of action that seems to lie outside traditionally permitted limits. This is so in two respects: first, in its disregard for the distinction between combatants and uninvolved civilians; second, in its recourse to suicide attacks. Either of these alone is problematic, but the combination seems to violate clear precepts of Islam. And some mullahs have made clear that someone who kills himself with the aim of taking with him not even enemy soldiers but defenseless civilians cannot claim the title of shahid.

But the striking fact is how little impact these rulings have had in many Muslim societies. Not only are they totally ignored in the street, as it were, where young Palestinians still refer to suicide bombers, whose only victims may be teenagers at a disco, as "martyrs," but many of the religious authorities in these "hot" societies go along with the public rather than endorsing the best jurisprudence. What is happening here? May it not be that "Islamic" action is being driven by the sense that "we" are being despised and mishandled by "them," quite like nationalist reactions that have become very familiar to us? To take an example from Christendom: the clergy of all the combatants in the First World War, with very few honorable exceptions, bestowed God's blessing on their nation's armies. From a certain distance, the betrayal of their Christian commitment is only too painfully obvious.

Moreover, seeing nationalism, proletarian internationalism, and religious fundamentalisms in the same register may help us to understand their interaction, that they are often, in fact, fighting for the same space. Arab nationalism gives way to Islamic integrism,[104] just as the demise of Soviet Marxism opens the way for virulent nationalisms. The search for a categorical identity, to answer the call for difference and become the bearer of a sought-after dignity, can take many forms. It is understandable that the discrediting of some must strengthen the appeal of others. This discussion yields a rather mixed picture. It cautions us against taking "religion" to be a clearly identifiable phenomenon, once and for all, responding to a single inner dynamic. It ought to be clear that there is more than one dynamic going on today in connection with religion. We must be particularly aware of this if we want to do something to overcome the violence that is often associated with religious differences.

But perhaps we can understand the multiple dynamic with the aid of the tripartite scheme roughly elaborated above. In line with the second term, religion can be a (would be) political identity, of a state, or an alliance of states; this marker can provide the sense of dignity and also the collective efficacy that many people feel are lacking in their world as older forms break down. In the terms of the discussion earlier, religion can be the basis of a "neo-Durkheimian" identity, and this can bring with it hostility or opposition to other groups in the way that national identities often do.

In line with the third term, religion can be felt to be the bulwark of a moral-civilizational order. This can be felt with special acuity in cases where "globalization," migration, and economic development are eroding a traditional way of life.

But there remains the first term: religious belief and piety can also be actuated by other motives, a felt need for anchoring, a desire to come closer to God or whatever is seen as the source of spiritual strength, a sense of emptiness in one's present life, and so on.

Now, these sources can operate together. The second and third are often linked, for instance. Some Islamist identities that focus on attaining political power do so with the idea that Islamic law and civilization is the highest or only true one and see themselves as fighting back the corruption and immorality of Western culture. But this kind of linkage is less evident in the mobilizations undertaken by the RSS and the BJP, which are more purely of the second, political type.

What makes the proclivity to violence of these forms, of the second—and perhaps especially the second—allied with the third? This is a deep question, which needs much more study. But I believe that much would be gained by studying the roots of the perennial attraction of scapegoating. This seems to have something to do with the way we can establish our own sense of purity, goodness, and integrity through the violent separation or expulsion of a contrast case, taken as the embodiment of impurity, evil, and chaos. Reactions of this kind can be discovered in the earliest societies. What is astonishing is that they have somehow survived the progress of "civilization" and "enlightenment" and even the utter rejection of all religion, as the twentieth-century histories of Russia, China, Cambodia, and so on, can attest. In the light of what are millennial histories of scapegoating and holy wars, it is not surprising that our ills are often attributed to a source in an enemy who wants to destroy us and whom we must combat. We should measure how overwhelming the temptation can be to go along with this kind of (often murderous) mobilization, where it comes across as the only way to recover orientation, dignity, or agency.[105]

Now, plainly religion as political identity and as the bulwark of a moral-civilizational identity can also be commingled with other, more "spiritual" motives; it can be part of my search for personal piety. But it is also not surprising that this search often finds itself in opposition to the use of religion to forge political identity. People may sense that the search for identity and "our" religion may contradict the demands of a genuine deepening of piety. This seems to be the case with the women's mosque movement in Egypt, as studied by Saba Mahmood.[106] These women want to resist the "folklorization" of Islamic practice. They are not into pride in the symbols of Islam but are trying to discover the full, transformative meaning of its practices.

The same unease leads the Iranian dissident 'Abdolkarim Soroush to distinguish Islam as an identity from Islam as truth. Only the latter is really valid in his eyes.[107] A similar logic leads many pious Hindus, some following Gandhi, vigorously to oppose the BJP.

I have argued that there is a particularly modern dynamic that can issue in "religious" hatred and violence, but that is in some ways rather alien to religion in its devotional thrust. There are clear cases in which this alien nature stands out, but there are also very mixed cases, in which religious movements are traversed by a number of different demands—of fidelity to the past, of piety, of recovering social discipline and order, as well as of the power and dignity of "peoples." In these cases, there is no single dynamic at work.

This may be hard to sort out in practice, but it has important policy consequences. Where the dynamic of identity struggles has an important role to play, there is no point in seeking the source in theology. What may be needed is the classic kit for coping with extreme identity strife: trying to give more space to complex, or "hybrid," identities that can diffuse and buffer the standoff. Thus one of the big threats to the BJP's mobilization behind "Hindutva" comes from the scheduled castes and Other Backward Classes in India, for whom this kind of pan-caste solidarity is, understandably, very dubious. From this, it is to be hoped, new kinds of alliances can be made that will blunt the drive to exclusion.

ANOTHER SET of interesting reflections is inspired by reading Birgit Meyer's interesting study, *Translating the Devil*. She relates how a form of North German Pietist Protestantism is transformed in the African context, particularly in that a much greater role is attributed to the devil and his minions, and much greater efforts are made to separate the faithful from these and to exorcise them. Here we have a new mode of the presence (and probably future) of a past. But the past is that of this Nordic Protestantism, and of Christianity in general. Something substantially similar to what these African churches are now doing was already undertaken in the early Christian church, and also has analogies to the post-Reformation period in Europe.

What happened in each of these cases is that the spirits and gods recognized in the earlier "pagan" setting, instead of being simply declared nonexistent, as most modern Western Christians (not to speak of atheists) would say, are understood to be very real, but to be evil, enemies of God and of Christ. We can readily surmise that this reflects a world in which the old religion is still very much alive, in which even converts find it hard to separate themselves from it, and in which therefore both "pagans" and converts live in an enchanted world as porous selves. Just declaring the old gods nonexistent is not only hard to believe but doesn't do justice to the struggle in which converts are still engaged.

There is a parallel to the Reformation period, when a great disenchantment was undertaken by elites and imposed—with only partial success—on the population. The latter lived in a thoroughly enchanted world, inhabited by spirits and the site of magic. The attack on this world couldn't credibly take the form of simple denial, and so it involved a radical change of sign. Magic was formerly both white and black, benign and malign. The new dispensation wanted to deny white magic altogether; all forms of it were declared malign.[108]

This was accompanied by an intensification of concern with witches and witchcraft throughout the whole period of the Reformation. This runs counter to the Whig scenario, which sees Protestantism as more "enlightened" than Catholicism, and then Deism as more enlightened than Protestantism, and so on. A kink appears in the sequencing of this master narrative when we find that Thomas Aquinas seems to have had a more "enlightened" view of witchcraft than, say, Bodin.

What is remarkable about Meyer's account is that, although the practices of exorcism among African converts have some parallels with German peasants in the nineteenth century, this whole aspect of the home religion had not been communicated by the missionaries. It was re-created in situ.

So we might think of the intense concern with the devil and with witchcraft as a transition phenomenon, while the old context is still there and has to be fought. Meyer describes the cures from devil possession as bringing about an individuation, loosening ties with the extended kin within which the old religion operates.[109] One could imagine that, over time, individuation would be accompanied, as in the West, by a buffered identity, and the sense of the presence of the spirits would fade.

The interesting issue is whether this expectation is correct. Are all regions of the world fated to head toward the predicament of Western modernity, with a disenchanted world, a strong sense of a self-sufficient immanent order, and a staunchly buffered identity? If one holds that this is the "normal" human situation, only impeded in the past by ignorance and/or "superstition," then this may sound likely. But one conclusion that one might draw from the narrative I have been sketching is that all the "forward" movements are bought at a price: the axial revolutions with their notions of our higher good; Western reform with its abolition of enchantment and the repression of collective ritual; the creation of the immanent order. All these "advances" are met at various points with enthusiasm, but a profound ambivalence remains. This expresses itself in nostalgia, the sense that something is missing, a hankering after some richer meaning.

How we can extrapolate from a story of unmitigated advance is different from how we might imagine such a history of ambivalence continuing. In particular, this makes a big difference when it comes to predicting what varieties of religious life can show themselves to be viable over the long term in human history. We have been too long mesmerized by one master narrative of the history of one civilization. We don't even have the concepts to state the differences between civilizations or societies with very different religious forms. (Or perhaps I should say, more modestly, that I haven't grasped these myself. But I may not be totally alone in this.) The varieties of religious past that have a future may be much greater than we have been led to suspect.

CHAPTER TWELVE

Disenchantment-Reenchantment

I

These terms are often used together, the first designating one of the main features of the process we know as secularization, the second a supposed undoing of the first, which can be either desired or feared, according to one's point of view.

But their relation is more complicated than this. In some sense, it can be argued, the process of disenchantment is irreversible. The aspiration to reenchant (or the apprehended danger this threatens) points to a different process, which may indeed reproduce features analogous to the enchanted world, but does not in any simple sense restore it.

Let's speak of "the enchanted world" to designate those features which disenchantment did away with. There are two main ones.

The first feature of this world is that it was one filled with spirits and moral forces, and one moreover in which these forces impinged on human beings; that is, the boundary between the self and these forces was somewhat porous. There were spirits of the wood, or of the wilderness areas. There were objects with powers to wreak good or ill, such as relics (good) and love potions (not so unambiguously good). I speak of "moral" forces to mark this point, that the causality of certain physical objects was directed to good or ill. So a phial of water from Canterbury (which must contain some blood of the martyr Thomas à Becket) could have a curative effect on any ill you were suffering from. In this it was quite unlike a modern medical drug which "targets" certain maladies and conditions, owing to its chemical constitution.

One could sum this up by saying that this was a world of "magic." This is implied in our term "disenchantment," which can be thought of as a process of removing the magic. This is even clearer in the original German: Weber's "Entzauberung" contains the word "Zauber" (magic). But this is less illuminating than it seems. The process of disenchantment, carried out first for religious reasons, consisted of delegitimating all the practices for dealing with spirits and forces, because they allegedly either neglected the power of God, or directly went against it. Rituals of this kind were supposed to have power in themselves and hence were blasphemous. All such rituals were put into a category of "magic." The category was constituted by the rejection, rather than providing a clear reason for the rejection. It then carries on in Western culture even after the decline of faith—for example, James George Frazer's distinction between magic and religion. Only when Westerners attempted to make ethnographic studies of non-Western societies did it become clear how inadequate and unstable this category is.

I talked about not being able to go back. But surely lots of our contemporaries are already "back" in this world. They believe in and practice certain rituals to restore health or give them success. The mentality survives, even if underground. That is true; much survives of the earlier epoch. But the big change, which would be hard to undo, is that which has replaced the porous selves of yore with what I would describe as "buffered" selves.

Let's look again at the enchanted world, the world of spirits, demons, moral forces which our predecessors acknowledged. The process of disenchantment is the disappearance of this world, and the substitution of what we live today: a world in which the only locus of thoughts, feelings, and spiritual élan is what we call minds; the only minds in the cosmos are those of humans (grosso modo, with apologies to possible Martians or extraterrestrials); and minds are bounded, so that these thoughts, feelings, and so forth are situated "within" them. What am I gesturing at with the expression "thoughts, et cetera"? I mean, of course, the perceptions we have as well as the beliefs or propositions which we hold or entertain about the world and ourselves. But I also mean our responses, the significance, importance, meaning, we find in things. I want to use for these the generic term *meaning*, even though there is in principle a danger of confusion with linguistic meaning. Here I'm using it in the sense in which we talk about "the meaning of life" or of a relationship as having great "meaning" for us.

Now the crucial difference between the mind-centered view and the enchanted world emerges when we look at meanings in this sense. According to the former view, meanings are "in the mind," in the sense that things only have the meaning they do in that they awaken a certain response in us, and this has to do with our nature as creatures who are thus capable of such responses, which means creatures with feelings, with desires, with aversions— that is, beings endowed with minds, in the broadest sense.

I must stress again that this is a way of understanding things which is prior to explication in different philosophical theories, materialist, idealist, monist, dualist. We can take a strict materialist view, and hold that our responses are to be explained by the functions things have for us as organisms, and further by the kinds of neurophysiological responses which their perception triggers. We are still explaining the meanings of things by our responses, and these responses are "within" us, in the sense that they depend on the way we have been "programmed" or "wired up" inside.

The materialist fantasy, that we could for all we know be brains in a vat, being manipulated by some mad scientist, depends for its sense on this view that the material sufficient condition for thoughts of all kinds is within the cranium. Hence convincing thoughts about a nonexistent world could be produced by generating the right brain states. The inside/outside geography, and the boundary dividing them, which is crucial to the mind outlook is reproduced in this materialist explication of it.

But in the enchanted world, meanings are not only in the mind in this sense, certainly not in the human mind. If we look at the lives of ordinary people—and even to a large degree of élites—500 years ago, we can see in a myriad ways how this was so. First, as I said above, they lived in a world of spirits, both good and bad. The bad ones include Satan, of course, but beside him, the world was full of a host of demons, threatening from all sides: demons and spirits of the forest and wilderness, but also those which can threaten us in our everyday lives.

Spirit agents were also numerous on the good side. Not just God, but also his saints, to whom one prayed, and whose shrines one visited in certain cases, in hopes of a cure, or in thanks for a cure already prayed for and granted, or for rescue from extreme danger, for example, at sea.

These extrahuman agencies are perhaps not so strange to us. They violate the second point of the modern outlook I mentioned above, namely, that (as we ordinarily tend to believe) the only minds in the cosmos are humans; but they nevertheless seem to offer a picture of minds, somewhat like ours, in which meanings, in the form of benevolent or malevolent intent can reside.

But seeing things this way understates the strangeness of the enchanted world. Thus precisely in this cult of the saints, we can see how the forces here were not all agents, subjectivities, who could decide to confer a favor. But power also resided in things.[1] For the curative action of saints was often linked to centers where their relics resided: either some piece of their body (supposedly) or some object which had been connected with them in life, like (in the case of Christ) pieces of the true cross or the sweat-cloth which Saint Veronica had used to wipe his face, and which was on display on certain occasions in Rome. And we can add to this other objects which had been endowed with sacramental power, like the Host, or candles which had been blessed at Candlemas. These objects were loci of spiritual power, which is why they had to be treated with care, and if abused could wreak terrible damage.

In fact, in the enchanted world, the line between personal agency and impersonal force was not at all clearly drawn. We see this again in the case of relics. The cures effected by them, or the curse laid on people who stole them or otherwise mishandled them, were seen both as emanating from them, as loci of power, and also as coming from the good will, or anger, of the saint they belonged to. Indeed, we can say that in this world, there is a whole gamut of forces, ranging from (to take the evil side for a moment) superagents like Satan himself, forever plotting to encompass our damnation, down to minor demons, like spirits of the wood, which are almost indistinguishable from the loci they inhabit, and magic potions which bring sickness or death. This illustrates a point which I want to bring out here, and to which I will recur shortly, that the enchanted world, in contrast to our universe of buffered selves and "minds," shows a perplexing absence of certain boundaries which seem to us essential.

So in the premodern world, meanings are not only in minds, but can reside in things, or in various kinds of extrahuman but intracosmic subjects. We can bring out the contrast with today in two dimensions, by looking at two kinds of powers that these things/subjects possess.

The first is the power to impose a certain meaning on us. Now in a sense, something like this happens today all the time, in that certain responses are involuntarily triggered in us by what happens in our world. Misfortunes befall us and we are sad; great events befall us and we rejoice. But the way in which things with power affected us in the enchanted world has no analogies in our understanding today.

For us, things in the world, those which are neither human beings nor expressions of human beings, are "outside" of the mind. They may in their own way impinge on the mind in two possible ways: (1) We may observe these things and therefore change our view of the world or be stirred up in ways that we otherwise wouldn't be; or (2) since we are ourselves as bodies continuous with these external things, and in constant exchange with them, and since our mental condition is responsive causally to our bodily condition in a host of ways (something we are aware of without espousing any particular theory of what exactly causes what), our strength, moods, motivations, and so forth can be affected, and are continually being affected by what happens outside.

But in all these cases, that these responses arise in us, that things take on these meanings, is a function of how we as minds, or organisms secreting minds, operate. By contrast, in the enchanted world, the meaning is already there in the object/agent; it is there quite independently of us; it would be there even if we didn't exist. And this means that the object/agent can communicate this meaning to us, impose it on us, in a third way, by bringing us, as it were, into its field of force. It can in this way even impose quite alien meanings on us, ones that we would not normally have, given our nature; as well as, in positive cases, strengthening our endogenous good responses.

In other words, the world doesn't just affect us by presenting us with certain states of affairs, which we react to from out of our own nature, or by bringing about some chemical-organic condition in us, which in virtue of the way we operate produces, say, euphoria or depression. In all these cases, the meaning as it were only comes into existence as the world impinges on the mind/organism. It is in this sense endogenous. But in the enchanted world, the meaning exists already outside of us, prior to contact; it can take us over, we can fall into its field of force. It comes on us from the outside.

The second feature of the earlier world which disenchantment sidelined is similar in import to the first. In another way, it placed meaning within the cosmos. Only this is a feature of elite culture. I am not speaking of popular "magic" and the sensibility of porous selves, but rather of high theory. The cosmos reflected and manifested a Great Chain of Being. Being itself existed on several levels, and the cosmos manifested this hierarchy, both in its overall structure and again in its different partial domains. The same superiority of dignity and rule that the soul manifests over the body reappears in the state in the preeminence of the king, in the animal realm in that of the lion, among birds and fishes in the supreme status of eagle and dolphin. These features "correspond" to each other in the different domains. The whole is bound together by relations of hierarchical complementarity, which should be reproduced in a well-ordered state.

Once again, to point up the contrast with our world, we can say that in the enchanted world, charged things have a causal power which matches their incorporated meaning. The High Renaissance theory of the correspondences, which while more an élite than a popular belief, partakes of the same enchanted logic, is full of such causal links mediated by meaning. Why does mercury cure venereal disease? Because this is contracted in the market, and Hermes is the God of markets. This way of thinking is totally different from our post-Galilean, mind-centered disenchantment. If thoughts and meanings are only in minds, then there can be no "charged" objects, and the causal relations between things cannot be in any way dependent on their meanings, which must be projected on them from our minds. In other words, the physical world, outside the mind, must proceed by causal laws which in no way turn on the moral meanings things have for us.

We can see how elite theory and popular sensibility interpenetrated and strengthened each other. The high theory was easier to believe in a world of enchanted sensibility. And the theory itself could draw on some of features of popular lore, giving them a new rationale and systematic form.

This second feature is easier to imagine recovering in our world. Certainly many people hold "wacky" theories. But a wholesale acceptance of this outlook as a hegemonic one is surely unthinkable in the post-Galilean world.

2

Now what do people who look to "reenchantment" seek? In a sense, it is the same fundamental feature, but differently conceived. In other words, they bridle at the idea that the universe in which we find ourselves is totally devoid of human meaning. Of course, instrumental meaning can be attributed to various features of our natural surroundings, in virtue of their serving or impeding our organic needs, but any human meaning must be simply a subjective projection. By "human meaning," I mean what we try to define when we identify the ends of life; through judgments like: this is really meaningful as a way of life; or this life is really worth living; or this form of being is a real fulfillment, or a higher way of being. Derivatively, we can attribute human meaning to the things which surround us because of their role in these ends or purposes. A statement like Thoreau's "in wildness is the preservation of the world" is such an attribution of meaning. It is the kind of statement which proponents of reenchantment often want to make.

This sense of loss was frequently expressed in the Romantic era. Take Schiller's poem *The Gods of Greece:*

> Da der Dichtung zauberische Hülle
> Sich noch lieblich um die Wahrheit wand,
> Durch die Schöpfung floss da Lebensfülle,
> Und was nie empfinden wird, empfand.
> An der Liebe Busen sie zu drücken,
> Gab man höhern Adel der Natur,
> Alles wies den eingeweihten Blicken,
> Alles eines Gottes Spur.

> (When poetry's magic cloak
> Still with delight enfolded truth
> Life's fullness flowed through creation

And there felt what never more will feel.
Man acknowledged a higher nobility in Nature
To press her to love's breast;
Everything to the initiate's eye
Showed the trace of a God.)

But this communion has now been destroyed; we face a "God-shorn nature":

Unbewusst der Freuden die sie schenket,
Nie entzückt von ihrer Herrlichkeit,
Nie gewahr des Geistes, der sie lenket,
Sel'ger nie durch meine Seligkeit,
Fühllos selbst für ihres Künstlers Ehre,
Gleich dem toten Schlag der Pendeluhr,
Dient sie knechtisch dem Gesetzt der Schwere,
Die entgötterte Natur.

(Unconscious of the joys she dispenses
Never enraptured by her own magnificence
Never aware of the spirit which guides her
Never more blessed through my blessedness
Insensible of her maker's glory
Like the dead stroke of the pendulum
She slavishly obeys the law of gravity,
A Nature shorn of the divine.)

And so what seems wrong with total disenchantment? What makes people seek reenchantment? Now the complaint which one finds again and again in what I will call loosely the post-"Romantic" period targets a reading of our modern condition in which all human meanings are simply projected. That is, they are seen as arbitrarily conferred by human subjects. None would be valid universally. Universal agreement on these meanings would result from de facto convergence of our projections. Thoreau's statement about wilderness would have to be read as one such subjective projection rather than claiming validity for all human beings.

But this projectivist outlook doesn't follow from disenchantment in the double sense outlined above. True, human meanings are no longer seen as residing in the object, even in the absence of human agents. These meanings arise for us as agents-in-the-world. But it doesn't follow from this that they are arbitrarily conferred.

There is a massive slippage in the reasoning here, which has frequently accompanied the modern turn to the subject. In the field of epistemology, this turn (Descartes, Locke) first of all generated a view of knowledge as a correct portrayal of external reality residing in the mind. But this reflexive turn to examine our experience, carried through more fully, ended up dispelling this illusion. Our grasp of the world is not simply a representation within us. It resides rather in our dealing with reality. We are being in the world (Heidegger's *Inderweltsein*), or being to the world (Merleau-Ponty's *être au monde*).

Some similar working through needs to be done in this domain of human meanings. Otherwise we are living with a distorted view of ourselves.

A word about the relation of this debate to that between theists and atheists. Obviously the former will not consent to the notion that there is no meaning in reality in abstraction from human agents; and I myself am not accepting this. But this doesn't make it any the less interesting for me to enquire how we can discover in human experience what meanings must be recognized as universally valid. The debate between theists and atheists can be better conducted once we have established what these meanings are. Without taking this first step we are living a distorted form of the human condition, where instrumentalist deviations can put in danger the very survival of the planet.

So the issue about reenchantment can be put this way: when we have left the "enchanted" world of spirits, and no longer believe in the Great Chain, what sense can we make of the notion that nature or the universe which surrounds us is the locus of human meanings which are "objective," in the sense that they are not just arbitrarily projected through choice or contingent desire?

Put another way, the attribution of these meanings counts for us as strong evaluations. The distinction between strong and weak evaluation that I'm adverting to here comes to this. A weak evaluation is one which depends on choices that we may not make, or our espousing ends which we may not accept. We can thus defeat the claim that something should have value for us, by choosing another end, or repudiating the one on which this value depends. In the case of strong evaluations, we cannot so release ourselves, and our attempt to do so reflects negatively on us.

This distinction for the moral realm can be illustrated by Kant's contrast between categorical and hypothetical imperatives. If someone says, "Invest in real estate" (admittedly not a smart idea today, but often sound advice), you can defeat the imperative by saying, "I'm rich enough already," or "I'm dedicated to a life of poverty." But if someone says, "Act to reduce unnecessary suffering," you couldn't release yourself by pleading that you have other goals in life. You would need an argument to the effect that reducing suffering wasn't good, because, for example, it leads to a world of "last men," or blocks the way to the Übermensch.

But of course strong evaluations can be made outside the moral realm, in aesthetics, for instance. A judgment that some work or scene is beautiful would be strong if it carried the implication that those who could not concur were defective in their perception of beauty, rather than just being disinterested in this kind of thing.

The attribution of human meaning to (things in) the universe as a strong evaluation straddles the gap between the moral and the aesthetic. It concerns perhaps the ethical in the broad sense, where we make judgments about what a really good or properly human life consists in.

With these reflections as background, let's try to look at the debates about disenchantment and reenchantment. I follow here the excellent discussion by George Levine in his recent book.[2] The debate starts from the claim, made by many people, both atheists and theists and some people in between, that the combination of Weberian rationalization and post-Galilean science with the accompanying decline of religion has left us with a world deprived of meaning, and offering no consolation. The situation of moderns is thought to be very different in this regard from that of people in all previous ages and cultures. A debate may then break out over what we can or ought to do about this: face the empty world with resolute courage, or call into question the rejection of religion, or perhaps find some new sources of meaning.

But one might instead question this "Weberian" picture.[3] Is this really our predicament? Do we not now experience wonder at the vast yet intricate universe and the manifold forms of life, at the very spectacle of the evolution of higher forms out of lower ones? Do we not find beauty in all this? In this case, a part of the very change which is held to have disenchanted the world, here that bit of modern science which we call the theory of evolution, has in fact given us further, deeper cause to wonder at the universe. As Levine puts it, the world hasn't lost meaning; "it is stunning, beautiful, scary, fascinating, dangerous, seductive, real."[4] The first four of these epithets might be thought to be rather aesthetic than ethical. But one can argue that this sense of greatness and beauty fosters a love of the world which is one of the wellsprings of generosity. As Kant saw, the inspiration we draw from "the starry skies above" is akin to that we sense before "the moral law within."[5]

In fact, from the very beginning, materialism has generated a sense of awe at the universe and at our genesis out of it. One can find this in Lucretius, but this sense intensifies and develops in the eighteenth century, as the materialist outlook takes on shape and consistency. This vision solidified, but it also deepened.

We are alone in the universe, and this is frightening, but it can also be exhilarating. There is a certain joy in solitude, particularly for the buffered identity. The thrill at being alone is part sense of freedom, part the intense poignancy of this fragile moment, the *dies* (day) that you must *carpere* (seize). All meaning is here, in this small speck. Pascal got at some of this with his image of the human being as a thinking reed.

The new cosmic imaginary adds a further dimension to this. Having come to sense how vast the universe is in time and space, how deep its micro-constitution goes into the infinitesimal, and feeling thus both our insignificance and fragility, we also see what a remarkable thing it is that out of this immense, purposeless machine, life and then feeling, imagination, and thought emerge.

Here is where a religious person will easily confess a sense of mystery. Materialists often want to repudiate this; science in its progress recognizes no mysteries, only temporary puzzles. But nevertheless, the sense that our thinking, feeling life plunges its roots into a system of such unimaginable depths, that consciousness can emerge out of this, fills them too with awe.

Our wonder at our dark genesis, and the conflict we can feel around it, is well captured by a writer of our day. Douglas Hofstadter recognizes that certain people

> have an instinctive horror of any "explaining away" of the soul. I don't know why some people have this horror while others, like me, find in reductionism the ultimate religion. Perhaps my lifelong training in physics and science in general has given me a deep awe at seeing how the most substantial and familiar of objects or experiences fades away, as one approaches the infinitesimal scale, into an eerily insubstantial ether, a myriad of ephemeral swirling vortices of nearly incomprehensible mathematical activity. This in me evokes a cosmic awe. To me, reductionism doesn't "explain away"; rather, it adds mystery.[6]

But this awe is modulated, and intensified, by a sense of kinship, of belonging integrally to these depths. And this allows us to recapture the sense of connection and solidarity with all existence which arose in the eighteenth century out of our sense of dark genesis, but now with an incomparably greater sense of the width and profundity of its reach.[7]

And so materialism has become deeper, richer, but also more varied in its forms, as protagonists take different stands to the complex facets I have just been trying to lay out. The reasons to opt for unbelief go beyond our judgments about religion, and the supposed deliverances of "science." They include also the moral meanings which we now find in the universe and our genesis out of it. Materialism is now nourished by certain ways of living in, and further developing, our cosmic imaginary; certain ways of inflecting our sense of the purposelessness of this vast universe, our awe at and sense of kinship with it.

But one cannot just stop here. A hostile critic will object that these are just *feelings*. We sense depth and greatness, but does this correspond to reality? Is there a reality to which these feelings can correspond, if we do away with all religion and metaphysics? To which one can reply in turn that just having discovered a new and (supposedly) more correct explanation of things shouldn't alter in any way the awe or admiration we feel before these things. Thus, in this case, where we explain the shape of the universe, or the origins of life, we can split completely (1) our account of the origins of things from (2) our sense of the significance they bear.

Now there is some truth in this reply, but the matter is more complicated than it implies. When we talk of our sense of wonder at the greatness and complexity of the universe, or of the love of the world it inspires in us, these are what I called above strong evaluations. They carry the sense that wonder is what one should feel, that someone who fails to sense this is missing something, is somehow insensitive to an object which really commands admiration. In this it is quite unlike one's preference, say, for flavors of ice cream, to take a really trivial and hence clear contrast case. I like strawberry and you vanilla. It would be absurd to accuse each other of not seeing something.

Let's take up this point with another contrast. The understanding behind strong evaluations is that they track some reality. A question can be raised: is that object really worthy of respect, or of wonder? That object may inspire love in you, but does it merit love? Obviously these arguments are central to ethical life. Yes, one should do the courageous thing, but is that (blindly charging the enemy) really courage? Be generous, but is that (spending from the public relations budget to raise the profile of the company) really generosity? Now take a (rather shocking) contrast: we feel nausea at certain things; we can call these "nauseating." Does it make sense to argue about what is *really* nauseating? I am thinking of the literal applications to substances whose sight or smell is unbearable; of course there are moral applications, as when I say that government policy is nauseating. Clearly the answer is "no" in the straightforward, literal cases. What nauseates us is a brute fact; some things just trigger this response, others not. If there are interpersonal differences, they also are a matter of brute fact. There is no arbitrating them.

These contrasts point up the fact that underlying strong evaluations there is supposed to be a truth of the matter. And this can't be separated from facts about how our reactions are to be explained. Put simply, our moral reactions suppose that they are responses to some reality, and can be criticized for misapprehension of this reality. But in the case of nausea, there is no room for this account; the issue of reality can't get a purchase.

Now if we keep this distinction in mind, we might agree that there is indeed no reason why switching from a theistic to a materialist account of reality should undercut our wonder at the universe, although the account of what properly inspires wonder will be different, and will connect to different things for the theist and atheist, respectively.

But take something like a sociobiological account which claims to show that human behavior, like all animal behavior, is really driven by "selfish" genes. There is indeed an "altruist" pattern of action, where one agent benefits another to his own detriment, but there is no real difference in the underlying motivation. This has to undercut part of the crucial background understanding of those who admire altruism. Why? Because admiring altruism is not just finding this pattern of action useful; it is also holding that the motivation which powers it is in some ways higher, more noble, more admirable. A claim like this can only make sense against a background view of human motivation as capable of transformation so as to be more and more drawn by the higher, so that ultimately our pattern of action is changed. The background is also richer than a simple hierarchy of motives; there is invariably some account of why one motive is higher: because it brings true harmony, corresponds to our real self, brings about a unity and harmony between human beings which answers one of our deepest longings—and so on through a wide range of alternatives. It is this whole background outlook which is negated and made impossible by the claim that we are always and inalterably at base "egoistic."

One can see a parallel case in one of Nietzsche's lines of attack against Christianity. Christians speak of "charity," of "love," of turning the other cheek. But in fact this is a lie. Because really we are all actuated by the Will to Power. Christian behavior is in fact motivated by a desire to get back at, and perhaps even get control over, those who have bested them in the power stakes. Now from the Christian point of view, going the second mile, pushing further in self-giving love, makes sense, because it can be a step on a transformation which makes us more Christlike, more Godlike. If this entire prospect is a delusion, if we are all inalterably and equally actuated by the Will to Power, then the aspiration is vain, the whole outlook collapses. It is just an extra ironic twist in Nietzsche's argument that he shows that "love" here is really driven by its opposite, ressentiment and hatred.

Thus, while it is certainly right to say that disenchantment, in the double sense above, and a rejection of religion, can't by themselves undercut very powerful human meanings, like a sense of wonder, love of the world and of others, and the like, it is clear that certain kinds of reductive accounts of human life and action do rule these out. We can't just say that explanations of why we experience these meanings are irrelevant to their validity; that they stand on their own, because we *feel* them strongly. Our attributing these meanings makes a stronger claim. It lies in their nature as strong evaluations to claim truth, reality, or objective rightness.

That is why those who experience the wonder at reality that I described above feel the need to make sense of this, to articulate it. We saw above that a whole background understanding underlies the different ethics of altruism.

This background will be different for theists and for atheists, but neither can rest simply on the bare reaction. One could argue that in human life such reactions are primary, and that all attempts to develop philosophical and religious theories flow from the need to articulate them. But these articulations are not simply derivative and secondary. Each way of giving expression to what appears as a similar reaction modifies it, develops it, gives it a different thrust. Thus we see how today in the sphere of humanitarian work, people of all convictions, religious and nonreligious, work side by side. They are in a sense actuated by the same impulse, but some very different ethics lie behind the common dedication in each case: different views of human life, of the possibilities of transformation, of the modes of spiritual or mental discipline that are to be engaged in, and so on.

But these articulations are never complete. They leave gaps where mystery intrudes, where the claims to truth are not fully grounded, where seeming refutation or contradictions lie half visible. In a sense, all require some degree of faith that these difficulties could in principle be resolved. And this is true as much of the naturalist and materialist ones as of the "faith-based" ones. Indeed, though the gaps and the uncertainties lie in different places, this term could apply to all humanitarian efforts, however motivated.

Some might be astonished that something like a truth claim can ever be made in the moral or ethical domain. How can one ever prove conclusively that some direction of human transformation, toward sainthood, or Buddhahood, or a pure Kantian will, can really be accomplished, that there aren't decisive obstacles on the way? Indeed, this cannot be shown in the classical "scientific" way, that one find some reality which corresponds to and thus verifies the hope. Some (the companions of the Buddha, the disciples of Christ) believed themselves to have seen such a reality, but this cannot simply be manifested to other who have not. In fact, a good deal of our confidence in our own faiths comes through another route, the unmasking of our illusions, which allows us to abandon earlier, more questionable views. This process is, of course, never complete, but views which can survive such winnowing of illusion are less incredible than those which cannot.[8]

3

The above discussion can perhaps help to define better the following question: in what way does a scientific account of the world "disenchant" it beyond recall, that is, beyond any possibility of what we have been calling reenchantment? Clearly the simple fact that we understand better how different species evolved, however "mechanistic" the process identified, cannot take away from our wonder at the scope and intricacy of the resultant system. We are faced, however we understand it, with the fact that we can thus respond with wonder; we might want to add that anyone with sufficient knowledge, training, and consciousness cannot but feel this wonder.

Where then can the potential conflict lie? It lies in the fact that this wonder is lived by us as a strong evaluation; one that in some ways ennobles our lives, a wonder whose absence betokens a lack in the person left indifferent by these marvels. Now like all strong evaluations by which we give sense to and live our lives, this would run athwart a certain kind of reductive explanation, not of the evolution of birds on pacific islands, but of our own psychology and behavior.

Wherein does this conflict reside? A response which we understand as a strong evaluation supposes the following ontology: (1) This response genuinely motivates us, it is not simply a cover, or a rationalization, or a screen for some other drive; (2) it can fail to occur on some occasions or in some people, but this betokens some limitation, blindness, or insensitivity on their part; (3) in other words, there is something objectively right about this response; (4) we can and ought to challenge ourselves to cultivate this response, to refine or improve our perception of its proper objects. This four-point feature represents a package, reflecting our sense that this evaluation is founded. In Bernard Williams's terms, our moral and other strong evaluations claim to be "world-guided."[9]

Now an account in blind, mechanistic terms of the evolution of the birds poses no essential threat to my wonder—although a conflict may in fact arise here if my sense of awe is bound up with a belief in conscious design. But an account of my psychology and action, and hence of the production of this response on certain occasions, which admitted only "blind," efficient causes, does create a conflict, as we saw with the case of altruistic motivation above. Here is where the issue of reduction crucially enters.

The question of reductive explanation arises when we have two accounts of what would seem to be the same range of phenomena (where "same" can be glossed in terms of spatio-temporal coordinates or other uncontroversial ways of identifying the same objects). Now accounts couched in terms of post-Galilean science clearly are intended to avoid teleology or intentionality, purpose or evaluation as causally relevant factors, whereas accounts of what we are doing which recognize strong evaluation make essential reference to such factors. The issue about reductive explanation is whether we can give an adequate explanation of the phenomena we describe in the "upper" language (e.g., people reacting to the universe with a sense of wonder) entirely in the terms of the "lower" language (post-Galilean science). This would mean, inter alia, that we could provide necessary and sufficient conditions for all states described in the upper language in the terms of the lower language. But then the claim, made on behalf of the "upper" phenomena, that they operate on genuinely different principles than those adequately explained by the lower language would be voided.

Of course, some philosophers would want to deny any difference in ontology between humans and machines. The only difference between humans and machines, which seem to exhibit purposive behavior—as, for example, in guided missiles and computers—apart from a difference of complexity, lies in the stance that we assume to them. As observers we can adopt the "intentional" stance to both human and missile, or we can see them as mechanisms, which is the more fruitful language for explaining what they do, but both are explained by the same principles. Could we then attribute to more complex robots consciousness and self-feeling? Why not? argues Daniel Dennett.[10] Perhaps the robot feels that it is striving to do its task conscientiously. But apart from the difficulty of attributing consciousness and feeling to beings made of plastic and silicone, this inner sense would be in the robot purely epiphenomenal, perhaps itself built in an extra feat of engineering but not essential to the account of what it is doing.

But our whole moral-evaluative lives rest on the opposite understanding. Evaluations motivate, and they reflect a perception of their objects which can be more or less adequate.

It is in fact extraordinary how blithely some philosophers can talk of reductive explanation as a virtually certain prospect, given all that we know about human life and evolution. A neurobiological account of human conscious action, in terms of how we are "wired," would operate primarily on the level of the individual organism, and explain social combinations in terms of the interactions between these. But human culture is in fact developed in societies. As Merlin Donald has pointed out, no human being invents language, much less human culture, on his or her own. Left to themselves, abandoned children, or those who are unreachable, like Helen Keller, never take the step to language and the conscious grasp of things which language enables.[11] What is more, the "wiring" of the brains of young infants is to a significant extent determined in the course of their early upbringing by the kinds of things they learn, which themselves vary from culture to culture. No one can simply deny a priori that all this can be captured in terms of a monological, purely efficient causal account of the formation and operation of the brain and nervous system, but it is not easy to see how this can be accomplished.

On top of this, we have the fact that cultural evolution has brought about new strong evaluations, such as those we live by today, like democracy and universal human rights, and we have quite an agenda for anyone who would give a more circumstantial account of the evolution of humankind. This is a tremendously valuable goal, but it is not immediately obvious how we should go about realizing it.

It follows from the above that the issues of disenchantment and reenchantment arise on at least two levels. First, there is the question of whether disenchantment in the senses I described at the outset, that is, the dissipation of the enchanted world, the denial of the Great Chain, plus the widespread rejection of Western theism, have not voided the universe of any human meaning. In particular, it has been claimed here that there is no further basis for a sense of awe and wonder at the universe, which in turn can inspire in human beings love and even gratitude toward the greater whole in which they are set. The answer to this is that undoubtedly some modes of wonder, articulated in a certain manner, will be decisively undercut. But the question remains open whether other forms, based on our own experience of being in the world, can be recovered. It seems to me that the answer here is affirmative.

But there is a quite different way in which the deliverances of "science" could undercut this affirmative response, and that is by a certain form of reductive explanation, not of the universe, but of human life. This is perhaps one of the most burning intellectual issues in modern culture.

Of course, to revert to the first issue, there remains a question whether purely anthropocentric articulations can do justice to our sense of wonder, and other related evaluations. This will remain a bone of contention between people in different positions—religious, secular, spiritual, indeed of an almost unlimited variety. The discussion between us promises to be fruitful; there is a virtual infinity of insights here, of which no single view has the monopoly. But all of these depend on a rejection of a reductive account of human life.

CHAPTER THIRTEEN

What Does Secularism Mean?

I

We live in a world in which ideas, institutions, artistic styles, and formulae for production and living circulate among societies and civilizations that are very different in their historical roots and traditional forms. Parliamentary democracy spread outward from England, among other countries, to India; likewise, the practice of nonviolent civil disobedience spread from its origins in the struggle for Indian independence to many other places, including Martin Luther King Jr.'s civil rights movement, Manila in 1983, and eventually the Velvet and Orange Revolutions of our time.

But these ideas and forms of practice don't just change place as solid blocks; they are modified, reinterpreted, given new meanings, in each transfer. This can lead to tremendous confusion when we try to follow these shifts and understand them. One such confusion comes from taking the word itself too seriously; the name may be the same, but the reality will often be different.

This is evident in the case of the word "secular." We think of "secularization" as a selfsame process that can occur anywhere (and, according to some people, *is* occurring everywhere). And we think of secularist regimes as an option for any country, whether or not they are actually adopted. And certainly, these *words* crop up everywhere. But do they really mean the same thing in each iteration? Are there not, rather, subtle differences, which can bedevil cross-cultural discussions of these matters?

I think that there are, and that they do create problems for our understanding. Either we stumble through tangles of cross-purposes or else a rather minimal awareness of significant differences can lead us to draw far-reaching conclusions that are very far from the realities we seek to describe. Such is the case, for instance, when people argue that since the "secular" is an old category of Christian culture, and since Islam doesn't seem to have a corresponding category, therefore Islamic societies cannot adopt secular regimes. Obviously, they would not be just like those in Christendom, but maybe the idea, rather than being locally restricted, can travel across borders in an inventive and imaginative way.

Let's look at some of the features of the "secular" as a category that developed within Latin Christendom. First, it was one term of a dyad. The secular had to do with the "century"—that is, with profane time—and it was contrasted with what related to the eternal, or to sacred time.[1] Certain times, places, persons, institutions, and actions were seen as closely related to the sacred or higher time, and others as pertaining to profane time alone. That's why the same distinction could often be made by use of the dyad "spiritual/temporal" (e.g., the state as the "temporal arm" of the church). Ordinary parish priests are thus "secular" because they operate out there in the "century," as against those in monastic institutions—"regular" priests—who live by the rules of their order.

So there is an obvious meaning of "secularization" that dates from the aftermath of the Reformation. It refers specifically, in this sense, to when certain functions, properties, and institutions were transferred from church control to that of laymen.

These moves were originally made within a system held in place by the overarching dyad; things were moved from one niche to another within a standing system of niches. This configuration of the "secular," where it still holds, can make secularization a relatively undramatic affair, a rearrangement of the furniture in a space the basic features of which remain unchanged.

But from the seventeenth century on, a new possibility gradually arose—a conception of social life in which the "secular" was all there was. Since "secular" originally referred to profane or ordinary time, in contradistinction to higher times, what was necessary was to come to understand profane time without any reference to higher times. The word could go on being used, but its meaning was profoundly changed, because its counterpoint had been fundamentally altered. The contrast was no longer with another temporal dimension, in which "spiritual" institutions had their niche; rather, the secular was, in its new sense, opposed to any claim made in the name of something transcendent of this world and its interests. Needless to say, those who imagined a "secular" world in this sense saw such claims as ultimately unfounded and only to be tolerated to the extent that they did not challenge the interests of worldly powers and human well-being.

Because many people went on believing in the transcendent, however, it was necessary that churches continue to have a place in the social order. They could be essential in their own way to the functioning of society, but this functioning was to be understood exclusively in terms of "this-worldly" goals and values (peace, prosperity, growth, flourishing, etc.).

This shift entailed two important changes: first, it brought a new conception of good social and political order, which was unconnected to either the traditional ethics of the good life or the specifically Christian notion of perfection (sainthood). This was the new post-Grotian idea of a society formed of and by individuals in order to meet their needs for security and the means to life. The criterion of a good society in this outlook, mutual benefit, was not only emphatically "this-worldly" but also unconcerned with "virtue" in the traditional sense.

The breaking away of a specifically "earthly" criterion figured within a broader distinction, one that divided "this world," or the immanent, from the transcendent. This very clear-cut distinction is itself a product of the development of Latin Christendom, and has become part of our way of seeing things in the West. We tend to apply it universally, even though no distinction this hard and fast has existed in any other human culture in history. What does seem, indeed, to exist universally is some distinction between higher beings (spirits) and realms, and the everyday world we see immediately around us. But these are not usually sorted out into two distinct domains, such that the lower one can be taken as a system understandable purely in its own terms. Rather, the levels usually interpenetrate, and the lower cannot be understood without reference to the higher. To take an example from the realm of philosophy, for Plato, the existence and development of the things around us can only be understood in terms of their corresponding Ideas, and these exist in a realm outside time. The clear separation of an immanent from a transcendent order is one of the inventions (for better or worse) of Latin Christendom.

The new understanding of the secular that I have been describing builds on this separation. It affirms, in effect, that the "lower"—immanent or secular—order is all that there is and that the higher—or transcendent—is a human invention. Obviously, the prior invention of a clear-cut distinction between these levels prepared the ground for the "declaration of independence" of the immanent.

AT FIRST, the independence claimed on the part of the immanent was limited and partial. In the "Deist" version of this claim, widespread in the eighteenth century, God was seen as the artificer of the immanent order. Since he is creator, the natural order stands as a proof of his existence; and since the proper human order of mutual benefit is one that He designs and recommends, we follow His will in building it. Furthermore, it is still affirmed that He backs up His law with the rewards and punishments of the next life.

Thus, some religion, or a certain piety, is a necessary condition of good order. Locke will thus exclude from toleration not only Catholics, but also atheists. This is the positive relation of God to good order, but religion can also have negative effects. Religious authority can enter into competition with secular rulers; it can demand things of the faithful that go beyond, or even against, the demands of good order; it can make irrational claims. So it remains to purge society of "superstition," "fanaticism," and "enthusiasm."

The attempts of eighteenth-century "enlightened" rulers, such as Frederick the Great and Joseph II, to "rationalize" religious institutions—in effect, treating the Church as a department of the state—belong to this earlier phase of secularization in the West. So too, in a quite different fashion, does the founding of the American republic, with its separation of church and state. But the first unambiguous assertion of the self-sufficiency of the secular came with the radical phases of the French Revolution.

The polemical assertion of secularity returns in the Third Republic, whose "laïcité" is founded on the ideas of the self-sufficiency of the secular and the exclusion of religion. Needless to say, this spirit goes marching on in contemporary France, as one can see in the ongoing debate over banning the Muslim headscarf. The insistence is still that the public spaces in which citizens meet must be purified of any religious reference.

AND SO THE HISTORY of the term "secular" in the West is complex and ambiguous. It starts off as one term in a dyad that distinguishes two dimensions of existence, identifying them by the particular type of time that is essential to each. But from the foundation of this clear distinction between the immanent and the transcendent there develops another dyad, in which "secular" refers to what pertains to a self-sufficient, immanent sphere, and is contrasted with what relates to the transcendent realm (often identified as "religious"). This binary can then undergo a further mutation, via a denial of the transcendent level, into a dyad in which one term refers to the real ("secular"), and the other to what is merely invented ("religious"); or where "secular" refers to the institutions we really require to live in "this world," and "religious" or "ecclesial" to optional accessories, which often disturb the course of this-worldly life.

Through this double mutation, the dyad itself is profoundly transformed; in the first case, both sides are real and indispensable dimensions of life and society. The dyad is thus "internal," in the sense that each term is impossible without its other, like right and left or up and down. After the mutations, the dyad becomes "external"; secular and religious are opposed as true and false or necessary and superfluous. The goal of policy becomes, in many cases, to abolish one while conserving the other.

IN SOME WAYS, the post-Deist modes of secularism transpose features of the Deist template described above. In the Jacobin outlook, the Designer is now Nature, and so the "piety" required is a humanist ideology based on the natural. What is unacceptable, in turn, is any form of "public" religion. Faith must be relegated to the private sphere. Following this view, there must be a coherent *morale indépendante,* a self-sufficient social morality without transcendent reference. This demand, in turn, encourages the idea that there is such a thing as "reason alone" *(die blosse Vernunft),* that is, reason unaided by any "extra" premises derived from Revelation or any other allegedly transcendent source. Variants of these claims resurface often in contemporary discussions of secularism in the West.[2]

The Deist template has helped to define "good," or "acceptable," religion for much of the Western discussion of the last few centuries. A good, or proper, religion is a set of beliefs in God or some other transcendent power, which entails an acceptable or, in some versions, a "rational" morality. It is devoid of any elements that do not contribute to this morality, and thus of "superstition." It is also necessarily opposed to "fanaticism" and "enthusiasm" because these involve by definition a challenge by religious authority to what "reason alone" shows to be the proper order of society.[3]

Religion can thus be an aid to social order by inculcating the right principles, but it must avoid becoming a threat to this order by launching a challenge against it. Thus Locke is ready to tolerate various religious views, but he excepts from this benign treatment atheists (whose nonbelief in an afterlife undermines their readiness to keep their promises and respect good order) and Catholics (who could not but challenge the established order).

In both these ways, positive and negative, the essential impact of good religion takes place *in foro interno:* on one hand, it generates the right moral motivation; on the other, by remaining within the mind and soul of the subject, it refrains from challenging the external order. So public ritual can be an essential element of this "rational" religion only if it can help by celebrating public order or by stimulating inner moral motivation.

EVENTUALLY THIS CONSTELLATION of terms, including "secular" and "religious," with all of its baggage of ambiguity and deep assumptions concerning the clear division between immanent and transcendent, on one hand, and public and private, on the other, begins to travel. It is no surprise, then, that it causes immense confusion. Westerners themselves are frequently confused about their own history. One way of understanding the development of Western secularism is to see the separation of church and state and the removal of religion into a "private" sphere where it cannot interfere with public life as a result of the earlier distinction between the secular (or temporal) and the sacred (or eternal). The former would thus be, in retrospect, the ultimately satisfactory solution, whereby religion is finally relegated to the margins of political life.

But these stages are not clearly distinguished.[4] Thus American secularists often totally confuse the separation of church and state from that of religion and state. (John Rawls at one point wanted to ban all reference to the grounds of people's "comprehensive views"—these included religious views—from public discourse.) Moreover, the whole constellation generates disastrously ethnocentric judgments. If the canonical background for a satisfactory secularist regime is the three-stage history described above—distinction of church and state, separation of church and state, and, finally, sidelining of religion from the state and from public life—then obviously Islamic societies can never make it.

Similarly, one often hears the judgment that Chinese imperial society was already "secular," totally ignoring the tremendous role played by the immanent/transcendent split in the Western concept, which had no analogue in traditional China. Ashis Nandy, in discussing the problems that arise out of the multiple uses of the term "secular," shows the confusions that are often involved in analogous statements about the Indian case (e.g., that the emperor Asoka was "secular," or that the Mughal emperor Akbar established a "secular" form of rule).

But this kind of (mis)statement can also reflect a certain wisdom. In fact, Nandy distinguishes two quite different notions that consciously or unconsciously inform the Indian discussion. There is, first, the "scientific-rational" sense of the term, in which secularism is closely identified with modernity; and, second, a variety of "accommodative" meanings, which are rooted in indigenous traditions. The first attempts to free public life from religion; the second seeks rather to open spaces "for a continuous dialogue among religious traditions and between the religious and the secular."[5]

The invocation of Akbar's rule as "secular" can thus function as a creative and productive way of redefining the term. Such redefinitions, starting from the problems that contemporary societies have to solve, often conceive of secularity as an attempt to find fair and harmonious modes of coexistence between religious communities, and leave the connotations of the word "secular" as they have evolved through Western history quietly to the side. This takes account of the fact that formulae for mutually beneficent living together have evolved in many different religious traditions and are not the monopoly of those whose outlook has been formed by the modern, Western dyad, in which the secular lays claim to exclusive reality.[6]

2

It is generally agreed that modern democracies have to be "secular." As we have just seen, a certain ethnocentricity attaches to this term. But even in the Western context it is far from limpid. What in fact does it mean? I believe that there are at least two models abroad today of what constitutes a secular regime.

Both involve some kind of separation of church and state. The state can't be officially linked to some religious confession, except in a vestigial and largely symbolic sense, as in England or Scandinavia. But secularism requires more than this. The pluralism of society requires that there be some kind of neutrality, or "principled distance," to use Rajeev Bhargava's term.[7]

If we try to examine it further, secularism involves in fact a complex requirement. There is more than one good sought here. We can single out three, which we can class in the three categories of the French Revolutionary trinity: liberty, equality, fraternity: (1) No one must be forced in the domain of religion, or basic belief. This is what is often defined a religious liberty, including, of course, the freedom not to believe. This is what is also described as the "free exercise" of religion, in the terms of the U.S. First Amendment. (2) There must be equality between people of different faiths or basic belief; no religious outlook or (religious or areligious) Weltanschauung can enjoy a privileged status, let alone be adopted as the official view of the state. Then, (3) all spiritual families must be heard, included in the ongoing process of determining what the society is about (its political identity), and how it is going to realize these goals (the exact regime of rights and privileges). This (stretching the point a little) is what corresponds to "fraternity."

These goals can, of course, conflict; sometimes we have to balance the goods involved here. Moreover, I believe that we might add a fourth goal: that we try as much as possible to maintain relations of harmony and comity between the supporters of different religions and Weltanschauungen (maybe this is what really deserves to be called "fraternity," but I am still attached to the neatness of the above schema, with only the three traditional goods).

Sometimes the claim seems to be made, on behalf of one or another definition of secularism, that it can resolve the question of how to realize these goals in the domain of timeless principle, and that no further input or negotiation is required to define them for our society now. The basis for these principles can be found in reason alone, or in some outlook which is itself free from religion, purely *laïque*. Jacobins are on this wavelength, as was the first Rawls.

The problem with this is that (a) there is no such set of timeless principles which can be determined, at least in the detail they must be for a given political system, by pure reason alone; and (b) situations differ very much, and require different kinds of concrete realization of agreed general principles; so that some degree of working out is necessary in each situation. It follows that (c) dictating the principles from some supposedly higher authority above the fray violates (3) above. It deprives certain spiritual families of a voice in this working out. And therefore (d) this leaves us very often with difficult conflicts and dilemmas between our basic goals.

We have a good illustration of (b), in the way that the issues concerning secularism have evolved in different Western societies in recent decades, because the faiths represented in those societies have changed. We need to alter the way in which we proceed when the range of religions or basic philosophies expands: for example, contemporary Europe or America with the arrival of substantive communities of Muslims.

In relation to (c), we have the recent legislation in France against wearing the hijab in schools. Normally, this kind of thing needs to be negotiated. The host country is often forced to send a double message: (i) you can't do that here (e.g., kill blaspheming authors, practice female genital mutilation), and (ii) we invite you to be part of our consensus-building process. These tend to run against each other; (i) hinders and renders (ii) less plausible. All the more reason to avoid where possible the unilateral application of (i). Of course, sometimes it is not possible. Certain basic laws have to be observed. But the general principle is that religious groups must be seen as much as interlocutors and as little as menace as the situation allows.

These groups also evolve if they're in a process of redefinition of this kind in a democratic, liberal context. José Casanova has pointed out how American Catholicism was originally targeted in the nineteenth century as inassimilable to democratic mores, in ways very analogous to the suspicions which nag people over Islam today. The subsequent history has shown how American Catholicism evolved, and in the process changed world Catholicism in significant ways. There is no reason written into the essence of things why a similar evolution cannot take place in Muslim communities.[8] If this doesn't happen, it will in all likelihood be because of prejudice and bad management.

Now I believe that one of our basic difficulties in dealing with these problems is that we have the wrong model, which has a continuing hold on our minds. We think that secularism (or laïcité) has to do with the relation of the state and religion; whereas in fact it has to do with the (correct) response of the democratic state to diversity. If we look at the three goals above, they have in common that they are concerned with (1) protecting people in their belonging and/or practice of whatever outlook they choose or find themselves in; with (2) treating people equally whatever their option; and with (3) giving them all a hearing. There is no reason to single out religion, as against nonreligious, "secular" (in another widely used sense), or atheist viewpoints.

Indeed, the point of state neutrality is precisely to avoid favoring or disfavoring not just religion positions, but any basic position, religious or nonreligious. We can't favor Christianity over Islam, nor can we favor religion over nonbelief in religion, or vice versa.

One of the ways of demonstrating the superiority of the three-principle model of secularism, over what religion fixates on, is that it would never allow one to misrecognize the regime founded by Atatürk as genuinely secular, making light as it does of the fundamental principles, and even of the separation of state and religious institutions.

This also shows the value of the late-Rawlsian formulation for a secular state. This cleaves very strongly to certain political principles: human rights, equality, the rule of law, democracy. These are the very basis of the state, which must support them. But this political ethic can be and is shared by people of very different basic outlooks (what Rawls calls "comprehensive views of the good"). A Kantian will justify the rights to life and freedom by pointing to the dignity of rational agency; a Utilitarian will speak of the necessity to treat beings who can experience joy and suffering in such a way as to maximize the first and minimize the second. A Christian will speak of humans as made in the image of God. They concur on the principles, but differ on the deeper reasons for holding to this ethic. The state must uphold the ethic, but must refrain from favoring any of the deeper reasons.

3

The idea that secularism makes a special case of religion arises from the history of its coming to be in the West (as does, indeed, the name). To put it briefly, there are two important founding contexts for this kind of regime, the United States and France. In the United States, the whole range of comprehensive views, or deeper reasons, were in the original case variants of (Protestant) Christianity, stretching to a smattering of Deists. Subsequent history has widened the palette of views beyond Christianity, and then beyond religion. But in the original case, the positions between which the state must be neutral were all religious. Hence the First Amendment: Congress shall pass no law establishing religion or impeding the free exercise thereof (or something like this).

The word "secularism" didn't appear in the early decades of American public life. But this was the sign that a basic problem had not yet been faced. Because the First Amendment concerned the separation of church and state, it opened the possibility of giving a place to religion which no one would accept today. Thus in the 1830s, a judge of the Supreme Court could argue that while the First Amendment forbade the identification of the federal government with any church, since all the churches were Christian (and in effect Protestant), one could invoke the principles of Christianity in interpreting the law.

For Judge Joseph Story, the goal of the First Amendment was "to exclude all rivalry among Christian sects," but nevertheless "Christianity ought to receive encouragement from the state." Christianity was essential to the state because the belief in "a future state of rewards and punishments" is "indispensable to the administration of justice." What is more, "it is impossible for those who believe in the truth of Christianity, as a divine revelation, to doubt, that it is a special duty of government to foster, and encourage it among the citizens."[9]

This primacy of Christianity was upheld even later in the nineteenth century. As late as 1890, thirty-seven of the forty-two existing states recognized the authority of God in the preambles or in the text of their constitutions. A unanimous judgment of the Supreme Court of 1892 declared that if one wanted to describe "of American life as expressed by its laws, its business, its customs and its society, we find everywhere a clear recognition of the same truth . . . that this is a Christian nation" (*Church of the Holy Trinity v. United States*, 143 U.S. 457 at 471).

In the latter part of the century, resistance began to build to this conception, but the National Reform Association (NRA) was founded in 1863 with the following goal:

> The object of this Society shall be to maintain existing Christian features in the American government . . . to secure such an amendment to the Constitution of the United States as will declare the nation's allegiance to Jesus Christ and its acceptance of the moral laws of the Christian religion, and so as to indicate that this is a Christian nation, and place all the Christian laws, institutions, and usages of our government on an undeniable legal basis in the fundamental law of the land.

After 1870, the battle was joined between the supporters of this narrow view, on one hand, and those who wanted a real opening to all other religions and also to nonreligion. These included not only Jews, but also Catholics who (rightly) saw the "Christianity" of the NRA as excluding them. It was in this battle that the word "secular" first appears on the American scene as a key term, and very often in its polemical sense of non- or anti-religious.[10]

IN THE FRENCH CASE, laïcité came about in a struggle *against* a powerful church. The strong temptation was for the state itself to stand on a moral basis independent from religion. Marcel Gauchet shows how Renouvier laid the grounds for the outlook of the Third Republic radicals in their battle against the church. The state has to be "moral et enseignant" (moral and instructive). It has "charge d'âmes aussi bien que toute Église ou communauté, mais à titre plus universel" (charge of souls just as does the church or religious community, but a more universal claim). Morality is the key criterion. In order not to be under the church, the state must have "une morale indépendante de toute religion" (a morality independent of all religion), and enjoy a "suprématie morale" (moral supremacy) in relation to all religions. The basis of this morality is liberty. In order to hold its own before religion, the morality underlying the state has to be based on more than just utility or feeling; it needs a real "théologie rationnelle," like that of Kant.[11] The wisdom of Jules Ferry, and later of Aristide Briand and Jean Jaurès, saved France at the time of the Separation (1905) from such a lopsided regime, but the notion stuck that laïcité was all about controlling and managing religion.

If we move, however, beyond such originating contexts, and look at the kinds of societies in which we are now living in the West, the first feature that strikes us is the wide diversity, not only of religious views, but also of those which involve no religion, not to speak of those which are unclassifiable in this dichotomy. Reasons (1), (2), and (3) above require that we treat evenhandedly all of these.

4

This fixation on religion is complex, and it is bound up with two other features we often find in the debates on secularism: the first is the tendency to define secularism or laïcité in terms of some institutional arrangement, rather than starting from the goals as I proposed above. And so you hear mantra-type formulae, like "the separation of church and state," or the necessity of removing religion from public space ("les espaces de la République," as in the recent French debate). The second follows from the first, or may easily seem to. If the whole matter is defined by one institutional formula, then one must just determine which arrangement of things best meets this formula, and there is no need to think further. One cannot find oneself in a dilemma, as will easily happen if one is pursuing more than one goal, because here there is just one master formula.

Hence one often hears these mantras employed as argument stoppers, the ultimate decisive response which annuls all objections. In the United States, people invoke the "Wall of Separation" as the ultimate criterion, and hyper-Republicans in France cite laïcité as the final word. (Of course, if one consulted the First Amendment of the U.S. Constitution, one would find two goals mentioned: the rejection of establishment and the assurance of "free exercise." It is not inconceivable that these could conflict.)

This kind of move amounts, from the standpoint I'm adopting here, to a fetishization of the favored institutional arrangements. Whereas one should start from the goals and derive the concrete arrangements from these. It is not that some separation of church and state, some mutual autonomy of governing and religious institutions, will not be an inescapable feature of any secularist regime. And the same goes for the neutrality of the public institutions. These are both indispensable. But what these requirements mean in practice ought to be determined by how we can maximize our three (or four) basic goals.

Take for example the wearing of the hijab by Muslim women in public schools, which has been a hot issue in a number of Western democracies. In France, pupils in public schools were famously forbidden the headscarf, seen as a "signe religieux ostantatoire" (ostentatious religious sign), according to the notorious Loi Stasi of 2004. In certain German Länder, pupils can wear it, but teachers are not allowed to do so. In the United Kingdom and other countries, there is no general interdict, but individual schools can decide.

What are the reasons for this variation? Plainly in all these cases, legislators and administrators were trying to balance two goals. One was the maintenance of neutrality in public institutions seen (rightly) as an essential entailment of goal (2): equality between all basic beliefs. The other was goal (1), ensuring the maximum possible religious liberty, or, in its most general form, liberty of conscience. Goal (1) seems to push us toward permitting the hijab anywhere. But various arguments were made to override this in the French and German cases. For the Germans, what was disturbing was that someone in authority in a public institution should be religiously marked, as it were. In the French case, an attempt was made to cast doubt on the proposition that wearing the hijab was a free act. There were dark suggestions that the girls were being forced by their families or by their male peers to adopt this dress code. That was one argument which was frequently used, however dubious it might appear in the light of the sociological research carried out among the pupils themselves, which the Stasi Commission largely ignored.

The other main argument was that wearing the headscarf in school was less an act of piety than a statement of hostility against the Republic and its essential institution of laïcité. This was the meaning behind the introduction of the concept of "signe ostantatoire." A smaller discrete sign would be no problem, argued the Stasi Commission, but these attention-grabbing features of dress were meant to make a highly controversial statement. It was in vain that Muslim women protested that "le foulard n'est pas un signe" (the headscarf is not a sign).

So on one level, we can see that these different national answers to the same question reflect different takes on how to balance the two main goals of a secular regime. But on another level, the dilemma and its resolution remain hidden under the illusion that there is only one principle here, say, laïcité and its corollary of the neutrality of public institutions or spaces ("les espaces de la République"). It's just a matter of applying an essential feature of our republican regime; there is no need or place for choice, or the weighing of different aims.

Perhaps the most pernicious feature of this fetishization is that it tends to hide from view the real dilemmas which we encounter in this realm, and which leap into view once we recognize the plurality of principles at stake.

5

We should be aware that this fetishization reflects a deep feature of life in modern democracies. We can see why as soon as we ponder what is involved in self-government, what is implied in the basic mode of legitimation of states that they are founded on popular sovereignty. For the people to be sovereign, it needs to form an entity and have a personality.

The revolutions which ushered in regimes of popular sovereignty transferred the ruling power from a king onto a "nation" or a "people." In the process, they invented a new kind of collective agency. These terms existed before, but the thing they now indicated, this new kind of agency, was something unprecedented, at least in the immediate context of early modern Europe. Thus the notion of a "people" could certainly be applied to the ensemble of subjects of the kingdom, or to the non-élite strata of society, but prior to the turnover it hadn't indicated an entity which could decide and act together, to whom one could attribute a *will*.

But for people to act together, in other words, to deliberate in order to form a common will on which they will act, requires a high degree of common commitment, a sense of common identification. A society of this kind presupposes trust, the basic trust that members and constituent groups have to have, the confidence that they are really part of the process, that they will be listened to and their views taken account of by others. Without this mutual commitment, this trust will be fatally eroded.

And so we have in the modern age a new kind of collective agency. It is one with which its members identify, typically as the realization/bulwark of their freedom, and/or the locus of their national/cultural expression (or, most often, some combination of the two). Of course, in premodern societies, too, people often "identified" with the regime, with sacred kings, or with hierarchical orders. They were often willing subjects. But in the democratic age we identify as free agents. That is why the notion of popular will plays a crucial role in the legitimating idea.[12]

This means that the modern democratic state has generally accepted common purposes, or reference points, the features whereby it can lay claim to being the bulwark of freedom and locus of expression of its citizens. Whether or not these claims are actually founded, the state must be so imagined by its citizens if it is to be legitimate.

So a question can arise for the modern state for which there is no analogue in most premodern forms: What, or whom, is this state for? Whose freedom? Whose expression? The question seems to make no sense applied to, say, the Austrian or Turkish empires—unless one answered the "whom for?" question by referring to the Habsburg or Ottoman dynasties; and this would hardly give you their legitimating ideas.

This is the sense in which a modern state has what I want to call a political identity, defined as the generally accepted answer to the "what/whom for?" question. This is distinct from the identities of its members, that is, the reference points, many and varied, which for each of these defines what is important in their lives. There better be some overlap, of course, if these members are to feel strongly identified with the state, but the identities of individuals and constituent groups will generally be richer and more complex, as well as being often quite different from each other.[13]

IN OTHER WORDS, a modern democratic state demands a "people" with a strong collective identity. Democracy obliges us to show much more solidarity and much more commitment to one another in our joint political project than was demanded by the hierarchical and authoritarian societies of yesteryear. In the good old days of the Austro-Hungarian Empire, the Polish peasant in Galicia could be altogether oblivious of the Hungarian country squire, the bourgeois of Prague, or the Viennese worker, without this in the slightest threatening the stability of the state. On the contrary. This condition of things only becomes untenable when ideas about popular government start to circulate. This is the moment when subgroups which will not, or cannot, be bound together start to demand their own states. This is the era of nationalism, of the breakup of empires.

I have been discussing the political necessity of a strong common identity for modern democratic states in terms of the requirement of forming a people, a deliberative unit. But this is also evident in a number of other ways. Thinkers in the civic humanist tradition, from Aristotle through to Arendt, have noted that free societies require a higher level of commitment and participation than despotic or authoritarian ones. Citizens have to do for themselves, as it were, what otherwise the rulers do for them. But this will only happen if these citizens feel a strong bond of identification with their political community, and hence with those who share with them in this.

From another angle again, because these societies require strong commitment to do the common work, and because a situation in which some carried the burdens of participation and others just enjoyed the benefits would be intolerable, free societies require a high level of mutual trust. In other words, they are extremely vulnerable to mistrust on the part of some citizens in relation to others, that the latter are not really assuming their commitments—for example, that others are not paying their taxes, or are cheating on welfare, or as employers are benefitting from a good labor market without assuming any of the social costs. This kind of mistrust creates extreme tension and threatens to unravel the whole skein of the mores of commitment which democratic societies need to operate. A continuing and constantly renewed mutual commitment is an essential basis for taking the measures needed to renew this trust.

The relation between nation and state is often considered from a unilateral point of view, as if it were always the nation which sought to provide itself with a state. But there is also the opposite process. In order to remain viable, states sometimes seek to create a feeling of common belonging. This is an important theme in the history of Canada, for example. To form a state, in the democratic era, a society is forced to undertake the difficult and never-to-be-completed task of defining its collective identity.

Thus what I have been calling political identity is extremely important in modern democratic states. And this identity is usually defined partly in terms of certain basic principles (democracy, human rights, equality), and partly in terms of their historical, or linguistic, or religious traditions. It is understandable that features of this identity can take on a quasi-sacred status, for to alter or undermine them can seem to threaten the very basis of unity without which a democratic state cannot function.

It is in this context that certain historical institutional arrangements can appear untouchable. They may appear as an essential part of the basic principles of the regime, but they will also come to be seen as a key component of its historic identity. This is what one sees with laïcité as invoked by many French *républicains*. The irony is that in the face of a modern politics of (multicultural) identity, they invoke this principle as a crucial feature of (French) identity. This is unfortunate, but very understandable. It is one illustration of a general truth: that contemporary democracies, as they progressively diversify, will have to undergo redefinitions of their historical identities, which may be far-reaching and painful.

6

At this point, I would like to discuss an interesting point that Jürgen Habermas reminds us of in his paper "Das Politische": originally political authority was defined and justified in cosmic-religious terms. It was defined within the terms of a "political theology."[14] But Habermas seems to think that modern secular states might do altogether without some analogous concept, and this seems to me not quite right.

The crucial move that we see in the modern West from the seventeenth century, the move that takes us out of the cosmic-religious conceptions of order, establishes a new "bottom-up" view of society, as existing for the protection and mutual benefit of its (equal) members. There is a strong normative view attached to this new conception, which I've called the "modern moral order."[15] It enshrines basically three principles (on one possible enumeration): (1) the rights and liberties of the members, (2) the equality among them (which has of course been variously interpreted, and has mutated toward more radical conceptions over time), and (3) the principle that rule is based on consent (which has also been defended in more and less radical forms).

These basic norms have been worked out in a host of different philosophical anthropologies, and according to very different concepts of human sociability. It very soon transcended the atomism that narrowed the vision of its early formulators, like Locke and Hobbes. But the basic norms remain, and are more or less inseparable from modern liberal democracies.

The rejection of cosmic-religious embedding thus was accomplished by a new conception of "the political," a new basic norm, which as Lefort suggests involved its own representation of political authority, but one in which the central spot remains paradoxically empty. If the notion of sovereignty is retained, no one person or group can be identified with it.

Democratic societies are organized not necessarily around a "civil religion," as Rousseau claimed, but certainly around a strong "philosophy of civility," enshrining the three norms, which in contemporary societies are often expressed as (1) human rights, (2) equality and nondiscrimination, and (3) democracy.

But in certain cases, there can be a civil religion: a religious view incorporating and justifying the philosophy of civility. This was arguably so for the young American republic. It was adopting a form which was clearly part of God's providential plan for mankind ("We hold these truths to be self-evident, that men were *created* equal"). Or it can alternatively be part of a non- or even anti-religious ideology, as with the First French Republic. One can even argue that all-englobing views of this kind seem more "natural" to many of our contemporaries. After all, the principles of our civil philosophy seem to call for deeper grounding. If it's very important that we agree on the principles, then surely things are much more stable if we also accept a common grounding. Or so it may appear, and the centuries-long tradition of political life seems to testify for this idea.

For indeed the overlapping consensus between different founding views on a common philosophy of civility is something quite new in history, and relatively untried. It is consequently hazardous. And besides, we often suspect that those with different basic views can't really subscribe to these principles, not the way we do (because, as "we" know, "atheists can't have principles"; or as (another) "we" knows, "religions are all against liberty and/or equality").

The problem is that a really diverse democracy can't revert to a civil religion, or anti-religion, however comforting this might be, without betraying its own principles. We are condemned to live an overlapping consensus.

7

We have seen how this strongly motivated move to fetishize our historical arrangements can prevent our seeing our secular regime in a more fruitful light, which foregrounds the basic goals we are seeking, and which allows us to recognize and reason about the dilemmas which we face. But this connects to the other main cause of confusion I cited above, our fixation on religion as the problem. In fact, we have moved in many Western countries from an original phase in which secularism was a hard-won achievement warding off some form of religious domination, to a phase of such widespread diversity of basic beliefs, religious and areligious, that only clear focus on the need to balance freedom of conscience and equality of respect can allow us to take the measure of the situation. Otherwise we risk needlessly limiting the religious freedom of immigrant minorities, on the strength of our historic institutional arrangements, while sending a message to these same minorities that they by no means enjoy equal status with the long-established mainstream.

Think of the argument of the German Länder that forbade the headscarf for teachers. These are authority figures, surely; but is our idea that only unmarked people can be authority figures? That those whose religious practices make them stand out in this context don't belong in positions of authority in this society? This is maybe the wrong message to inculcate in children in a rapidly diversifying society.

But the fixation on religion as the problem is not just a historical relic. Much of our thought and some of our major thinkers remain stuck in the old rut. They want to make a special thing of religion, but not always for very flattering reasons.

What are we to think of the idea, entertained by Rawls for a time, that one can legitimately ask of a religiously and philosophically diverse democracy that everyone deliberate in a language of reason alone, leaving their religious views in the vestibule of the public sphere? The tyrannical nature of this demand was rapidly appreciated by Rawls, to his credit. But we ought to ask why the proposition arose in the first place. Rawls's point in suggesting this restriction was that everyone should use a language with which they could reasonably expect their fellow citizens to agree. The idea seems to be something like this: secular reason is a language that everyone speaks and can argue and be convinced in. Religious languages operate outside of this discourse, by introducing extraneous premises which only believers can accept. So let's all talk the common language.

What underpins this notion is something like an epistemic distinction. There is secular reason which everyone can use and reach conclusions by—conclusions, that is, with which everyone can agree. Then there are special languages, which introduce extra assumptions, which might even contradict those of ordinary secular reason. These are much more epistemically fragile; in fact you won't be convinced by them unless you already hold them. So religious reason either comes to the same conclusions as secular reason, but then it is superfluous; or it comes to contrary conclusions, and then it is dangerous and disruptive. This is why it needs to be sidelined.

As for Habermas, he has always marked an epistemic break between secular reason and religious thought, with the advantage on the side of the first. Secular reason suffices to arrive at the normative conclusions we need, such as establishing the legitimacy of the democratic state, and defining our political ethic. Recently, his position on religious discourse has evolved considerably, to the point of recognizing that its "Potential macht die religiöse Rede bei entsprechenden politischen Fragen zu einem ernsthaften Kandidaten für mögliche Wahrheitsgehalte" (its potential makes religious speech with respect to corresponding political questions a serious candidate for possible truth-contents). But the basic epistemic distinction still holds for him. Thus when it comes to the official language of the state, religious references have to be expunged: "Im Parlament muss beispielsweise die Geschäftsordnung den Presidenten ermächtigen, religiöse Stellungnahmen und Rechtfertigungen aus dem Protokoll zu streichen" (In Parliament, for example, the rules of procedure must empower the house leader to strike religious positions or justifications from the official transcript).[16]

Do these positions of Rawls and Habermas show that they have not yet understood the normative basis for the contemporary secular state? I believe that they are on to something, in that there are zones of a secular state in which the language used has to be neutral. But these do not include citizen deliberation, as Rawls at first thought, or even deliberation in the legislature, as Habermas seems to think from the above quote. This zone can be described as the official language of the state: the language in which legislation, administrative decrees, and court judgments must be couched. It is self-evident that a law before Parliament couldn't contain a justifying clause of the type "Whereas the Bible tells us that . . ." And the same goes, mutatis mutandis, for the justification of a judicial decision in the court's verdict. But this has nothing to do with the specific nature of religious language. It would be equally improper to have a legislative clause: "Whereas Marx has shown that religion is the opium of the people," or "Whereas Kant has shown that the only thing good without qualification is a good will." The grounds for both these kinds of exclusions is the neutrality of the state.

The state can be neither Christian nor Muslim nor Jewish, but by the same token it should also be neither Marxist nor Kantian nor Utilitarian. Of course, the democratic state will end up passing laws which (in the best case) reflect the actual convictions of its citizens, which will be either Christian, or Muslim, and so forth, through the whole gamut of views held in a modern society. But the decisions can't be framed in a way which gives special recognition to one of these views. This is not easy to do; the lines are hard to draw, and they must always be drawn anew. But such is the nature of the enterprise that is the modern secular state. And what better alternative is there for diverse democracies?[17]

Now the notion that state neutrality is basically a response to diversity has trouble making headway among "secular" people in the West, who remain oddly fixated on religion as something strange and perhaps even threatening. This stance is fed by all the conflicts, past and present, of liberal states with religion, but also by a specifically epistemic distinction: religiously informed thought is somehow less *rational* than purely "secular" reasoning. The attitude has a political ground (religion as threat), but also an epistemological one (religion as a faulty mode of reason).[18]

I believe we can see these two motifs in a popular contemporary book, Mark Lilla's *The Stillborn God*. On one hand, Lilla wants to claim that there is a great gulf between thinking informed by political theology and "thinking and talking about politics exclusively in human terms."[19] Moderns have effected "the liberation, isolation, and clarification of distinctively political questions, apart from speculations about the divine nexus. Politics became, intellectually speaking, its own realm deserving independent investigation and serving the limited aim of providing the peace and plenty necessary for human dignity. That was the Great Separation."[20] Such metaphors of radical separation imply that human-centered political thought is a more reliable guide to answer the questions in its domain than theories informed by political theology.

So much for the epistemological ranking. But then toward the end of his book, Lilla calls on us not to lose our nerve and allow the Great Separation to be reversed,[21] which seems to imply that there are dangers in doing so. The return of religion in this sense would be full of menace.[22]

8

This phenomenon deserves fuller examination. Ideally we should look carefully at the double grounds for this stance of distrust, comment on these, and then say something about the possible negative political consequences of maintaining this stance. But in this chapter, I shall only really have space to look at the roots of the epistemological ground.

I think this has its source in what one might call a myth of the Enlightenment. There certainly is a common view which sees the Enlightenment *(Aufklärung, Lumières)* as a passage from darkness to light, that is, as an absolute, unmitigated move from a realm of thought full of error and illusion to one where the truth is at last available. To this one must immediately add that a counterview defines "reactionary" thought: the Enlightenment would be an unqualified move into error, a massive forgetting of salutary and necessary truths about the human condition.

In the polemics around modernity, more nuanced understandings tend to get driven to the wall, and these two slug it out. Matthew Arnold's phrase about "ignorant armies clashing by night" comes irresistibly to mind.

But what I want to do here, rather than bemoaning this fact, is to try to explain what underlies the understanding of the Enlightenment as an absolute, unmitigated step forward. This is what I see as the "myth" of the Enlightenment. (One can't resist this jab, because "myth" is often cited as what the Enlightenment has saved us from.)

This is worth doing, I believe, because the myth is more widespread than one might think. Even sophisticated thinkers, who might repudiate it when it is presented as a general proposition, seem to be leaning on it in other contexts.

Thus there is a version of what the Enlightenment represents which sees it as our stepping out of a realm in which Revelation, or religion in general, counted as a source of insight about human affairs, into a realm in which these are now understood in purely this-worldly or human terms. Of course, that some people have made this passage is not what is in dispute. What is questionable is the idea that this move involves the self-evident epistemic gain of our setting aside consideration of dubious truth and relevance and concentrating on matters which we can settle and which are obviously relevant. This is often represented as a move from Revelation to reason alone (Kant's "blosse Vernunft").

Clearer examples are found in contemporary political thinkers—for instance, Rawls and Habermas. For all their differences, they seem to reserve a special status for nonreligiously informed reason (let's call this "reason alone"), as though this latter were able to resolve certain moral-political issues (a) in a way which can legitimately satisfy any honest, unconfused thinker, and (b) where religiously based conclusions will always be dubious, and in the end only convincing to people who have already accepted the dogmas in question.

This surely is what lies behind the idea I mentioned above (Section 6), entertained for a time in different form by both thinkers, that one can restrict the use of religious language in the sphere of public reason. We must mention again that this proposition has been largely dropped by both; but we can see that the proposition itself makes no sense, unless something like (a) + (b) above is true. Rawls's point in suggesting this restriction was that public reason must be couched in terms which could in principle be universally agreed upon. The notion was that the only terms meeting this standard were those of reason alone (a), while religious language by its very nature would fail to do so (b).

BEFORE PROCEEDING FURTHER, I should just say that this distinction in rational credibility between religious and nonreligious discourse, supposed by (a) + (b), seems to me utterly without foundation. It may turn out at the end of the day that religion is founded on an illusion, and hence that what is derived from it is less credible. But until we actually reach that place, there is no a priori reason for greater suspicion being directed at it. The credibility of this distinction depends on the view that some quite "this-worldly" argument *suffices* to establish certain moral-political conclusions. I mean "satisfy" in the sense of (a) above: that it should legitimately be convincing to any honest, unconfused thinker. There are propositions of this kind, ranging from "$2 + 2 = 4$" all the way to some of the better-founded deliverances of modern natural science. But the key beliefs we need, for instance, to establish our basic political morality are not among them. The two most widespread this-worldly philosophies in our contemporary world, utilitarianism and Kantianism, in their different versions, both have points at which they fail to convince honest and unconfused people. If we take key statements of our contemporary political morality, such as those attributing rights to human beings as such, say the right to life, I cannot see how the fact that we are desiring/enjoying/suffering beings, or the perception that we are rational agents, should be any surer basis for this right than the fact that we are made in the image of God. Of course, our being capable of suffering is one of those basic unchallengeable propositions, in the sense of (a), as our being creatures of God is not, but what is less sure is what follows normatively from the first claim.

Of course, this distinction would be much more credible if one had a "secular" argument for rights which was watertight. And this probably accounts for the difference between me and Habermas on this score. He finds this secure foundation in a "discourse ethic," which I unfortunately find quite unconvincing.

The (a) + (b) distinction, applied to the moral-political domain, is one of the fruits of the Enlightenment myth; or perhaps one should say it is one of the forms which this myth takes. It would be interesting to trace the rise of this illusion, through a series of moves which were in part well founded, and in part themselves grounded on illusions. In another essay,[23] I identified three, of which the first two are relatively well traced, and the third requires more elaborate description. I'll briefly mention the first two here.

First comes (1) foundationalism, which one sees most famously with Descartes. This combines a supposedly indubitable starting point (the particulate ideas in the mind) with an infallible method (that of clear and distinct ideas) and thus should yield conclusions which would live up to claim (a). But this comes unstuck, in two places. The indubitable starting points can be challenged by a determined scepticism, such as we find in Hume; and the method relies much too much on a priori argument, and not enough on empirical input.

But even though his foundationalism and his a priori physics were rejected, Descartes left behind (i) a belief in the importance of finding the correct method, and (ii) the crucial account which underpins the notion of reason alone. He claimed to be prescinding from all external authority, whether emanating from society or tradition, whether inculcated by parents or teachers, and to rely only on what monological reason can verify as certain. The proper use of reason is sharply distinguished from what we receive from authority. In the Western tradition, this supposedly external imposition comes to include, indeed to find its paradigm in, religious revelation. As the Marquis de Condorcet put it, in his account of the progress of the human mind:

> Il fut enfin permis de proclamer hautement ce droit si longtemps méconnu de soumettre toutes les opinions à notre propre raison, c'est-à-dire d'employer, pour saisir la vérité, le seul instrument qui nous ait été donné pour la reconnaître. Chaque homme apprit, avec une sorte d'orgueil, que la nature ne l'avait pas absolument destiné à croire sur la parole d'autrui; et la superstition del'Antiquité, l'abaissement de la raison devant le délire d'une foi surnaturelle disparurent de la société comme de la philosophie.[24]
>
> (It was finally permitted to resolutely proclaim this right, so long unrecognized, to submit all opinions to our own reason, that is to say, to employ, for seizing on the truth, the sole instrument that we have been given for recognition. Each man learned, with a certain pride, that his nature was not absolutely destined to believe in the words of others; and the superstition of antiquity, the abasement of reason before the delirium of a supernatural faith, disappeared from society as from philosophy.)

Our reasoning power is here defined as autonomous and self-sufficient. Proper reason takes nothing on "faith" in any sense of the word. We might call this the principle of "self-sufficient reason." The story of its rise and its self-emancipation comes to be seen as a kind of coming of age of humanity. As Kant put it, not long after Condorcet wrote, enlightenment is the emergence of human beings from a state of tutelage for which they were themselves responsible, a *selbstbeschuldigte Unmündigkeit* (a self-responsible nonage). The slogan of the age was *sapere aude:* Dare to know.[25]

The first crucial move is that to self-sufficient reason. The next (2) was to point to natural science as a model for the science of society, the move we see in Hobbes, for instance. I shall not pursue this further here, because reductive views of social science have less credibility today, although they are, alas, still present on the scene.

This whole matter deserves much further consideration, more than I can give it here. But I am convinced that this further examination would lend even more credibility to the revisionary polysemy I am proposing here, which amounts to this: what deserve to be called "secularist" regimes in contemporary democracy have to be conceived not primarily as bulwarks against religion but as good-faith attempts to secure the three (or four) basic goals I outlined at the start of this chapter. And this means that they attempt to shape their institutional arrangements, not to remain true to hallowed tradition, but to maximize the basic goals of liberty and equality between basic beliefs.

CHAPTER FOURTEEN

Die Blosse Vernunft
("Reason Alone")

I

Is there a myth of the Enlightenment? There certainly is a common view which sees the Enlightenment *(Aufklärung, Lumières)* as a passage from darkness to light, that is, as an absolute, unmitigated move from a realm of thought full of error and illusion to one where the truth is at last available. To this one must immediately add that a counterview defines "reactionary" thought: the Enlightenment would be an unqualified move into error, a massive forgetting of salutary and necessary truths about the human condition.

In the polemics around modernity, more nuanced understandings tend to get driven to the wall, and these two slug it out. Matthew Arnold's phrase about "ignorant armies clashing by night" comes irresistibly to mind.

What are the more nuanced views? First, of course, they include those interpretations of modern history which allow for plural versions of the Enlightenment (John Pocock, Gertrude Himmelfarb).[1] But they also include interpretations which see enlightenment, singular or plural, as involving important gains, for instance, discoveries of truth, or framing of new and advantageous conceptualizations, which also brought certain losses, occluding or forgetting some understandings or virtues which were in our world before. This doesn't rule out an overall positive judgment of the change(s), but it does pose the question of what we might do to recover some of what we have lost while not sacrificing the gains.

A good example of this kind of thing is Tocqueville's thoughts about democracy. This vast movement of social leveling is seen by him as inevitable and laudable. He even speaks of it as providential at one point.[2] But he is also keenly aware of what has been lost with the way of life of the ci-devant aristocracy, a certain heroic sense of one's own dignity, of which freedom and courageous service were essential parts. This awareness of loss doesn't remain at the level of nostalgic feeling. Tocqueville wants to find ways of recreating something analogous in the democratic age, and this he finds precisely in the life of active citizen engagement, the exercise of what he calls political liberty. By analogy with Tocqueville's stance toward democracy, we might say that there is a way of being "for" the Enlightenment, either tout court or in one of its variants, which doesn't see it an unmitigated move forward, but rather is aware of losses incurred in its wake, and thus puts on the agenda the question of how perhaps some of these losses might be made up.

This is where I would situate my own view. But what I want to do here, rather than expounding this view, is to try to explain what underlies the understanding of the Enlightenment as an absolute, unmitigated step forward. This is what I see as the "myth" of the Enlightenment. (One can't resist this jab, because "myth" is often cited as what the Enlightenment has saved us from.)

This is worth doing, I believe, because the myth is more widespread than one might think. Even sophisticated thinkers, who might repudiate it when it is presented as a general proposition, seem to be leaning on it in other contexts.

Thus there is a version of what the Enlightenment represents which sees it as our stepping out of a realm in which Revelation, or religion in general, counted as a source of insight about human affairs, into a realm in which these are now understood in purely this-worldly or human terms. Of course, that some people have made this passage is not what is in dispute. What is questionable is the idea that this move involves the self-evident epistemic gain of our setting aside consideration of dubious truth and relevance and concentrating on matters which we can settle and which are obviously relevant. This is often represented as a move from Revelation to reason alone (Kant's "blosse Vernunft").

We see this kind of idea at work in a book like Mark Lilla's *Stillborn God*, although in some passages he writes as though this is a choice that we must make, rather than being imposed by reason. However the very idea that there is a clear distinction between political thought where theological considerations are at work, and political thought where these are banned is redolent of a certain myth of reason. Lilla wants to claim that there is a great gulf between thinking informed by political theology and "thinking and talking about politics exclusively in human terms."[3] Moderns have effected "the liberation, isolation, and clarification of distinctively political questions, apart from speculations about the divine nexus. Politics became, intellectually speaking, its own realm deserving independent investigation and serving the limited aim of providing the peace and plenty necessary for human dignity. That was the Great Separation."[4] Such metaphors of radical separation imply that human-centered political thought is a more reliable guide to answer the questions in its domain than theories informed by political theology.

Clearer examples are found in contemporary political thinkers, for instance, John Rawls and Jürgen Habermas. For all their differences, they seem to reserve a special status for nonreligiously informed reason (let's call this "reason alone"), as though this latter were able to resolve certain moral-political issues (a) in a way which can legitimately satisfy any honest, unconfused thinker, and (b) where religiously based conclusions will always be dubious, and in the end only convincing to people who have already accepted the dogmas in question.

Hence the idea, entertained by Rawls for a time, that one can legitimately ask of a religiously and philosophically diverse democracy that everyone deliberate in a language of reason alone, leaving their religious views in the vestibule of the public sphere. The tyrannical nature of this demand was rapidly appreciated by Rawls, to his credit. But the proposition itself makes no sense, unless something like (a) + (b) above is true. Rawls's point in suggesting this restriction was that everyone should use a language with which they could reasonably expect their fellow citizens to agree. That this requirement allows for reason alone while excluding religious language is the substance of (a) and (b).

As for Habermas, his position on religious discourse has considerably evolved, to the point of recognizing that its "Potential macht die religiöse Rede bei entsprechenden politischen Fragen zu einem ernsthaften Kandidaten für mögliche Wahrheitsgehalte" (potential makes religious speech with respect to corresponding political questions a serious candidate for possible truth-contents). But the basic epistemic distinction still holds for him. Thus when it comes to the official language of the state, religious references have to be expunged: "Im Parlament muss beispielsweise die Geschäftsordnung den Präsidenten ermächtigen, religiöse Stellungnahmen und Rechtfertigungen aus dem Protokoll zu streichen" (In Parliament, for example, the rules of procedure must empower the house leader to strike religious positions or justifications from the official transcript).[5]

Before proceeding further, I should just say that this distinction in rational credibility between religious and nonreligious discourse, supposed by (a) + (b), seems to me utterly without foundation. It may turn out at the end of the day that religion is founded on an illusion, and hence that what is derived from it is less credible. But until we actually reach that place, there is no a priori reason for greater suspicion being directed at it. The credibility of this distinction depends on the view that some quite "this-worldly" argument *suffices* to establish certain moral-political conclusions. I mean "satisfy" in the sense of (a): it should legitimately be convincing to any honest, unconfused thinker. There are propositions of this kind, ranging from "$2+2=4$" all the way to some of the better-founded deliverances of modern natural science. But the key beliefs we need, for instance, to establish our basic political morality are not among them. The two most widespread this-worldly philosophies in our contemporary world, utilitarianism and Kantianism, in their different versions, all have points at which they fail to convince honest and unconfused people. If we take key statements of our contemporary political morality, such as those attributing rights to human beings as such, say the right to life, I cannot see how the fact that we are desiring/enjoying/suffering beings, or the perception that we are rational agents, should be any surer basis for this right than the fact that we are made in the image of God. Of course, our being capable of suffering is one of those basic unchallengeable propositions, in the sense of (a), as our being creatures of God is not, but what is less sure is what follows normatively from the first claim.

To propound the distinction is much easier if you think you already have a "secular" argument for rights which is watertight, as Habermas does for his "discourse ethic" (which I unfortunately find quite unconvincing).

The (a) + (b) distinction, applied to the moral-political domain, is one of the fruits of the Enlightenment myth; or perhaps one should say that it is one of the forms which this myth takes. In the following pages, I will try to trace the rise of this illusion, through a series of moves which were in part well founded, and in part themselves grounded on illusions. I identify three here, of which the first two are relatively well traced, and so I shall be briefer with them, and concentrate on the third.

The first one (1) originates in Cartesian foundationalism. This famously combines a supposedly indubitable starting point (the particulate ideas in the mind) with an infallible method (that of clear and distinct ideas) and thus should yield conclusions which would live up to claim (a). But this comes unstuck in two places. The indubitable starting points can be challenged by a determined scepticism, such as we find in Hume; and the method relies much too much on a priori argument, and not enough on empirical input.

But even though his foundationalism and his a priori physics were rejected, Descartes left behind (i) a belief in the importance of finding the correct method, and (ii) the crucial account which underpins the notion of reason alone. He claimed to be prescinding from all external authority, whether emanating from society or tradition, whether inculcated by parents or teachers, and to rely only on what monological reason can verify as certain. The proper use of reason is sharply distinguished from what we receive from authority. In the Western tradition, this supposedly external imposition comes to include, indeed to find its paradigm in, religious revelation. As the Marquis de Condorcet put it, in his account of the progress of the human mind:

> Il fut enfin permis de proclamer hautement ce droit si longtemps méconnu de soumettre toutes les opinions à notre propre raison, c'est-à-dire d'employer, pour saisir la vérité, le seul instrument qui nous ait été donné pour la reconnaître. Chaque homme apprit, avec une sorte d'orgueil, que la nature ne l'avait pas absolument destiné à croire sur la parole d'autrui; et la superstition de l'Antiquité, l'abaissement de la raison devant le délire d'une foi surnaturelle disparurent de la société comme de la philosophie.[6]
>
> (It was finally permitted to resolutely proclaim this right, so long unrecognized, to submit all opinions to our own reason, that is to say, to employ, for seizing on the truth, the sole instrument that we have been given for recognition. Each man learned, with a certain pride, that his nature was not absolutely destined to believe in the words of others; and the superstition of antiquity, the abasement of reason before the delirium of a supernatural faith, disappeared from society as from philosophy.)

Our reasoning power is here defined as autonomous and self-sufficient. Proper reason takes nothing on "faith" in any sense of the word. We might call this the principle of "self-sufficient reason." The story of its rise and its self-emancipation comes to be seen as a kind of coming of age of humanity. As Kant put it, not long after Condorcet wrote, enlightenment is the emergence of human beings from a state of tutelage for which they were themselves responsible, a *selbstbeschuldigte Unmündigkeit* (a self-responsible nonage). The slogan of the age was *sapere aude:* Dare to know.[7]

The first crucial move is that to self-sufficient reason. It was inaugurated by Descartes, but the method he proposed came very soon under attack. A rival method came to dominate the scene, that of empiricism, famously defined by John Locke. This in effect considers itself justified in ignoring the radical sceptical objection to its starting point. Simple ideas cannot be gone behind; the mind can't help receiving them, and hence they are the unavoidable starting points. It is of no use to question them further. But a better method than the Cartesian can be devised, one which patiently tracks the actual correlations found in experience.

Here empiricism finds some support in (2) post-Galilean natural science, or hopes to do so. The notion is that there is a method, which anchors its conclusions in facts of observation, which everyone but radical sceptics accepts as meeting the (a) standard. According to one very simple, empiricist, version, it simply notes and records correlations of such facts, and/or orders them by more complex intervening entities which are themselves unobservable.

This very naïve understanding of science has been replaced by more adequate ones which take account of the fact that the scientific treatment of observable fact is shaped by a larger picture of how things work, and how the events we observe are to be causally explained. This wider picture is often referred to today as a "paradigm," following the influential work of Thomas Kuhn. Certain advances in science may be impossible as long as one is working with an inadequate paradigm, and a new surge forward becomes possible with a paradigm change. Thus to recur to the famous example: in Aristotelian mechanics, the principle *no mobile without mover* was considered valid. Each movement had to have a presently operating cause. This made it impossible to understand the movement of projectiles or cannonballs. What makes them go on moving when they leave the hand or cannon? There was no possible resolution of these questions as long as the paradigm remained intact. These movements constituted anomalies for the theory. Only when one shifted to the inertial paradigm was it possible to make sense of these movements, of their trajectory, and what brought them to an end.

Following this understanding of the role of paradigms, we have the picture of a science which, basing itself in undeniable (in the sense of [a]) elements of experience, attempts to offer efficient causal explanations of these events. Although this science can only proceed by devising explanatory frameworks within which to cast the events observed, these can be discriminated by their ability to deal with the issues of explanation without running into unsolvable anomalies. The supersession of one paradigm by another can be justified by the anomalies resolved in the move. We are far from the foundationalism of Descartes, but we still have a domain in which we can say that well-established conclusions deserve the kind of credit claimed in (a).

Now (1) and (2), and particularly (2), have had a powerful effect on the modern imagination. Natural science has become for many the paradigm of the successful acquisition of knowledge, while dealing with only this-worldly materials. In a way, the rise of post-Galilean natural science offers a scenario which fits perfectly the Enlightenment myth of an unmitigated advance. Taking the explanation of the phenomena of the natural world out of the Platonic-Aristotelian framework, where Forms shape the material universe, and into the domain of efficient-causal relations within this universe, allowed for a Great Leap Forward, which continues to this day. Since the Forms, at least in their Platonic variant, are other-worldly (outside of time), this can be configured as a move from darkness to light, leaving the shadowy, other-worldly realm and throwing clear light on the world which surrounds us. Have we not earned the right to talk of a clear epistemic superiority of this-worldly reason over other-worldly belief? Undoubtedly in a sense, yes. But this is not the same dichotomy that we were dealing with above, where the terms were reason and revelation or reason and religion. The refutation of Aristotelian physics is one thing, that of all religions quite another. So different are these issues that we can note that the refutation of Aristotelian and Platonic views of the cosmos was at least cheered on, and partly undertaken, by Christian thinkers of a certain persuasion. One can cite, for example, Marin Mersenne, who was in correspondence with all the important scientific thinkers of his time (the mid-seventeenth century), and particularly close to Descartes, who on theological grounds was deeply suspicious of the late-Renaissance theories of an animated universe. The drive here was the same as that toward disenchantment in the reforming movements, both Catholic and Protestant, of this period, which strove to ban a series of practices, retrospectively condemned as "magic" (hence the Weberian term "Entzauberung," which we translate as "disenchantment"). The ground in all these cases was that attributing such power to worldly processes either denied or defied the sovereign power of God.

In spite of this crucial facet of our history, the confusion which lumps enchantment with religion in general is widespread, and is part of what underlies the claim that "science has refuted religion." From which it is perhaps an easy step to the view that the (a) + (b) distinction, which clearly holds of post-Galilean natural science in relation to Platonic-Aristotelian Form theory, also applies somehow to the moral and political. But one can also take this further step in another way, by espousing a notion of reductive explanation whereby the methods of natural science already do or will eventually suffice to explain the phenomena of human life. That would be, indeed, the shortest route to this facet of the Enlightenment myth. I will return to this below.

2

These are the moves which underpin what I have called the (3) modern idea of moral order.[8] This was most clearly stated in the new theories of natural law which emerged in the seventeenth century, largely as a response to the domestic and international disorder wrought by the wars of religion. Hugo Grotius and John Locke are the most important theorists of reference for our purposes here.

Grotius derives the normative order underlying political society from the nature of its constitutive members. Human beings are rational, sociable agents who are meant to collaborate in peace to their mutual benefit.

Starting from the seventeenth century, this idea has come more and more to dominate our political thinking, and the way we imagine our society. It starts off in Grotius's version as a theory of what political society is, that is, what it is in aid of, and how it comes to be. But any theory of this kind also offers inescapably an idea of moral order. It tells us something about how we ought to live together in society.

The picture of society is that of individuals who come together to form a political entity, against a certain preexisting moral background, and with certain ends in view. The moral background is one of natural rights; these people already have certain moral obligations toward each other. The ends sought are certain common benefits, of which security is the most important.

The underlying idea of moral order stresses the rights and obligations which we have as individuals in regard to each other, even prior to or outside of the political bond. Political obligations are seen as an extension or application of these more fundamental moral ties. Political authority itself is legitimate only because it was consented to by individuals (the original contract), and this contract creates binding obligations in virtue of the preexisting principle that promises ought to be kept.

More important to our lives today is the manner in which this idea of order has become more and more central to our notions of society and polity, remaking them in the process. And in the course of this expansion, it has moved from being a theory, animating the discourse of a few experts, and become integral to our social imaginary, that is, the way in which our contemporaries imagine the societies they inhabit and sustain. I want to describe this process in more detail later.

A crucial point which ought to be evident from the foregoing is that the notion of moral order I am using here goes beyond some proposed schedule of norms which ought to govern our mutual relations and/or political life. What an understanding of moral order adds to an awareness and acceptance of norms is an identification of features of the world, or divine action, or human life which make certain norms both right and (up to the point indicated) realizable. In other words, the image of order carries a definition not only of what is right, but of the context in which it makes sense to strive for and hope to realize the right (at least partially).

Now it is clear that the images of moral order which descend through a series of transformations from that inscribed in the natural law theories of Grotius and Locke are rather different from those embedded in the social imaginary of the premodern age.

Two important types of premodern moral order are worth singling out here, because we can see them being gradually taken over, displaced, or marginalized by the Grotian-Lockean strand during the transition to political modernity. One is based on the idea of the law of a people, which has governed this people since time out of mind, and which in a sense defines it as a people. This idea seems to have been widespread among the Indo-European tribes who at various stages erupted into Europe. It was very powerful in seventeenth-century

England, under the guise of the Ancient Constitution, and became one of the key justifying ideas of the rebellion against the king.[9]

This case should be enough to show that these notions are not always conservative in import; but we should also include in this category the sense of normative order which seems to have been carried on through generations in peasant communities, and out of which they developed a picture of the "moral economy," from which they could criticize the burdens laid on them by landlords, or the exactions levied on them by state and church.[10] Here again, the recurring idea seems to have been that an original acceptable distribution of burdens had been displaced by usurpation, and ought to be rolled back.

The other type is organized around a notion of a hierarchy in society which expresses and corresponds to a hierarchy in the cosmos. These were often theorized in language drawn from the Platonic-Aristotelian concept of Form, but the underlying notion also emerges strongly in theories of correspondence: for example, the king is in his kingdom, as the lion among animals, the eagle among birds, and so forth. It is out of this outlook that the idea emerges that disorders in the human realm will resonate in nature, because the very order of things is threatened. The night on which Duncan was murdered was disturbed by "lamenting heard i' the air; strange screams of death," and it remained dark even though day should have started. On the previous Tuesday, a falcon had been killed by a mousing owl; and Duncan's horses turned wild in the night, "Contending 'gainst obedience, as they would / Make war with mankind."[11]

In both these cases, and particularly in the second, we have an order which tends to impose itself by the course of things; violations are met with backlash which transcends the merely human realm. This seems to be a very common feature in premodern ideas of moral order. Anaximander likens any deviation from the course of nature to injustice, and says that things which resist it must eventually "pay penalty and retribution to each other for their injustice according to the assessment of time."[12] Heraclitus speaks of the order of things in similar terms, when he says that if ever the sun should deviate from its appointed course, the Furies would seize it and drag it back.[13] And of course, the Platonic forms are active in shaping the things and events in the world of change.

In these cases, it is very clear that a moral order is more than just a set of norms; that it also contains what we might call an "ontic" component, identifying features of the world which make the norms realizable. Now the modern order which descends from Grotius and Locke is not self-realizing in the sense invoked by Hesiod or Plato, or the cosmic reactions to Duncan's murder. It is therefore tempting to think that our modern notions of moral order lack altogether an ontic component. But this would be a mistake, as I hope to show later. There is an important difference, but it lies in the fact that this component is now a feature about us humans, rather than one touching God or the cosmos, and not in the supposed absence altogether of an ontic dimension.

Now what is peculiar to our modern understanding of order stands out most clearly if we focus on how the idealizations of natural law theory differ from those which were dominant before. Premodern social imaginaries, especially those of the second type mentioned above, were structured by various modes of hierarchical complementarity. Society was seen as made up of different orders. These needed and complemented each other. But this didn't mean that their relations were truly mutual, because they didn't exist on the same level. They formed rather a hierarchy in which some had greater dignity and value than the others. An example is the often repeated medieval idealization of the society of three orders, oratores, bellatores, laboratores: those who pray, those who fight, and those who work. It was clear that each needed the others, but there was no doubt that we have here a descending scale of dignity; some functions were in their essence higher than others.

Now it is crucial to this kind of ideal that the distribution of functions is itself a key part of the normative order. It is not just that each order ought to perform its characteristic function for the others, granted they have entered these relations of exchange, while we keep the possibility open that things might be arranged rather differently, for example, in a world where everyone does some praying, some fighting, and some working. No, the hierarchical differentiation itself is seen as the proper order of things. It was part of the nature or form of society. In the Platonic and neo-Platonic traditions, as I have just mentioned, this form was already at work in the world, and any attempt to deviate from it turned reality against itself. Society would be denatured in the attempt. Hence the tremendous power of the organic metaphor in these earlier theories. The organism seems the paradigm locus of forms at work, striving to heal its wounds and cure its maladies. And at the same time, the arrangement of functions which it exhibits is not simply contingent; it is "normal" and right. That the feet are below the head is how it should be.

The modern idealization of order departs radically from this. It is not just that there is no place for a Platonic-type form at work; but connected to this, whatever distribution of functions a society might develop is deemed contingent; it will be justified or not instrumentally; it cannot itself define the good. The basic normative principle is, indeed, that the members of society serve each other's needs, help each other, in short, behave like the rational and sociable creatures that they are. In this way, they complement each other. But the particular functional differentiation which they need to take on to do this most effectively is endowed with no essential worth. It is adventitious, and potentially changeable. In some cases, it may be merely temporary, as with the principle of the ancient polis, that we may be rulers and ruled in turn. In other cases, it requires lifetime specialization, but there is no inherent value in this, and all callings are equal in the sight of God. In one way or the other, the modern order gives no ontological status to hierarchy, or any particular structure of differentiation.

In other words, the basic point of the new normative order was the mutual respect and mutual service of the individuals who make up society. The actual structures were meant to serve these ends, and were judged instrumentally in this light. The difference might be obscured by the fact that the older orders also ensured a kind of mutual service; the clergy prays for the laity, and the laity defend/work for the clergy. But the crucial point is just this division into types in their hierarchical ordering, whereas on the new understanding we start with individuals and their debt of mutual service, and the divisions fall out as they can most effectively discharge this debt.

Thus Plato, in book II of the *Republic,* starts out by reasoning from the non-self-sufficiency of the individual to the need for an order of mutual service. But quite rapidly it becomes clear that it is the structure of this order which is the basic point. And the last doubt is removed when we see that this order is meant to stand in analogy and interaction with the normative order in the soul. By contrast, in the modern ideal, the whole point is the mutual respect and service, however achieved.

I have mentioned two differences which distinguish this ideal from the earlier, Platonic-modeled orders of hierarchical complementarity: the Form is no longer at work in reality, and the distribution of functions is not itself normative. A third difference goes along with this. For the Platonic-derived theories, the mutual service which the classes render to each other when they stand in the right relation includes bringing them to the condition of their highest virtue; indeed, this is the service which the whole order, as it were, renders to all its members. But in the modern ideal, the mutual respect and service is directed toward serving our ordinary goals, life, liberty, sustenance of self and family. The organization of society, I said above, is judged not on its inherent form, but instrumentally. But now we can add that what this organization is instrumental to concerns the very basic conditions of existence as free agents, rather than the excellence of virtue—although we may judge that we need a high degree of virtue to play our proper part in this.

Our primary service to each other was thus (to use the language of a later age) the provision of collective security, to render our lives and property safe under law. But we also serve each other in practicing economic exchange. These two main ends, security and prosperity, are now the principal goals of organized society, which itself can come to be seen as something in the nature of a profitable exchange between its constituent members. The ideal social order is one in which our purposes mesh, and each in furthering himself helps the others.

This ideal order was not thought to be a mere human invention. Rather it was designed by God, an order in which everything coheres according to God's purposes. Later in the eighteenth century, the same model is projected on the cosmos, in a vision of the universe as a set of perfectly interlocking parts, in which the purposes of each kind of creature mesh with those of all the others.

This order sets the goal for our constructive activity, insofar as it lies within our power to upset it, or realize it. Of course, when we look at the whole, we see how much the order is already realized, but when we cast our eye on human affairs, we see how much we have deviated from it and upset it; it becomes the norm to which we should strive to return.

This order was thought to be evident in the nature of things. Of course, if we consult revelation, we will also find the demand formulated there that we abide by it. But reason alone can tell us God's purposes. Living things, including ourselves, strive to preserve themselves. This is God's doing:

> God having made Man, and planted in him, as in all other Animals, a strong desire of Self-preservation, and furnished the World with things fit for Food and Rayment and other Necessaries of Life, Subservient to his design, that Man should live and abide for some time upon the Face of the Earth, and not that so curious and wonderful a piece of Workmanship by its own Negligence, or want of Necessities, should perish again . . . : God . . . spoke to him, (that is) directed him by his Senses and Reason, . . . to the use of those things which were serviceable for his Subsistence, and given him as the means of his Preservation. . . . For the desire, strong desire of Preserving his Life and Being having been planted in him, as a Principle of Action by God himself, Reason, which was the voice of God in him, could not but teach him and assure him, that pursuing that natural Inclination he had to preserve his Being, he followed the Will of his Maker.[14]

Being endowed with reason, we see that not only our lives but that of all humans are to be preserved. And in addition, God made us sociable beings. So that "every one as he is bound to preserve himself, and not quit his Station wilfully; so by the like reason when his Preservation comes not in competition, ought he, as much as he can, to preserve the rest of Mankind."[15]

Similarly Locke reasons that God gave us our powers of reason and discipline so that we could most effectively go about the business of preserving ourselves. It follows that we ought to be "Industrious and Rational."[16] The ethic of discipline and improvement is itself a requirement of the natural order that God had designed. The imposition of order by human will is itself called for by his scheme.

We can see in Locke's formulation how much he sees mutual service in terms of profitable exchange. "Economic" (that is, ordered, peaceful, productive) activity has become the model for human behavior, and the key for harmonious coexistence. In contrast to the theories of hierarchical complementarity, we meet in a zone of concord and mutual service, not to the extent that we transcend our ordinary goals and purposes, but, on the contrary, in the process of carrying them out according to God's design.

Now this idealization was at the outset profoundly out of sync with the way things in fact ran, thus with the effective social imaginary on just about every level of society. Hierarchical complementarity was the principle on which people's lives effectively operated, all the way from the kingdom, to the city, to the diocese, to the parish, to the clan and the family. We still have some lively sense of this disparity in the case of the family, because it is really only in our time that the older images of hierarchical complementarity between men and women are being comprehensively challenged. But this is a late stage on a "long march," a process in which the modern idealization, advancing along the three axes I mentioned above, has connected up with and transformed our social imaginary on virtually every level, with revolutionary consequences.

The very revolutionary nature of the consequences ensured that those who first took up this theory would fail to see its application in a host of areas which seem obvious to us today. The powerful hold of hierarchically complementary forms of life, in the family, between master and servant in the household, between lord and peasant on the domain, between educated élite and the masses, made it seem "evident" that the new principle of order ought to be applied within certain bounds. This was often not even perceived as a restriction. What seems to us flagrant inconsistency when eighteenth-century Whigs defended their oligarchic power in the name of the "people," for instance, was for the Whig leaders themselves just common sense.

In fact, they were drawing on an older understanding of "people," one stemming from a premodern notion of order, of the first type I mentioned above, where a people is constituted as such by a law which already exists, "since time out of mind." This law can confer leadership on some elements, who thus quite naturally speak for the "people." Even revolutions (or what we consider such) in early modern Europe were carried out under this understanding—as, for instance, the Monarchomachs in the French Wars of Religion, who accorded the right to rebel not to the unorganized masses, but to the "subordinate magistrates." This was also the basis of Parliament's rebellion against Charles I.

And this long march is perhaps only ending today. Or perhaps we too are victims of a mental restriction, for which our posterity will accuse us of inconsistency or hypocrisy. In any case, some very important tracts of this journey have happened only very recently. I have mentioned contemporary gender relations in this regard. But we should also remember that it wasn't very long ago when whole segments of our supposedly modern society remained outside of this modern social imaginary. Eugen Weber has shown how many communities of French peasants were transformed only late in the last century, and inducted into France as a nation of 40 million individual citizens.[17] He makes plain how much their previous mode of life depended on complementary modes of action which were far from equal, especially but not only between the sexes; there was also the fate of younger siblings, who renounced their share of the inheritance in order to keep the family property together and viable. In a world of indigence and insecurity, of perpetually threatening dearth, the rules of family and community seemed the only guarantee of survival. Modern modes of individualism seemed a luxury, a dangerous indulgence.

This is easy to forget, because once we are well installed in the modern social imaginary, it seems the only possible one, the only one which makes sense. After all, are we not all individuals? Do we not associate in society for our mutual benefit? How else to measure social life?

This makes it very easy for us to entertain a quite distorted view of the process; and this in two respects. First, we tend to read the march of this new principle of order, and its displacing of traditional modes of complementarity, as the rise of "individualism" at the expense of "community"; whereas the new understanding of the individual has as its inevitable flip side a new understanding of sociality, the society of mutual benefit, whose functional differentiations are ultimately contingent, and whose members are fundamentally equal. This is what I have been insisting on in these pages, just because it generally gets lost from view. The individual seems primary, because we read the displacement of older forms of complementarity as the erosion of community as such. We seem to be left with a standing problem of how to induce or force the individual into some kind of social order, to make him conform and obey the rules.

This recurrent experience of breakdown is real enough. But it shouldn't mask from us the fact that modernity is also the rise of new principles of sociality. Breakdown occurs, as we can see with the case of the French Revolution, because people are often expelled from their old forms, through war, revolution, or rapid economic change, before they can find their feet in the new structures, that is, connect some transformed practices to the new principles to form a viable social imaginary. But this doesn't show that modern individualism is by its very essence a solvent of community. Nor that the modern political predicament is that defined by Thomas Hobbes: how do we rescue atomic individuals from the prisoners' dilemma? The real, recurring problem has been better defined by Tocqueville or, in our day, François Furet.

The second distortion is the familiar one. The modern principle seems to us so self-evident—are we not by nature and essence individuals?—that we are tempted by a "subtraction" account of the rise of modernity. We just needed to liberate ourselves from the old horizons, and then the mutual service conception of order was the obvious alternative left. It needed no inventive insight or constructive effort. Individualism and mutual benefit are the evident residual ideas which remain after you have sloughed off the older religions and metaphysics.

But the reverse is the case. Humans have lived for most of their history in modes of complementarity, mixed with a greater or lesser degree of hierarchy. There have been islands of equality, like that of the citizens of the polis, but they are set in a sea of hierarchy, once you replace them in the bigger picture. Not to speak of how alien these societies were to modern individualism. What is rather surprising is that it was possible to win through to modern individualism; not just on the level of theory, but also transforming and penetrating the social imaginary. Now that this imaginary has become linked with societies of unprecedented power in human history, it seems impossible and mad to try to resist. But we mustn't fall into the anachronism of thinking that this was always the case.

The best antidote to this error is to bring to mind again some of the phases of the long and often conflictual march by which this theory has ended up achieving such a hold on our imagination.

I will be doing some of this as my argument proceeds. But at this stage, I want to pull together the preceding discussion and outline the main features of this modern understanding of moral order. This can be sketched in three points, to which I will then add a fourth:

(1) The original idealization of this order of mutual benefit comes in a theory of rights and of legitimate rule. It starts with individuals, and conceives society as established for their sake. Political society is seen as an instrument for something prepolitical.

This individualism signifies a rejection of the previously dominant notion of hierarchy, according to which a human being can only be a proper moral agent embedded in a larger social whole, whose very nature is to exhibit a hierarchical complementarity. In its original form, the Grotian-Lockean theory stands against all those views, of which Aristotle's is the most prominent, which deny that one can be a fully competent human subject outside of society.

As this idea of order advances, and generates new "redactions," it becomes connected again with a philosophical anthropology which defines humans as social beings, incapable of functioning morally on their own. Rousseau, Hegel, Marx provide earlier examples, and they are followed by a host of thinkers in our day. But I see these still as redactions of the modern idea, because what they posit as a well-ordered society incorporates relations of mutual service between equal individuals as a crucial element. This is the goal, even for those who think that the "bourgeois individual" is a fiction, and that the goal can be

achieved only in a communist society. Even connected to ethical concepts antithetical to those of the natural law theorists, and, indeed, closer to the Aristotle they rejected, the kernel of the modern idea remains an idée force in our
world.

(2) As an instrument, political society enables these individuals to serve each
other for mutual benefit; both in providing security, and in fostering exchange
and prosperity. Any differentiations within it are to be justified by this telos;
no hierarchical or other form is intrinsically good.

The significance of this, as we saw above, is that the mutual service centers
on the needs of ordinary life, rather than aiming to secure for them the highest
virtue. It aims to secure their conditions of existence as free agents. Now here,
too, later redactions involve a revision. With Rousseau, for instance, freedom
itself becomes the basis for a new definition of virtue, and an order of true
mutual benefit becomes inseparable from one which secures the virtue of self-
dependence. But Rousseau and those who followed him still put the central
emphasis on securing freedom, equality, and the needs of ordinary life.

(3) The theory starts with individuals, whom political society must serve.
More important, this service is defined in terms of the defense of individuals'
rights. And freedom is central to these rights. The importance of freedom is
attested in the requirement that political society be founded on the consent of
those bound by it.

If we reflect on the context in which this theory was operative, we can see
that the crucial emphasis on freedom was overdetermined. The order of mutual benefit is an ideal to be constructed. It serves as a guide for those who
want to establish a stable peace, and then remake society to bring it closer to its
norms. The proponents of the theory already see themselves as agents who
through disengaged, disciplined action can reform their own lives, as well as the
larger social order. They are buffered, disciplined selves. Free agency is central
to their self-understanding. The emphasis on rights, and the primacy of freedom among them, doesn't just stem from the principle that society should exist
for the sake of its members; it also reflects the holders' sense of their own agency,
and of the situation which that agency normatively demands in the world,
namely, freedom.

Thus the ethic at work here should be defined just as much in terms of this
condition of agency as in terms of the demands of the ideal order. We should
best think of it as an ethic of freedom and mutual benefit. Both terms in this
expression are essential. And that is why consent plays such an important role
in the political theories which derive from this ethic.

Summing up, we can say that (1) the order of mutual benefit holds between
individuals (or at least moral agents who are independent of larger hierarchical
orders); (2) the benefits crucially include life and the means to life, however

securing these relates to the practice of virtue; and (3) it is meant to secure freedom, and easily finds expression in terms of rights. To these we can add a fourth point: (4) these rights, this freedom, and this mutual benefit are to be secured for all participants equally. Exactly what is meant by equality will vary, but that it must be affirmed in some form follows from the rejection of hierarchical order. These are the crucial features, the constants that recur in the modern idea of moral order, through its varying "redactions."

My claim here is that this notion of order has entered the social imaginary of the modern West, and to some extent also beyond. In particular, it has given us certain standard ways of grasping a society, as an economy, as a public sphere, and as a state created by, and serving as instrument of, a "people." What is more, these and other analytic categories connected to this notion have come to seem to us "natural"; they are more than the correlates of a particular way of looking at and imagining society but are there in the nature of social reality.

3

This can make it easily comprehensible that the Grotian move has come to be seen by many as another facet of the Enlightenment. That is, it is seen as a move of unmitigated epistemic gain, one from darkness to light. The "darkness" consists in the invoking of such strange metaphysical entities as a law which holds since time out of mind, regardless of the incompatible positive legislation which may have crept in for a time; or of a cosmic order arranging different levels of being in a hierarchy. The "light" consists in the clear analysis of worldly reality, in which societies are nothing more than aggregations of human beings. The move, in other words, is from the mental world of the Great Chain of Being to that of Hobbes's *Leviathan*.[18] Because the new era now has a scientific way of studying society (however much social scientists may disagree about how to analyze and explain things), we can relegate all the earlier stuff about Gods, Great Chains, and the like. Look, for example, at Trevor-Roper's introduction to Edward Gibbon's *Decline and Fall*. In Trevor-Roper's view, Gibbon in projecting his "philosophical history" followed his predecessors, is venturing to "handle Church history in a secular spirit, to see the Church not as a repository of truth (or error), but as a human society subject to the same social laws as other societies."[19] The opposition is clear. There is "social science" with its "laws," and then there is another view or discourse, which imports some criteria, unsubstantiated by science, in order to discriminate truth and error. The deliverances of social science can meet the claim (a), that is, they can legitimately satisfy any honest, unconfused thinker; while the other discourse of truth and error falls under the strictures of (b), that is, its conclusions will always be dubious and in the end only convincing to people who have already accepted the criteria in question.

In short, the claim to an (a) + (b) distinction made here (3) parallels that made on behalf of post-Galilean natural science (2). Obviously (3) is all the stronger if backed by (2), but even by itself it seems to justify the application of the (a) + (b) distinction to moral and political matters.

I have been speaking in these last paragraphs of claims made on behalf of what we usually call social science, but I have come to them via a discussion of the Grotian turn, because I believe that this turn, understood as a step into this-worldly Enlightenment, is part of the background which lends credibility to these claims. At a certain point, we stepped out of the shadow of super-worldly frameworks, and saw reality for what it was. We could think of Gibbon and Montesquieu as being in our modern enlightened space, or we could think of Hobbes as making the crucial move, but the step to analyzing societies as the ways in which human persons live together under rules, free from a background of cosmic or divine order, is in some ways the key shift.

Of course, if we think of the step outside higher orders as what matters, there is no reason not to give Machiavelli pride of place, and people often do. He in fact precedes Grotius by a century. And he is indeed operating in a very different conceptual framework, which owes a lot to the civic humanist tradition that comes from the ancients. But the Grotian line is, I believe, crucial to the illusion of a modern reason which can make claims of force (a) about political morality. It is this analysis which gives the specific background for so much of our contemporary, now close to unquestioned, political morality: human rights, equality, popular sovereignty. I would even want to argue that the Grotian definition of the human predicament provides the key background, via Rousseau, for Kant's moral and political theory. That it provides the framework for the other widespread secular theory of morality, utilitarianism, seems obvious.

I have been trying to give an account of that facet of the Enlightenment myth which holds that "reason alone" can yield us truths about morality and political theory that cannot be added to, and may even be obscured by introducing putative truths of religion or metaphysics, whether stemming from "Revelation" or other forms of supramundane insight. The claim in other words is that an (a) + (b) distinction holds in this moral-political realm, too, as well as it indisputably does in the realm of natural science. I have been arguing that three moves combine to make this claim look plausible: (1) the principle of self-sufficient reason; (2) the model of natural science; and (3) the modern post-Grotian understanding of society as made up of individuals, where good order demands that their relations conduce to mutual benefit.

But there are two major variants, two ways of combining the elements to produce the desired result. The first variant can be called the Condorcet version. This uses all three moves. It sees natural science as an exercise in self-sufficient reason, and it then proposes to apply the methods of natural science to solve the normative questions of social and political life. This can appear an unproblematic move, because we now "know" that society is made up of individuals, and that a good society protects the rights of these individuals and establishes relations which ensure mutual benefit. What relations effectively secure these ends is a matter for empirical social science, which is as unproblematically an exercise of self-sufficient reason as physics.

But not everyone can accept this quick assimilation of social or human to natural science. The reasoning underlying this involves various moments of slippage. We indeed saw with (2) that (i) it is with post-Galilean natural science that the Enlightenment myth comes true. It may indeed be that the frameworks of Platonic or Aristotelian forms which this science relegates still have something important to teach us, about ontology, or morals, or aesthetics. But the liberation of a field of explanation of material reality in efficient-causal terms has greatly increased our knowledge and understanding of this reality, not to speak of the greatly magnified control which has resulted. We saw, however, (ii) that the dethroning of Aristotle by Galileo is far from being the same thing as the sidelining of religion by science. And in addition, (iii) there is no road from (i) to a reasoning about moral and political matters which might have force (a), until, that is, materialist reductive accounts of human life become available, and we are at least several centuries from that (supposed) day.

We should be clear that point (ii) above holds as much of the Grotian move as of the Galilean. As often as we may hear contemporaries say that with modernity, we realized that there was no divinely sanctioned social order, and that we now have to devise laws on our own, human authority, this was far from the conclusions drawn in earlier centuries. As I mentioned above, the modern natural law was seen either as something which flowed from a human condition designed by Providence, or else as something commanded by God. The latter seems to have been the view of Locke and Samuel von Pufendorf; the former seems to underlie a document like the American Declaration of Independence. Of course, the commands of God were not necessarily delivered by Revelation; for Locke it was sufficient that his will could be read off his creation. But we are far from having taken a step outside all religious frameworks.

But more: we cannot make on behalf of social science point (i) made above about natural science. It isn't grounded on an unmitigated epistemic step forward. It is true that something of the sort can be claimed for certain of the paniculate observations of social science. The tracing of voting patterns over time, the incidence of poverty, the reporting on the state of public opinion— these are all matters in which it is in principle possible to establish propositions which no one can dispute (even though there is often dispute over individual claims here). But social science which attempts to explain these patterns cannot rest content with such particulate findings. These have to figure in some explanatory framework, provide the material for answering certain kinds of questions and not others. And once you come to the level of paradigms, there is no agreement.

Whether we think of the original Grotian model as worked out by Hobbes and Locke, with its basically atomistic bent, or we think of the critiques of this model which have tried to overcome the problems of atomism, with Montesquieu, Rousseau, Fichte, Hegel, Marx, on to Durkheim and Weber, it is clear that there has never been, and probably never will be, any convergence on a paradigm. Of course, one could protest that natural sciences too have been through paradigm changes, but this is not the same thing. In natural sciences, there tends to be at any one time convergence on a paradigm. This may later be upset because of the anomalies it encounters, but then typically the crisis is resolved when the troubled paradigm is superseded by another. In social sciences, there has never been convergence, and it is hard to identify moves which can be unambiguously called supersessions. The Grotian move, as before it the Machiavellian one, and after it the trail of grand theories of societies, has never generated an unmitigated epistemic gain, except in the eyes of its partisans. But this is precisely the (b) status which is always attributed to religiously enframed accounts. Social science offers no contrast case.

But now we get close to pinpointing the difficulty. The grand theories in social science are separated by their philosophical anthropologies, their conception of how humans relate in societies, of the fundamental goals which humans pursue, of the distinction between sacred and profane, and so on. But these are also the considerations that underlie various accounts of ethics and morals, as well as of the virtues of societies. Social science cannot establish a reasoning on the political-moral with (a) force, because the field is divided between rival anthropologies, each of which secretes its own understanding of the human moral-social predicament. The question about point (iii) above doesn't even arise.

And just to drive the point home, in this clash of rival views, lay or this-worldly anthropologies enjoy no epistemic preference over theological or religious ones. The whole putative (a) + (b) distinction between religious views and this-worldly reasoning turns out to be a mirage.

The obvious difficulties with the Condorcet variant have led to a second variant, which I will call the neo-Kantian (though Rousseau and others also deserve credit). This drops move (2) and builds a new variant of self-sufficient reason which it derives in its own way from the Grotian turn. If societies are made up of individuals with claims, and indeed equal claims since there is no way to discriminate some as higher or more worthy than others, then reason alone seems to be telling us that an adequate norm will be one which serves all equally. This general idea can be cashed out in various ways: valid norms are universalizable maxims, or are norms we would all accept under the veil of ignorance, or are ones which all those affected could accept given ideal conditions of free exchange, or are ones which we could reasonably ask others to accept granted we seek such norms, and so on.

This second variant has jettisoned a lot of the ballast which has dragged the Condorcet variant down to the bottom of the shallow seas of utility. It is quite independent of any supposed reduction of human to natural science. It puts together moves (1) and (3) to create principles which may indeed need social science to be applied but can be enunciated independently. But it may easily fail to carry conviction because of its too great dependence on the Grotian turn. Is it really true that the major features of the good society or the just society turn on the defense of rights, equality, and arrangements of mutual benefit? This is a conclusion that it is still very hard to class in category (a), along with the truths of mathematics and natural science. The second variant is also turning out to be a mirage.

But like any mirage, it can look very solid from a distance, that is, if one doesn't examine closely what could ground it. It lives more by the suggestive force of narratives which have been spun around its three key motifs: (1) Cartesian foundationalism and its attendant rationalism, (2) the coming of post-Galilean science, and (3) the Grotian reconstruction of social theory, and the field of social science debate it has opened up, to name them in ascending order of their persuasive force. If you stand back far enough, it can appear that the Grotian turn, which was this-worldly indeed in relation to theories of the Great Chain, inaugurated an age of disenchantment, in which humans found themselves alone in an indifferent universe, condemned to make up the rules as they go along. And then the narrative locks in, which can carry us to the delicious illusions of a self-sufficient reason *(blosse Vernunft)*.

CHAPTER FIFTEEN

Perils of Moralism

A GREAT DEAL of effort in modern liberal society is invested in defining and applying codes of conduct. First, at the highest theoretical level, much contemporary moral theory assumes that morality can be defined in terms of a code of obligatory and forbidden actions, a code moreover which can be generated from a single source or principle. Hence the major importance in our philosophy departments of the battle between Utilitarians and (post-)Kantians; they agree that there must be a single principle from which one can generate all and only obligatory actions, but they wage a vigorous polemic over the nature of this principle. On one hand, there are those who opt for some or other mode of calculation of utility (rule utilitarianism, act utilitarianism, utilities as preferences, and so forth). On the other hand, we find those whose criterion lies in some form of universality, be it the original Kantian sort (acting by universalizable maxims) or more sophisticated modern versions: as, for example, that norm is right which is agreed by all those affected (Habermas); or that act is right which you could justify to those affected (Scanlon). The constant here is the identification of morality with a unified code, generated from a single source.

But if you move out of the academy into the political realm, you are struck with a similar (and related) code fixation. This is interwoven with the legal entrenchment of certain fundamental principles of our society, whose most prominent and visible form is the constitutionalization of various charters of rights and nondiscrimination, which is a central feature of our world. This leads to a more and more elaborate definition of legally binding codes. But this approach extends in spirit beyond the political sphere. It is taken for granted that the way to achieve certain important collective goods, like tolerance and mutual respect, lies in a code of behavior, like the "speech codes" which some campuses have put in place. The contours of disrespect are codified, so that they can be forbidden, and if necessary sanctioned. Thus will our society march forward.

Oĸ. wʜᴀᴛ's wʀᴏɴɢ with this? In this first section, I'd like to present some obvious and often rehearsed objections to this way of proceeding. Then in later sections, I want to try to go deeper into our culture and history to trace the sources of this code fixation, and some of the forms of resistance to it. At the end, I will try to articulate some specifically Christian concerns about it.

I

Why can't our moral/ethical life ever be adequately captured in a code? Here are some of the reasons:

(1) The Aristotle reason: situations and events are unforseeably various; no set of formulae will ever capture all of them. Any prefixed code will have to be adjusted to new situations. That is why the good person with phronêsis really operates on a deep sense of the goods concerned, plus a flexible ability to discern what the new situation requires.

(2) The plurality of goods (also Aristotle): there is more than one good; this is not recognized by Kant and Bentham and all those who try to derive morality from a single-source principle. These goods can conflict in certain circumstances: liberty and equality; justice and mercy; commutative justice and comity; efficient success and compassionate understanding; getting things done bureaucratically (requiring categories, rules) and treating everyone as a unique person; and so on.

(3) Now this feature (2) intensifies (1). It creates dilemmas; and dilemmatic situations differ in nonpredictable ways. So we need phronêsis even more. We need a sense of the two goods in conflict here, and of the weight of each demand in the tension in relation to its own kind. If one is really weighty, and the other relatively trivial, we know which way to lean.

So different examples of the "same" dilemma call for different resolutions. But there is more. It is in the nature of dilemmas that even in a concrete case, they may admit of more than one solution. That is, the "same" dilemma, defined by the goods in conflict, and in this concrete case, may admit of more than one solution, like quadratic equations with two unknowns. Why?

Because we are dealing not only with goods (justice and mercy, liberty and equality), but with the claims of certain people, certain agents. How they chose or can be induced to treat their own claims can have a fateful effect on the outcome. Someone has suffered a historical wrong; commutative justice demands redress. But there are other considerations. What might be considered full redress, if we just look at the nature of the wrong, will have other effects, which may be damaging to parties who are either innocent, or whose guilt is not all that total. This is obviously what arises in cases of historical redress: as in reparations payments to historical victims; or in cases of transition from a despotic exploitative regime to a more open, democratic, egalitarian one. In this latter case, we have also to consider the effects of full reparations on the future coexistence of the descendants of exploiters and exploited in the new regime.

Now one "right" solution might be an all-things-considered award to the victims, in a context where the two parties remain locked in conflict, at arm's length. But if they can be brought together, can talk, become motivated to try to find some good future basis for their common existence, then one may emerge with quite a different "award" or solution. Cases of contemporary transitional justice come to mind, like the Truth and Reconciliation Commission (TRC) in South Africa. Of course, big questions arise about this: did the victims really agree? Who exactly were the victims? Were they rushed, pushed, forced into conceding too much? And so on. But the basic idea behind this kind of procedure was to get the ex-victims to accept that they could have a maximum of one kind of closure (the truth about what happened) at the cost of renouncing a lot that they could quite legitimately claim of another kind: punishment of the perpetrators, an eye for an eye. The aim was to find an "award" which allowed also for a reconciliation, and therefore living together on a new footing.

The important point here is this: that one reason dilemmas admit of more than one solution is that they are frequently also conflicts between claimants, and these can be differently seen or interpreted by those involved. But further, by moving the interpretations in a certain direction, the same dilemma can be resolved in a less costly way to the two goods. That is, one resolution may be the only right one here, because the parties remain rigidly hostile and opposed to each other, insisting on their full "rights"; as a result, the "award" to the victim is on one sense higher, therefore hurting the perpetrator more; but the resulting hostility also deprives the victims and their successors of the goods of comity and collaboration. As against this, the operation of a TRC can lift us to a new point where the issue is not so totally zero-sum. It can bring about, in relation to the first situation of total hostility, a win-win move.

(4) Generalizing this, we can see that dilemmas have to be understood in a kind of two-dimensional space. The horizontal space gives you the dimension in which you have to find the point of resolution, the fair "award," between two parties. The vertical space opens the possibility that by rising higher, you'll accede to a new horizontal space where the resolution will be less painful or damaging for both parties.

Examples of this abound in modern politics. A "fair" resolution for Bosnia after the terrible mutual killing is perhaps this strange tripartite state with separate cantons and a triune presidency, and a great deal of uncertainty and instability. But imagine that, over time, some trust can be reestablished between the parties; then one can see the possibility of moving toward a more normal federal system.

That is why the great benefactors in politics—Mandela, Tutu—are those whose charismatic interventions help a society to move up in this space.

Put another way, we can say that dilemmas of this kind are also trilemmas, or double dilemmas. First, we have to judge between claims A and B; but then we also have to decide whether we will go for the best "award" between A and B on the level we're now on, or try to induce people to rise to another level. Great leaders here have a mixture of shrewd judgment of where people can be induced to go, as well as great charismatic power to lead them there. Mandela again.

(5) The vertical dimension I've been talking about here is one of reconciliation and trust. And this whole discussion shows how Christian faith can never be decanted into a fixed code. Because it always places our actions in two dimensions, one of right action, and also an eschatological dimension. This is also a dimension of reconciliation and trust, but it points beyond any merely intrahistorical perspective of possible reconciliation. It can, however, inspire vertical moves in history, like those of Mandela and Tutu. (Tutu's faith commitment is well known; I don't know what Nelson Mandela actually believes, but his whole move was obviously deeply inspired by Christianity, if only historically; forgiveness is a key category, however downplayed as a term here.)

The New Testament is full of indications of this. Take the owner of the vineyard who invited workers in at the beginning of the day, then successively at later hours until the end. His proposal to pay everyone one denarius is obviously outrageous as a suggestion for the basis of wages policy in a stable society; hence the protests of those who came at the beginning of the day. But the parable opens the eschatological dimension of the Kingdom of God: at the height of that vertical space, that's the only appropriate distribution. God operates in that vertical dimension, as well as being with us horizontally in the person of Christ.[1]

But that means that there aren't any formulae for acting as Christians in the world. Take the best code possible in today's circumstances, or what passes for such. The question always arises: could one, by transcending/amending/re-interpreting the code, move us all vertically? Christ is constantly doing that in the Gospel.

One "solution" adopted in the past was marking out different roles. The clergy couldn't do certain things which were permitted to the laity, like, for instance, partaking in battle. But we tend to distrust that today. And a more exigent demand of Christian pacifism would wipe out this distinction. But is that the right move?

2

My claim above was that modern liberal society tends toward a kind of "code fetishism," or nomolatry. It tends to forget the background which makes sense of any code—the variety of goods which rules and norms are meant to realize—as well as the vertical dimension which arises above all these.

We can see this above in relation to contemporary Anglo-Saxon moral philosophy, as well as in the drive to codification in liberal society.

But the sources go back deeper in our culture. I want to argue that it was a turn in Latin Christendom which sent us down this road. This was the drive to reform in its various stages and variants—not just the Protestant Reformation, but a series of moves on both sides of the confessional divide. The attempt was always to make people over as more perfect practicing Christians, through articulating codes and inculcating disciplines. Until the Christian life became more and more identified with these codes and disciplines.

In other words, this code-centrism came about as the by-product of an attempt to make over the lives of Christians, and their social order, so as to make them conform thoroughly to the demands of the Gospel. I am talking not of a particular, revolutionary moment, but of a long, ascending series of attempts to establish a Christian order, of which the Reformation is a key phase. These attempts show a progressive impatience with older modes of postaxial religion, in which certain collective, ritualistic forms of earlier religions existed in uneasy coexistence with the demands of individual devotion and ethical reform which came from the "higher" revelations. In Latin Christendom, the attempt was to recover and impose on everyone a more individually committed and Christocentric religion of devotion and action, and to repress or even abolish older, supposedly "magical" or "superstitious" forms of collective ritual practice.

Allied with a neo-Stoic outlook, this became the charter for a series of attempts to establish new forms of social order, drawing on new disciplines

(Foucault enters the story here), which helped to reduce violence and disorder, and to create populations of relatively pacific and productive artisans and peasants, who were more and more induced/forced into the new forms of devotional practice and moral behavior, be this in Protestant England, Holland, the American colonies, Counter-Reformation France, or the Germany of the *Polizeistaat*.

My hypothesis is that this new creation of a civilized, "polite" order succeeded beyond what its first originators could have hoped for, and that this in turn led to a new reading of what a Christian order might be, one which was seen more and more in "immanent" terms (polite, civilized order *is* the Christian order). This version of Christianity was shorn of much of its "transcendent" content, and was thus open to a new departure, in which the understanding of good order (what I call the "modern moral order") could be embraced outside of the original theological, providential framework, and in certain cases even against it (as with Voltaire, Gibbon, and, in another way, Hume).

Disbelief in God arises in close symbiosis with this belief in a moral order of rights-bearing individuals, who are destined (by God or Nature) to act for mutual benefit, an order which thus rejects the earlier honor ethic that exalted the warrior, as it also tends to occlude any transcendent horizon. (We see one good formulation of this notion of order in Locke's *Second Treatise*.) This understanding of order has profoundly shaped the forms of social imaginary which dominate in the modern West: the market economy, the public sphere, the sovereign "people."[2]

The process was completed when these disciplined forms of life began to be seen as not needing any transcendent endorsement; they could be made the content of an exclusive humanism. As a matter of fact, as, for instance, Hume and Gibbon argued, they were liable to be destabilized by any appeal to the transcendent, which tended to breed "fanaticism" and/or "enthusiasm." With this modern enclosed humanism, the vertical dimension is largely eclipsed, or else disappears altogether.

This involved a change in the foreground understanding of Christian life; but even more fatefully a deep change in the background understanding. The premodern sense that any code can hold only in a larger order that transcends the code, articulated in such events as Carnival or hierarchical reversals, which Victor Turner has so brilliantly analyzed, has almost totally faded from our world.

3

Code fetishism means that the entire spiritual dimension of human life is captured in a moral code. Kant proposes perhaps the most moving form of this (but perhaps the capture wasn't complete in his case). His followers today, be they Rawls or Habermas or others again, carry on this reduction (although Habermas seems to have had recent second thoughts).

Modern culture is marked by a series of revolts against this moralism, in both its Christian and non-Christian forms. Think of the great late nineteenth-century reaction in England against evangelical "puritanism" that we associate with names as diverse as Arnold, Wilde, and later Bloomsbury; or think of Ibsen; or of Nietzsche and all those who follow him, including those rebelling against the various disciplines that have helped constitute this modern moralization, such as our contemporary, Michel Foucault.

But these reactions start earlier. The code-centered notion of order and its attendant disciplines begin to generate negative reactions from the eighteenth century on. These form, for instance, the central themes of the Romantic period. Many people found it hard to believe, even preposterous, that the achievement of this code-bound life should exhaust the significance of human existence. It's almost as though each form of protest were adding its own verse to the famous Peggy Lee song: "Is that all there is?"

The reactions were in fact plural, and not all in one direction. Some wanted to return to, recover, or reconceive forms of Christian faith which acknowledged transcendence. But others tried rather to reconceptualize immanence, giving rise to what could be called the "immanent counter-Enlightenment."[3] What may seem to call for a return to belief may give rise also to new forms of unbelief, and vice versa.

The multiplicity of the reactions, and multiple directions in which they can be carried out, has meant a steadily widening gamut of different possible positions in our civilization, something I have called "the nova effect." We can get a sense of this if we look at the dynamic of this movement in somewhat finer detail. The whole package—disciplined, buffered identity, contained within the code of freedom and mutual benefit—has given rise to a gamut of negative reactions, sometimes leveled at the package itself, sometimes against one or other part of it, sometimes against particular solutions which arise from it. I want to look at least at some of these, and follow out a little the path of the polemics, as the nova expands, along several axes at once.

Disintricating these axes will be difficult. In the actual struggles, there has often been more than one issue at stake. I am going to have to make a number of analytic distinctions, which are bound to seem rather artificial when we look at any particular thinker or movement. But this move is justified, because the strands, while always connected, combine in a number of different ways.

It might help to group the axes into two spaces. The first (i) takes up critiques of the buffered self and modern order as too narrow, self-enclosed, denying a greater reality both within and without. They are often optimistic, and point toward ways of healing through openness or completion. The second batch (ii), on the contrary, tends to see this modern outlook as too facile and optimistic. It frequently points to irremediable division, and can introduce a note of tragedy.

i

(1) One of the central themes of the Romantic age was a critique leveled at the disengaged, disciplined, buffered self, and the world it had built. The accusation was that it had repressed or denied feeling; or, alternatively, that it had divided us, confined us in a dessicating reason which had alienated us from our deeper emotions. Now this critique in fact went back some considerable way. Shaftesbury had reacted to the calculating hedonism of Locke and rehabilitated the "generous affection" of which the soul is capable.[4] His was part of the inspiration behind the moral sense school. Later Rousseau in his own eloquent way protested against the narrow reasons of self-interest, which divide us from each other and stifle the reasons of the heart. The great importance laid on deep feeling as a facet of human excellence, on sentiment, on sensibility, reflected in part a reaction to the excessive demands of ordering reason. All this forms the background to the classical statements of the Romantic period, like Schiller's in his *Aesthetic Education,* which posits the goal of overcoming this internal division as the way to wholeness and freedom, the very height of human excellence.

Now this reaction could be part of a way back out of rationalist Deism into orthodox belief. This is what it was for the Pietist movement. True religion couldn't consist in this intellectual fascination with doctrine; it had to engage the whole heart, or it was nothing. Spener pronounced his lapidary judgment on the apologetic obsessions of establishment theologians: "Whoever would prove the existence of God, he is already an atheist."[5] This religion of the heart was passed on to Wesley and Methodism, where it took ecstatic, often spectacular forms, deeply disturbing to those who feared above all "enthusiasm."

But the same reaction could lead in a quite different direction. The tyranny of reason over feeling in the context of much traditional morality involved a condemnation of base desire. The rehabilitation of ordinary feeling could therefore take the form of a rejection of this moral tradition, and also of the Christianity which seemed to underlie it, with its picture of human nature as damaged and depraved. So Rousseau's Deism sloughed off the doctrine of original sin. And others would follow this lead down the path to a humanism in which natural, spontaneous desire was the source of healing.

The same response could lead in two diametrically opposed directions, bringing us both John Wesley (and today's Pentecostal movements) and D. H. Lawrence (and various twentieth-century cults of liberated sexuality)—not to speak of all the mediating links between these two Englishmen living a century and a half apart.

(2) Another closely related line of attack against the buffered identity and its model of order, the one most central to this discussion, charged its adherents with moralism. In a sense, this too goes quite far back. Already the "reasonable" religion which emerges out of the English civil war and its aftermath in that country tended toward moralism. Our duty to God consisted in establishing and conforming to the moral order he had designed for us. The proofs of his existence and goodness pointed to his design of a world in which this order was appropriate, and his endorsing of it through the rewards and punishments he offers us. What had got lost was the sense that devotion to God, for its own sake, was the center of the religious life.

In a sense, this objection overlaps the previous one, could even be seen as the same charge taken from a different angle. It protests against a life totally absorbed in conforming to certain rules. The sense is that something central is missing here, some great purpose, some élan, some fulfillment, without which life has lost its point.

Seen in a Christian perspective, this missing centerpiece is the love of God, and this could give us an alternative way of describing Wesley's rebellion against the established piety of his day. But the same charge can be taken up in a different perspective, in the name of an integral, fulfilled human nature, for instance, as we see it with Schiller. Simply imposing moral rules gives us a kind of unfreedom, a realm of necessity. If we impose them on ourselves, this means that we have created a kind of "master within."[6] True freedom requires that we go beyond morality to the harmonious realization of our whole nature, which we achieve in "play."

This appeal against the moral to a genuine self-realization can then be played out in a host of forms, both spiritual and naturalistic, as with see with Nietzsche, among others—and, of course, with Lawrence. Indeed, since moralism is one of the recurring forms generated out of the modern order of freedom and benefit, including its contemporary unbelieving Utilitarian and post-Kantian modes, this response is still being generated, and in a host of different directions. The nova effect goes on.

(3) But returning to the eighteenth century, we can see that these two objections could and often did combine with a third: the sense that the understanding

of benevolence, of charity, is too pale and tame in mainstream Deism/humanism. The movement toward Deism, and eventually to the skeptical Enlightenment stance of a Hume or a Gibbon, involved some exclusion of practices which were previously seen as central to the love of and devotion to God, and their condemnation as excessive, extravagant, harmful, or "enthusiastic."[7] A more demanding piety rebels at these restrictions. And so evangelicals felt called upon to throw themselves into causes which most mainstream churchmen were willing to leave alone, most notably the abolition of slavery. To the less stringent, more Establishment-friendly, mainstream notion of order, it seemed excessive to upset production and property rights, and long-settled ways, to such an extent, for such a reason.

But the call of a more demanding form of justice/benevolence also gave rise to new and more radical modes of humanism. Again Rousseau is a hinge figure. He spoke up, very eloquently and persuasively, for a more demanding standard of justice and benevolence, and he was the inspiration of a whole tradition of radical humanist views, starting with those of the French revolutionaries who swore by him.

And the succession from Rousseau also has to include Kant. Here again, someone on the verge of Deism, in a sense; but one who very sharply defined the inner source of the moral law, and made morality identical to autonomy. In spite of the continuing place of God and immortality in his scheme, Kant is a crucial figure in the development of exclusive humanism, just because he articulates so strongly the power of inner sources of morality.

And yet, we cannot be surprised when we learn that Kant came from a Pietist background. His philosophy goes on breathing this sense of the stringent demands of God and the good, even while he puts his Pietistic faith through an anthropocentric turn. We have a moving field of forces here, in which more than one constellation is possible, and more, in which the constellations frequently mutate.

(4) I have by no means exhausted the reactions to the buffered identity and moral order. The Romantic movement carried a multiplicity of protests in its current. Some have been mentioned, but I want to touch on one more here. This is a reaction to the buffered self as such. It is the sense that in closing ourselves to the enchanted world, we have been cut off from a great source of life and meaning, which is there for us in nature. Not that this was seen as an invitation to return to the past. On the contrary, the Romantics rather explored new ways to recover the link with nature, mediated by our expressive powers.

Now there is a feature of this facet which is especially worth mention. It is the malaise at the adoption of a purely instrumental, "rational" stance toward the world of human life. The close link to (4) comes in the fact that it is usually this stance which is indicted as what has in fact closed us off from Nature and the current of life within us and without. But still, the attack on the instrumental stance takes up another side of this self-closure which has had its own devastating consequences. In the effort to control our lives, or control Nature, we have destroyed much that is deep and valuable in them. We have been blinded to the importance of equilibria which can be upset, but can't be created by instrumental rationality. The most important of these in the contemporary debates is obviously the one touching the ecological balance of our entire biosphere. The line of protest which I am invoking here has been absolutely crucial to the ecological movements of our time. Some of these are grounded, of course, on instrumental rational considerations, but an important part of the whole ecological movement draws on the sense that there is something fundamentally wrong, blind, hubristic, even impious in taking this stance to the world, in which the environment is seen exclusively in terms of the human purposes to which it can be put.

Needless to say, this reaction too can take unbelieving as well as Christian forms.

ii

(5) Something which may also go with a strong piety—but may not—is the rejection of the Deistic notion of Providence as just too absurdly, self-indulgently optimistic. Everything fits together for the good. It is all too pat, and seems to deny the tragedy, the pain, the unresolved suffering which we all know is there. The most famous occasion for this objection was the Lisbon earthquake of 1757. And the most famous articulation of it is probably Voltaire's in *Candide,* which shows right off how this response doesn't have to feed a sense of piety. On the contrary, it can be used to put on trial the whole notion of Providence and, beyond it, of belief in God as such. This has perhaps been its most important effect in the last two centuries. A very common objection of unbelief to Christianity has been that it offers a childishly benign view of human life, where everything will come right in the end, something which the really mature person cannot believe, and is willing to do without, having the courage to face reality as it is. This was in fact one of the main motors impelling those who moved from Deism to exclusive humanism in the eighteenth century.

In part, this bespeaks a one-sided definition of Christianity in terms of providential Deism, particularly in the context of apologetic, as Buckley has shown.[8] It shows the importance of the order of historical events, and the key role played by Deism in the development of the modern debate. But it also is somewhat justified by the continuing place of a liberal, sanitized Christianity, which doesn't quite know what to do with suffering.

There is something deep in this objection. Deism or Christianity is taxed with unrealism; but there is also a moral objection here. Unrealism doesn't always have to be a moral matter. Some may even admire Christians or anarchists for their Utopian hopes, and their willingness to fight for things which others recognize as impossible of attainment. But in the case of Panglossian optimism, the unrealism is held to betoken an immaturity, a lack of courage, and inability to face things.

Moreover, it is held in some way to cheapen life, to render it shallow. Recognizing the tragedy in life is not just having the nerve to face it; it is also acknowledging some of its depth and grandeur. There is depth, because suffering can make plain to us some of the meaning of life which we couldn't appreciate before, when it all seemed swimmingly benign; this is, after all, what tragedy as an art form explores. There is grandeur because of the way suffering is sometimes borne, or fought against. So in a curious way, a picture of life as potentially frictionless bliss robs us of something.

This is undoubtedly what Nietzsche was getting at in *The Genealogy of Morals,* where he says that what humans can't stand is not suffering, but meaningless suffering. They need to give a meaning to it. And he mentions specifically what we could call the judicial-penal model, the idea that we suffer because we have sinned, as an example of a belief which comes to be accredited partly because it makes sense of what is otherwise unbearable.[9]

Nietzsche is on to something here, although I have reservations about the idea that there is a demand for meaning as such, as it were, any meaning, as against something more specific. This is rather endemic to our modern humanist consciousness of religion, and gives a particular (and I think dubious) twist to the hunger for religion in human beings. Nietzsche is followed in this, among others, by Weber, and also Gauchet.

But nevertheless there is something important here. A too benign picture of the human condition leaves something crucial out, something that matters to us. There is a dark side to creation, to use this (Barthian?) expression; along with joy, there is massive innocent suffering; and then on top of this, the suffering is denied, the story of the victims is distorted, eventually forgotten, never rectified or compensated. Along with communion, there is division, alienation, spite, mutual forgetfulness, never reconciled and brought together again.

Even where a voice of faith wants to deny that this is the last word, as with Christianity, we cannot set aside the fact that this is what we live, that we regularly experience this as ultimate. All great religions recognize this, and place their hopes in a beyond which doesn't simply deny this, which takes its reality seriously.

An image like the dance of Shiva, which brings destruction as well as creation in its wake, or a goddess like Kali is a reflection of this. And so, for all its faults, was the juridical-penal model. It offered an articulation of the dark side of creation. Simply negating it, as many of us modern Christians are tempted to do, leaves a vacuum. Or it leaves rather an unbelievably benign picture, which cannot but provoke people either to unbelief or to a return to this hyper-Augustinian mode of faith, unless it leads to a recovery of the mystery of the Crucifixion, of world-healing through the suffering of the God-man. Certainly this central mystery of Christian faith becomes invisible if one tries to paint the dark out of Creation.

(6) There is another reaction which has arisen against precisely the models of benevolence and universalism in Deism and humanism. This is an attack that sees them as leveling down. Everybody is to be equal, and the old virtues of aristocracy—the virtues of heroism, for instance, the warrior virtues—are no longer valued.

In this objection, the tilt in modern humanism and "civilization" toward equality is taken together with the valuing of peace over war, with the affirmation of the "bourgeois" virtues of production, and the relief of suffering; this is put in the context of the rejection of "extravagance" and "excess"; and the whole is condemned for leveling, for pusillanimity, for a negation of any high, demanding ideal, for the negation of all heroism.

We can see this in reactionary thinkers, like de Maistre but also in Tocqueville; in Baudelaire, but also in Nietzsche; in Maurras, and also in Sorel. It can not only place itself on Left and Right (although perhaps it has been more evident in the twentieth century on the Right); but it also can take pious forms (where are the great vocations of asceticism and self-giving?), as well as fiercely anti-Christian forms (Nietzsche, who sees all this modern liberal egalitarianism as Christianity continued by other means).

It goes without saying that (6) easily combines with (5), but the objection lies on a different axis, and therefore I distinguish them.

(7) Closely related to both of these is a critique of the understanding of happiness implicit in modern ideas of order. This, especially in its most simplistic, down-to-earth, or sensuous forms, as with certain kinds of utilitarianism, is often attacked as too flat, shallow, even demeaning. Moreover, it is held not just to reflect an intellectual error, an erroneous theory of happiness; it can also be the charter of a debased practice which threatens to spread in the modern world and to degrade human life. Humans so reduced will end up finding the point of their existence in "les petits et vulgaires plaisirs," which Tocqueville saw as the only remaining concern of the subjects of soft despotism;[10] or in the even more horrifying vision of Nietzsche, these reduced beings would end up as "last men."[11]

In the curved space of modern controversy, this axis clearly interweaves with the previous two. In one way, it clearly lies close to (6), in that this idea of happiness is being judged as base, unworthy of humanity; in another way, it can connect to (5), and be denounced as profoundly illusory, unrealistic. Human beings, however much they try, cannot really be happy this way. Their attempt to be so will be frustrated, either by the natural, unavoidable occurrence of suffering and death, or by the stifled sense within them that they were born for something higher. This latter criticism has been frequently leveled by Christian writers, but it can also be seen as implicit in Nietzsche's scornful picture of the last man.

These last three axes define types of controversy, rather than identifying fixed positions. That is, a given critical position may itself be attacked from a more exigent standpoint as being open to the same criticism. Thus, taking (7) as our example, the lowest-level hedonistic definition of a Helvétius can be spurned as debased by a Rousseau, who will introduce a range of higher sentiments as well as an intrinsic love of virtue into his picture of human happiness. But from a more tragic standpoint, this harmonious fulfillment in a virtuous republic may seem quite Utopian, and in the light of a more stringent demand for self-overcoming, it may seem too indulgent, insufficiently heroic, all too human.

These potential shifts in a more or less radical direction crop up in most of the axes I am identifying here. The Utilitarian Enlightenment was insufficiently spiritual for Madame de Staël and Benjamin Constant, but they in turn appeared too crassly humanist to a Chateaubriand. And so on.

(8) Another related line of attack concerns death. Modern humanism tends to develop a notion of human flourishing which has no place for death. Death is simply the negation, the ultimate negation, of flourishing; it must be combated and held off till the very last moment. Against this, there have developed a whole range of views in the post-Enlightenment world, which while remaining atheist, or at least ambivalent and unclear about transcendence, have seen in death, at least the moment of death, or the standpoint of death, a privileged position, one at which the meaning, the point of life, comes clear, or can be more closely attained than in the fullness of life.

Mallarmé, Heidegger, Camus, Celan, Beckett: the important thing is that these have not been marginal, forgotten figures, but their work has seized the imagination of their age. We don't fully understand this, but we have to take it into account in any attempt to understand the face-off between humanism and faith. Strangely, many things reminiscent of the religious tradition emerge in these and other writers, while it is also in some cases clear that they mean to reject religion, at least as it has been understood.

4

In the previous two sections, I have been trying to offer a pencil sketch of the development which leads up to our modern liberal society, and the modes of exclusive humanism which play an important role in it. In terms of my narrative, a crucial turn was the development, in the seventeenth and eighteenth centuries, of an outlook, sometimes Christian and theist, but always verging on Deism, which identified the demands of Christian faith with a certain mode of social order, one of mutual benefit among rights-bearing individuals; this was the civilized order of "polite" society. We are still living with the aspiration to this order—although it has been reconceptualized a number of times since the eighteenth century and is now conceived more radically and more universally. But for many people, it has been disconnected from its Christian and providentialist roots, and in some cases, Christian faith is even seen as a danger and potential obstacle to it. This order, or certain variants of it, and the accompanying demands for discipline, rational control, and the denial of aspirations which seem to go beyond and threaten it, has also awakened great unease, and a gamut of critical positions, of which some (e.g., Rousseau, Marx) seem to call for a radicalized version of it; and others (especially Nietzsche) for a root and branch rejection. The many-sided battle around this order—how to conceive it, how to ground it (e.g., in God, or against God), or even whether to uphold or destroy it—has defined the great continuing Kulturkampf of the last two centuries of Western civilization.

But from our point of view here, the crucial move was the original identification of the demands of Christian faith with a civilizational order, whose demands could be exhaustively expressed in such purely "immanent" terms, such as mutual benefit or the upholding of rights (immensely valuable as these are). The effect of this was to close off a horizon of further transformation, the kind of thing visible in the life, for instance, of a Francis of Assisi. This kind of aspiration came to be seen as a gratuitous and senseless asceticism, unpleasant, troubling, and perhaps even dangerous to civilizational order, cultivating the "monkish virtues" which Hume identified and condemned.

But this meant that what I called above the vertical dimension, in which our relations can be potentially transformed, and our moral predicament altered, was severely foreshortened, to the point frequently of virtual disappearance. This is the context in which code fixation can take hold. Once you cease to see your moral dilemmas as double, in the sense described above, that is, as situated in two dimensions, that of the two conflicting claims, on one hand, and that of the potential vertical movement, on the other, they begin to seem much more tractable. It takes only a burst of confidence in procedural reason (never in short supply in modern culture), to believe that they can be arbitrated finally and decisively by a rationally derived code. This is the foreshortened vision that many of our contemporaries have come to see as unproblematic reality.

Hence the great weakness of modern moralism discussed in Section 1, that it sweeps dilemmas under the carpet, particularly the ones involving verticality. That is, it cannot take account of the importance of vertical movement, because it doesn't see the vertical dimension. This would pose one sort of problem if its view of the capacities of human nature were very low. But in fact, modern humanism very often makes an extremely high set of demands of people—a selective one, indeed, but very high in the areas selected. People are thought to be capable of a very strong sense of equality, an absence of discrimination on the basis of gender, race, and so forth, and to be able to eschew violence and violent reactions, and so on. On the other side, they are not seen to be susceptible to a radical change in their motivations. They are thought to be ready as they are, given appropriate training and institutions, to reach a very high standard on the "liberal" requirements.

A combination of high demands and utter insensitivity to a vertical dimension of transformation leads to some terrible consequences. (1) Take violence. There seem to be gender differences here (although one may be taken to task for saying so). Men, particularly young men, are frequently recruitable for some combative causes, as we see daily in our contemporary world. But the remedy often proposed is to train them in the proper way. To the extent that violence is a male pattern, we should be able to train it out. Don't let little boys play with tanks, guns, and so forth. Or on a rougher level, try to shame young men into renouncing various forms of violence.

All this would constitute the best way of dealing with this problem, if one assumes a one-dimensional motivation. But there are certain views of vertical transformation which, if true, show it to be highly questionable. Perhaps what needs to happen to the propensity for violent, combative, forceful action is not to discredit it, but to turn it inside out, transform it into an energy with a quite different focus. We see something like this happening with the conversion of Ignatius Loyola, from soldier into apostle.

If instead of this you try to control young men by shame, you may be just stoking up trouble for all of us. Especially when we think of the work of James Gilligan,[12] which shows how much early humiliation can predispose people to later violence. Of course, we have the making of a classical dilemma here. Not everyone can become a Loyola, certainly not right now. We may need to use shame to control some pretty nasty behavior which threatens right away in the schoolyard, for instance. But at least recognize the dilemma; and this the code fetishist mind-set finds very difficult to do.

(2) So we could argue from this example that modern nomolatry can make you very imprudent in the motivations you encourage or intensify in order to

realize the good. Here's another example. I remember a conversation with a leading figure of the Society of Engaged Buddhists, the Thai thinker Sulak. He had been traveling in Europe, and naturally he went to the convention of the German Greens (Engaged Buddhists are very strong on ecological issues). He didn't mind the program, but what surprised and disturbed him was the tone of anger and indignation in all the speeches. Didn't they see that stoking up anger made them part of the problem, not of the solution? As a Westerner who has spent much time in Left movements, I could understand what he meant. (But the Right is no better, be it said.) It is generally thought that the more clearly you see the right, and the more committed you are to it, the more you will be moved by anger and indignation at all the violations of it that one sees around you. The pure in heart are in a perpetual flaming rage, according to this view.

An openness to the vertical dimension—which raises the question, how do we all have to change, in our most basic motivation, in order to live up the ideals we've set for ourselves?—would alert one to the dangers of this cultivation of anger. Certainly Buddhist verticality is very clear on how destructive this can be.

(3) We can move from Sulak to René Girard: Girard has shown brilliantly how the age-old temptations to scapegoating, and to purification of our society/world by eliminating evil elements, can survive into the modern age of supposed rationality and disenchantment. The very moment when we feel the purest ourselves is when we're hammering the really bad guys, making war on Milošević, or fighting the "axis of evil." We at last know who are making the world worse, and who thus needs to be conquered or eliminated. We make a feast of our righteous anger. This is the moment when we're readiest to allow ourselves the worst atrocities. And not even notice it, at least at the time.[13]

Of course, this is not the monopoly of exclusive humanists. We Christians set the template in our civilization with the Crusades and anti-Semitism, among other things. Reading the Gospel makes you shudder in astonishment that Christians were capable of falling into this kind of perversion, which the Crucifixion story seems so directly to warn against. But we did. A very sobering thought. Somehow we were blindsided.

Now modern humanists, thinking that all this scapegoat stuff depends on irrational religious beliefs, think that they are immune to it, and they too are blindsided. Welcome to the human race; and thus to the predicament of sin.

(4) Now to Dostoyevsky, who saw how precisely this combination of high demands and blindness to the vertical dimension can prepare the ground for the most terrible atrocities. The very estimate of human potential, without aid

of grace, prepares the way for a terrible disillusionment when flesh-and-blood human beings can't seem to rise to the occasion. The high image mutates into anger and contempt for the actual human material that revolutionaries have to work with. This anger and contempt ends up licensing almost limitless violence and repression in the name of the radiant future one is aiming at. The astonishing thing about Dostoyevsky, as Solzhenitsyn has pointed out, is that he foresaw so much that would happen in Russia in the following century, on the basis of such a minute sample of revolutionary movements.

The slogan of Dostoyevsky's revolutionaries is that "no one is to blame." Evil comes from the working out of certain social laws. Things just have to be reconstructed in order to make these laws work for us. Blame and guilt are part of the discourse of myth and superstition that we have to put behind us. The slogan of his heroes is "we are all to blame"; the recognition that we are all complicit in sin is the gateway to grace, and hence the transformation which can take us out of the structures of evil. We are at the antipodes to self-righteous anger. We join Sulak, but for specifically Christian reasons.[14]

(5) Nomolatry makes us unaware of the vertical dimension, and hence what it takes to change ourselves. It also encourages a "one size fits all" approach: a rule is a rule. It cannot understand how there can be vocations which are valid, even while being in some profound way antithetical to each other. For instance, celibate and noncelibate vocations. One side must be wrong. Hence the response of many outsiders to the present travails of the Catholic Church over sexual harassment and pedophilia. It all comes from demanding celibacy of the clergy. Of course, there is some truth in the charge that these abuses sometimes come from the breakdown of celibate vocations. But I'm talking about something deeper: the inability to understand how there could be such radically different modes of life, equally important and valid, equally essential.

If the code suffices, it dictates one or the other thing (either celibacy is "higher," or it's just an aberration, or a proper life, minus something). But in an economy of human transformation, where we all have to move higher, but where we can't have everything together now, it makes sense for some people to strike out and blaze trails, and they can blaze farther in some directions because they're renouncing others. This can serve to nudge us all upward. Celibacy is just one example of this. There are other kinds of voluntary modes of poverty, stripping down of one's life, which permit one to open out new forms of agape. But if we just think of the ways in which celibates have enriched the common spiritual life of all Christians, the point should be evident.

(6) Another facet of this same blindness is that modern code fetishism can't see how each self-transformation can feed into, inspire, and nourish those of

others. It doesn't see how there can be sharing, communion at this level of being changed by God.

MODERN NOMOLATRY dumbs us down, morally and spiritually. It can make us entirely fail to see certain dilemmas: like those speech codes which so rigidly control for expressions of contempt that they severely limit frank exchange. It especially blinds us to the dilemmas arising from the vertical dimension. And in particular, it can make us blind to the issue of moral motivation. Humanitarian action hits a ceiling, to the extent that we aren't yet capable of loving human beings as they are; to the extent that we need idealizations; or that with the collapse of our ideal images, we can feel only disdain, contempt, or hatred. How do we become more capable of this? Most contemporary moral philosophy ignores this question; cannot even see its pertinence.[15]

5

I've been criticizing forms of modern humanism. But the various churches of Latin Christendom pioneered in this.[16] Think of the tremendous investment of nineteenth-century evangelicalism into a code of "respectability," plus temperance, plus Sabbath-observing. Indeed, some of this was overdetermined. Temperance was what many newly arrived workers needed in order to be able to hack it in the disordered industrial cities, to keep a job, to get ahead. The same is true today of many slums, of ghettos in the First World, and even more in the Third. But the code so often ends up swallowing the faith. The next generation comes to find the disciplines second nature; they want to relax some of the extreme prohibitions. They don't need the powerful emotions of amazing grace in order to get on with their lives. But they now have trouble seeing what other point the faith has; so they fall away altogether.

On the Catholic side, there is a kind of creeping nomolatry through the Catholic Reformation; more and more coding and rules; what you have to do, have to avoid, to stay in good standing.[17] People driven out of the Church because they engaged in dancing (as in nineteenth-century France), or because their married life is "irregular" (ongoing today). We are sacrificing pastoral goals to the maintenance of a rigid code of don'ts.

Over against a great deal of pastoral wisdom and charity on the ground, the official pronouncements of the Church today still reflect our own historic forms of code fetishism. We helped create this modern culture, and for a large part we have trouble helping it free itself from its crippling lack of moral vision; because for a large part, we come back at the narrow code with our own countercode. Instead of helping people to move ahead on their own rocky path to sanctification, the official stance often consists in posing a lot of prerequisites they have to pass in order to join the course. Then when we publicly and lamentably fail to live up to our own prerequisites, we provoke more Schadenfreude than compassionate understanding.

If we want a countermodel, look at Taizé;[18] look at the World Youth Days, which were deeply influenced by Taizé. If John Paul II was one of the great Christian leaders of our time, as I think he was, perhaps it is, among other things, the John Paul of the World Youth Days who is to be followed rather than the figure at the center of a Vatican orbiting in a stratosphere from which the contours of the pastoral ground become invisible.

CHAPTER SIXTEEN

What Was the Axial Revolution?

I

Any view about the long-term history of religion turns on an interpretation of
the axial age. What was the nature of the axial revolution? This is sometimes
spoken of the coming to be of a new tension "between the transcendental and
mundane orders," involving a new conception of the "transcendental."[1] But
"transcendental" has more than one meaning. It can designate something like
a "going beyond" the human world or the cosmos (1). But it also can mean the
discovery or invention of a new standpoint from which the existing order in
the cosmos or society can be criticized or denounced (2). Moreover, these two
meanings can be linked. The place or being beyond the cosmos may yield the
new locus from which critique becomes possible. The Hebrew prophets con-
demning the practices of Israel in the name of God come to mind.

Again, potentially linked to these two is another change: the introduction
of second-order thinking (3), in which the formulae we use to describe or operate in the world themselves come under critical examination.

Possibly linked with these three is another change: what Jan Assmann calls
"implied globality" (4).[2] The notion here is that the transcendent being, or the
principles of criticism, may be seen as of relevance not just to our society, but
to the whole of humanity. But the link with our own society may be weakened
in another way. Any of the above changes may bring with them a new notion
of the philosophical or religious vocation of individuals. Indeed, the changes

may themselves be introduced by such individuals who invent or discover new forms of religious or philosophical life. The Buddha or Socrates come to mind. This can be the origin point of a process of disembedding (5), a process I would like to deal with in the following discussion.

These five may be seen as rival accounts of what axiality consists in, but it might be better to see them as potentially linked changes, in which case the issue between them would be more like this: which of these changes provides the best starting point from which to understand the linkages in the whole set?

Without wanting to challenge any of these readings, I would like to suggest a sixth way of conceiving the change. It was a shift from a mode of religious life which involved "feeding the gods," where the understanding of human good was that of prospering or flourishing (as this was understood); and where the "gods" or spirits were not necessarily unambiguously on the side of human good; to a mode in which (a) there is notion of a higher, more complete human good, a notion of complete virtue, or even of a salvation beyond human flourishing (Buddha); while at the same time (b) the higher powers according to this view are unambiguously on the side of human good. What may survive is a notion of Satan or Mara, spirits which are not ambivalent, but rather totally against human good. I make some of the links clear from the outset, because I would like to present this change in our understanding of the good (6) as a facet of the change I call disembedding (5).

2

The full scale of this far-reaching change becomes clearer if we focus on some features of the religious life of earlier, smaller-scale societies, insofar as we can trace this. There must have been a phase in which all humans lived in such small-scale societies, even though much of the life of this epoch can only be guessed at. If we examine (what we know of) these earlier forms of religion (which coincide partly with what Robert Bellah called "archaic religion"),[3] we note how profoundly these forms of life "embed" the agent. And that in three crucial ways.

First, socially: in Paleolithic and even certain Neolithic tribal societies, religious life is inseparably linked with social life. This meant first of all that the primary agency of important religious action—invoking, praying to, sacrificing to, or propitiating Gods or spirits; coming close to these powers, getting healing, protection from them, divining under their guidance, and so forth—was the social group as a whole, or some more specialized agency recognized as acting for the group. In early religion, we primarily relate to God as a society.

This kind of collective ritual action, where the principal agents are acting on behalf of a community, which also in its own way becomes involved in the action, seems to figure virtually everywhere in early religion, and continues in some ways up till our day. Certainly it goes on occupying an important place as long as people live in an enchanted world. The ceremony of "beating the bounds" of the agricultural village, for instance, involved the whole parish, and could only be effective as a collective act of this whole.[4]

This embedding in social ritual usually carries with it another feature. Just because the most important religious action was that of the collective, and because it often required that certain functionaries—priests, shamans, medicine men, diviners, chiefs, and so on—fill crucial roles in the action, the social order in which these roles were defined tended to be sacrosanct. This is, of course, the aspect of religious life which was most centrally identified and pilloried by the radical Enlightenment. The crime laid bare here was the entrenchment of forms of inequality, domination, and exploitation through their identification with the untouchable, sacred structure of things. Hence the longing to see the day "when the last king had been strangled in the entrails of the last priest." But this identification is in fact very old, and goes back to a time when many of the later, more egregious and vicious forms of inequality had not yet been developed, before there were kings and hierarchies of priests.

Behind the issue of inequality and justice lies something deeper, which touches what we would call today the "identity" of the human beings in those earlier societies. Just because their most important actions were the doings of whole groups (tribe, clan, subtribe, lineage), articulated in a certain way (the actions were led by chiefs, shamans, masters of the fishing spear), they couldn't conceive of themselves as potentially disconnected from this social matrix. It would probably never even occur to them to try.

Embedding thus in society. But this also brings with it an embedding in the cosmos. For in early religion, the spirits and forces with whom we are dealing are in numerous ways intricated in the world. We can see this if we look at the enchanted world of our medieval ancestors: for all that the God they worshipped transcended the world, they nevertheless also had to do with intracosmic spirits, and they dealt with causal powers which were embedded in things: relics, sacred places, and the like. In early religion, even the high gods are often identified with certain features of the world; and where the phenomenon which has come to be called "totemism" exists, we can even say that some feature of the world, an animal or plant species, for instance, is central to the identity of a group.[5] It may even be that a particular geographical terrain is essential to our religious life. Certain places are sacred. Or the layout of the land speaks to us of the original disposition of things in sacred time. We relate to the ancestors and to this higher time through this landscape.[6]

Besides this relation to society and the cosmos, there is a third form of embedding in existing reality which we can see in early religion. This is what makes the most striking contrast with what we tend to think of as the "higher" religions. What the people ask for when they invoke or placate divinities and powers is prosperity, health, long life, fertility; what they ask to be preserved from is disease, dearth, sterility, premature death. There is a certain understanding of human flourishing here which we can immediately understand, and which, however much we might want to add to it, seems to us quite "natural." What there isn't, and what seems central to the later "higher" religions, is the idea that we have to question radically this ordinary understanding, that we are called in some way to go beyond it.

This is not to say that human flourishing is the end sought by all things. The divine may also have other purposes, some of which impact harmfully on us. There is a sense in which, for early religions, the divine is always more than just well-disposed toward us; it may also be in some ways indifferent; or there may also be hostility, jealousy, or anger, which we have to deflect. Although benevolence, in principle, may have the upper hand, this process may have to be helped along, by propitiation, or even by the action of "trickster" figures. But through all this, what remains true is that divinity's benign purposes are defined in terms of ordinary human flourishing. Again, there may be capacities which some people can attain, which go way beyond the ordinary human ones, which, say, prophets or shamans have. But these in the end subserve well-being as ordinarily understood.

By contrast, with Christianity or Buddhism, for instance, there is a notion of our good which goes beyond human flourishing, which we may gain even while failing utterly on the scales of human flourishing, even *through* such a failing (like dying young on a cross); or which involves leaving the field of flourishing altogether (ending the cycle of rebirth). The paradox of Christianity, in relation to early religion, is that, on one hand, it seems to assert the unconditional benevolence of God toward humans; there is none of the ambivalence of early divinity in this respect; yet, on the other hand, it redefines our ends so as to take us beyond flourishing.

In this respect, early religion has something in common with modern exclusive humanism, and this has been felt and expressed in the sympathy of many modern post-Enlightenment people for "paganism"; "pagan self-assertion," thought John Stuart Mill, was much superior to "Christian self-denial."[7] (This is related to, but not quite the same as, the sympathy felt for "polytheism," which I want to discuss later.) What makes modern humanism unprecedented, of course, is the idea that this flourishing involves no relation to anything higher.

The portrait of the early triple embeddedness is well-drawn by Francis Oakley, in his discussion of the history of monarchy:

Kingship . . . emerged from an "archaic" mentality that appears to have been thoroughly monistic, to have perceived no impermeable barrier between the human and divine, to have intuited the divine as immanent in the cyclic rhythms of the natural world and civil society as somehow enmeshed in these natural processes, and to have viewed its primary function, therefore, as a fundamentally religious one, involving the preservation of the cosmic order and the "harmonious integration" of human beings with the natural world.[8]

Human agents are embedded in society, society in the cosmos, and the cosmos incorporates the divine.

Now as earlier mentions suggest, I have been speaking of "early religion" to contrast with what many people have called "post-axial" religions.[9] The reference is to what Karl Jaspers called the "axial age,"[10] the extraordinary period in the last millennium B.C.E. when various "higher" forms of religion appeared seemingly independently in different civilizations, marked by such founding figures as Confucius, Gautama, Socrates, and the Hebrew prophets.

The surprising feature of the axial religions, compared with what went before, what would in other words have made them hard to predict beforehand, is that they initiate a break in all three dimensions of embeddedness: social order, cosmos, human good. Not in all cases and all at once: perhaps in some ways Buddhism is the most far-reaching, because it radically undercuts the second dimension: the order of the world itself is called into question, because the wheel of rebirth means suffering. In Christianity there is something analogous: our world is disordered and must be made anew. But some postaxial outlooks keep the sense of relation to an ordered cosmos, as we see in very different ways with Confucius and Plato; however, they mark a distinction between this and the actual, highly imperfect social order, so that the close link to the cosmos through collective religious life is made problematic.

But perhaps the most fundamental novelty of all is the revisionary stance toward the human good in axial religions. More or less radically, they all call into question the received, seemingly unquestionable understandings of human flourishing and hence inevitably also the structures of society and the features of the cosmos through which this flourishing was supposedly achieved. The change was double, as I mentioned above. On one hand, the "transcendent" realm, the world of God, or gods, of spirits, or Heaven, however defined, which previously contained elements which were both favorable and unfavorable to the human good, becomes unambiguously affirmative of this good. But on the other hand, both the crucial terms here, both the transcendent and the human good, are reconceived in the process.

We have already noted the changes in the first term. The transcendent may now be quite beyond or outside of the cosmos, as with the Creator God of

Genesis, or the Nirvana of Buddhism. Or if it remains cosmic, it loses its original ambivalent character, and exhibits an order of unalloyed goodness, as with the "Heaven," guarantor of just rule in Chinese thought,[11] or the order of Ideas of Plato, whose key is the Good.

But the second term must perforce also change. The highest human goal can no longer just be to flourish, as it was before. Either a new goal is posited, of a salvation which takes us beyond what we usually understand as human flourishing. Or else Heaven or the Good lays the demand on us to imitate or embody its unambiguous goodness, and hence to alter the mundane order of things down here. This may, indeed usually does, involve flourishing on a wider scale, but our own flourishing (as individual, family, clan, or tribe) can no longer be our highest goal. And of course, this may be expressed by a redefinition of what "flourishing" consists in.

Seen from another angle, this means a change in our attitude to evil as the destructive, harm-inflicting side of reality. This is no longer just part of the order of things, to be accepted as such. Something has to be done about it. This may be conceived as an escape through self-transformation, or it may be seen as a struggle to contain or eliminate the bad, but in either case evil is not something just to be lived with as part of the inevitable balance of things. Of course, the very sense of the term "evil" also changes here, once it is no longer just the negative side of the cosmos, and comes to be branded as an imperfection.[12]

We might try to put the contrast in this way: unlike postaxial religion, early religion involved an acceptance of the order of things, in the three dimensions I have been discussing. In a remarkable series of articles on Australian Aboriginal religion, W. E. H. Stanner speaks of "the mood of assent" which is central to this spirituality. Aboriginals had not set up the "kind of quarrel with life" which springs from the various postaxial religious initiatives.[13] The contrast is in some ways easy to miss, because Aboriginal mythology, in relating the way in which the order of things came to be in the Dream Time—the original time out of time, which is also "everywhen"—contains a number of stories of catastrophe, brought on by trickery, deceit, and violence, from which human life recouped and reemerged, but in an impaired and divided fashion, so that there remains the intrinsic connection between life and suffering, and unity is inseparable from division. Now this may seem reminiscent of other stories of a Fall, including that related in Genesis. But in contrast with what Christianity has made of this last, for the Aboriginals the imperative to "follow up" the Dreaming, to recover through ritual and insight their contact with the order of the original time, relates to this riven and impaired dispensation, in which good and evil are interwoven. There is no question of reparation of the original rift, or of a compensation, or of making good of the original loss. What is more, ritual and the wisdom that goes with it can even bring them to accept the inexorable, and "celebrate joyously what could not be changed."[14] The original catastrophe doesn't separate or alienate us from the sacred or Higher, as in the Genesis story; it rather contributes to shaping the sacred order we are trying to "follow up."

I CAN PERHAPS sum up this postaxial notion of higher good, in terms of four features. (a) It is defined as going beyond (whatever is locally understood as) ordinary human flourishing: long life, prosperity, freedom from disease, drought, natural catastrophe, and so on. (b) There were vocations with special higher powers before, like shamans, for instance; but now the higher good doesn't just consist of special powers; it is in some sense a goal for all human beings. This is so even if this aspect is downplayed or countervailed by notions of hierarchy. Thus for Plato, the philosophical life is not for everyone; but at the same time it amounts to the fullest realization of the nature which all human beings share. (c) This good is our goal as human beings in virtue of the way things are—whether the demands of God, or the nature of things, or the Fourfold Noble Truth, or whatever. In consequence, the goal is endorsed by whatever higher beings, gods, spirits, or the cosmos, are recognized by the culture concerned. This contrasts with the pre-axial ambivalence of many of these beings to human flourishing. (d) Grounded in the way things are, endorsed by higher powers, this goal is unitary, harmonious, and inwardly consistent.

3

The resulting religious life in the postaxial age combines elements of the pre-axial in some kind of amalgam, often unstable. The postaxial pushes toward individual spiritual "virtuosi," to use Max Weber's phrase (which includes monks, Bhikkus, Platonist sages, and so on). The great "higher" religions, which become entrenched within and help to shape civilizations, have this hybrid character and the resultant tensions.

Axial religion didn't in fact do away with early religious life. It doesn't at once totally change the religious life of whole societies. But it does open new possibilities of disembedded religion: seeking a relation to the divine or the higher, which severely revises the going notions of flourishing, or even goes beyond them, and can be carried through by individuals on their own, and/or in new kinds of sociality, unlinked to the established sacred order. So, monks, Bhikkus, sanyassi, and devotees of some avatar or God strike out on their own; and from this springs unprecedented modes of sociality: initiation groups, sects of devotees, the sangha, monastic orders, and so on.

In all these cases, there is some kind of hiatus, difference, or even break in relation to the religious life of the whole larger society. This may itself be to some extent differentiated, with different strata, castes, or classes, and a new religious outlook may lodge in one of them. But very often a new devotion may cut across all of these, particularly where there is a break in the third dimension, with a "higher" idea of the human good.

There is inevitably a tension here, but there often is also an attempt to secure the unity of the whole, to recover some sense of complementarity between the different religious forms. So that those who are fully dedicated to the "higher" forms can, on one hand, be seen as a standing reproach to those who remain in the earlier forms, supplicating the powers for human flourishing, and, on the other hand, nevertheless can also be seen as in a relationship of mutual help with them. The laity feed the monks, and by this they earn "merit," which can be understood as taking them a little farther along the "higher" road, but also serves to protect them against the dangers of life, and increases their health, prosperity, fertility.

So strong is the pull toward complementarity that even in those cases where a "higher" religion took over the whole society, as we see with Buddhism, Christianity, and Islam, and there is nothing supposedly left to contrast with, the difference between dedicated minorities of religious "virtuosi" (to use Max Weber's term again) and the mass religion of the social sacred, still largely oriented to flourishing, survived or reconstituted itself, with the same combination of strain, on one hand, and hierarchical complementarity, on the other.

From our modern perspective, with 20:20 hindsight, it appears as though the axial spiritualities were prevented from producing their full disembedding effect because they were, so to speak, hemmed in by the force of the majority religious life, which remained firmly in the old mold. They did bring about a certain form of religious individualism, but this was what Louis Dumont called the charter for "l'individu hors du monde":[15] that is, it was the way of life of elite minorities, and it was in some ways marginal to, or in some tension with, the "world," where this means not just the cosmos which is ordered in relation to the Higher or the Sacred but also the society which is ordered in relation to both the cosmos and the sacred. This "world" was still a matrix of embeddedness, and it still provided the inescapable framework for social life, including that of the individuals who tried to turn their backs on it, insofar as they remained in some sense within its reach.[16]

I HAVE DESCRIBED these as "unstable" amalgams, but this feature is perhaps a potentiality, which isn't always actualized. Let's look at some of the possible sites of tension in these religious forms.

First, (i) to return to the reference to "polytheism" above, the new understanding of our higher good which is itself endorsed by God or the cosmos, Heaven, or some other higher reality, is itself unitary and coherent. The good human being for Plato was harmonious; to attain Nirvana is to come to perfect peace; the sage is in ideal equilibrium. This contrasts very sharply with a potentiality of pre-axial religions, realized in certain forms of polytheism. The demands of higher beings on us may be in tension with each other. Insofar as our good (flourishing) is bound up with our meeting these demands, the human good itself can be seen as combining elements which are at best in tension, in more dire straits even contradictory.

Take the story of Hippolytos, dragged into the disastrous love triangle with his father and Phaedra, in which he loses his life. Hippolytos is portrayed as devoted to Artemis, so devoted that he is celibate. But this too great attachment is bound to rouse the jealousy of Aphrodite, the goddess of marriage and sexual love. Her hand is visible in the love entanglement into which he is unwittingly and unwillingly drawn, and which costs him his life.

There is an ambivalence in the story. There is something heroic and admirable in Hippolytos' single-mindedness. In a sense it aspires to go above the human condition. For mortals the prudent thing is to "pay one's dues" to all the immortals, and to navigate at our own level between the rocks they lay out for us. Perhaps a similar moral can be drawn from the story of Oedipus, whose ability to see overt reality with exceptional acuity is paid for by a blindness to the inarticulate depths (which Tiresias for his part is aware of).

We might recognize a "disenchanted" analogue of this insight in, for instance, the philosophy of Isaiah Berlin, with his insistence on the potential conflict between the goods we subscribe to.

ANOTHER POTENTIAL SITE of instability is (ii) what I described above as the second level of embedding, that of social order in cosmic order. Axial revolutions, which relate to a new, unitary higher good, transform this cosmic embedding. The surrounding order now perhaps really merits the attribute "cosmic" with the full resonance of harmonious unity which attaches to this Greek term. Previously, the various gods, spirits, or higher beings could make incompatible demands on humans, as we have just seen, and were not all unambiguously favorable to human welfare. Now the proper cosmic order is frequently unified and aligned with the higher human good; indeed the cosmic frame can set the standard by which human social orders are to be judged and criticized. In some cases, as with Buddhism or the Hebrew Bible, the potentiality is opened for a standpoint of critique that can judge the condition of the cosmos itself. But this didn't inhibit the development of a normative understanding of cosmic order even in the civilizations animated by Buddhism, or by post-biblical revelations.[17]

These postaxial "higher" religions can still have a place for spirits who are ill disposed toward the human good, such as Satan or Mara. But now they are classed as radical enemies of the normative order, and are destined in the end to be defeated. Or else a god can retain his or her Janus-faced ambivalence, as with Pattini or the Isvara form of Shiva in Sri Lankan Buddhism; but the destructive side is clearly marked as against and the restorative side as for the normative order.[18] Or else, taking purchase in a higher good from which the cosmos itself can be judged, a god who wreaks destruction of worldly things can be seen as working for the good, as doing a work of purification, as with certain understandings of Siva or Kali.

But the cosmic battle itself is not the site of potential instability. This lies rather in the fact that the two-tiered normative order, that of society in cosmos, can itself be seen as not fully self-sufficient, as needing to draw on its opposite, its negation to sustain itself.

I want to mention two types, which deserve much fuller discussion, but which I can only briefly discuss here:

(1) The equilibrium in tension of Latin Christendom emerged and became evident in Carnival and similar festivities, such as the feasts of misrule, or boy bishops, and the like. These were periods in which the ordinary order of things was inverted, or "the world was turned upside down." For a while, there was a ludic interval, in which people played out a condition of reversal of the usual order. Boys wore the miter, or fools were made kings for a day; what was ordinarily revered was mocked, and people permitted themselves various forms of license, not just sexually but also in close-to-violent acts and the like.

(2) The example of the second type is drawn from Sri Lankan Buddhism. I am drawing on Bruce Kapferer's fascinating study of sorcery and exorcism.[19] A sorcerer's spell binds me, impedes, even paralyzes my life. It cuts me off from the sources of health and goodness. In this way, it contravenes the normative order. The origin stories, which are called on to understand sorcery and to underpin the ceremonies of exorcism, make this relation clear. They relate ur-events in which the ideal normative order was attacked and deeply damaged. These provide the paradigm for the sorcerer's aggression. And the myths also relate how the damage was undone. But in these it becomes clear that the healing could only be effected and the order restored by drawing on the same power of sorcery which disrupted the order in the first place. This ambivalent stance toward the sorcerer's power is reenacted in the various rites of exorcism.

Thus on one level it is clear that there is an ideal, Buddha-inspired normative order, that established by King Mahasammata in the beginning. This is utterly opposed to the forces of disruption which various demon-figures attempt to inflict. But on another level, the act of restoration has to draw on these same forces. Restorer figures are ambivalently placed toward this order, as their myths of origin indicate.[20]

We get a result which is similar and yet different from the previous type. As with Carnival, we reveal the normative order to be not really self-sufficient. It must somehow draw on its opposite. But where with Carnival (at least as read by Turner) the opposite of order is simply its dissolution, a chaos which contains restorative powers, here we are dealing with its active negation. Order must draw on the forces of its enemy. In both cases, the tension, which can easily be seen as a contradiction, is a source of potential instability.

4

In Latin Christendom, we get an upsetting of this shaky equilibrium, in the long movement of reform (beginning with Hildebrand, but carrying through the Reformation, Counter-Reformation, and so on). Here the site of the previous instability, the two-tiered order of society in cosmos, is what is undermined and then destroyed.

What had yet to happen in the first postaxial millennium was for the two-tiered matrix to be itself transformed, to be made over according to some of the principles of axial spirituality, so that the "world" itself would come to be seen as constituted by individuals. This would be the charter for "l'individu dans le monde," in Dumont's terms: the agent who in his ordinary "worldly" life sees himself as primordially an individual, that is, the human agent of modernity.

And something like this did come about in the long movement of reform in Latin Christendom from the eleventh century. This involved the development among important élites of a buffered identity, impervious to the enchanted cosmos. This both animated and was rendered firmer by disciplines of thought and conduct. These disciplines in turn aimed not only at the reform of personal conduct, but at reforming and remaking societies so as to render them more peaceful, more ordered, more industrious.

The newly remade society was to embody unequivocally the demands of the Gospel in a stable and, as it was increasingly understood, a rational order. This had no place for the ambivalent complementarities of the older enchanted world: between worldly life and monastic renunciation, between proper order and its periodic suspension in Carnival, between the acknowledged power of sprits and forces and their relegation by divine power. The new order was coherent, uncompromising, all of a piece. Disenchantment brought a new uniformity of purpose and principle.

The progressive imposition of this order meant the end of the unstable post-axial equilibrium. The compromise between the individuated religion of devotion, obedience, or rationally understood virtue, on one hand, and the collective often cosmos-related rituals of whole societies, on the other, was broken, and in favor of the former. Disenchantment, reform, and personal religion went together. Just as the church was at its most perfect when each of its members adhered to it based on their own individual responsibility—and in certain places, like Congregational Connecticut, this became an explicit requirement of membership—so society itself comes to be reconceived as made up of individuals. The great disembedding, as I propose to call it, implicit in the axial revolution, reaches its logical conclusion.

This involved the growth and entrenchment of a new self-understanding of our social existence, one which gave an unprecedented primacy to the individual.

This project of transformation was an attempt to make over society in a thoroughgoing way according to the demands of a Christian order, while purging it of its connection to an enchanted cosmos, and removing all vestiges of the old complementarities, between spiritual and temporal, between life devoted to God and life in the "world," between order and the chaos on which it draws.

This project was thoroughly disembedding just by virtue of its form or mode of operation: the disciplined remaking of behavior and social forms through objectification and an instrumental stance. But its ends were also intrinsically concerned with disembedding. This is clear with the drive to disenchantment, which destroys the second dimension of embeddedness; but we can also see it in the Christian context. In one way, Christianity here operates like any axial spirituality; indeed, it operates in conjunction with another such, namely, Stoicism. But there also were specifically Christian modes. The New Testament is full of calls to leave or relativize solidarities of family, clan, society, to be part of the Kingdom. We see this seriously reflected in the way certain Protestant churches operated, where one was not simply a member by virtue of birth, but had to join by answering a personal call. This in turn helped to give force to a conception of society as founded on covenant, and hence as ultimately constituted by the decision of free individuals.

This is a relatively obvious filiation. But my thesis is that the effect of the Christian, or Christian-Stoic, attempt to remake society in bringing about the modern "individual in the world" was much more pervasive, and multitracked. It helped to nudge first the moral, then the social imaginary in the direction of modern individualism. This becomes evident in the new conception of moral order which we see emerging in modern natural law theory. This was heavily indebted to Stoicism, and its originators were arguably the Netherlands neo-Stoics Justus Lipsius and Hugo Grotius. But this was a Christianized Stoicism, and a modern one, in the sense that it gave a crucial place to a willed remaking of human society.

So the great disembedding occurs as a revolution in our understanding of moral order. And it goes on being accompanied by ideas of moral order. This revolution disembeds us from the cosmic sacred; altogether, and not just partially and for certain people as in earlier postaxial moves. It disembeds us from the social sacred and posits a new relation to God, as designer. This new relation will in fact turn out to be dispensable, because the design underlying the moral order can be seen as directed to ordinary human flourishing. This, the transcendent aspect of the axial revolution, is partly rolled back, or can be, given a neat separation of this-worldly from other-worldly good. But only partly, because notions of flourishing remain under surveillance in our modern moral view: they have to fit with the demands of the moral order itself, of justice, equality, nondomination, if they are to escape condemnation. Our notions of flourishing can thus always be revised. This belongs to our postaxial condition.

5

The developments I have described in the last section not only show up certain instabilities of postaxial religion but liquidated the whole unstable amalgam which was their locus. And along with this, they also eliminated instabilities (i) and (ii). We now live within the primacy of moral codes which are meant to define the entirety of our moral obligation, and to have ironed out all contradictions and tensions. The big question which is posed by this entire evolution is whether we have gained or lost crucial insights into the human condition through the transformations they have wrought.

This raises a crucial question about the place of the axial transformation in human history. Granted that these introduced changes were of immense importance in human history (which is why we think it worthwhile to define just what those changes were), what are we to think of the pre-axial life which they transformed?

Is this merely superseded, relegated to an unrecoverable past? Or is it in various ways still present, and inescapably so, in postaxial life? Robert Bellah's crucial insight, formulated in the phrase that "nothing is ever lost," points us toward some version of the second answer. Following him, I would find it incredible that our history has been one of unadulterated gain, for this would mean that the features I have outlined in the pre-axial past have been indeed well lost.

Notes

1. Iris Murdoch and Moral Philosophy

1. Cambridge, MA: Harvard University Press, 1989, chap. 4.
2. Aristotle, *Ethics* VI, 1140b10–20.
3. *Ethics* (Harmondsworth, England: Penguin Books, 1977), part 2.
4. I argue this in "Explanation and Practical Reason," in *The Quality of Life,* ed. Martha Nussbaum and Amartya Sen (Oxford: Clarendon Press), 1993.
5. Jim Miller, *The Passion of Michel Foucault* (New York: Simon & Schuster, 1993).
6. René Girard, *The Scapegoat,* trans. Yvonne Freccero (Baltimore: Johns Hopkins University Press, 1986).

2. Understanding the Other

1. *Wahrheit und Methode, Gesammelte Werke* 1 (Tübingen: J. C. B. Mohr [Paul Siebeck], 1986), 360; *Truth and Method,* 2nd rev. ed., trans. Joel Weinsheimer and Donald Marshall (New York: Continuum, 1989), 354.
2. *Wahrheit und Methode,* 361; *Truth and Method,* 355.
3. *Wahrheit und Methode,* 304; *Truth and Method,* 299.
4. *Wahrheit und Methode,* 311; *Truth and Method,* 306.
5. *Wahrheit und Methode,* 309; *Truth and Method,* 304.
6. "On the Very Idea of a Conceptual Scheme," in *Inquiries into Truth and Interpretation* (Oxford: Clarendon Press, 1984).
7. Ibid., 198.
8. *Wahrheit und Methode,* 366; *Truth and Method,* 360.
9. *Wahrheit und Methode,* 367; *Truth and Method,* 361.

3. Language Not Mysterious?

This essay has greatly benefited from the discussion of an earlier version with the members of the Phiolosophisches Institut of the Freie Universität, Berlin.

1. *Essai sur l'origine des Connoissances humaines,* 2.1.1.
2. Harvard University Press, 2002.
3. The example is taken here from John Searle, *Speech Acts* (Cambridge: Cambridge University Press, 1969), chap. 2.
4. See *Also sprach Zarathustra,* "Nachtlied," book 4; also Mahler's Third Symphony.
5. *Making It Explicit* (Cambridge, MA: Harvard University Press, 1994), 64; see also *Articulating Reasons* (Cambridge, MA: Harvard University Press, 2000), 26.
6. *Die Religion innerhalb der Grenzen der blossen Vernunft, Kants Werke* (Akademie Ausgabe, Berlin: Walter de Gruyter, 1968), 6:1–202.
7. See the discussion in *Sources of the Self* (Cambridge, MA: Harvard University Press, 1989), chap. 8.
8. See Merlin Donald, *Origins of the Modern Mind* (Cambridge, MA: Harvard University Press, 1991).
9. "Was ist Aufklärung," in *Kants Werke* (Akademie Ausgabe, Berlin: Walter de Gruyter, 1968), 8:33–42.
10. Steven Pinker, *The Language Instinct* (New York: Morrow, 1994), 16: "A common language connects the members of a community into an information-sharing network with formidable collective powers." The example he gives in the text is not mammoth hunting, but our Paleolithic ancestors stampeding horses over a cliff. The bones of the victims are "fossils of ancient co-operation and shared ingenuity." This example is the occasion for a short scientistic sermon. Language, he says, "does not call for sequestering the study of humans from the domain of biology, for a magnificent ability unique to a particular living species is far from unique in the animal kingdom. Some kinds of bats home in on flying insects using Doppler sonar. Some kinds of migratory birds navigate thousands of miles by calibrating the positions of the constellations against the time of day and year. In nature's talent show we are simply a species of primate with our own act, a knack for communicating information about who did what to whom by modulating the sounds we make when we exhale" (p. 19). It is typical of Pinker's approach that he identifies the issue whether the study of humanity "should be sequestered from the domain of biology" (which few in their right minds would propose), with the issue whether a reductive theory of language entirely focused on the factual-practical is viable (which is highly dubious).
11. *Making It Explicit,* 626.
12. *Articulating Reasons,* 26.
13. *Making It Explicit,* 626.
14. Pound, "Hugh Selwyn Mauberley."
15. *Making It Explicit,* 626. Italics in original.
16. Ibid., 64.
17. A similar point is made by Charles Larmore, in his *Les Pratiques du Moi* (Paris: Presses Universitaires de France, 2004), 148.

4. Celan and the Recovery of Language

1. *Die Kunstlehre*, 81–82; I have chosen "symbol" as the key word, even though it was not the only one used, and the usage within and across writers was varied and not always consistent. Sometimes the word "allegory" was used for the same thing, which was highly confusing, since "symbol" as a vehicle for this key idea was defined in contrast to "allegory" (under another description). Confusion is potentially further compounded by the fact that this term is also used in a host of different ways by others (its use in the expression "symbolic logic" seems utterly antipodal to the sense it bears for the Romantics). But we need a word for our discussion, and let it be "symbol."

2. See Stephen Gill, *Wordsworth and the Victorians* (Oxford: Clarendon Press, 1998).

3. See John Felstiner, *Paul Celan: Poet, Survivor, Jew* (New Haven, CT: Yale University Press, 1995), 136, 163 (hereafter referred to simply as Felstiner).

4. Paul Celan, *Der Meridian* (Frankfurt: S. Fischer Verlag, 1961). Page references in the text are to this edition.

5. Translations from John Felstiner, *Selected Poems and Prose of Paul Celan* (New York: Norton, 2001), 409.

6. I have developed this point further in *Sources of the Self* (Cambridge, MA: Harvard University Press, 1989), chap. 21.

7. "Le Tombeau d'Edgar Poe," line 6.

8. This idea of the importance of the addressee, even beyond our contemporaries the super-addressee, was also developed by M. M. Bakhtin.

9. Felstiner, 140–141.

10. Ferdinand de Saussure, *Cours de Linguistique générale* (Paris: Payot, 1978), 155–156.

11. Dostoyevsky in *The Devils* illustrates the whole cycle. Stavrogin excites both Kirilov and the young Verkhovensky to different modes of destruction, which they see as exalted goals. But when the ideas trickle down to materialist ideologues like Shigalyov, the whole socialist project is reduced to a matter of disengaged social engineering. A terrible despotism is being planned but as though it were a question of the working over of inert matter. Horror and exaltation have both been swallowed up in an idiotic insensitivity.

12. J. M Coetzee, "In the Midst of Losses," *New York Review of Books*, July 5, 2001, p. 5.

13. Translations from Felstiner, *Selected Poems and Prose of Paul Celan*, 413.

14. Translations of this poem from ibid., 204–208.

15. Translation from ibid., 128–131.

16. Translation modified from *Stéphane Mallarmé: Selected Poems*, trans. Henry Weinfield (Berkeley: University of California Press, 1994), 12.

17. Letter of March 1866 to Henri Cazalis, reproduced in S. Mallarmé, *Correspondance: 1862–71* (Paris: Gallimard, 1959), 188. *Propos sur la Poésie*, 66.

18. Modified from *Selected Letters of Stéphane Mallarmé*, ed. and trans. Rosemary Lloyd (Chicago: University of Chicago Press, 1988), 74.

19. Translations from Felstiner, *Selected Poems and Prose of Paul Celan*, 157, 135.

20. Translation from ibid., 195.

21. See Felstiner, 188.

22. Without knowing whether they had any contact with each other, there is a strikingly similar icon in the work of the Polish poet Zbigniew Herbert:

> The stone
> is a perfect creature
>
> equal to itself
> obedient to its limits
>
> filled exactly
> with a stony meaning.

Czesław Miłosz, *The History of Polish Literature* (New York: Macmillan, 1969), 471–472.

23. See Felstiner, chap. 13.
24. Paul Celan, "Weggebeizt," from the collection *Atemwende,* in *Gesammelte Werke* (Frankfurt: Suhrkamp, 1983), 2:31; trans. Michael Hamburger in *Poems of Paul Celan* (New York: Persea Books, 1988), 230.
25. Paul Celan, "Fadensonnen," from *Atemwende,* in *Gesammelte Werke* 2:26; trans. M. Hamburger in *Poems of Paul Celan,* 226.
26. Felstiner, 287.

5. Nationalism and Modernity

1. We might follow Ernest Gellner in defining nationalism as the "political principle, which holds that the political and the national unit should be congruent" (*Nations and Nationalism* [Ithaca, NY: Cornell University Press, 1983], 1). The basic idea is that a people, defined antecedently by unity of culture, language, or religion, should be allowed to give themselves their own political forms. This certainly picks out a class of movements, sentiments, political *idées-forces* in the contemporary world, namely, those related to that principle. The question I'm raising is whether they all have the same causes and are moved by the same dynamic.
2. I am drawing here on ibid.
3. Ibid., 39.
4. I have borrowed this terminology from Craig Calhoun. See, for instance, his "Nationalism and Ethnicity," *American Review of Sociology,* no. 19 (1993): 230. I have drawn heavily on Calhoun's work in my characterization of "direct-access" societies that follows.
5. Gellner, *Nations and Nationalism,* 18. I have dwelt at length here on only one facet of Gellner's theory, the emphasis on the homogenization functionally essential to a modern economy. But the move to modern, homogenized society was driven by other things as well. The modern European bureaucratic state has been growing for a number of centuries, increasing its outreach, invading the lives of its citizens, administering its territories, far and near, by uniform principles. Not all of this was powered by economic motives (though much undoubtedly was). But the upshot essentially provides the basis from which Gellner's account takes off: this historical development has given us the homogeneous state with its uniform official language and culture, indispensable to our kind of economy as well as to our type of polity and our administrative procedures. And it is this that accounts for nationalism.
6. Eugen Weber, *Peasants into Frenchmen* (Stanford, CA: Stanford University Press, 1976).

7. Benedict Anderson, *Imagined Communities: Reflections on the Origin and Spread of Nationalism,* rev. ed. (London: Verso, 1991).

8. Ibid., 37.

9. Calhoun, "Nationalism and Ethnicity," 234–235. I want to reiterate how much the discussion in this section owes to Calhoun's recent work.

10. I haven't discussed the case of nondemocratic regimes based on popular will, but these plainly push in the same direction, indeed, even further and faster. Because their emanation from the common will is essential to their legitimacy, they cannot leave their citizens alone in a condition of obedient passivity, as earlier despotic regimes were content to do. They must always mobilize the citizens into repeated expressions of unshakable, unanimous will: phony elections, demonstrations, May Day parades, and the like. This is the essence of modern "totalitarianism" in its distinction from earlier despotism.

    Calhoun in "Nationalism and Ethnicity" stresses, however, how easily the search for national identity, even in democratic contexts, leads to an attempt to induce people to suppress their other (gender, religious, minority-cultural) identities in favor of a "national" one. The modern quest for patriotism is full of dangers.

11. Many nationalisms are "produced," however, at an earlier phase in which a movement begins to unite disparate populations under the same banner in the name of a supposed common history. Thus many official languages today have resulted from the imposition of one dialect as the "true" language on whole peoples who earlier spoke a scattering of similar dialects. National vernaculars have almost always had to be "invented" in this sense.

    Too much has perhaps been made of this point in a spirit of debunking nationalist claims. A lot of nationalist history hovers between myth and lies. But as Calhoun cogently argues, this doesn't by itself invalidate the claims that contemporaries may make in terms of their shared sense of national identity: "Ethnicity or cultural traditions are bases for nationalism when they effectively constitute historical memory, when they inculcate it as habitus, . . . not when (or because) the historical origins they claim are accurate" ("Nationalism and Ethnicity," 222).

12. This does not have to be a political society. It can be a dispersed common agency, like a religious or ethnic group.

13. See Charles Taylor, "The Politics of Recognition," in *Multiculturalism and "The Politics of Recognition,"* ed. Amy Gutmann (Princeton, NJ: Princeton University Press, 1992), 25–73.

14. Especially Frantz Fanon, *Les Damnés de la Terre* (Paris: Maspéro, 1975).

15. Fortunately, this tactic doesn't always succeed. There are signs that ties between Hindus and Sikhs in the Punjab were in many cases strong enough to withstand the atrocities perpetrated by murderous bands of Khalistan supporters, though a self-feeding process of distrust and division was clearly the aim of these terrible acts. Again, after the massacres of partition in 1947, the communities in India seemed to draw back from the brink. Secularism was strengthened for a while. It took some time for the forces of Hindu chauvinism to make the progress they have registered recently.

16. See Liah Greenfeld, "Transcending the Nation's Worth," *Daedalus* 122, no. 3 (Summer 1993): 47–62. A fuller account of her view is given in *Nationalism: Five Roads to Modernity* (Cambridge, MA: Harvard University Press, 1992).

17. See Martin Kramer, "Arab Nationalism: Mistaken Identity," *Daedalus* 122, no. 3 (Summer 1993): 171–206.

6. Conditions of an Unforced Consensus on Human Rights

1. John Rawls, *Political Liberalisms* (New York: Columbia University Press, 1993), lecture IV.

2. From the Introduction to UNESCO, *Human Rights: Comments and Interpretations* (London: Allan Wingate, 1949), 10–11; cited in Abdullahi An-Na'im, "Towards a Cross-Cultural Approach to Defining International Standards of Human Rights: The Meaning of Cruel, Inhuman, or Degrading Treatment or Punishment," in *Human Rights in Cross-Cultural Perspectives,* ed. Abdullahi Ahmed An-Na'im (Philadelphia: University of Pennsylvania Press, 1992), 28–29.

3. Jack Donnelly, *Universal Human Rights in Theory and Practice* (Ithaca, NY: Cornell University Press, 1989), 28–37.

4. See chapter 4 in *The East Asian Challenge to Human Rights,* ed. Joanne R. Bauer and Daniel A. Bell (New York: Cambridge University Press, 1999), 124–144.

5. See Sidney Jones, "The Impact of Asian Economic Growth on Human Rights," *Asia Project Working Paper Series* (New York: Council on Foreign Relations, January 1995), 9.

6. "I find parts of [the American system] totally unacceptable: guns, drugs, violent crime, vagrancy, unbecoming behaviour in public—in sum, the breakdown of civil society. The expansion of the right of the individual to behave or misbehave as he pleases has come at the expense of orderly society. In the East the main object is to have a well-ordered society so that everybody can have maximum enjoyment of his freedoms. This freedom can only exist in an ordered state and not in a natural state of contention." See Fareed Zakaria, "Culture Is Destiny: A Conversation with Lee Kuan Yew," *Foreign Affairs,* March/April 1994, p. 111.

7. This is why Locke had to introduce a restrictive adjective to block this option of waiver, when he spoke of "inalienable rights." The notion of inalienability had no place in earlier natural right discourse, because this had no option of waiver.

8. According to Louis Henkin, "The Human Rights Idea in Contemporary China: A Comparative Perspective," in R. Randle Edwards, Louis Henkin, and Andrew J. Nathan, *Human Rights in Contemporary China* (New York: Columbia University Press, 1986), 21:

> In the Chinese tradition the individual was not central, and no conception of individual rights existed in the sense known to the United States. The individual's participation in society was not voluntary, and the legitimacy of government did not depend on his consent or the consent of the whole people of individuals. . . .
>
> In traditional China, the idea was not individual liberty or equality but order and harmony, not individual independence but selflessness and cooperation, not freedom of individual conscience but conformity to orthodox truth. . . . The purpose of society was not to preserve and promote individual liberty but to maintain the harmony of the hierarchical order and to see to it that truth prevailed.

9. See Sulak Sivarakza, "Buddhism and Human Rights in Siam" (unpublished paper presented at Bangkok Workshop of the Human Rights Initiative, Carnegie Council on Ethics and International Affairs, March 1996), 4–5. Sulak wonders whether the Western concept of freedom, closely allied with that of right, "has reached an end point in environmental degradation."

10. "L'égalité place les homes à côté les uns des autres, sans rien commun qui les retienne. Le despotisme élève des barrières entre eux et les sépare. Elle les dispose ne point songer à leurs semblables et il leur fait une sorte de vertu publique de l'indifférance." (Equality places people next to each other, without a common link that really keeps them together. Despotism elevates barriers between people and keeps them apart. It predisposes individuals not to think of their compatriots and makes a kind of public virtue out of their indifference.) *La Démocratic en Amérique,* vol. 2, Ile partie, chapitre IV (Paris: Édition Garnier-Flammarion, 1981), 131.

11. I have talked about substantially similar issues in somewhat different terms in the last chapter of *The Malaise of Modernity* (Toronto: Anansi Press, 1991), and in "Liberalism and the Public Sphere," *Philosophical Arguments* (Cambridge, MA: Harvard University Press, 1995), chap. 13.

12. That is what is so dangerous to public order in cases like the 1995 O. J. Simpson trial, which both show up and further entrench a deep lack of respect for and trust in the judicial process.

13. There is a Western analogue in the positive part played by Juan Carlos during the coup in Madrid in 1974.

14. See Stanley Tambiah, *World Conqueror and World Renouncer* (New York: Cambridge University Press, 1976).

15. See the discussion in John Girling, *Thailand: Society and Politics* (Ithaca, NY: Cornell University Press, 1981), 154–157. Frank Reynolds in his "Legitimation and Rebellion: Thailand's Civic Religion and the Student Uprising of October, 1973," in *Religion and Legitimation of Power in Thailand, Laos, and Burma,* ed. Bardwell L. Smith (Chambersburg, PA: Anima Books, 1978), discusses the use by the student demonstrators of the symbols of "Nation, Religion, Monarchy."

16. Richard Gombrich and Gananath Obeyesekere, *Buddhism Transformed: Religious Change in Sri Lanka* (Princeton, NJ: Princeton University Press, 1988), chap. 6 and 7.

17. See Sulak Sivaraksa, *Seeds of Power: A Buddhist Vision for Renewing Society* (Berkeley, CA: Parallax Press, 1992), chap. 9.

18. See ibid., esp. part 2.

19. See the discussion in Vitit Muntarbhorn and Charles Taylor, *Roads to Democracy: Human Rights and Democratic Development in Thailand* (Bangkok and Montreal: International Centre for Human Rights and Democratic Development, July 1994), part 3.

20. *Kants Werke,* vol. 6, *Kritik der Urteilskraft* (Berlin: Walter de Gruyter, 1964), part 1, book 2, sections 28–29.

21. *Grundlegung zur Metaphysik der Sitten,* Berlin Academy ed. (Berlin: Walter de Gruyter, 1968), 4:434.

22. See the discussion in Joseph Chan, "The Asian Challenge to Universal Human Rights: A Philosophical Appraisal," in *Human Rights and International Relations in the Asia-Pacific Region,* ed. James T. H. Tang (London: Pinter, 1995).

23. A good example is Pierre Bourdieu's description of the "correspondences" between the male-female difference and different colors, cardinal points, and oppositions like wet-dry, up-down, etc. See his *Outline of a Theory of Practice* (Cambridge: Cambridge University Press, 1977), chap. 3.

24. See, e.g., Sudhir Kakar, *The Inner World* (Delhi: Oxford University Press, 1978), who claims that Hindu culture foregrounds a love story of the young married couple, already with children, as against the prevalent Western tale of the love intrigue that leads to marriage.

25. See his "Towards a Cross-Cultural Approach to Defining International Standards of Human Rights," chapter 1 in *Human Rights in Cross-Cultural Perspectives: A Quest for Consensus,* ed. Abdullahi Ahmed An-Na'im (Philadelphia: University of Pennsylvania Press, 1992); also see chapter 6 in ibid.

26. Foucault, *Surveiller et Punir* (Paris: Gallimard, 1976).

27. Tocqueville was already aware of the change when he commented on a passage from Mme. de Sévigny in *La Démocratie en Amérique.*

28. See Charles Taylor, *Sources of the Self* (Cambridge, MA: Harvard University Press, 1989), chap. 13.

29. I have discussed at greater length the two opposed understandings of the rise of modernity that are invoked here in "Modernity and the Rise of the Public Sphere," in *The Tanner Lectures on Human Values,* ed. Grethe B. Peterson (Salt Lake City: University of Utah Press, 1993).

7. Democratic Exclusion (and Its Remedies?)

1. And in fact, the drive to democracy took a predominantly "national" form. Logically, it is perfectly possible that the democratic challenge to a multinational authoritarian regime, for example, Austria and Turkey, should take the form of a multinational citizenship in a pan-imperial "people." But in fact, attempts at this usually fail, and the peoples take their own road into freedom. So the Czechs declined being part of a democratized empire in the Paulskirche in 1848; and the Young Turk attempt at an Ottoman citizenship foundered, and made way for a fierce Turkish nationalism.

2. Rousseau, who laid bare very early the logic of this idea, saw that a democratic sovereign couldn't just be an "aggregation," as with our earlier lecture audience; it has to be an "association," that is, a strong collective agency, a "corps moral et collectif" with "son unité, son moi common, sa vie et sa volonté." This last term is the key one, because what gives this body its personality is a "volonté générale." *Contrat Social,* book I, chap. 6.

3. I have discussed this relation in "Les Sources de l'identité moderne," in Mikhaël Elbaz, Andrée Fortin, and Guy Laforest, eds. *Les Frontières de l'Identité: Modernité et postmodernisme au Québec* (Sainte-Foy: Presses de l'Université Laval, 1996), 347–364.

4. Michael Sandel, *Democracy's Discontent* (Cambridge, MA: Harvard University Press, 1996).

5. *Le Cruset français* (Paris: Le Seuil, 1989).

6. Ernest Gellner, *Nations and Nationalism* (Ithaca, NY: Cornell University Press, 1983), 1.

7. See *Sources of the Self* (Cambridge, MA: Harvard University Press, 1989), chap. 3.

8. Religious Mobilizations

1. Ernst Kantorowicz, *The King's Two Bodies* (Princeton, NJ: Princeton University Press, 1997).
2. I have discussed this at greater length in *Modern Social Imaginaries* (Durham, NC: Duke University Press, 2004).
3. Robert Bellah, "Civil Religion in America," in *Beyond Belief: Essays on Religion in a Post-Traditional World* (New York: Harper and Row, 1970).
4. See ibid., chap. 9.
5. For a fuller discussion of this term, see my *Varieties of Religion Today* (Cambridge, MA: Harvard University Press, 2002), chap. 3.
6. The connection of Christianity with decency in England has been noted by David Martin in *Dilemmas of Contemporary Religion* (Oxford: Blackwell, 1978), 122.
7. This whole issue of violence in modernity deserves further extensive treatment, especially taking account of the pathbreaking work of René Girard.
8. I have drawn here on the valuable discussions in Hugh McLeod's *Religion and the People of Western Europe* (Oxford: Oxford University Press, 1997), 36–43; John Wolffe's *God and Greater Britain: Religion and National Life in Britain and Ireland, 1843–1945* (London: Routledge, 1994), 20–30; and David Hempton's *Religion and Political Culture in Britain and Ireland: From the Glorious Revolution to the Decline of Empire* (Cambridge: Cambridge University Press, 1996), chap. 2.
9. Joyce Appleby, *Inheriting the Revolution: The First Generation of Americans* (Cambridge, MA: Harvard University Press, 2000), 206.
10. Callum Brown, *The Death of Christian Britain* (London: Routledge, 2001), chap. 4–5.
11. See David Martin's *Tongues of Fire: The Explosion of Protestantism in Latin America* (Oxford: Blackwell, 1990) and *Pentecostalism: The World Their Parish* (Oxford: Blackwell, 2002).
12. Sociologists have noticed similar effects flowing from strong (re)conversions to Islam in contemporary France; see Danièle Hervieu-Léger, *Le pèlerin et le converti* [The pilgrim and the convert] (Paris: Flammarion, 1999), 142–143.
13. Philippe Boutry, *Prêtres et paroisses* [Priests and parishes] (Paris: Cerf, 1986), 344, also 380, where he speaks of the self-given "mission morale, sociale, et pour tout dire civilisatrice de l'Église dans le 'monde.'" Yves-Marie Hilaire evokes the same idea in *Une Chrétienneté au XIXe Siècle* [A Christendom in the nineteenth century] (Lille, France: PUL, 1977), 1:305.
14. Jeffrey Cox, *The English Churches in a Secular Society* (New York: Oxford University Press, 1982), 271.
15. Ibid., 109–110.
16. Steve Bruce, *Religion in the Modern World* (Oxford: Oxford University Press, 1996), chap. 1.
17. Ibid., chap. 6.
18. This is close to a thesis made by Martin in *Tongues of Fire,* 56, 68.
19. Again, there is a similarity to the thesis outlined by Martin, if I understand him correctly, in *Tongues of Fire,* 53.
20. This hot identity may also help to explain the differences between Europe and America that emerged on the occasion of the recent war in Iraq. Some commentators have tried

to capture this in the memorable phrase "Americans are from Mars, Europeans are from Venus." See Robert Kagan, "The U.S.-Europe Divide," *Washington Post,* May 26, 2002.

9. A Catholic Modernity?

This lecture was given at the University of Dayton on the occasion of the presentation of the Marianist Award to Charles Taylor, January 25, 1996.

1. This is not to say that we cannot claim in certain areas to have gained certain insights and settled certain questions that still troubled our ancestors. For instance, we are able to see the Inquisition clearly for the unevangelical horror that it was. But this doesn't exclude our having a lot to learn from earlier ages as well, even from people who also made the mistake of supporting the Inquisition.
2. Henri Bremond, *Histoire littéraire du sentient religieux en France depuis la fin des guerres de religion jusqu'à nos jours* (Paris: A. Colin, 1967–1968).
3. See *Sources of the Self* (Cambridge, MA: Harvard University Press, 1989), chap. 13.
4. Cf. Daniel Callahan, *Setting Limits: Medical Goals in an Aging Society* (Washington, DC: Georgetown University Press, 1995).
5. James Miller, *The Passion of Michel Foucault* (New York: Simon & Schuster, 1993).
6. See René Girard, *La Violence et le Sacré* (Paris: Grasset, 1972) and *Le Bouc Emissaire* (Paris: Grasset, 1982).
7. Fyodor Dostoevsky, *The Devils,* trans. David Magarshack (Harmondsworth, England: Penguin, 1971), 404.
8. I have discussed this in *The Malaise of Modernity* (Toronto: Anansi, 1991); American edition: *The Ethics of Authenticity* (Cambridge, MA: Harvard University Press, 1992).
9. Ibid.

10. Notes on the Sources of Violence

1. James Gilligan, *Violence* (New York: Vintage, 1996).
2. Chris Hedges, *War Is a Force That Gives Us Meaning* (New York: Public Affairs, 2002), 89. In *Humanity* (New Haven, CT: Yale University Press, 1999), Jonathan Glover points to the same sense of excitement at power, which some people experience in combat. War, he quotes a Vietnam veteran, "is, for men, at some terrible level the closest thing to what childbirth is for women: the initiation into the power of life and death. It's like lifting off a corner of the universe and looking at what's underneath" (p. 56).
3. Hedges also notes this, in *War Is a Force,* 98–105.
4. John Keegan, *A History of Warfare* (London: Hutchinson, 1993).
5. Sudhir Kakar, *The Colors of Violence: Cultural Identities, Religion and Conflict* (Chicago: University of Chicago Press, 1996), 81.
6. See the importance of "Daransetzen": "Und es ist allein das Daransetzen des Lebens, wodurch die Freiheit, wodurch es bewährt wird, dass dem Selbstbewusstsein nicht das *Sein,* nicht die *unmittelbare* Weise, wie es auftritt, nicht sein Versenktsein in die Ausbreitung des Lebens das Wesen,—sondern das an ihm nichts vorhanden, was für es nicht verschwindendes Moment wäre, das es nur reines *Fürsichsein* ist"; *Die Phänomenologie des Geistes* (Hamburg: Felix Meiner Verlag, 1952), 144.

7. This interweaving of the warrior code of honor, the vendetta, and sacred violence is evident in the Palestine-Israel conflict. It emerges also in this telling quote from a leader in the communal riots in Hyderabad: "Riots are like one-day cricket matches where the killings are the runs. You have to score at least one more than the opposing team. The whole honour of your nation (quam) depends on not scoring less than the opponent"; from Sudhir Kakar, *Colors of Violence,* 57.

8. See, among others, *Le Bouc émissaire* (Paris: Grasset, 1982) and the more recent *Je vois Satan tomber comme l'éclair* (Paris: Grasset, 1999).

9. It is in this context that I would like to understand the thesis about monotheism and violence of Regina Schwartz's interesting and suggestive work, *The Curse of Cain* (Chicago: University of Chicago Press, 1997). I am suggesting that the phenomenon is perhaps more widespread and general than she proposes.

10. E. P. Thompson, "The Moral Economy of the English Crowd in the Eighteenth Century," *Past and Present* 50 (1971): 76–136.

11. See Albert Soboul, "Violences collectives et rapports sociaux: Les foules révolutionnaires," in *La Révolution française* (Paris: Gallimard, 1981), 577–578; and François Furet and Denis Richet, *La Révolution française* (Paris: Hachette [Pluriel], 1999), 206–207. The idea that someone must always be to blame for catastrophic events is, of course, common in many "primitive" cultures; see, for instance, E. Evans-Pritchard, *Witchcraft, Oracles and Magic among the Azande* (Oxford: Oxford University Press, 1937).

12. Cited in Georges Lefebvre, *Quatre-Vingt-neuf* (Paris: Éditions Sociales, 1970), 245–246.

13. From Patrice Gueniffey, *La Politique de la Terreur* (Paris: Fayard, 2000), 311–313. I have drawn a great deal on the interesting discussion in this book.

14. See again ibid., 310. He shows the same demonization of opposition in the case of the mass killings in La Vendée. The people here were described as animals, dehumanized as a preparation for massacre. There is a continuity with the prerevolutionary language of élites describing the people (ibid., 255–261).

15. Eric Hobsbawm, *Nations and Nationalism since 1780* (Cambridge: Cambridge University Press, 1992).

16. I have described elsewhere how religion slides to becoming a marker for identity. See volume 15 of the journal *Transit* (1996), published by IWM, Vienna.

17. I have discussed this drive to exclusion at greater length in Chapter 7.

18. See Craig Calhoun, "Nationalism and Ethnicity," *American Review of Sociology,* no. 9 (1993): 230. The discussion in this section owes a great deal to Calhoun's recent work.

19. I have learned a great deal from the interesting discussion in Kakar, *Colors of Violence,* esp. chap. 6.

20. I have discussed this at greater length in "The Immanent Counter-Enlightenment," in *Canadian Political Philosophy,* ed. Ronald Beiner and Wayne Norman (Don Mills, Ont.: Oxford University Press, 2001), 386–400.

21. See *Je vois Satan,* chap. 13.

22. David Martin, *Dilemmas of Contemporary Religion* (Oxford: B. Blackwell, 1978), 94.

23. For an interesting discussion of the advantages and dangers of a commission in the same vein as the Truth and Reconciliation Commission, see Rajeev Bhargava, "Restoring Decency to Barbaric Societies," in *Truth and Justice,* ed. Robert Rotberg and Dennis Thompson (Princeton, NJ: Princeton University Press, 2000), 45–67.

24. Chris Hedges, *War Is a Force.*

11. The Future of the Religious Past

1. Robert Tombs, *France: 1814–1914* (London: Longman, 1996), 135, places the high-water mark at 1880; Gérard Cholvy and Yves-Marie Hillaire, *Histoire religieuse de la France contemporaine: 1800–1880* (Paris: Privat, 1985), 317, set it earlier, around 1860. I have split the difference.

2. See John McManners's essay in *The Oxford History of Christianity,* ed. John McManners (Oxford: Oxford University Press, 1993), 277–228.

3. See Robert Bellah, "Religious Evolution," chap. 2 of his *Beyond Belief: Essays on Religion in a Post-Traditional World* (New York: Harper & Row, 1970).

4. Godfrey Lienhardt, *Divinity and Experience* (Oxford: Oxford University Press, 1961), 233–235.

5. Ibid., 292.

6. As a matter of fact, it has been argued (e.g., by Pierre Clastres, *La société contre l'État: Recherches d'anthropologie politique* [Paris: Minuit, 1974]) that the earliest forms of this religion were highly egalitarian in relation to later developments, just because the pervasive sense of a sacred order left little room for personal decision on the part of those charged with special functions. They couldn't yet parlay these into personal power.

7. See, e.g., Lienhardt, *Divinity and Experience,* chap. 3; and Roger Caillois, *L'homme et le sacré* (Paris: Gallimard, 1963), chap. 3.

8. This is a much commented-upon feature of Aboriginal religion in Australia; see Lucien Lévy-Bruhl, *L'expérience mystique et les symboles chez les primitifs* (Paris: Alcan, 1937), 180ff.; Caillois, *L'homme et le sacré,* 143–155; W. E. H. Stanner, "On Aboriginal Religion," a series of six articles in *Oceania* 30–33 (1959–1963). The same connection to the land has been noted with the Okanagan in British Columbia; see Jerry Mander and Edward Goldsmith, *The Case against the Global Economy* (San Francisco: Sierra Club Books, 1996), chap. 39.

9. William Kingdom Clifford, *Ethics of Belief and Other Essays,* ed. Leslie Stephen and Sir Frederick Pollock (London: Watts, 1947).

10. Birgit Meyer, *Translating the Devil* (Trenton, NJ: Africa World Press, 1999), 181.

11. See the discussion of possession in ibid., 205–206.

12. John Stuart Mill, *On Liberty,* in *Three Essays* (Oxford: Oxford University Press 1975), 77.

13. See, e.g., S. N. Eisenstadt, ed., *The Origins and Diversity of Axial Age Civilizations* (Albany: State University of New York Press, 1986); see also Bellah, *Beyond Belief.*

14. Karl Jaspers, *Vom Ursprung und Ziel der Geschichte* (Zurich: Artemis, 1949).

15. Stanner, "On Aboriginal Religion"; the expression quoted figures in article 11, *Oceania* 30, no. 4 (June 1960): 276. See also, by the same author, "The Dreaming," in *Reader in Comparative Religion,* ed. W. Lessa and E. Z. Vogt (Evanston, IL: Row, Peterson, 1958), 158–167.

16. Stanner, "On Aboriginal Religion," article 6, *Oceania* 33, no. 4 (June 1963): 269.

17. I have been greatly helped here by the much richer account of religious development in Robert Bellah's "Religious Evolution," in his *Beyond Belief.* My contrast is much simpler than the series of stages that Bellah identifies; the "primitive" and the "archaic" are fused in my category of "early" religion. My point is to bring into sharp relief the disembedding thrust of the axial formulations.

18. See Marcel Gauchet, *Le désenchantement du monde* (Paris: Gallimard 1985), chap. 2.

19. Louis Dumont, "De l'individu-hors-du-monde à l'individu-dans-le-monde," in *Essais sur l'individualisme* (Paris: Seuil, 1983).

20. I have developed this at greater length in *Modern Social Imaginaries* (Durham, NC: Duke University Press, 2004).

21. Danièle Hervieu-Léger, *Catholicisme, la fin d'un monde* (Paris: Bayard, 2003).

22. See Robert Bellah, "Civil Religion in America," in *Beyond Belief,* chap. 9.

23. See my *The Varieties of Religion Today* (Cambridge, MA: Harvard University Press, 2002).

24. See, e.g., David Martin, *Tongues of Fire* (Oxford: Basil Blackwell, 1990), and *A General Theory of Secularization* (Oxford: Basil Blackwell, 1978).

25. See Gordon Wood, *The Radicalism of the American Revolution* (New York: Vintage, 1993).

26. But even so, the very poor tended to be touched by these movements in England less than more skilled workers. See Hugh McLeod, *Secularization in Western Europe, 1848—1914* (New York: St. Martin's Press, 2000), chap. 3; also his *Religion and the People of Western Europe, 1789–1989* (Oxford: Oxford University Press, 1997), chap. 4; and David Hempton, *Religion and Political Culture in Britain and Ireland* (Cambridge: Cambridge University Press, 1996), 29 and chap. 6.

27. I have drawn here, inter alia, on the valuable discussions in McLeod, *Religion and the People of Western Europe,* 36–43; John Wolffe, *God and Greater Britain: Religion and National Life in Britain and Ireland, 1843–1945* (London: Routledge, 1994), 20–30; and Hempton, *Religion and Political Culture,* chap. 2.

28. Joyce Appleby, *Inheriting the Revolution: The First Generation of Americans* (Cambridge, MA: Harvard University Press, 2000), 206.

29. Callum Brown, *The Death of Christian Britain* (London: Routledge, 2001).

30. See David Martin, *Tongues of Fire,* and *Pentecostalism: The World Their Parish* (Oxford: Basil Blackwell, 2002).

31. Sociologists have noticed similar effects flowing from strong (re)conversions to Islam in contemporary France; see Danièle Hervieu-Léger, *Le pèlerin et le converti* (Paris: Flammarion, 1999), 142–143.

32. The connection of Christianity with decency in England has been noted by David Martin, *Dilemmas of Contemporary Religion* (Oxford: Basil Blackwell, 1978), 22.

33. This whole issue of violence in modernity deserves further extensive treatment, especially taking account of the pathbreaking work of René Girard.

34. See Philippe Chenaux, *Entre Maurras et Maritain* (Paris: Cerf, 1999).

35. Philippe Boutry, *Prêtres et paroisses au pays du curé d'Ars* (Paris: Cerf, 1986), also speaks of the campaigns of cures against *les abus,* principally dancing, theater, and working on Sunday (579).

36. Cf. Richard Hoggart, *The Uses of Literacy* (London: Chatto & Windus, 1957); Yves Lambert, *Dieu change en Bretagne* (Paris: Cerf, 1985).

37. Michael Sandel, *Democracy's Discontent* (Cambridge, MA: Harvard University Press, 1996), 209–210.

38. Michel Winock, *Le siècle des intellectuels* (Paris: Seuil, 1997), 582.

39. François Furet, *Le passé d'une illusion* (Paris: Gallimard, 1996), points out how remarkable the allegiance was and the sense of belonging that sustained it.

40. Luc Ferry, in his very interesting *L'Homme-Dieu ou le sens de la vie* (Paris: Grasset, 1996), chap. 1, picks up on this phenomenon under the title "the refusal of authority." I agree with much of what he says, but I think he overintellectualizes this reaction by relating it directly to Descartes, instead of seeing its expressivist roots.

41. Sir George Trevelyan, in a lecture at the Festival for Mind, Body, and Spirit, quoted in Paul Heelas, *The New Age Movement* (Oxford: Basil Blackwell, 1996), 21. The injunction, one might say, represents only a New Age outlook. But in this respect, the various New Age movements accentuate much more widely held attitudes, as Heelas argues in chap. 6. In 1978, for instance, a Gallup poll found that 80 percent of Americans agreed that "an individual should arrive at his or her own religious beliefs independent of any churches or synagogues" (Heelas, 164; also cited in Robert Bellah et al., *Habits of the Heart* [Berkeley: University of California Press, 1985], 228).

42. The excellent book by José Casanova, *Public Religions in the Modern World* (Chicago: University of Chicago Press, 1994), shows how diverse our religious predicament is. If we ever came to live in a predicament totally defined by the post-Durkheimian understanding, there would probably be no further space for religion in the public sphere. Spiritual life would be entirely privatized, in keeping with the norms of a certain procedural liberalism that is very widespread today. But Casanova traces, in fact, a "deprivatization" of religion, that is, an attempt by churches and religious bodies to intervene again in the political life of their societies. Examples include the Christian Right and the Catholic bishops' letters in the United States, which I have just mentioned. It is unlikely (and also undesirable) that this kind of thing will ever cease. But the situation in which these interventions take place is defined by the end of a uniform Durkheimian dispensation and the growing acceptance among many people of a post-Durkheimian understanding.

43. Hempton, *Religion and Political Culture*, 18 and 132–133.

44. Mill, *On Liberty*; see McLeod, *Religion and the People of Western Europe*, 114; Jeffrey Cox, *The English Churches in a Secular Society: Lambeth, 1870–1930* (New York: Oxford University Press, 1982), 275.

45. Martin, *Pentecostalism*, 14–15.

46. Of course, the sexual revolution could itself be taken as the axis of a master narrative or subtraction story, and it was frequently interpreted in this way in the 1960s, See, e.g., Charles A. Reich, *The Greening of America* (New York: Random House, 1970). Parallel to stories claiming that science shows that religion is wrong, and once people remove the obstacles to seeing this, they can't go back; or that people in the end want autonomy, and once they see through the false reasons underlying authority, they can't go back; there is another possible story: people desire unchecked sexual fulfillment, and once they see that they have been denied this by unfounded restrictions, there is no going back. This is certainly how things felt to a lot of young people in, say, Berkeley or the Latin Quarter in 1968. But this outlook hasn't worn very well. In fact, most people quickly perceived that things are much more complicated.

47. Martin, *Pentecostalism*, 98–106.

48. See Brown, *The Death of Christian Britain*, esp. chaps. 4 and 5.

49. I have discussed this at greater length in my *Modern Social Imaginaries*.

50. Boutry, *Prêtres et paroisses*, 578.

51. Ibid., part 3, chaps. 1 and 4. There are also interesting discussions of this gender split in practice in McLeod, *Religion and the People of Western Europe*, 128; Leonore Davidoff

and Catherine Hall, *Family Fortunes* (London: Routledge, 1987), chap. 2; and Thomas Kselman, "The Varieties of Religious Experience in Urban France," in *European Religion in the Age of Great Cities, 1830–1930*, ed. Hugh McLeod (London: Routledge, 1995), chap. 6.

52. Hervieu-Léger, in *Catholicisme*, speaks of an "exculturation," a move beyond and outside of the culture that the Catholic Church helped form over centuries in France and that was shared by the "Republican" opponents of the Church. See esp. chaps. 3–6.

53. Quoted in Brown, *The Death of Christian Britain*, 180.

54. See Yves-Marie Hilaire, *Une Chrétienneté au XIXe siècle?* (Lille: PUL, 1977), 1:74–80,

55. Grace Davie, *Religion in Modern Europe* (Oxford: Oxford University Press, 2000), 63–64.

56. John Bossy, *Christianity in the West, 1400–1700* (Oxford: Oxford University Press, 1985), 35; Ralph Gibson, *A Social History of French Catholicism, 1789–1914* (London: Routledge, 1989), 24.

57. Bossy, *Christianity in the West*, 37.

58. Jean Delumeau, *Le péché et la peur* (Paris: Fayard, 1983); also Gibson, *A Social History*, 241ff.

59. Quoted in Gibson, *A Social History*, 246.

60. E. Germain, *Parler du salut?* (Paris: Beauchesne, 1967), 295; quoted, along with a very interesting discussion, in Gibson, *A Social History*, 244.

61. Hervieu-Léger, *Catholicisme*, 248.

62. Gibson, *A Social History*, 188; Delumeau, *Le péché et la peur*, chap. 17, 517–519, 525.

63. Martin, *Pentecostalism*, 21.

64. Michael Hornsby-Smith, "Recent Transformations in English Catholicism," in *Religion and Modernization: Sociologists and historians debate the secularization thesis*, ed. Steve Bruce (Oxford: Clarendon Press, 1992), chap. 6.

65. See Steve Bruce, *Religion in the Modern World* (Oxford: Oxford University Press, 1996), 33, 137ff.; Sylvie Denèfle, *Sociologie de la secularisation* (Paris: L'Harmattan, 1997).

66. For example, the *Gallup Political and Economic Index* (394, June 1993) reports that in Britain 40 percent believe in "some sort of spirit or lifeforce," as opposed to 30 percent who have faith in a "personal God"; cited in Heelas, *The New Age Movement*, 166. Analogous figures have been found in Sweden and France; see Hervieu-Léger, *Le pélerin et le converti*, 44–46.

67. The move of many Western societies into what I have been calling a "post-Durkheimian" dispensation has obviously facilitated their move toward "multiculturalism," at the same time as this has become a more urgent issue because of the increasing diversity of their populations. But multiculturalism has also produced strains, which are often exacerbated by the continuing hold of one or another "Durkheimian" understandings on important segments of the population. Christian conservatives are made edgy by rampant expressivism in the United States, and many French people find it hard to see their country as containing an important Muslim component, so long have they related to it as an essentially Catholic country or as one defined by the constitutive tension between Catholicism and *laïcité*.

68. Hervieu-Léger, *Le pélerin et le convent*, 41, 56; Grace Davie, *Religion in Britain since 1945: Relieving without Belonging* (Oxford: Basil Blackwell, 1994). A discussion of the

special Scandinavian pattern can be found in Hervieu-Léger, *Le pélerin et le converti,* 57; and Davie, *Religion in Modern Europe,* 3.

69. William James, *The Varieties of Religious Experience* (Harmondsworth, England: Penguin Books, 1982).

70. Boutry, *Prêtres et paroisses,* tells of the "attitudes of reservation, of suspicion, and even of refusal" by clergy in the face of many of the practices of folk religion (481). McLeod *(Religion and the People of Western Europe,* 64–65) quotes the bitter statement of another French curé in 1907: "Not a single man does his Easter Duties, but it's a curious fact that they all take part in processions."

71. Jim Obelkevich, *Religion and Rural Society: South Lindsey, 1825–1875* (London: Oxford University Press, 1976), 83–84.

72. Maurice Agulhon, *La république au village* (Paris: Seuil, 1979), 172.

73. Ibid., 644, also 578–595 and 625–651.

74. Gibson, *A Social History,* 144.

75. See the interesting discussion in Thomas Kselman, *Miracles and Prophecies in Nineteenth-Century France* (New Brunswick, NJ: Rutgers University Press, 1983), chap. 6.

76. Victor Turner, *The Ritual Process: Structure and Counter-Structure* (London: Routledge & Kegan Paul, 1969).

77. Hervieu-Léger, *Le pélerin et le converti,* 100–108.

78. See Davie, *Religion in Britain since 1945;* and Wolffe, *God and Greater Britain.* The term *diffusive Christianity* was coined by Cox, *English Churches in a Secular Society,* chap. 4.

79. Wolffe, *God and Greater Britain,* 92–93. Hempton, *Religion and Political Culture,* 136–137, gives another account of this diffused understanding of Christianity, while stressing that all the terms we invent to describe it, including *believing without belonging* and *diffusive Christianity* itself, are insufficiently flexible to capture the complex reality. Hempton also points out the importance of religious music, particularly hymn singing, in this culture.

80. Wolffe, *God and Greater Britain,* 92–93. Boutry, *Prêtres et paroisses,* makes a parallel remark about the period 1840–1860 in the Ain Department (but this was not exceptional in this respect in France): "Never, perhaps, in the long history of the Catholic Church, will the lived reality of the ministry have coincided more exactly with its ideal, never will the life of village priests approach so closely to the model of the 'good priest,' developed three centuries earlier by the Fathers of the Council of Trent" (243).

81. Davie, *Religion in Britain since 1945,* 69–70. For the numbers, see her tables.

82. Ibid., 88–91.

83. See Grace Davie, *Europe: The Exceptional Case* (London: Darton, Longman & Todd, 2002), 46.

84. Perhaps a "cold" form of their erstwhile religious identity can be observed among Québécois; on the occasion of the deconfessionalization of the public schools in the 1990s, lots of quite nonpracticing parents expressed anxiety about the possible suppression of religious education for their children in school. They feared being unable to inculcate proper moral guidelines in their children without the backing this education could provide.

85. Steve Brace, *Religion in the Modern World* (Oxford: Oxford University Press, 1996), chap. 6.
86. This is close to the thesis outlined by Martin, if I understand him correctly, in *A General Theory of Secularization,* 53.
87. Again, there is a similarity to a thesis of Martin's; see ibid., 56, 68.
88. This "hot" identity may also help to explain the differences between Europe and America that emerged on the occasion of the recent war in Iraq. Some commentators have tried to capture this in the following memorable phrase: "Americans are from Mars, Europeans from Venus." See Robert Kagan, *Of Paradise and Power: America and Europe in the New World Order* (New York: Alfred A. Knopf, 2003).
89. S. N. Eisenstadt, *Japanese Civilization: A Comparative View* (Chicago: University of Chicago Press, 1996).
90. Saba Mahmood, *Pious Formations: The Islamic Revival and the Subject of Feminism* (Princeton, NJ: Princeton University Press, 2004).
91. Moussa Kömeçoğlu, in *Islam in Public,* ed. Nilüfer Göle and Ludwig Amman (Istanbul: Bilgi University Press, 2006), 369–394.
92. Ugur Kömeçoğlu, in *Islam in Public,* ed. Göle and Amman, 173.
93. For a further discussion of this distinction between network and categorical identities, see Craig Calhoun, *Nationalism* (Minneapolis: University of Minnesota Press, 1997), chap. 2. I am indebted to Calhoun's work throughout this discussion.
94. D. Eikelman and J. Anderson, eds., *New Media in the Muslim World: The Emerging Public Sphere* (Bloomington: Indiana University Press, 1999).
95. See Nilüfer Göle, *Musulmanes et Modernes* (Paris: La Découverte, 1993).
96. See, e.g., Craig Calhoun, "Nationalism and Ethnicity," *American Review of Sociology,* no. 9 (1993): 230.
97. See, esp. for the Sri Lankan case, Stanley Tambiah, *Buddhism Betrayed? Religion, Politics, and Violence in Sri Lanka* (Chicago: University of Chicago Press, 1992).
98. Montesquieu, *L'esprit des lois,* book 5, chap. 1.
99. Immanuel Kant, *Grundlegung zur Metaphysik der Sitten,* Berlin Academy ed. (Berlin: Walter de Gruyter, 1968), 4:434.
100. This doesn't have to be a political society. It can be a dispersed common agency, like a religious confession, or an ethnic group.
101. See my "The Politics of Recognition," in *Multiculturalism: Examining the Politics of Recognition,* ed. Amy Gutmann (Princeton, NJ: Princeton University Press, 1992).
102. See esp. Frantz Fanon, *Les damnés de la terre* (Paris: Maspéro, 1968).
103. I owe a lot here to the interesting discussion by Nilüfer Göle about this whole topic, both in the Turkish and in the broader Islamic context. See *Musulmanes et Modernes.*
104. See Martin Kramer, "Arab Nationalism: Mistaken Identity," *Daedalus* 122, no. 3 (Summer 1993): 171–206.
105. I have learned a great deal from the interesting discussion in Sudhir Kakar, *The Colors of Violence* (Chicago: University of Chicago Press, 1996), esp. chap. 6; and also from René Girard: e.g., *Le bouc émissaire* (Paris: Grasset, 1982) and *Je vois Satan tomber comme l'éclair* (Paris: Grasset, 1999). I have tried to discuss these issues in Chapter 10.
106. See Saba Mahmood, "Ethical Formation and Politics of Individual Autonomy in Contemporary Egypt," *Social Research* 70, no. 3 (Fall 2003): 837–866.

107. 'Abdolkarim Soroush, *Reason, Freedom, and Democracy in Islam* (Oxford: Oxford University Press, 2000), 24.
108. See Keith Thomas, *Religion and the Decline of Magic* (New York: Scribner, 1971).
109. Meyer, *Translating the Devil,* 162, 170, 212–216.

12. Disenchantment-Reenchantment

1. "There was a force in all things, animate, and, to our view, inanimate: water, trees, substances, words; and there was a mutual influence among things. There were also human and supra- or extra-human beings, who exercised power of different kinds and at different levels: saints, witches, ghosts, spirits and less palpable entities." Stephen Wilson, *The Magical Universe* (London: Hambledon & London, 2000), xvii.
2. George Levine, *Darwin Loves You* (Princeton, NJ: Princeton University Press, 2006), esp. chap. 1.
3. The quotation marks here express some questioning of whether this picture of disenchantment is really Weber's, but we don't need to settle that here.
4. Levine, *Darwin Loves You,* 29.
5. "Zwei Dinge erfüllen das Gemüth mit immer neuer und zunehmender Bewunderung und Ehrfurcht, je öfter und anhaltender sich das Nachdenken damit beschäftigt: *der bestirnte Himmel über mir und das moralische Gesetz in mir*"; *Kritik der praktischen Vernunft,* Berlin Academy edition (Berlin: Walter Gruyter, 1968), p. 161.
6. Douglas Hofstadter, "Reductionism and Religion," *Behavioral and Brain Sciences* 3 (1980): 434.
7. The awe, but also the sense of connection, emerges in these reflections of Charles Lindbergh:

> I know myself as mortal, but this raises the question: "What is I?" Am I an individual, or am I an evolving life stream composed of countless selves? . . . As one identity, I was born in ad 1902. But as ad twentieth-century man, I am billions of years old. The life I consider as myself has existed through past eons with unbroken continuity. Individuals are custodians of the life stream— temporal manifestations of far greater being, forming from and returning to their essence like so many dreams. . . . I recall standing on the edge of a deep valley in the Hawaiian island of Maui, thinking that a life stream is like a mountain river—springing from hidden sources, born out of the earth, touched by stars, merging, blending, evolving in the shape momentarily seen.

> He sums up: "I am form and I am formless. I am life and I am matter, mortal and immortal. I am one and I am many—myself and humanity in flux. . . . After my death, the molecules of my being will return to the earth and sky. They came from the stars. I am of the stars." Quoted in Gore Vidal, "The Eagle Is Grounded," *Times Literary Supplement,* no. 4987, October 30, 1998, p. 6.

> We can see how Lindbergh stands fully within the modern cosmic imaginary. His experience of nature, for example, on Maui, immediately suggests to him the depth of the universe and our dark genesis from it.

8. I have developed this point at greater length in "Explanation and Practical Reason," in *Philosophical Arguments* (Cambridge, MA: Harvard University Press, 1995), 34–60.

9. Bernard Williams, *Ethics and the Limits of Philosophy* (Cambridge, MA: Harvard University Press, 1985).

10. Daniel Dennett, *Consciousness Explained* (Boston: Little, Brown, 1991).

11. Merlin Donald, *Origins of the Modern Mind* (Cambridge, MA: Harvard University Press, 1991) and *A Mind So Rare* (New York: Norton, 2001).

13. What Does Secularism Mean?

1. See the discussion of profane and sacred times in my *A Secular Age* (Cambridge, MA: Harvard University Press, 2007), 54–61.

2. I have discussed this at greater length in Chapter 14.

3. For a fuller discussion of the modern idea of moral order, see my *Modern Social Imaginaries* (Durham, NC: Duke University Press, 2004).

4. Thus, American secularists often totally confuse the separation of church and state from that of religion and state. For instance, Rawls at one point wanted to ban all reference to the grounds of people's "comprehensive views" (these of course included religious views) from public discourse.

5. Ashis Nandy, "The Politics of Secularism and the Recovery of Religious Tolerance," in *Time Warps* (Piscataway, NJ: Rutgers University Press, 2002), chap. 3, esp. pp. 68–69 and 80.

6. Ibid., 85. Amartya Sen also makes use of a similar point about Akbar's rule to establish the roots of certain modes of secularism in Indian history. See *The Argumentative Indian: Writings on Indian History, Culture, and Identity* (New York: Farrar, Straus and Giroux, 2005). For an excellent example of such a creative redefinition, see Rajeev Bhargava, "What Is Secularism For?" in *Secularism and Its Critics,* ed. Rajeev Bhargava (Delhi: Oxford University Press, 1998).

7. Bhargava, "What Is Secularism For?" 586–652 (see esp. 493–494 and 520 for "principled distance"); and "The Distinctiveness of Indian Secularism," in *The Future of Secularism,* ed. T. N. Srinavasan (Delhi: Oxford University Press, 1997), 39–41.

8. José Casanova (forthcoming).

9. Andrew Koppelman, "Rawls and Habermas," personal communication.

10. Christian Smith, *The Secular Revolution* (Berkeley: University of California Press, 2003). See also Tisa Wenger, "Rewriting the First Amendment: Competing American Secularisms, 1850–1900," in *Public Religion, Secularism, and Democracy,* ed. Linell Cady and Elizabeth Shakman Hurd (London: Routledge Press, 2010).

11. Marcel Gauchet, *La Religion dans la Démocratie* (Paris: Gallimard, 1998), 47–50.

12. Rousseau, who laid bare very early the logic of this idea, saw that a democratic sovereign couldn't just be an "aggregation"; it has to be an "association," that is, a strong collective agency, a "corps moral et collectif" (moral and collective body) with "son unité, son moi commun, sa vie et sa volonté" (its unity, its common self, its life and its will). This last term is the key one, because what gives this body its personality is a "volonté générale" (general will). *Contrat Social,* book I, chap. 6.

13. I have discussed this relation in "Les Sources de l'identité moderne," in *Les Frontières de l'Identité: Modernité et postmodernisme au Québec,* ed. Mikhaël Elbaz, Andrée Fortin, and Guy Laforest (Sainte-Foy, Québec: Presses de l'Université Laval, 1996), 347–364.

14. "In dieser symbolischen Dimension entsteht jene legitimationswirksame Legierung aus Politik und Religion, auf sich der Begriff des Politischen bezieht" ("Hence this symbolic dimension is a manifestation of that fusion of politics and religion to which the concept of 'the political' refers"). Jürgen Habermas, "The Political," forthcoming.

15. See Taylor, *Modern Social Imaginaries.*

16. Jürgen Habermas, *Zwischen Naturalismus und Religion* (Frankfurt: Suhrkamp Verlag, 2005), 137. Of course, Habermas is right: official language in diverse democracies must avoid certain religious references (although this shouldn't be stretched to include assembly debates); this is not because they are specifically religious, but rather because they are not shared. It would be just as unacceptable for, say, legislation to be justified by a "whereas" clause referring to an atheist philosophy, as by such a clause referring to the authority of the Bible.

17. I am not sure whether I am disagreeing with Habermas or whether the difference in formulation really amounts to a difference in practice. We both recognize contexts in which the language of the state has to respect a reserve of neutrality, and others in which freedom of speech is unlimited. We differ perhaps more in our rationales than in the practice we recommend.

18. Sometimes the obligation of citizens to address their compatriots in the language of secular reason is grounded in an obligation to make one's position intelligible to them. "The self-understanding of the constitutional state has developed within the framework of a contractualist tradition that relies on 'natural reason,' in other words solely on public arguments to which all persons are supposed to have equal access." See Jürgen Habermas, "Religion in the Public Sphere," *European Journal of Philosophy* 14, no. 1 (2006): 5. But what argument is there to think that "natural reason" offered us a kind of ideological Esperanto? Were Martin Luther King's secular compatriots unable to understand what he was arguing for when he put the case for equality in biblical terms? Would more people have got the point had he invoked Kant? And besides, how does one distinguish religious from secular language? Is the Golden Rule clearly a move in either one or the other direction?

19. Mark Lilla, *The Stillborn God* (New York: Alfred A. Knopf, 2007), 5.

20. Ibid., 162.

21. Ibid., 305–306.

22. Habermas is an exceptional figure in many respects, of course, but here I want to point out that although he is a major thinker in the epistemological distinction between religion and reason (for which I will subsequently criticize him), he most emphatically does not share the political mistrust of religion that often goes with this.

23. See Chapter 14.

24. Nicolas de Caritat, marquis de Condorcet, *Esquisse d'un tableau historique des progrès de l'esprit humain* (Paris: Flammarion, 1988), 225. I have learned a great deal from the interesting discussion in Vincent Descombes, *Le raisonnement de l'ours* (Paris: Seuil, 2007), 163–178.

25. Immanuel Kant, "Was ist Aufklärung?" in *Kants Werke,* Akademie Textausgabe (Berlin: Walter de Gruyter, 1968), 8:33.

14. *Die Blosse Vernunft* ("Reason Alone")

1. John Pocock, *Barbarism and Religion,* vol. 1, *The Enlightenments of Edward Gibbon* (Cambridge: Cambridge University Press, 1999); Gertrude Himmelfarb, *The Roads to Modernity: The British, French, and American Enlightenments* (New York: Knopf, 2004).

2. Alexis de Tocqueville, *La Démocratie en Amérique* (Paris: Garnier-Flammarion, 1981).

3. Mark Lilla, *The Stillborn God* (New York: Alfred A. Knopf, 2007), 5.

4. Ibid., p. 162.

5. J. Habermas, *Zwischen Naturalismus une Religion* (Frankfurt: Suhrkamp, 2005), 137. Of course, Habermas is right: official language in diverse democracies must avoid certain religious references (although this shouldn't be stretched to include assembly debates); this is not because they are specifically *religious,* but rather because they are not shared. It would be just as unacceptable for, say, legislation to be justified by a "whereas" clause referring to an atheist philosophy, as by such a clause referring to the authority of the Bible.

6. Condorcet, *Esquisse d'un tableau historique des progrès de l'esprit humain* (Paris: Flammarion, 1988), 225. I have learned a great deal from the interesting discussion in Vincent Descombes, *Le raisonnement de l'ours* (Paris: Seuil, 2007), 163–178.

7. Immanuel Kant, "Was ist Aufklärung?" in *Kants Werke,* Akademie Textausgabe (Berlin: Walter de Gruyter, 1968) 8:33.

8. I have discussed this at much greater length in *Modern Social Imaginaries* (Durham, NC: Duke University Press, 2004).

9. See J. G. A. Pocock, *The Ancient Constitution and the Feudal Law,* 2nd ed. (Cambridge: Cambridge University Press, 1987).

10. The term "moral economy" is borrowed from E. P. Thompson, "The Moral Economy of the English Crowd in the Eighteenth Century," *Past and Present* 50 (1971): 76–136.

11. *Macbeth,* 2.3.56; 2.4.17–18 (see my book *Sources of the Self: The Making of the Modern Identity* (Cambridge, MA: Harvard University Press, 1989), 298.

12. Quoted in Louis Dupré, *Passage to Modernity* (New Haven, CT: Yale University Press, 1993), 19.

13. "The sun will not overstep his measures; if he does, the Erinyes, the handmaids of Justice, will find him out." Quoted in George Sabine, *A History of Political Theory,* 3rd ed. (New York: Holt Rinehart & Winston, 1961), 26.

14. *Locke's Two Treatises,* I, chap. 9, para. 86, p. 223.

15. Ibid., II, chap. 2, para. 6, p. 289; see also II, chap. 11, para. 135, p. 376; and *Some Thoughts concerning Education,* para. 116.

16. Ibid., II, chap. 5, para. 34, p. 309.

17. See Eugen Weber, *Peasants into Frenchmen* (London: Chatto & Windus, 1979), chap. 28.

18. See the discussion in Lilla's *The Stillborn God.*

19. Edward Gibbon, *The Decline and Fall of the Roman Empire,* ed. H. R. Trevor-Roper (New York: Twayne, 1963), x.

15. Perils of Moralism

1. In a profound discussion of the parable of the Good Samaritan, Paul Thibaud makes the remark that the Samaritan's response should not simply be seen as a one-off act. It inaugurates a new relation. "Cette relation s'étend dans le temps, elle peut connaître des étapes comme le montre l'évocation de la convalescence à l'auberge, elle inaugure un temps meilleur, unissant les protagonistes dans la perspective d'un avenir commun. L'horizon qui s'offre n'est pas un horizon apocalyptique, comme dans nombre d'autres paraboles évangéliques, c'est un horizon historique, d'amélioration du monde." ("This relation continues, as we see in the evocation of the victim's convalescence at the inn; it inaugurates a new phase, which unites the protagonists in a common future. The horizon here is not an apocalyptic one, as in many other gospel parables; it is an historic one, making for a better world.") "L'Autre et le Prochain" ("The Other and the Neighbor"). I might add, and Thibaud might well agree here, that this historical horizon makes sense for Christians in relation to the deeper, apocalyptic one.

2. See my *Modern Social Imaginaries* (Durham, NC: Duke University Press, 2004).

3. I have developed this theme in "The Immanent Counter-Enlightenment," in *Canadian Political Philosophy: Contemporary Reflections,* ed. Ronald Beiner and Wayne Norman (Dons Mills, Ont.: Oxford University Press, 2001), 386–400.

4. "Philosophical Regimen," in *Life, Unpublished Letters, and Philosophical Regimen of Anthony, Earl of Shaftesbury,* ed. Benjamin Rand (London: S. Sonnenschein, 1900), 54.

5. Nicholaus Ludwig von Zinzendorf, a Pietist thinker of the eighteenth century. The quote appears in his *Ergänzungbände zu den Hauptschriften,* ed. Erich Bayreuther and Gerhard Meyer (Hildesheim, 1964), vol. 3, p. 181.

6. *Letters on the Aesthetic Education of Man,* ed. and trans. Elizabeth Wilkinson and L. A. Willoughby (Oxford: Clarendon Press, 1967), letter VI.

7. Cf. Hume's listing—and castigation—of the "monkish virtues"; *Enquiry concerning the Principles of Morals,* in David Hume, *Enquiries,* ed. L. A. Selby-Bigge, 2nd ed. (1902; repr., Oxford: Clarendon Press, 1970), paragraph 270.

8. Michael Buckley, *At the Origins of Modern Atheism* (New Haven, CT: Yale University Press, 1987), passim.

9. *Zur Genealogie der Moral,* III, 28: "Die Sinnlosigkeit des Leidens, nicht das Leiden, war der Fluch, der bisher über der Menschheit ausgebreitet lag" (Munich: Goldmann, Gelbe Taschenbücher), vol. 991, p. 135.

10. Alexis de Tocqueville, *La Démocratie en Amérique* (Paris: Garnier-Flammarion, 1981), vol. 2, part 2, chap. 2, p. 385.

11. See *Also Sprach Zarathustra,* Zarathustra's Vorrede, section 5 (Munich: Gelbe Taschenbücher), vol. 403, p. 16.

12. James Gilligan, *Violence* (New York: Vintage, 1996).

13. I have developed this further in Chapter 10.

14. I have discussed this further in Chapter 9.

15. A very honorable exception is Jonathan Glover, *Humanity* (New Haven, CT: Yale University Press, 1999). True, in keeping with his naturalistic stance, he has to repudiate the vertical dimension as conceived here; but his work has the great merit of having posed the question of the moral motivations which might save us from repeating some of the worst atrocities of the previous century.

16. A profound and insightful statement of the thesis I am struggling to articulate here comes in his posthumous work, *The Corruption of Christianity,* ed. David Cayley (Toronto: Anansi Press, forthcoming), publication of the Canadian Broadcasting Corporation in the series "Ideas," January 2000. See also *The Rivers North of the Future: The Testament of Ivan Illich,* as told to David Cayley (Toronto: Anansi, 2005).

17. See Maximos Davies, "Celibacy in Context," in *First Things,* December 2002, 13–15. The author, a monk of the Eastern rite, contrasts the Eastern Church's conception of clerical celibacy within a "culture of asceticism" to the Western Catholic focus on rules and legal requirements.

18. A good account of the Taizé center can be found in Danièle Hervieu-Léger, *Le Pélerin et le Converti* (Paris: Flammarion, 1999), 100–108.

16. What Was the Axial Revolution?

This chapter is partly based on my book *A Secular Age* (Cambridge, MA: Harvard University Press, 2007), especially chapter 3. I develop further here the thesis I advanced there.

1. S. N. Eisenstadt, ed., *The Origins and Diversity of Axial Age Civilizations* (Albany: State University of New York Press, 1986), 1.

2. See Jan Assmann, "Cultural Memory and the Myth of the Axial Age," in *The Axial Age and Its Consequences,* ed. Robert N. Bellah (Cambridge, MA: Harvard University Press, forthcoming).

3. See his "Religious Evolution," chap. 2 of *Beyond Belief* (New York: Harper & Row, 1970).

4. Robert Bellah, in his article "What Is Axial about the Axial Age?" *Archives européennes de Sociologie* 46, no. 1 (2005): 69–89, makes a similar point about what he calls "tribal religion": "Ritual in tribal societies involves the participation of all or most members of the group" (69). He contrasts these with "archaic societies," which term designates the large-scale states that arose in the ancient world, and subjugated many of the smaller face-to-face societies. These were hierarchical, and their crucial rituals focused on crucial figures, kings or priests. But the face-to-face rituals continued, down at the base, and in Bellah's mind, do so right up to our time. I have been greatly helped here by the much richer account of religious development in Robert Bellah's work: first in his "Religious Evolution" in *Beyond Belief,* and more recently in the article quoted above. The contrast I want to make in this chapter is much simpler than the series of stages which Bellah identifies; the "tribal" and the "archaic" are fused in my category of "early" or "pre-axial" religion. My point is to bring into sharp relief the disembedding thrust of the axial formulations.

5. See, e.g., Godfrey Lienhardt, *Divinity and Experience* (Oxford University Press, 1961), chap. 3; Roger Caillois, *L'Homme et le Sacré* (Paris: Gallimard, 1963), chap. 3.

6. This is a much commented upon feature of Aboriginal religion in Australia; see Lucien Lévy-Bruhl, *L'Expérience mystique et les Symboles chez les Primitifs* (Paris: Alcan, 1937), 180ff.; Caillois, *L'Homme et le Sacré,* 143–145; W. E. H. Stanner, "On Aboriginal Religion," a series of six articles in *Oceania* 30–33, (1959–1963). The same connection to the land has been noted with the Okanagan in British Columbia; see J. Mander and E. Goldsmith, *The Case against the Global Economy* (San Francisco: Sierra Club Books, 1996), chap. 39.

7. John Stuart Mill, *On Liberty,* in *Three Essays* (Oxford: Oxford University Press, 1975), 77.

8. Francis Oakley, *Kingship* (Oxford: Blackwell, 2006), 7. Bellah makes a fundamentally similar point, I believe, in "What Is Axial": "Both tribal and archaic religions are 'cosmological,' in that supernature, nature and society were all fused in a single cosmos" (70).

9. See for instance, Eisenstadt, *The Origins and Diversity of Axial Age Civilizations;* see also Bellah, "What Is Axial."

10. Karl Jaspers, *Vom Ursprung und Ziel der Geschichte* (Zurich: Artemis, 1949). In using these terms, "axial" and "postaxial," I am groping for an expression to distinguish two quite different forms of religious life, one of which goes back much further than the other. But I am not necessarily accepting much of what Jaspers associated with this term. For instance, I have no final view on whether we can identify a particular "Axial Age" *(Achsenzeit)* when these important changes occurred in civilizations far removed from each other more or less simultaneously. The issue of what these important changes consists in has recently come back to the center of scholarly attention, along with the renewed concern with defining different civilizational traditions, after a long infertile period in which Western thinkers remained spellbound by the extraordinary idea that there was a single path, from "tradition" to "modernity," which all societies were bound to travel, some much earlier than others. See, for instance, Johann Arnason, S. N. Eisenstadt, and Björn Wittrock, *Axial Civilizations and World History* (Leiden: Brill, 2005). I don't want to take a stand in their very interesting debates, for instance, that between Eisenstadt and Wittrock, about which changes were crucial to the transitions. For my purposes in this book, the contrast between pre- and postaxial is defined by the features I enumerate in my text.

11. See Cho-Yun Hsu, "Historical Conditions of the Emergence and Crystallization of the Confucian System," in *Axial Age Civilizations,* ed. S. N. Eisenstadt, 306–324.

12. In this sense, I agree with Shmuel Eisenstadt's formulation of one of the key changes of the axial period, "the emergence, conceptualization and institutionalization of a basic tension between the transcendental and mundane orders"; with, of course, the understanding that the "transcendental" order itself changes when the tension arises. Eisenstadt, *Axial Age Civilizations,* 1.

13. W. E. Stanner, "On Aboriginal Religion"; the expression quoted figures in article 2, *Oceania* 30, no. 4 (June 1960): 276. See also by the same author "The Dreaming," in *Reader in Comparative Religion,* ed. W. Lessa and E. Z. Vogt (Evanston, IL: Row, Peterson, 1958), 158–167.

14. Stanner, "On Aboriginal Religion," article 6, *Oceania* 33, no. 4 (June 1963): 269.

15. Louis Dumont, "De l'individu-hors-du-monde à l'individu-dans-le-monde," in *Essais sur l'individualisme* (Paris: Seuil, 1983).

16. I want to take account of Stanley Tambiah's reservations about Dumont's formula "individual outside the world" in relation to the Buddhist renouncer; see S. J. Tambiah, "The Reflexive and Institutional Achievements of Early Buddhism", in *Axial Age Civilizations,* ed. S. N. Eisenstadt, 466. The Bhikku is outside the "world," in the sense of the life of the society relating to the cosmos and gods. But this doesn't prevent, even perhaps renders inevitable, (a) a new kind of sociability in which renouncers come together (the Sangha), and (b) relations of complementarity between renouncers and

those in the world, whereby the latter can have some part in what the renouncers are directly seeking ("merit"), or even (although this may appear a deviation) whereby the spiritual power of monks can be directed to the ordinary life goals of the laity.

17. I have discussed this at greater length in *A Secular Age,* 45–54.
18. Bruce Kapferer, *The Feast of the Sorcerer: Practices of Consciousness and Power* (Chicago: University of Chicago Press, 1997).
19. Ibid.
20. Ibid., chap. 3.

Credits

I acknowledge the following sources in which my previously published material first appeared.

Chapter 1: Originally published in *Iris Murdoch and the Search for Human Goodness,* ed. Maria Antonaccio and William Schweiker (Chicago: University of Chicago Press, 1996), 3–28. Copyright © 1996 by the University of Chicago.

Chapter 2: Originally published in *Gadamer's Century: Essays in Honor of Hans-Georg Gadamer,* ed. Jeff Malpas et al. (Cambridge, MA: MIT Press, 2002), 279–297. Copyright © 2002 by the Massachusetts Institute of Technology.

Chapter 3: Originally published in *Deutsche Zeitschrift fur Philosophie,* Bd. 56, Heft 1 (Berlin: Akademie Verlag, 2008), 3–19.

Chapter 5: Originally published in *The Morality of Nationalism,* ed. Robert McKim and Jeff McMahan (New York: Oxford University Press, 1997), 31–55. Copyright © 1997 by Oxford University Press. Reprinted by permission of Oxford University Press.

Chapter 6: Originally published in *The East Asian Challenge to Human Rights,* ed. Joanne R. Bauer and Daniel A. Bell (New York: Cambridge University Press, 1999), 124–144. Copyright © 1999 by Carnegie Council on Ethics and International Affairs. Reprinted with the permission of Cambridge University Press.

Chapter 7: Originally published in *Multiculturalism, Liberalism, and Democracy,* ed. Rajeev Bhargava et al. (New York: Oxford University Press, 1999), 135–163. Papers originally presented at a seminar organized by the Centre for Studies in Social Sciences, Calcutta, India.

Chapter 8: Originally published in *Public Culture* 18, no. 2 (Spring 2006): 281–300. Copyright © 2006 by Duke University Press. Reprinted by permission of Duke University Press.

Chapter 9: Originally published in *A Catholic Modernity? Charles Taylor's Marianist Award Lecture,* edited and with an introduction by James L. Heft, S. M., with responses by William M. Shea et al. (New York: Oxford University Press, 1999), 13–37. Copyright © 1999 by Oxford University Press. Reprinted by permission of Oxford University Press.

Chapter 10: Originally published in *Beyond Violence: Religious Sources of Social Transformation in Judaism, Christianity, Islam,* ed. James L. Heft (New York: Fordham University Press 2004), 15–42. Copyright © 2004 by Fordham University Press.

Chapter 11: Originally published in *Religion: Beyond a Concept,* ed. Hent de Vries (New York: Fordham University Press, 2008), 178–244. Copyright © 2008 by Fordham University Press.

Chapter 12: To be published in *Secular Enchantment*, ed. George Levine (Princeton, NJ: Princeton University Press, 2011). Copyright © 2011 by Princeton University Press. Reprinted by permission of Princeton University Press.

Index